THE COMPLETE ENCYCLOPEDIA OF
BEER

BERRY VERHOEF

THE COMPLETE ENCYCLOPEDIA OF
BEER

BERRY VERHOEF

BARNES
&NOBLE
BOOKS
NEW YORK

This edition published by Barnes & Noble, Inc.,
by arrangement with Rebo International b.v.

2002 Barnes & Noble Books

ISBN 0–7607–32922

Copyright © Rebo International b.v., Lisse, The Netherlands
1st printing

Text: Berry Verhoef
Translated by Stephen Challacombe for Bookpros.co.uk
Editing and production: TextCase, Grongingen, The Netherlands
Cover design by Minkowsky graphic designers, Enkhuizen, The Netherlands
Lay-out and composition: Studio Imago, Amersfoort, The Netherlands

Contents

Foreword

"People get what they deserve," is an appalling attitude yet I expect to lend the notion further support during the course of this book. Although I do not get the impression that things are getting any better, I regularly refuse to accept a Westmalle Dubbel served icy cold. There is no greater injustice for good beer than the serving of a Westmalle Dubbel at a temperature of 5°C (41°F). Immediate dismissal ought to be the minimum consequence for those who perpetrate such a heinous act. But this does not happen. After a copious exchange of words with the bar person and their manager I more often than not am advised: "But we keep all our beer chilled because nobody wants warm beer." This is even true of the British, who still have a reputation (no longer deserved in all but the better real ale pubs) for serving warm beer. I usually end up choosing a pilsener-type or lager, brewed to be drunk cold.

Fortunately there are increasing numbers of places where the beer is better respected. The choice of beer on offer is also much wider in many of these bars than the staple product of the country. The Belgians led the way with menu cards for beer to help selection and many other countries have seen a growth in venues with a broad choice. Many bars feature "guest beers" of the month which creates the opportunity for a greater number of people to become enthusiasts for its specific taste. Conscious choice of a beer for its taste also tends to avoid the excesses of consuming a large quantity of beer for its effect. Drinkers are more engaged in tasting, assessing, and enjoying their beer. There is a beer for everyone's taste, including those who claim not to like beer. Not all beer is bitter in taste and there are beers with sweet or sour flavors, often with herbal or spicy undertones.

This book is primarily aimed at those beers that you can buy to take home, so that everyone can learn more about beer – on their own or in the company of friends – and choose those with the most to offer. Taste is a personal thing and judgments about taste can vary from person-to-person but the general descriptions of the beers in this book give an impression of the type of beer under discussion. I hope this book may lead the reader to great enjoyment of beer.

Cheers!
Berry Verhoef

The story behind beer

BREWERIES

Everybody knows that beer is brewed in a brewery and yet few people have ever been inside one or know what a fermentation vessel looks like. Most breweries organize tours to help foster closer ties with their consumers but not all breweries are alike of course. Production capacity is one area of significant difference between breweries. The varying scales of brewing are reflected in the categories listed below.

HOME BREWER

Any enthusiast who brews beer at home with pots and pans for their own consumption falls into this category. Home brewers do not brew for sale but for their immediate circle of family and friends. Most home brewers produce ales because of the problems of cooling the wort and keeping of newly brewed beer. Hobby shops supply special brewing

kits with everything needed so that a home brewer can readily make their own beer with a minimum level of investment. The brewery itself will often be the kitchen, shed, or garage using large pans or slightly more professional equipment. A good many micro-brewers started out as home brewers. Most home brewers produce of the order of 16–20 pints (10 liters) at a time.

Pub Brewery

A development of recent years has been the growth of small-scale breweries attached to pubs and other bars just as the innkeepers of old once brewed their own beer for their customers. Occasionally such a pub brewery is part of a chain of pubs or bars but more often they are independent breweries that supply beer just for their own customer's glasses. Beer cannot get fresher than this. These in-house breweries often offer a choice of two set beers with a third choice constantly changing. Customers get the chance to sample a wide range of different types of beers through this "beer of the week" or "beer of the month."

Micro-Brewery

Micro-breweries often see-saw between being a commercial venture and a hobby. If a home brewer manages to make repeat batches of successful beer and then sets up his or her equipment somewhere other than the kitchen or shed and starts to sell the surplus one can refer to a micro-brewery.

In the nineteenth century most beer came from small-scale breweries that brewed for the local people and it was not uncommon for even small villages to have more than one brewery. During the industrial revolution and the arrival of light ales, increases in the scale of production became essential. Large groups of workers sought as much beer as possible at the cheapest possible price. Because many of these workers were not local to the area the local character of individual beers became less important and increasing numbers of small brewers were swallowed up by larger concerns.

The siting of the micro-brewery can barely be seen from the street. There is a small tiled space behind the steel doors just sufficient to house the necessary equipment.

Today small breweries have created a niche in the beer market by offering something different from the large-scale brewers. Partially influenced by organizations set-up by beer lovers, these breweries have often turned their attention to the traditions of the past. The brewers of these small operations usually have to brew their beer with simple equipment and it is quite common for them to disappear within a year, either through under or over estimating demand. A few manage to establish themselves and even grow into a true brewery. There are companies who will install complete brewing installations but most micro-brewers create their own on the basis of a discarded fermentation vessel. A micro-brewer might brew fifty thousand to one million liters (13,210–264,200 gallons) in a year and this will generally be ale although a few brew lager type beers.

REGIONAL BREWERY

It is difficult to precisely define the line between a regional brewer and the large national and international concerns. The overall size of the country and structure of its beer market naturally has much to do with whether a brewery is regional or otherwise. National distribution is easy in a country such as The Netherlands but entirely different in the USA or China.

Regional brewers once accounted for the majority of breweries and of beer brewed but they

Small family brewers are often traditionally sited in the heart of a village, next to the church.

have been under constant threat in the past fifty years. Many of the regional brewers operated in precisely the same market as the "big boys" who grew ever larger through mergers and acquisitions. The economies of scale offered by their size enabled these breweries to supply their beer at keen prices and they were able to use their financial muscle to tie pubs and other bars to them as outlets.

Many regional breweries have survived in Germany because of the German attitude towards their beer but also because the size of the German market did not encourage the German brewers into international markets or national distribution. Regional brewing was a simple affair in the former Soviet Union for the breweries were instructed to brew the same types and volumes of beer as before state control. There was no need for growth since there was no competition. Some countries such as Canada and Switzerland have had measures in place for many years to protect regional breweries. These measures, which in Canada prevented beer being sold outside the province in which it was brewed, had the opposite effect with breweries establishing breweries in each province and becoming even more competitive. They were not effective in Switzerland either. Eventually most of the regional breweries just vanished. In the British Isles many suggest that the tied relationship between regional brewers and the public houses which are their main outlets has led to the survival of a number of regional breweries, most of which are family concerns. Distribution through tied

Small breweries do not carry out their own malting but buy malt from specialist suppliers.

houses provides a degree of assurance for the production volumes required provided that most beer is consumed in pubs and bars. Despite this though most of the public houses are also in the hands of the big brewers.

More usual throughout the world is for the regional breweries to be taken over by a much larger brewer which seeks to retain regional character in the retention of the local brewer's brand names – whether the related brewery is kept going or closed down. This shows that local character is one factor for consumers in their choice of beer. In the past twenty years a number of micro-breweries in the USA have grown to become regional brewers with sales often limited to one or two states but these are entirely different from the threatened regional brewers. These new brewers seek earnestly to keep "out of the hair" of the big brewers by brewing entirely different types of beer. The regional brewers of the past directly competed with the ever-expanding big brewers with very similar products. Just a few of them have managed to survive by differentiating themselves from these giant concerns.

LARGE-SCALE BREWERS

Large-scale breweries started to develop during the Industrial Revolution. The emergence of the more technically complicated Pilsener or lager beers contributed to the demand for greater economies of scale. One of the consequences of industrialization was the concentration of large numbers of predominantly male workers who felt

The large Bavaria brewing concern dominates the small village of Lieshout in The Netherlands and is an important regional employer.

a need to drink a jar of ale in the company of others. Technical developments enabled a large volume of beer to be brewed at a time. The building of railways, development of refrigeration, and invention of motor trucks enabled beer to be transported over large distances in a short period of time. All these developments of course required capital for investment and one means of acquiring sufficient capital was to merge with or take-over a number of other breweries. The larger sales volumes this caused enabled the investment to pay for itself more quickly. This set a ball rolling.

The smaller regional brewers which had not taken this course were gradually almost all swallowed up. The big brewers were constantly able to win markets from the smaller brewers because of their competitive advantages and these smaller breweries could not win new markets, hence investment became increasingly difficult. The result was that most of them were taken over by the giant breweries which often use a strong home market as a foundation for their international strength.

The size of the domestic market also has a bearing on the eagerness of a brewer to export. Brewers such as Carlsberg, Fosters, Heineken, Guinness and a few other brands have been driven by small home markets to seek expansion through export. Brands such as Budweiser, Brahma, and SAB were able to expand within their domestic markets to a size which made them world players. These brewers are now active in the new markets of the former Soviet Union and its satellites and China, benefiting from the growth these opening markets offer and probably getting still larger and stronger as a result. They have access to the capital to build new breweries and set-up distribution networks. These giant brewers, with the help of their marketing departments, manage to turn breweries that were on their knees into flourishing concerns.

It appears that this growth in economies of scale is not yet done. Even huge breweries with ten billion liters (2.6 billion gallons) deem it necessary to merge with one another in order to survive. It is likely that most beer in the world will soon be

Bavaria does its own malting. Grain arrives in bulk by canal in barges.

brewed by a small number of giant brewery concerns. Outside this mass market there are small niche markets for the small specialist brewers but here too there is a danger that the big brewers will introduce beers that they have largely ignored for so long – since brewing beer is something they certainly can do. If the specialist brewers grab too much of the overall market then the big concerns will certainly react, either by brewing similar products or by absorbing a specialist brewer within their corporate fold.

What happens in these areas is largely in the hands of the consumers themselves but consumers are easily influenced and fairly undiscerning.

Quite how this process of development of taste happens I have no idea but it must have something to do with familiarity. Few young boys really appreciate the bitter taste of beer while very few grown men dislike it. Practice makes perfect!

The grain is handled automatically: no more hauling of sacks.

The Bavaria brewery's maltings.

DRINKING AND TASTING BEER

The first role of beer is as a thirst quencher but the presence of alcohol gives the beverage an additional function. It is unfortunate when this aspect of beer is more important than its other qualities. Many drink beer without regard any regard for taste, frequently far too cold and the drinking of a cold beer with friends in a bar or al fresco is in itself an enjoyable pastime. Most drink a lager (or Pilsener) type of beer, leading to the world-wide success of "lagers", although some stalwarts among the British still steadfastly stick to traditional ales and bitters.

There are alternatives. The variety of different brews means there is a beer to suit every taste. If one lager is too bitter then perhaps a sweet malt beer will be more appealing. The reality is that most beer drinkers get no further than their everyday beer, and this is such a shame. Tasting of different beers is usually stimulated by friends or a well-informed barkeeper. Once drinkers start to drink beers for their taste, quantity is pushed into second place behind quality in the quest for the perfect brew. With experience one becomes increasingly more discerning and the taste develops. What might once have been deemed too bitter and not at all pleasing can become "a strong after taste of bitter hops that is ideally suited to the style of the beer."

GLASS

The choice of glass is just one of the elements that has a bearing on how well the beer is enjoyed. This may seem somewhat exaggerated but is true. The choice of the right type of glass allows the aroma of the beer to do what the brewer intended it to do: to mix as quickly as possible with the surroundings or to concentrate above the glass. The thickness of the glass and its shape have

Grain germinates on the floor of this brewery's maltings.

The germinated grain is turned automatically.

their bearing on both the color and taste experience.

Pilsener type (lager) beers are generally drunk out of small thin and straight glasses in most countries but the British generally prefer larger, thicker, and slightly tapered glasses of a pint or half pint (approx. 500 or 250 ml). German wheat beer is also served in half-liter glasses but ones that are tall and narrow, and frequently decorated. Belgian wheat beer is usually served in sturdy thick glasses of about 250 ml, the strongly fermented special brews are served in tulip-form glasses with narrow necks and Trappist and other monastic beers are mainly offered in broad rimmed goblets.

Glasses need to be very clean and thoroughly rinsed. Washing-up detergents can invisibly affect the taste, hence the need for rinsing. Do not use a teacloth to dry beer glasses that has been used to dry other dishes for it will contain too much detergent to dry the glass properly. Grease removes the froth off the head of beer which is not pleasing in the case of most beers and regarded as a sign of bad beer in many countries.

TEMPERATURE

There are special thermometers available to check the temperature of beer to be tasted but you can get by without such specialist equipment. The correct temperature for storage and for serving are not always the same. Most beers are best stored in a cellar with little daylight between 10 and 13°C (50 and 55.4°F). Certain lagers are best kept in a refrigerator though not for too long a period.

A micro-brewer's brewing vessel.

The temperature at which a beer is served varies with the type of beer. The colder the beer is served the more the elements in its taste are suppressed – but this might be the express intention. Wheat beer and alcohol-free beer are best served at about 4°C (39.2°F), many lagers between 6 and 8°C (42.8–46.4°F), and ales generally at about 10°C (50°F), while some special brews such as barley ale and other special grain brews are best served at room temperature. Serving beers at a warmer than usual temperature can lead to surprising results. The taste is much fuller and the beer's aroma develops more fully.

APPEARANCE

Our perception of beer is largely psychological. Color forms part of this impression and the liveliness of the beer together with its head of froth are also important. Few beer drinkers will think much of a pale yellow beer without a head and with just a few gas bubbles. Different beers need to have a particular color and liveliness and provided these are present then this part of the perception is acceptable.

Color depends on the malt that is used. The malt used in Pilsner or lager type beers imparts a light color, caramelized malt makes darker beer, and really dark or black malt makes the darkest beers. The color of the malt is determined by the temperature at which the malt was dried and the duration of the drying time. The proportions of these different types of malt finally determine the color of the beer. These colors are expressed in units according to a scale. The most widely used color scales are those of EBC and SRM. Terms such as white (or blonde), amber, copper, brown, or black together with the adjectives light and dark are much more readily understood. There are beers of course that are red are have a red glint to them.

AROMA

The smell or aroma of beer is another important element. There is more to the aroma than smell alone for much of what we experience as taste forms part of the aroma. The nose is far more receptive than our taste buds and it is difficult to determine where the difference between taste and smell begins and ends. Our sense of smell is recognition of chemical elements that are imprinted in our memories.

Beer clearly has aromas of malt and hops but smells such as banana, butter, apple, and cardboard are rather more unexpected but it so happens that the chemicals that we recognize as banana can also be present in beer, especially in German wheat beer. The presence of cardboard manifests itself in beer that is slightly stale. Buttery aromas are caused by chemicals that should disappear when the beer is stored. Because of the importance of smell in beer tasting having a cold makes it quite impossible to taste beer properly.

TASTE

Taste is in general terms experienced as one of four different types: sweet, salty, sour, and bitter. Saltiness is virtually never encountered in beer but these other taste experiences all occur to some extent. Sweetness is due to the malt extracts in beer since not all the sugar in malt ferments but sugar can also be added. Caramel (toffee), boiled sweet, and sugar sweetness can all occur and the combination of sugar and alcohol is not at all unknown. Bitterness comes from the oils in hops but the burnt malt can also impart bitterness somewhat akin to burnt toast. Bitterness can vary from a tart spicy bitterness to a fully-developed and strong floral bitterness. Sourness can be encountered in Belgian beer and also in German wheat beer. Some of the strong Lambic draught beers of Belgian can cause sucking in of the cheeks as if sucking on a lemon. There can also be slightly tart nuances that cause a dry sourness on the tongue.

Sweet and sour combine well together, this is as true of beer as it is for sweets. In order to allow

The sparkling brass and copper of this small family brewery emanates an aura of craftsmanship.

The modern technology and stainless steel of today's brewery have replaced the traditional coppers.

all the character of the beer's flavor to manifest itself it is best to swill the beer around your mouth. It is not sufficient just to let the beer pass over the tongue on its way down your throat if you wish to experience the full flavor. The receptors for sour flavors are sited at the side of the tongue while sweetness is detected by the front of the tongue and bitterness by the back of the tongue. The full flavors can be enjoyed if the beer is swilled around in the mouth before swallowing.

EFFECT IN THE MOUTH

Beers have different effects in the mouth which can be experienced as body, liveliness, dryness, warmth, contraction, balance, and aftertaste.

Body

A beer's body is one of the experiences we sense in our mouths. It is not the case that a beer has to be full bodied in order to be a good beer. Light lagers in particular that are intended to be guzzled down need to have a light body to make them easy to drink. Combined with the right hops a light lager can still be a very decent beer. On the other hand a heavy monastic beer absolutely must be full bodied. The fullness of body comes from the presence of proteins and sugars. A beer's body can vary from watery to syrupy.

Body cannot be assured by the mere addition of sugars, indeed the opposite is the case. Sugars are generally added because they ferment and this

results in increased alcohol without extra body. Where malt is used some of the natural sugar always remains unfermented, resulting in body. Determining a beer's body can be quite difficult since (quite fortunately) our senses are led astray by flavor and aroma in the beer.

Liveliness

Put a glass of English ale alongside a second fermentation Hefe Weizen and it will instantly be apparent what a difference the liveliness of a beer makes. The English ale contains virtually no carbon dioxide and hence it is easy to drink it down with great gulps while the sparkling nature of some wheat beers with their abundant carbon dioxide make it virtually impossible to drink the beer down quickly or to take more than small sips at one time. The carbon dioxide is a by-product of fermentation and the extent to which carbon dioxide is released contributes to its liveliness. Bottled beers that are fermented in the bottle are therefore always lively since the carbon dioxide cannot escape from the bottle and is absorbed in the beer. Sealed fermentation tanks have the same effect. Some brewers artificially increase the carbon dioxide in their beer. One of the first signs of a lively beer is of course the froth of its head but the mouth also quickly senses the difference between a lively beer and a flat one. Liveliness is neither a good or bad characteristic but must be appropriate to the type of beer.

Dryness

Dryness is an unexpected sensation in the mouth when drinking a liquid and yet some beers can create a strong sense of dryness in the mouth. These "dry" beers are not full-bodied but are mainly due to the presence of certain types of hop. Wine drinkers will be

Transferring the wort by pump is a simple but effective means for the micro-brewer.

The transfer of the mash, wort, and beer is done through a maze of piping at a large brewery such as that of Bavaria as seen in this glimpse into the brewing hall.

familiar with this sensation but the dry mouth feeling is not known to all beer drinkers. Certain English ales in particular are good examples of this characteristic and one of the first to be mentioned for this property is the Japanese Asahi beer but this is as much due to a complete absence of body as full or total fermentation.

Warmth

Alcohol can create a warm sensation in the mouth and this is particularly encountered with strong beers. In other words beers with 9% alcohol generally give a warmer feeling than those of 7% but this can easily be the other way around. The extent to which alcohol comes to the fore depends on other elements present in the beer.

Contraction

One of the sensations in the mouth that generally manifests itself towards the end of the taste, depending on the constituents of the beer, is a natural contraction of the mouth (as in the case of sucking a lemon) and it is caused by the presence of certain chemicals. Usually this sensation is regarded as a pleasing one.

Fermentation at this brewery occurs in open tanks without heating.

Balance

Balance relates to the proportions of the various constituents of beer in relation to one another. A well-balanced beer is always a good beer but a beer with a heavy predominance of e.g. a strong bitter taste is not necessarily a bad one. Balance is usually the result of the different taste constituents but the aroma also plays its part.

Aftertaste

New tastes can be experienced long after the beer has been swallowed, as if the brain has a delayed reaction. Bitterness in particular is one of the tastes that can be experienced late. The length of the aftertaste is one aspect on which beer can be judged in tastings. Taste which lingers often indicates high concentrations. Fruity sweetness can often be tasted on the lips for up to an hour and bitterness remains for quite some time. The aftertaste also influences the taste of subsequent mouthfuls of beer. The aftertaste can be a simple further development of the taste.

Fermentation in special plastic containers in a temperature controlled environment.

Fermentation at this brewery occurs in open tanks without heating.

Fermentation here takes place in long rows of cooled tanks.

TYPES OF BEER

Bottling at a micro-brewery.

ALES VERSUS LAGERS

The most basic categorization can be done on the manner in which the beer is fermented. Various types of yeast have differing temperatures at which they best work. A yeast culture that works at lower temperatures of 0–5°C (32–41°F) tends to sink to the bottom after it has done its work. Beer brewed in this way needs about four weeks to mature before it is sold. The beer is kept in cold storage during this time – once it was stored in deep cellars or natural caves – but today it is kept in special tanks. The German for store is lagern and it is from this that the popular name for this type of beer is derived. The origins of this type of beer are in Belgium, generally from monasteries.

Ale is a type of beer that is much older than lager and it is easier to brew. The term ale is derived from the Old English word alu (alo in Old Saxon). The first ales fermented spontaneously and did not have hops added to them. The froth from the fermentation on the top of the beer was scooped off to start the next brew. This is how top fermented ale came into being. Ale was not restricted to England since originally all beers, including German ones, were ales. The brewing of ale does not require much by way of technology or technique and the beer can be drunk within a couple of days of being brewed. Fermentation takes place at room temperature and no special cooling is required while the beer is conditioned. Ale is a popular brew for home brewers, micro-brewers, and still popular with people in Britain.

Storage is a major matter for this brewer.

Beer is brewed virtually throughout the world. With more or less the same ingredients, different brewers in various cultures brew an extraordinary diversity of types of beer. These differences stem from preparation of the basic ingredients in varying manners, other brewing methods, and also through the addition or otherwise of herbs and spices, fruit, sugar, or chemicals. Beer remains substantially the same though despite these variances and can be recognized readily as such. Because humans find it natural to classify everything, beer too is categorized. Beers are divided into a number of basic types on the basis of the ingredients used and the manner of brewing. This categorization is not rigid but it does provide some basis to understand what can be expected of a particular beer.

Storage, crates, bottles, and kegs are a major consideration for a big brewery.

Alt (ale)
SERVING TEMPERATURE 6–8°C (42.8–46.4°F)

Alt is a German type of ale that is especially popular in the area around Dusseldorf but a small number of micro-brewers in North America also brew alt. The word alt means old indicating a traditional type of top fermentation beer. Alt is stored at a temperature just above freezing for a period of three to eight weeks. The color of Alt generally tends towards bronze although certain Alt beers are a lighter amber color. Alt is predominantly a fresh but malty beer with suggestions of roasting or toast and bitter hop overtones.

Abbey beer (ale)
SERVING TEMPERATURE 12–18°C (53.6–64.4°F)

Abbey beer is closely related to Trappist but is not permitted to use this name. Both have their origins in monastic cloisters though some of today's present-day beers are brewed elsewhere under license. Many of the rest have no link with the monastic traditions whatsoever.

Alcohol-free (by dialysis)
SERVING TEMPERATURE 4–6°C (39.2–42.8°F)

Removal of a specific substance in a liquid solution can be done in a number of ways. One of these methods is dialysis, by use of a membrane. The principal is based on the different concentrations of a specific substance in two fluids that are separated by a membrane. The membrane separating the two liquid solutions permits specific substances to pass through it provided the concentration of these substances on both sides of the membrane is the same. It is in this way that alcohol-free beer is created.

The advantage of this method is that a beer can be brewed in the usual way (usually a Pilsener type) and the alcohol removed when it is fully fermented and matured, and has therefore also fully developed its flavor. Alcohol does have its effect on the taste and aroma of beer and hence alcohol-free beer tastes slightly different so that however good they may be, alcohol-free beers vary from their original source beer.

Micro-brewers often have a small-scale bottling operation, usually as a hand-me-down from a major brewery. Purchase of a full-automated bottling line is usually beyond the means of these small brewers.

American lager
SERVING TEMPERATURE 4–8°C (39.2–46.4°F)

American lager is a light type of lager brewed with corn (maize) or rice and with almost no presence of bitterness from hops. One of its most valuable qualities is the ease with which it can be drunk in volume. Generally most American lagers have higher levels of carbon dioxide than their European equivalents. Alcohol content (by volume) is more than 5%.

American malt liquor (lager)
SERVING TEMPERATURE 6–10°C (42.8–50°F)

Beer that contains more than 5% alcohol (the actual limit varies from state to state) is not permitted to be described as beer in the USA. Those brews above this level are termed malt liquor. Hence an imported Dortmunder "beer" will have to be sold as malt liquor but most imported beers ensure that

American ale
SERVING TEMPERATURE 10–15°C (50–59°F)

American ale varies is a number of ways from English ale. The hops used in American ale are generally more floral in aroma and the color of these ales vary from very pale to bronze. The Americans also brew extensively at high temperatures with "lager" yeasts. The malt in these ales is somewhat restrained but an ale must have a slightly fruity aroma.

American use the term ale to denote stronger beer and reserve the term beer for those with less than 5% alcohol, hence they regard ale as stronger.

The semi-automatic filling line of a brewery that does not bottle its own beer.

This brewery has its own separate bottling plant.

they remain under the legal threshold because the term malt liquor is not altogether positive because it also describes brews made with corn (maize) and sugar that are light bodied, with little hops, that are very high in alcohol.

Belgian ale
SERVING TEMPERATURE 6–12°C (42.8–53.6°F)

Belgian ale is the Belgian equivalent of English pale ale. It is amber in color and top fermented. This Belgian ale is very popular in both Belgium and The Netherlands. The mellow-sweet ale has a slightly fruity aroma with slight suggestions of burning and caramel. Hops are clearly present but do not dominate.

Belgian wheat beer (ale)
SERVING TEMPERATURE 4–6°C (39.2–42.8°F)

Belgian wheat beet or witbier (white beer) is entirely different from German wheat beer. It is brewed using 40–60% of wheat that has not been malted, malted barley, and sometimes some oats. Additions are hops, Curacao orange peel, and spices including coriander. Most of these ales are neither filtered or pasteurized and they are hence turbid and living types of beer.

Belgian witbiers are generally mild in flavor with hints of spice and citrus fruit, full-bodied, and very refreshing. They are mainly served very cool as a summer thirst quenchers.

Cleaning the crates.

A continuous stream of standard Euro bottles on their way to blue crates.

Bière de garde (ale)
SERVING TEMPERATURE 12–15°C (53.6–59°F)

The northern French equivalent of special Belgian beers is known as bière de garde or "beer for keeping". The name originates from the time when French farmers brewed beer in the spring to see them through the summer. This type of beer is brewed in several different ways, with high fermentation or low fermentation yeast at high temperatures. The manner of storage and maturing also differs. Some brewers mature their beer under cold conditions but others do so with warmth. Most of these beers have sugar added during bottling for additional fermentation in the bottle. These beers are recognizable by their Champagne-like bottles. The taste is sweet and malty with medium hoppiness and the necessary spiciness.

Bitter (ale)
SERVING TEMPERATURE 12–15°C (53.6–59°F)

Bitter is the daily thirst-quenching draught beer drunk by the British in their pubs. The bitterness is actually quite pleasing and mainly the dryness of hops and lack of sweetness. Most bitters are around 4% alcohol. Bitters are brewed with pale malt and generally with typically English hop sorts such as Fuggles and Golding. Bitter is a typical English still ale that is praised by the English and generally avoided by most northern Europeans.

Bock beer (malt lager)
SERVING TEMPERATURE 6–10°C (42.8–50°F)

This type of beer originated in Germany and is a fully bottom fermenting malted lager that varies from almost white to dark brown. Alcohol varies from 6–8%. Bock beer is always malty with restrained hop. There are various types of bock beer such as summer, May, autumn, double bock, and winter bock beers.

Cream ale (hybrid)
SERVING TEMPERATURE 6–8°C (46.4–50°F)

Cream ale is a light color (blonde) American beer that was originally brewed by brewers who did not have lager yeasts but wanted to compete with the pale colored lagers. Cream ale is now brewed in a variety of ways with ale yeast or lager yeast and the maturing period for these beverages can also differ. Some brewers even make both an ale and a lager. The ingredients used are the same as for American premium lagers. The alcohol level is around 5%.

Dortmunder (lager)
SERVING TEMPERATURE 6–8°C (46.4–50°F)

German-style lager mainly brewed around the Dortmund area and largely known as "Export". This type of lager is quite robust but pale with clear presence of malt and a moderate level of hops. Alcohol levels for these beers are just above 5%.

Can-filling line.

Distribution at the Bavaria brewery.

Dry beer (lager)
SERVING TEMPERATURE 4–6°C (39.2–42.8°F)

Dry beer was first developed in Japan as an accompaniment to Japanese fish dishes. It is a pale blonde lager with alcohol of 5%. The density of the beer is quite low and it is the intention that all sugar will have fermented to leave a pale and very clear liquid. Enzymes are sometimes added to aid this process that convert as many as possible of the otherwise non fermenting sugars into fermenting ones. Dry beer has small amounts of hops added to retain a rather neutral taste. It is mainly popular in Japan and the USA. The Germans brew a similar beer as a "diet pilsener".

Double bock (lager)
SERVING TEMPERATURE 10–15°C (50–59°F)

Double bock has a variety of colors and aromas and these are generally complex strong lagers with alcohol of 7–9%. There is a tradition in Germany (also adopted elsewhere) to use the suffix -ator to the name in honor of the Salvator or person who rescued the German Paulaner brewery. Double

Tasting area at a brewery.

The reception area of De Kroon brewery in The Netherlands.

bock is certainly stronger than a bock beer but not double strength.

Dunkel (dark lager)
SERVING TEMPERATURE 6–8°C (46.4–50°F)

The first beers brewed in the lager manner in Bavaria were dark beers and today's dunkel is a direct descendant of these beers. Their color tends towards bronze or dark brown and alcohol is around 5%. Dunkel beer is lightly malt with some burnt notes in the taste. Hops are distantly present but some dunkel beers are dryer than others.

Duvel (ale)
SERVING TEMPERATURE 6–15°C (46.4–59°F)

Duvel is a strong Belgian blonde or white beer originally brewed at the Moortgat brewery but now copied by other brewers with similar sounding names. True Duvel is both malty and hoppy, well balanced, with fruity nuances. A well brewed beer of the type does not regard a high level of alcohol as the prime objective. This type of beer is differentiated by the method of brewing in which fermentation takes place in three stages: a warm fermentation, followed by maturing at a cold temperature for about four weeks and then further fermentation in the bottle. Various different types of yeast are used and sugar is added at several stages. Duvel can be served either chilled or at ambient temperature.

Extra Special Bitter (ESB ale)
SERVING TEMPERATURE 12–15°C (53.6–59°F)

These beers are the premium versions of English bitters and possess greater density. Other descriptions include Special and XB. These indications are more a designation by each brewery of the categories of its different beers than any special position in the market place.

Faro (ale/spontaneous fermentation)
SERVING TEMPERATURE 10–12°C (50–53.6°F)

Faro ales have a very small position among the Belgian lambic ales. Sometimes these Faro ales are sweetened at bottling but sometimes this is done in the bottle or the glass. Various types of sugar are used to sweeten these lambic beers. This results in a robust sweet and sour beer with alcohol of 2–5%.

Barley wine (ale)
SERVING TEMPERATURE 12–18°C (53.6–64.4°F)

The British call their beer brewed with barley "barley wine" even though the beverage has none of the semblance of wine. Belgian brewers also use a similar name of gerstewijn – which is a literal translation – for their strongest ales that have a long maturing period and similar level of alcohol as wine. American micro-brewers have also discovered this type of brew and regard it as their specialty. A barley wine must possess complexity, alcoholic warmth, and a sweet taste of malt. Barley wine keeps a long time with some surviving for ten or twenty years. Alcohol content varies from 8–12%.

Geuze (spontaneous fermentation ale)
SERVING TEMPERATURE 12–15°C (53.6–59°F)

Geuze is a Brussels' type of lambic ale that is created by blending old and new lambic beers together. This imparts the liveliness of a young lambic ale with the character of an old one. Alcohol is in the region of 5%. Geuze is a true connoisseur's beer.

Helles (lager)
SERVING TEMPERATURE 6–8°C (46.4–50°F)

Helles is one of the "blonde" Bavarian beers for everyday drinking with alcohol of around 5%. This beer is also known as Münchener Hell. This beer has less hops in that Pilsener types with higher malt and is the Bavarian equivalent of a Pilsener.

Ice beer (lager)
SERVING TEMPERATURE 4–8°C (39.2–46.4°F)

The Canadian brewer Labatt was one of the first to introduce an ice beer. The beer is kept so cold that ice crystals form in the beer that are then

The Brouwerhuys Moorees brewery.

removed. In principal this method compares with distillation through boiling except that the freezing method leaves other substances behind in the beer that are desirable. The alcohol percentage is slightly higher than the original lager since alcohol has a lower freezing point and is therefore not removed with the ice crystals.

Imperial stout (ale)
SERVING TEMPERATURE 12–15°C (53.6–59°F)

A strong stout ale originally brewed to survive the long journey to Czarist Russia. Imported beers acquired a life of their own in Russia and were much imitated by various breweries. The strongest versions of this stout have lots of burnt flavors combined with alcohol, coffee, and bitter chocolate. Alcohol varies from 6–8%. The color is dark black.

IPA/India Pale Ale
SERVING TEMPERATURE 12–15°C (53.6–59°F)

During the days of the British empire many British people were spread around the globe. India was one of the largest and most important of her colonies. In order that these colonialists should not feel too homesick a stronger ale was brewed with plenty of hops that could survive the long journey by sea. Present-day IPA are strong ales with considerable bitterness of hops. The color varies from amber to bronze. This is another ale brewed by American micro-brewers.

Kölsch (Cologne ale)
SERVING TEMPERATURE 6–8°C (46.4–50°F)

The term Kölsch is legally protected by the brewers of the area around Cologne (Köln). A few American brewers describe their high fermentation "blonde" beers at "kälsch". This type of beer is a very light colored beer brewed with a little wheat. The alcohol content is around 5%. This beer is matured chilled following a heated fermentation. There is clear evidence of hops but not overwhelmingly so and Kölsch beer has a lively character.

Lambic (ale)
SERVING TEMPERATURE 10–15°C (50–59°F)

Lambic is a spontaneous fermentation ale from the Zenne area of Belgium close to Brussels. Lambic is a sour beer that has virtually no carbon dioxide. A small amount (10–20%) of wheat is used in the brewing of Lambic and the beer is then matured for several years in oak barrels in which fermentation continues. Lambic is rarely drunk in its original form but is generally used to produce Geuze, Faro, and Fruit Lambic beers (see there). The form known as kriek (a sour black cherry) is particularly popular in Belgium and The Netherlands.

Märzen (lager)
SERVING TEMPERATURE 6–8°C (46.4–50°F)

This type of beer is also known as Viennese or Oktoberfest (the annual October drinking festival in southern Germany and Austria). The beer was originally created by Anton Dreher and later developed by Sedlmayer specifically to be introduced at the Oktoberfest. These days this beer is amber-red with a sweet malt taste with alcohol above 5%. Its body is neither heavy or light. Its name is derived from the former practice that March was the last month before summer in which beer could be brewed.

Mild (ale)
SERVING TEMPERATURE 12–15°C (53.6–59°F)

Mild is a light English beer with alcohol of less than 4% that is also only mildly hopped. The color varies from pale amber to bronze and the taste is sweetly malty and the aroma can be fruity. For those who still drink it in Britain it is an everyday thirst quencher.

Oktoberfest (lager)
SERVING TEMPERATURE 6–8°C (46.4–50°F)

See Märzen.

Oatmeal stout (ale)
SERVING TEMPERATURE 10–12°C (50–53.6°F)

The ingredient that makes this stout different from others is the use of oatmeal. In other respects it is much like other stouts but it has a silky smoothness in the mouth. Oatmeal is a difficult grain to use in brewing, not least because of its tendency to bind together to form an impenetrable mass that is difficult to filter.

Pale ale
SERVING TEMPERATURE 12–15°C (53.6–59°F)

This is another classically English beer that generally ranges in color from light to dark amber with some examples of pale gold with a hint of red. At the time that pale ale was first introduced in the late eighteenth century the comparable stouts and milds were much darker beers. Pale ale today is akin to bitter and generally the draught form is known as bitter while bottled beers are termed pale ale. American ale was based on English pale ale but the British version contains more hops and has less body.

Pilsener (lager)
SERVING TEMPERATURE 6–8°C (46.4–50°F)

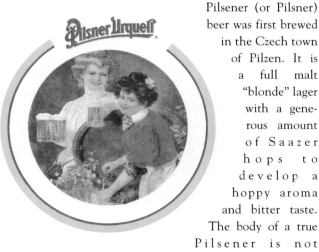

Pilsener (or Pilsner) beer was first brewed in the Czech town of Pilzen. It is a full malt "blonde" lager with a generous amount of Saazer hops to develop a hoppy aroma and bitter taste. The body of a true Pilsener is not particularly full-bodied

This beer is the origin of all Pilseners.

and the beer is not especially lively. Today the description Pilsener is found throughout the world on the labels of all manner of breweries. Many of these beers have little in common with a true Pilsener but there are some excellent imitations. All of them are in any event "blonde" lagers but often without full maltiness and hops. The Pilsener type of beer spread with the growth in interest in light-colored lagers of any type.

Porter (ale)
SERVING TEMPERATURE 12–15°C (53.6–59°F)

Porter is a milder and lighter variant of stout and is a top fermented dark (virtually black) beer with a roasted flavor. Generally the taste is slightly sweeter than that of a stout and usually more complex. Alcohol is normally below 5%. Porter was not brewed in the United Kingdom for a long time but is regaining popularity through micro-breweries in both the UK and USA.

Smoked beer (lager)
SERVING TEMPERATURE 6–8°C (46.4–50°F)

Smoked beer is an amber-colored lager that is brewed with malt that has been dried above a fire of beech wood but there are also versions for which the malt was dried over a peat fire. The taste and aroma of the beer are smoky. The presence of hops remains in the background.

Saison/Sezoens
SERVING TEMPERATURE 10–12°C (50–53.6°F)

By whichever name, this is a Belgian beer, brewed in the French-speaking part of the country, that is brewed for long keeping. This type of brew has a long tradition in that part of Belgium. The beer is golden "blonde" to amber and is a fairly strong top fermented ale that has a second fermentation in the bottle. Saison is sometimes brewed with the addition of herbs and spices.

Steam beer (hybrid)
SERVING TEMPERATURE 8–12°C (50–53.6°F)

The American version of steam beer is closely related to the Anchor brewery which has given this type of beer a new lease of life after it had all but vanished. In the late nineteenth century a number of US breweries did acquire lager-type yeast but did not have the necessary cooling facilities to brew lager. They use low shallow vats in which the beer was brewed for a relatively short time using lager yeast at a high temperature. Because the fermentation was not completed it continued in the vat. The name may be a reference to the liveliness of this type of beer. German steam beer or Dampfbier is top fermented but chilled during maturing and the name in Germany is more of a nostalgia for the old steam engines now in museums. Both Steam Beer and Dampfbier are protected names.

Stout (ale)
SERVING TEMPERATURE 10–12°C (50–53.6°F)

Stout is a strong ale with a strong roasted flavor. This ale of English/Irish origins uses some roasted barley in its brewing. Stout should be quite substantial but not too well-rounded. In addition to dryness and roasted flavors a good stout should be fruity and fresh and leave a smooth sensation in the mouth. The greatest influence in brewing of stout is Guinness that has developed a major world-wide name with this somewhat unusual brew. Alcohol is in the region of 5%.

Sweet stout
SERVING TEMPERATURE 10–12°C (50–53.6°F)

Lighter versions of stout were actually regarded as health drinks in the early twentieth century. Through the addition of lactose the impression was given that this stout was made using milk. The alcohol levels of sweet stouts vary from 3–4%. Sweet stout is pasteurized after addition of sugar to prevent further fermentation. Sweet stout is also known as "milk stout" and "cream stout".

Trappist (ale)
SERVING TEMPERATURE 10–15°C (50–59°F)

The designation "Trappist" is more an indication of the place of origin of a beer than its style or flavor. In any event such beers originate from breweries in monasteries in Westvleteren, Westmalle, Rochefort, Chimay, or Orval in Belgium or from the Dutch Trappist brewery of De Schaapskooi (the sheepfold). These beers differ from one another with colors ranging from blonde to almost black, in taste from sweet to bitter, and in alcoholic content from 5–10%. All Trappist beers are ales with strengths that vary and indicated by the terms enkel (single), dubbel (double), and tripel (triple) or with an old traditional Belgian original gravity figure. The name Trappist is protected and can only be used by these six breweries. Responsibility for brewing is still in the hands of monks and the brewing is done within the walls of the monasteries.

Viennese style
SERVING TEMPERATURE 6–8°C (46.4–50°F)

See Märzen.

Weissbier/Weizen (ale) (white beer/wheat beer)
SERVING TEMPERATURE 6°C (46.4°F)

This type of beer originated in Germany and is still very popular there. Weiss means white and weizen means wheat.

The Germans use both terms for this type of beer but weissbier does not necessarily mean that wheat is used in its brewing and there are also some dark brews known as weissbier. German wheat beer is brewed using top fermenting yeast but some have a bottom yeast added to them when they are bottled. These German wheat beers are above all intended as easy-drinking summer thirst quenchers with little sharpness to them. A typical aroma for

Hops are an important element in the brewing of beer.

Schwarzbier (black beer)

The bottom fermenting comparison with stout is the German Schwarzbier or black beer. It is an old traditional type of German beer that had lost its popularity in German until the Köstritzer brewery most closely associated with this type of beer became part of the Bittburg concern following the re-unification of Germany. This type of beer has won new popularity and is now brewed by many brewers. Black beer has also been brewed in Japan since the late nineteenth century and is still brewed there today on a small scale. Japanese black beer is brewed in the same way as the German version, although it is customary in Japan to use a small amount of rice in the brew. Both versions have about 5% alcohol and an emphasis on roasted malt.

these beers is that of cloves and the non-filtered versions of these beers are known as Hefe Weizen indicating that yeast (Hefe) is added. The filtered ones are known as Kristall Weizen. Weizenbier is also brewed by American micro-breweries although usually these lack the aroma of cloves.

Corn (maize) is used for many different purposes.

INGREDIENTS

GRAIN

Grain or cereal crops form the most important basic foodstuffs of humankind. Rice, corn (maize), barley, wheat, and oats are staple foods in both the rich and poor parts of the world. They are the source of important carbohydrates or energy foods. Beer can incorporate any of these grains among its nutrients and can therefore contribute to the daily intake of carbohydrates. The particular grain used to brew beer depends on the availability, ease of use for brewing, the brewer's own preferences, and sometimes the involvement of governments. Hence German brewers solely used barley unless they also happened to be brewers to the court of one of the monarchs. Some Belgian brewers only used wheat because this was the grain most readily available in their region. Many breweries use rice and corn (maize) because these are much cheaper but others use them because it is easier to brew clear beers with these cereals. Brewing with other grain types than barley or wheat is regarded by many as of lower quality and while not every brewer is solely concerned with quality, quality ingredients are needed for quality beer.

OATS

Oats are rarely used in brewing and where they are used the proportions used rarely exceed 10%. Oats are found in stout and certain Belgian beers. It is difficult for the brewer to create a mash with oats and they also contain a substantial amount of oil that has an adverse effect on the head of a beer.

CORN (MAIZE)

Corn (maize) is the cheapest provider of starch and it can account for up to 50% of the wort with some brewers. Corn produces a lighter body in beer its brews and is generally added in the form of cornflour from which the oil-bearing parts of the grain have been removed. Corn is not malted but cooked.

RICE

Many regard rice as an undesirable addition to beer but it can yield a drier and cleaner taste that many appreciate. The amount of rice used varies between 10–20% and is added in the form of either rice flakes or whole grains. Rice contains up to

70% starch and less than 10% protein. Rice needs to be cooked for a short time before it can be used. The conversion of the starch that is present in the rice is done with the help of enzymes in malt.

WHEAT

Wheat imparts a certain body and sharpness to a number of excellent types of beer. It is more difficult to brew with wheat than barley because it does not have a protective coating. German wheat beers used malted wheat but Belgian wheat beers and Lambic beers use wheat that has not been malted. The use of wheat also produces a firmer head on a beer and is the reason why certain beers use a small amount of wheat in their brewing. Wheat is almost always used in conjunction with malted barley. Because wheat is high in protein it is more difficult to produce a clear brew. When both baker and brewer had to rely upon local supplies of wheat, the baker had priority in years when the harvest was poor, with brewers getting only what was left over.

MALT

Once the brewer has decided on the type of grain or grains to be used that is not the end of the story. The manner in which the grain is prepared for brewing is at least as important. Grains such as barley, wheat, oats, and rye first have to be germinated in order to make them suitable for use. This is done by the maltster who wets the grain and then spreads it out in a warm space. Once the grain germinates the enzymes diatase and protease are activated that convert the stored energy into sugars and protein, which a germinating plant requires for its further development. The grain is then immediately dried to prevent the seed further developing into a plant. The manner in which this is done has a considerable bearing on the eventual color and flavor of the beer in which the malt is used.

AMBER MALT

This type of malt is often used to give beers a darker color. The malt is dried slowly and then roasted at a temperature of around 150°C (302°F). Amber malt is used only sparingly.

Pale malt

The pale type of malt is the most widely used and may be Pilsner malt, lager malt, or pale ale malt. These types of malt are dried slowly without the use of a high temperature which is raised in steps to a top of 80–85°C (176–185°F). This gradual warming enables the enzymes to continue to work whereas higher temperatures render them inoperative and the malt would become darker. It is for this reason that these pale malts form the basis for most beer. Beer cannot be brewed from the darker types of malt on its own.

Chocolate malt

This is a dark roasted malt that is malted at a very high temperature of up to 230°C (446°F) in which it is agitated. Chocolate malt has no active enzymes but it provides a dark brown to black color and a roasted flavor without being as harsh as black malt.

Crystallized malt

For this type of malt the grain is thoroughly soaked and then immediately heated to 150°C (302°F). This caramelizes or crystallizes the sugars in the malt. These sugars are not able to ferment and the malt has no active enzymes. For this reason crystallized malt does not consist of more than 20% of the wort. There is a great variety in colors and types of crystallized malt such as caramel and dark which are used to brew dark and strong ales. Crystallized malt imparts both fullness and sweetness to a beer.

Münchener malt

This "Munich" malt is dried at a higher temperature of up to 105°C (221°F) which gives it a somewhat darker color. This type of malt possesses sufficient enzymes to convert the starch but it is usually used in conjunction with "Pilsener" malt. Its main use is to darken beer and to increase the malt flavor.

Wheat malt

Wheat is malted for German wheat beers. The grains of wheat lack the hard coating of barley, making them more vulnerable during the malting process. Although wheat has sufficient enzymes for the fermentation process it is used with barley to produce a clearer brew. Up to 5% wheat malt is sometimes added to barley-based brews to improve the head of the beer.

Viennese malt

The foundation of Viennese type beers is Viennese malt, although other types of beer also use this kind of malt to impart a reddish-orange glow. Viennese malt is germinated at a slightly higher temperature than paler types but it has sufficient enzymes to be used on its own without the addition of other types of malt.

Black malt

The darkest type of malt is roasted for two hours at more than 200°C (392°F) until it is almost carbonized. It is used in small proportions of about 5% to produce a black color and a roasted taste.

SUGARS

The fermentation process is powered by sugar. There are various types of sugar and not all of them are converted by fermentation and this varies also according to the type of yeast used. These sugars include maltose, fructose, dextrin, galactose, raffinose, and meliobiose. Dextrin for example more or less does not ferment so that its presence in beer produces body rather than alcohol. Maltose or malt sugar is the principal form of sugar present in beer.

The sugars derived from the form of cereal used in brewing are produced by the modification of starch by enzymes but other by-products of this process are also present. If a brewer does not want these in his beer he can use sugar instead which more or less wholly ferments to produce alcohol and carbon dioxide. This choice results in a lighter-bodied beer that is less sweet. Strange as it may sound, sugar is actually added in the brewing process to make beer less sweet. Sugar is also added to beer by brewers during bottling. Many Belgian and British breweries use this practice to create secondary fermentation in the bottle.

HOPS

Quite how brewers got the notion to use the blossoms of the hop plant in their beer no-one knows. It is known that hops were being cultivated for this purpose some twelve hundred years ago. Various herbs and spices are used to flavor beer and it is likely that the properties of hops were well understood within the cloistered walls of the monasteries. The knowledge spread from the monasteries to the wider world so that the most appropriate flavoring for beer became known throughout Europe. This practice did not spread to the British though until later and use of hops only become commonplace in the British Isles in the late fifteenth century.

Hops impart bitterness, flavor, and aromas to beer like no other herb and also help to preserve the beer. This combination of properties has ensured that hops are added to beer almost throughout the entire world. Hop or Humulus lupus, grows in moderate climate zones. It is a climbing plant that can reach out for seven meters (23 ft). The plant climbs up wires or strings with little tendrils. In the wild this plant climbs its way up trees.

Hops can reach up to seven meters (23 ft) (right).

Hop plants are male or female but it is only the female plant that interests the brewer for this carries the flower form known as hops. These are picked by hand or machine and then dried with warm air which enables them to be kept for quite some time although quality deteriorates with age.

Hops are cultivated in Central Europe, England, the USA, and also in Australia and New Zealand. Famous name hops from Germany are their Hersbrucker, Tettnang, Spalt, and Hallertau. In the Czech Republic the best-known type grown is probably Saaz. English hops have names like Fuggles, Goldings, Brewer's Gold, and Northern Brewer. In the USA they grow Yakima valley, Willamette, Cascade, Cluster, Centennial, Chinnok, Mt. Hood, and Nugget. The Australians have their Pride of Ringwood.

These cultivated forms of hops get their names from either the area in which they were first grown or the nurseryman who developed them. These plants also find their way to other countries where they often acquire a quite different character. Different climate and soil in another country can

The female hops that are so important for today's beers.

Chili beer is bottled with a whole chili pepper that ensures a strong fiery taste.

often give the variety an entirely new character. Each types of hops has its own distinctive character which the brewers know. With this character, expressed in bitterness, the brewer can make a complex calculation to determine how much of the hops are required to reach a certain level of bitterness. The density of the wort itself, the amount of hops to be used, and the length of brewing time are all factors that have to be taken into consideration.

The form in which hops are used also varies between different brewers. Many traditional brewers swear by the use of whole hops but others use hops in pellet form. Hops are ground and then pressed into pellets that are vacuum packed for longer life. Hop extract is a liquid containing all the essential constituents of hops but there are also liquid forms that only impart aroma or bitterness.

The hops themselves consist of petals with a calyx on the outside. At the top of each sepal there are glands that contain lupinline. This is a substance comprising wax, resin, ethereal oils, sugar, and a number of other substances. The ethereal oils are the principal constituent in terms of their role in provision of taste and aroma.

In order that the bitterness from hops is transferred to the wort the hops need to brew with the wort for quite some time but this causes loss of the aromatic properties. For this reasons the hops that determine bitterness are added at the start of the process and those for aroma are added just before the end of the brewing process. Additional hops may be added during filtration for their aromatic properties. Another approach is the addition of hops during the time the beer is maturing or even when the kegs or barrels are being filled.

HERBS, SPICES, FRUIT, AND FLOWERS

Although hops are the most important additive to beer throughout the world there are many beers that are brewed with addition of other ingredients or even without hops.

Before hops became commonplace beer was brewed with a mixture of herbs that varied from area to area and from season to season.

The peel of bitter Curacao oranges is one of the ingredients of Hoegaarden type white beer.

The ingredients can include rosemary, coriander, bog myrtle, nutmeg, juniper and bay leaves, resin, and certain flowers. In addition to these flavorings brewers also use star anise, licorice, fennel, sweet flag root, ginger, and cumin. The Scottish brewer Bruce Williams uses heather flowers in his Heather Ale and in the USA there are chili beers with a whole chili in the bottle. Belgian wheat beers are flavoured with dried orange peel and coriander while cherries, peaches, and raspberries are popular flavorings for Belgian beers based on their lambic ales and normal ales. The Swiss Wadi-Brau adds hemp to the brew. Hemp and hops are closely related in the plant kingdom. German brewers reject any additive other than hops but are known to add a slice of lemon to their wheat beers. These various flavorings can produce some extremely interesting beers and provided they are not harmful to health they are to be welcomed as offering something for every taste.

The open fermentation vats of the Sierra-Nevada brewery.

WATER

Most of us regard water as commonplace. In spite of all the efforts of marketing men and women the majority of people living in well developed countries regard tap water as just as good as alternatives. We wash the car with it, water the garden, and drink it without any need to treat the water first. Such luxury is not available on tap throughout the entire world and was not available in the developed countries until recent times. In the Middles Ages beer was regarded as safer than water. Unlike water, beer had been boiled so that the majority of any bacteria had been killed.

Water comprises eight to ninety percent of beer. The water used for brewing comes from wells, springs, and from the mains water supply that gets its water from rivers, or from groundwater. What is

The Alfa brewery uses water from an officially recognized natural spring for its brewing (left).

in water can vary greatly from one area to another and it is the minerals and salts in water that largely determine the character of the beer that is made from it. Hard water is ideal for making ales but soft water is more suitable for the lighter lagers. Brewers have a number of ways they can modify their water for their different brews.

YEAST

Yeast is not really an ingredient in most beers. It is a single cell organism that converts sugar into alcohol and carbon dioxide. Yeast can be found almost everywhere because it is in the air. The ancient Egyptians relied on this for their brewing and present-day Belgian lambic beers still rely on naturally occurring beneficial yeast for fermentation. The first man-made controlled application of yeast occurred when brewers added the froth at the top of their fermentation vats to the following brew. This led to the top-working types of yeast gaining the upper hand.

With the invention of the microscope brewers discovered that the foaming top from fermentation consists of living organisms. Louis Pasteur was one of the first scientists to understand the working of yeast. The Buchner brothers discovered that yeast produced a specific enzyme in order to convert sugar into alcohol. A scientist name Emil Hansen who was employed by the Copenhagen Carlsberg brewers was one of the first to isolate a specific type of yeast. Yeast cultures can consist of a variety of different types but Hansen created pure cultures with which brewers had much greater control over the brewing process. Yeast can be somewhat unpredictable in its working and the unreliability factor is far greater with a number of different types of yeast than with just one. German monks learned that certain types of yeast were better at lower temperatures. In addition to storeage or lagern fermentation was also carried out in cold caves.

Experiments were carried out into cold fermentation at his Spaten brewery by Gabriel Seldmayer Junior. One of his apprentices was Jacob Christiaan Jacobsen who founded the Carlsberg brewery. Stories have it that Jacobsen took a culture of the bottom fermenting yeast with him to Copenhagen in a jar hidden in his hat. This type of yeast is known as *Saccharomyces uvarum* but it has also been known as *Saccharomyces carlsbergensis*. Top fermenting yeast is *Saccharomyces cerevisiae*. Top fermenting yeast works more quickly and at higher temperatures than the bottom fermenting kind, at 15–25°C (59–77°F). Once the fermentation has taken place a foaming layer is formed on the top of the wort. Bottom working yeast functions at 4–8°C (39.2–46.4°F). When bottom working yeast has fermented it sinks to the bottom from which the common name applied to it. This type of yeast

Modern brewers have the help of the latest automated equipment.

works more slowly but more thoroughly so that more sugar is converted. There are two phases to fermentation-aerobic (with oxygen) and anaerobic (without oxygen). During the aerobic phase the yeast is largely reproducing itself. Once it has exhausted the oxygen in the wort it then starts to convert sugar into carbon dioxide and alcohol with the help of certain enzymes.

Yeast is the essence of brewing and largely determines the character of the resulting beer but it is also susceptible to both infection and mutation and it is for this reason that a brewer will only use a culture up to five or six times. After this the brewer carefully creates a new culture from the pure basis culture. In addition to keeping cultures in their own laboratories, brewers also keep yeast cultures in special yeast banks. These can be turned to for yeast with precisely the same properties in the event of infection, a major fire, or some other calamity. Brewers such as the Dutch multi-national Heineken that brew in many centers throughout the world have new cultures flown to the world-wide breweries each week.

Malt is turned automatically at the Bavaria brewery.

This small roller mill may be old but it still works perfectly.

BREWING

Making beer is known as brewing. Technically the boiling of the wort is the actual brewing process but a brewer does somewhat more than this.

MALTING

Malting is the preparation of grain to make it suitable for use in brewing. Some breweries still produce their own malt but many leave it to other companies or in the case of multi-national breweries to a separate division. The purpose of malting is to activate the enzymes needed to convert starch into the essential soluble sugars. This is done by taking advantage of the initial growing phase of the plant that the grain represents. The grain is tricked into thinking it is spring by an increase in temperature and humidity. The dormant seed germinates in order to send its shoots above ground but the maltster has other ideas and halts germination when the grain has produced sufficient enzymes but before the new plant starts to draw on the reserves of sugar.

The maltster must carry out several tasks before the grain can be malted. With the aid of air blowers and sieves the grain is cleaned to rid it of dust, insects, sand, any foreign bodies, and any other seeds that may be present before it is stored. The storage period is necessary to give the grain the idea of a winter. Fresh grain does not germinate very well.

When the maltster needs to work with fresh grain it first needs to be steeped. The moisture content of the grain increases from 15 to 50% and by constant running water on the malt the acidity is kept low. The soaking time needed for grain varies from three to four days.

The most widely used malting methods these days are within special malting compartments or in drums. With the first of these the grain is piled up to a meter high (39 in) and the grain is turned by augers (spiral screws). Air is forced through ventilation grilles. The drum method is basically similar except that the grain is slowly turned in a large drum. The traditional method of malting is to spread grain out over the floor of a special malting kiln or malt house to a depth of 10–40 cm (4–16 in). The malt was once turned manually with a malt scoop but these days machine scoops do the job in traditional malt houses.

The turning of malt serves several purposes. It ensures that the grains germinate and develop uniformly and provides fresh oxygen so that the roots do not take hold of one another. The maltster can regularly mist the malt in order to control the humidity. This phase lasts from eight to fifteen days. The maltster checks progress of the malting by examining the roots, which may reach up to about three-quarters of the length of the grain. Where corn (maize) or rice is used in brewing no malting is required as boiling is sufficient.

DRYING

The next step in production of malt is its drying. This is necessary to halt the development of the germinating plant at the moment that the enzymes are active and before the grain has used too much of its food reserves. A further benefit of drying is that by reducing moisture content in the grain from 50% to 2% it can be stored longer.

The temperature at which the malt is dried has a direct bearing on the eventual color of the malt. These days maltsters use drum form hot air grain dryers but some malt is still traditionally dried or smoked in kilns over a wood or peat fire. Drying takes about two to four days, depending on the method used and the type of malt required.

MILLING

Malt is further treated by rolling in a mill before use so that the malt dissolves better. The mill usually consists of two large rollers which crush the malted grains between them. The inner soft part of the grain is crushed in this process but the chaff remains intact. This is important because the chaff helps the process of filtering during clarification of the beer. This milling process is carried out at the brewery just before the creation of the mash because once malt has been milled it is more readily prone to rot.

MASHING

We have now reached the point at which the brewer starts to introduce liquid. The crushed malt and water are combined together in a mash tun and brought to the appropriate temperature. The purpose is activation of the enzymes in the malt so that they will convert starch into sugars. For this reason the mash should taste sweet at the end of this process.

Brewers use one of two different methods of forming a mash: by infusion or decoction.

Infusion

With the infusion method the brewer uses just one mash tun and the mash is heated to 50–55°C (122–131°F). Some brewers refer to this stage of the mash as the "protein rest" and it last for about half an hour. At this temperature range the enzymes enable the release of proteins. By further heating the mash or adding more hot water, the temperature is then raised to about 65°C (149°F). This activates the ß amylase enzymes that degrade starch into maltose that will ferment. The temperature is then increased to 75°C (167°F) at which point a amylase converts the starch into the sugar dextrin, which does not ferment. This means that the control of the temperature and the duration at different temperatures determines the extent of sugars that do not ferment in the brew. High levels of maltose produce a thin beer that is high in alcohol while dextrin imparts sweetness and body.

Decoction

European brewers of lager in particular use the decoction method of mashing to create the mash. This requires two mash tuns. The biological process is the same as the infusion method but is done in a different way. A third of the mash at a time is transferred to the second mash tun and brought to the boil. The boiling liquid is then returned to the first tun and the mash is brought to the required temperature for the specific enzymes.

Fermentation is fascinating.

These cylindrical fermentation tanks for top fermentation were an innovation at the time of their installation at the Weistephan brewery in 1987.

CLARIFICATION

The mash is a cloudy mixture containing remnants of the malt that have not dissolved at the end of the mashing process. In order to achieve a clear beer these suspended solids such as the chaff from the malt needs to be filtered out. For this purpose the brewer takes advantage of the coarse nature of the chaff. Some brewers have a separate clarification tun into which the wort is pumped. These have a double bottom, the uppermost of which is finely slotted. The liquid drains through the slotted bottom into a sump from which it is pumped back to the tun. The chaff forms a sediment on the slotted bottom of the tank and acts as a very fine filter that traps all the suspended solids in the mash. This is one of the reasons why brewers have difficulty working with other types of grain with no chaff. Once the liquid that is being constantly circulated through this system is clear the circulation can be halted. At this point a great deal of sugar that the brewer does desire in his brew are also trapped by the chaff. The brewer therefore carefully rinses the chaff with hot water to separate the sugars from the chaff. The remaining waste is often used as cattle feed.

BREWING

Once the liquid from the mash has been clarified it is then referred to as the wort. The wort is transferred to the brewing vessel where the actual brewing process begins. The boiling of the wort is done for several reasons: firstly because it acts as a form of sterilization that kills of any bacteria and it stops the action of the enzymes. The protein present in the wort also swell up and gives greater body to the liquid. During the process of washing away the chaff the wort can become too watery but during the brewing process liquid evaporates and the beer is brought to the desired original gravity. This is variously shown on labels as "Original Gravity" or "O.G.", with a degree sign (°), or with an indication of percentage (%). This original gravity determines the eventual body of

Storage tanks at the Weihstephan brewery.

the beer and to some extent its proportion of alcohol. The original gravity though does not indicate what proportion of the sugar present is of the type that does not ferment.

Hops are now added to the wort. This is done at least an hour before the end of the brewing process because the bitter substances in the hops need this time to be absorbed. The aromatic substances largely vanish in the boiling process and hence hops are added just a quarter of an hour before the end of the brew to impart aroma. Generally beer is brewed (in other words boiled) for about one to one and a half hours.

FILTRATION

The wort is cloudy from particles of swollen proteins and the addition of hops at the end of the brewing period. Before the next stage of the process these suspended solids have to be removed. One traditional method is the use of a hop sieve.

The wort is transferred to another vessel with a slotted base above the actual bottom of the tank and is filtered just as the mash was earlier clarified. This time though the hop petals provide the filter. These can form a very thick filter on the bottom of the vessel. Some brewers use fresh hops as a filter – both for better filtration and to impart extra aroma. This method of filtration can only be carried out with whole hops.

The majority of large-scale breweries use a centrifuge to separate the solids from the wort. Like a whirlpool, the solids concentrate at the center and the clear liquid is allowed to drain off through the sides of the centrifuge vessel.

COOLING

Once the boiled wort has been clarified it can be fermented and this requires the correct temperature. The wort therefore has to be cooled. Waiting naturally for the wort to cool down would greatly increase risk of infection of the sterile wort and hence it has to be cooled as quickly as possible. This is done by passing the hot wort through a heat exchanger.

FERMENTATION

Fermentation is the most remarkable part of the brewing process. The notion that live yeast organisms turn a sweet liquid into beer and form a lively head on the top is quite fascinating. For a long time this process was shrouded in mystery and even today it is the most difficult stage for the brewer to control. Those producing lager have it slightly easier than the brewers of ales since the colder temperature keeps the yeast in check. The yeast that is added to the wort comes either from a new culture or from the previous brew. This starting culture of yeast is then added to the cool wort to begin the process of fermentation.

Cold fermentation

Fermentation using lager type yeast culture is carried out with the wort cooled to around 5°C (41°F). The culture is then added to the wort and the temperature is controlled because the yeast action can quickly raise the temperature of the wort in either an open or closed fermentation tank.

Initially yeast reproduces itself by using the sweet wort as a food source. This depletes the oxygen in the wort which prevents the organisms from reproducing and causes the actual fermentation to start. The yeast stimulates the production of enzymes and hence encourages the conversion of sugar into alcohol and carbon dioxide. Yeast works slowly but more thoroughly at lower temperatures. When the sugars that will ferment have been converted, so that there is no further nourishment for the lager yeast, it sinks to the bottom of the tank. Cold fermentation usually takes place in sealed tanks for a period of ten to fifteen days. This fermentation produces dry-

Most catering outlets sell beer on draft from casks. This cask-filling line at the Bittburger brewery can fill more than 1,300 casks per hour.

Beer is also sold in convenient cans, useful when traveling.

tasting beer because most of the sugar is converted by fermentation.

Warm fermentation

Warm fermentation takes place in open fermentation vessels. The wort is cooled to 15–20°C (59–68°F) before the yeast culture is added. The temperature of the wort can rise to 25°C (77°F) during fermentation. Warm fermentation happens much more rapidly than cold fermentation and is much livelier but far more sugar is left unfermented. Warm fermentation can be completed in between three and seven days. At the end of the fermentation the yeast lies on the surface in the form of a scum which the brewer can remove.

CONDITIONING IN STORE

The term lager is derived from the German lagern for storing beer in a cool place while it reaches condition. The idea was first used in Germany. After initial fermentation beer needs to be further conditioned. This is done in special tanks although some brewers use special vertical tanks in which both the fermentation and subsequent conditioning takes place. Others transfer the new beer to conditioning tanks or vats, some of which are still made of wood but most are stainless steel.

The conditioning process or – lagern as the Germans call it – is mainly intended to allow the beer an opportunity to continue fermenting so that carbon dioxide is created in the beer. Some brewers intentionally add a small amount of newly fermenting wort to encourage this. It is not just the traditional craft brewers who do this for this practice is also used to make American Budweiser. The American brewers of this beer use beech slats at the bottom of their lager tanks for the purposes of filtration. Top fermenting beers can take a week to reach condition but some are conditioned for a year or more. The temperature during this time

Glass is the most popular choice
for beer drunk at home (right).

Beers that have a second fermentation are allowed time to settle after bottling. This is done in warm room. Here the wheat beer of the Maisel Brothers is coming into condition.

varies around 25°C (77°F). Bottom fermenting beers are conditioned for three to twelve weeks at a temperature just above freezing. Here too certain beers are conditioned for longer at up to three years. There are beers though that are fermented with warmth but then conditioned at a cool temperature.

FILTRATION

Once the beer reaches condition it can be drunk but since most beers are drunk when clear there is still a final filtration process to undergo. This removes the remnants of yeast and flakes of protein from the beer. This is usually done with fine layers of chalk held between frames. The fine texture of the chalk with its minuscule fossilized skeletons of marine organisms ensures thorough filtering of the beer. Certain types of beer intentionally omit this final filtration so that further fermentation can take place.

PASTEURIZATION

Louis Pasteur made a major contribution to our knowledge of brewing. He discovered that heating kills micro-organisms such as bacteria and yeast. Many brewers have a negative attitude to pasteurization because they consider the process affects the flavor and aroma but others do not appear to have such qualms. It depends greatly on the brewery installation whether pasteurization can be safely omitted or not.

There are two methods of pasteurization: the tunnel method and flash method. With the flash pasteurization the beer is heated as it flows through hot water. One advantage of this approach is that it is of relatively short duration and fairly easy to

The warm storage area of a Dutch microbrewery.

contain some living yeast and not be pasteurized. These second fermentation beers are given sufficient time in the cellars of the breweries and bars for the fermentation to take place. The carbon dioxide that is created during fermentation cannot escape and hence the beer is very lively.

Belgian second fermentation beers and most German wheat beers are good examples of this type. Some British brewers add hops during filling for extra aroma but the vast majority of beers have no additives during bottling or the filling of casks.

The big brewers have fully automated bottling lines. The bottles are first thoroughly cleaned and then filled with carbon dioxide. The beer has minimal contact with oxygen during the filling process because beer in contact with oxygen during bottling oxidizes quickly. This is why most home brewed bottled beer that is filled by hand, and hence in contact with oxygen, can only be kept for a few days.

arrange but a disadvantage is that bottles, cans, and casks require separate sterilization, making the beer more vulnerable than with tunnel sterilization. With this method the bottles, cans, or casks slowly pass through a tunnel where they are heated to 60–80°C (140–176°F). This sterilizes the container as well as its contents and increases the life of the beer by a year.

BOTTLING AND FILLING

Few people have a pub on their doorstep that brews its own beer where they can buy beer on draught and so brewers have a number of ways of supplying beer for the home consumption and catering markets. Sometimes a small addition of sugar or unfermented wort is added during the filling of casks or bottles to cause further fermentation. The beer in question must of course

WEIGHTS AND MEASURES

The units of weights and measures are not universal throughout the world. Perhaps if Napoleon had conquered the entire world the matter would be different. The method of determining the percentage of alcohol in beer also differs between European and American practice. The Americans determine the original gravity (by weight) while the Europeans calculate the percentage by volume. Given that alcohol is lighter than water the results of these calculations consequently differ. The American system gives original gravity or alcohol by weight (ABW) and the European system is alcohol by volume (ABV).

UNITS OF VOLUME

1 liter	0.01 hectoliter	2.1133 US pints
		1.760 UK pints
1 hectoliter	100 liters	0.63 barrel
1 barrel	159 liters	1.59 hectoliters
1 US gallon	3.7853 liters	8 US pints
1 UK gallon	4.5459 liters	8 UK pints
1 US pint	0.4732 liters	
1 UK pint	0.5682 liters	

PERCENTAGES ALCOHOL

1% alcohol by volume	0.8% alcohol by weight (SG)
1% alcohol by weight	1.25% alcohol by volume

The following formula can be used to convert °Celsius to °Fahrenheit:

(x) °C multiply by 9 and divide by 5, then add 32 ($°F = °C \times 9/5 + 32$)

To convert °Fahrenheit to °Celsius:

(x) °Fahrenheit minus 32, multiply by 5 and divide by 9 ($°C = (°F - 32) \times 5/9$)

TEMPERATURE

1 °Celsius	33.8 °Fahrenheit
1 °Fahrenheit	-17.2 °Celsius
0 °Celsius	32 °Fahrenheit
0 °Fahrenheit	-17.8 °Celsius

Volume %	Weight %
1	0.8
2	1.6
3	2.4
4	3.2
5	4
6	4.8
7	5.6
8	6.4
9	7.2
10	8

°Celsius	°Fahrenheit
17.8	0
0	32
4	39.2
6	42.8
8	46.4
10	50
12	53.6
15	59
18	64.4
100	212

HOME BREWING

Provided there is space enough and the marriage is sound, a beer lover can easily brew his or her own ales.

The pale lager type of beer is quite difficult to approximate at home but top fermenting ales of many types are within the capability of a home brewer. Home brewing is not a particularly expensive hobby for the prices of special beers is higher than the cost of the raw materials a home brewer needs to produce a similar beer. Brewing your own beer can be very satisfying but be prepared for disappointing results. The brewing of beer demands considerable hygiene and even with great care beer can quickly go off. Brewing at home requires permits or licenses in some countries and in others is simply not allowed under the law, although this does not necessarily mean there is no home brewing in those countries.

The best start for a newcomer to home brewing is to read up on the subject from the many books that describe the process. The description of home brewing in this chapter does not seek to provide more than an impression of what is involved. Perhaps the next best step for the new home brewer is to join a club or association and perhaps to take out a subscription to a specialist magazine.

These steps can help the newcomer to avoid making some of the basic errors and clubs and associations can also advise about good value suppliers as well as providing useful hints, and brewing recipes.

A well-prepared beginner will have realized already that preparing his or her own malt is not straightforward, takes a great deal of time, and rarely produces results as good as those of professional maltsters. It is no shame to buy ready-prepared malt, indeed most breweries do likewise. Hops can also be purchased in a variety of forms: pellets, whole hops, and powdered. It is important to make sure you use quality ingredients, for these have a direct bearing on both the aroma and flavor of the beer you make. There are some excellent beer recipes available that are invaluable for the beginner. Yeast can be purchased in powdered or liquid form. So far as your water is concerned your water supplier should be able to provide you with information about the hardness of the water and such matters.

A newcomer to home brewing needs the following:
- large preserving pan of approx. 20 liters for brewing and also perhaps the mash
- large plastic container of approx. 25 liters that can be closed for use as a fermentation vessel
- coiled tubing to act as a water or air barrier to prevent infection of the wort
- hydrometer
- thermometer
- sulfite (for cleansing)
- accessories e.g. tubing, funnel, bucket, iodine, pH tester, scales, etc.

An experienced home brewer might add all manner of equipment to expand on these items and even produce his or her own malt and prepare the malt for brewing with a roller mill. At this stage hobby brewers needs to be certain they will continue with the pastime since costs can mount quickly. One such item might be a crown cork cap fitting device for bottles but the use of bottles with hinged stoppers is also possible.

Europe

Europe

England / The United Kingdom

While small countries like Denmark, Belgium, and The Netherlands have established export markets for their beers that have contributed to the international taste for beers, the United Kingdom – that once had such an extensive empire – has hardly spread the taste for its beer beyond the British Isles. Only in the USA, where there has been rapid growth in micro-breweries – that still only account for a tiny part of the market – has there been any interest in the "English-style" of ales. They stand in stark contrast in that country with the giant brands of lager that dominate the market. In Australia too – where the British roots are still apparent – it is lager-type beers that dominate. It is the British "island mentality" that has protected the "English ales" from continental influences–thank good-ness, for the land has a rich variety of ales from pretty insipid brews but many superb beers of outstanding flavors and aromas that virtually no lager-type beer can match in intensity and clarity.

British beer is an acquired taste. The still beer does not readily appeal to everyone but in part through the efforts of the Campaign for Real Ale (CAMRA) there are still many traditional ales that are well worth discovering.

CAMRA is an organization of beer lovers who banded together to save the traditional "real ale." By this they mean the traditional ales that are conditioned in the cask and not stored under pressure but need to be pumped from the barrel into the glass by hand. This type of beer was threatened because the big brewers could make money with less ado with modern-style brewing methods and ales. Real ale has a very short "shelf life" which demands a meticulous and expensive distribution system and good cellar management in the pubs. The filtered and pasteurized cask (or keg) beer under pressure has none of these problems. CAMRA has also helped to support as many small breweries as possible to continue brewing and new ones to set up in order to maintain the British tradition of "real ale."

Many of the rich assortment of inns or public houses (pubs for short) in Britain have a close relationship with a particular brewery. This can be in a number of ways.

There are so-called "tied houses" that are owned by a brewery or a management company that is ultimately owned by the holding company of a brewery. These are run by tenants who must pay rent to the company which owns them. Most are required not only to purchase their beer but also all other drinks from the brewery or management company.

Independent inns or pubs are known as "free houses." These are independently owned pubs which are free to buy their beers and other drinks from wherever they choose but in reality they are often not as free as it might seem for breweries often lend such publicans money for improvements or extensions in exchange for an agreement about the beers they sell.

A third type of pub is owned by a brewery or management company and run for them by a paid manager. This type of pub obviously has the closest relationship with its brewery or management company.

This relationship between pubs and breweries is a trading commodity and breweries sell pubs to one another or exchange them in order to strengthen their position in a particular area. When a brewery itself is taken over this also often brings with it that brewery's pubs and "tied houses." Breweries might be purchased for their outlets rather than the brewery itself – resulting in the closure of the brewery. This relationship between the breweries and their outlets is very important in the survival of the small family breweries. Should this link be removed – and the European Commission seems determined so to meddle – then many of these small breweries would be unable to compete against the financially stronger large brewing concerns. This would undoubtedly see the end of most of the small family brewers and the end of the much-loved traditional "real ales." The large-scale brewers do not trouble themselves with "real ales" although many allow them to be sold as "guest beers" in their pubs. These specialty beers

The towers of the Wadsworth brewery.

– that are rarely profitable for the major brewers – are usually supplied by small independent brewers.

Many of these traditional breweries have names made up of a couple of founders to which other activities such as the management of pubs, and wholesale distribution of wine and spirits, soft drinks, and imported beers may be added. Often the brewery itself will be known simple as "The Old Brewery" or "The Brewery."

The brewing industry saw rapid expansion in the late nineteenth century. Increased industrialization brought with it urbanization and concentrations of large numbers of thirsty workers. Many new breweries were built in the United Kingdom at this time to meet the growing demand. Many of these breweries were built in tower form that saved energy in the handling of raw materials, the wort, and the eventual beer. Gravity could be used from the top of the tower to move the products downwards through the process. The energy that was still required was provided by a steam engine and boilers but these have virtually all disappeared, although the tower breweries still exist. A fine example is that of the Wadsworth brewery in Devizes that still brews in the traditional manner, although the process shown has changed slightly due to changes in the taxation of beer, and other changes in brewing practice.

1.   THE INGREDIENTS

The ingredients of the Wadworth brewery are suitably treated mains water, malted barley, whole hops, cane sugar, and yeast.

2.   ROLLER MILLING

The malted barley is lifted to the top of the building and checked for purity. It is then passed through a roller mill to crush it so that it will more readily absorb liquid. Malt is crushed rather than ground to ensure that the chaff of the grain remains intact. The crushed malt is then transported to the mash tun.

3.   MASH TUN

Hot water is added to the crushed malt in the mash tun and this stimulates the conversion of starch in the grain into sugars. This process, in which the important constituents of the malt are absorbed in the liquid, is known as "mashing."

4.   CLARIFICATION VESSEL

The mash – known as the "wort" once it has been filtered – runs off by gravity through a small clarification vessel. The brewer then adds cane sugar to the wort which flows into the copper or brewing vessel by gravity.

5A.   BREWING COPPER

The Wadworth brewery's brewing copper is said to be the last open one of its kind in Britain. Here the hops are added and the wort is boiled for one and a half hours to impart the characteristics of the hops to the beer. Once more the wort runs off by gravity to the hopback.

5B.   HOPBACK

The hopback is another clarifying vat in which hops are used to filter the beer. Wadsworth add extra hops to the plates of the hopback – known as late hopping. Other brewers add additional hops at an earlier moment.

6A. COOLING

The beer is then pumped up the brewery tower through a cooler to bring it back to room temperature.

6B. COLLECTION VESSEL

The wort ends up in a collection vessel where it is aerated and yeast is added. It then runs off by gravity to the fermentation vessel.

7. MEASURING

Formerly the brewer determined the original gravity of the brew at this point (and made the necessary adjustments) in order to assess the duty that must be paid on the alcohol.

8. FERMENTATION

The primary fermentation takes place over two days. The foaming residue that forms on the surface is removed and the temperature of the beer is reduced to about 10°C (50°F) and is then left to ferment for a further five days.

9. QUALITY CONTROL

Close attention is paid to quality control, with regular checks throughout the brewing process.

10. REAL ALE

Real ales are transferred to wooden barrels with the addition of isinglass to help clarify the beer and a sugar preparation to foster further fermentation. Sometimes additional hops are added at this time.

11. KEG BEER

Beer that is to be supplied in kegs is first stored in chilled tanks at 0°C (32°F). Following this the beer is filtered before the kegs are filled.

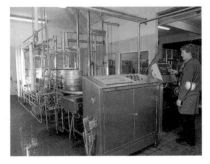

12. BOTTLED AND CANNED BEER

Beer for bottling or canning is treated in the same way as keg beer.

TYPES OF BEER

All the original types of beer with which the United Kingdom is richly endowed are top fermenting ales but lagers have gained wide popularity. In pubs, although lagers have made huge inroads, ales are still very popular and are responsible for a large share of the "on trade" market for beer consumed in pubs unlike other European countries where the "off trade" in bottles and cans for home consumption is most important. Alongside the traditional draught ales there has been a re-emergence in interest in the UK in recent years in bottled and canned special brews, both with and without second fermentation.

Bitter

Bitter is to the British man (and increasingly woman too) what a Pilsener is to a Dutch man. A pub without bitter would be akin to butcher without meat. It is as if the British have bitter flowing through their veins and this continues to be the single most important type of beer sold and drunk in Great Britain. Bitter's origins hark back to colonial times when strongly hopped and strongly alcoholic beers were brewed to withstand the rigors of long sea voyages so that the colonists would not be deprived of their English ales. The Indian Pales Ales (IPA) also owe their origins to this period.

There are other reasons though for the creation of a type of beer that on face value might be considered somewhat off-putting. This includes the development of more pungent types of hops.

Virtually every brewer now brews at least one bitter with a great variety of descriptions and names, such as Extra Special Bitter (ESB), Special Bitter, and Ordinary.

Brown ale

The best known brown ale is undoubtedly Newcastle Brown Ale, a malty but dry brown ale. This was originally launched in the North East of England to compete with the pale ales of the Midlands.

Mild

The popularity of mild was at its peak when Britain's industrialization was growing rapidly. The mild-tasting beer that is low in alcohol was drunk as a "pick-me-up" and because it was a cheap beer for those on low incomes. The term "mild" does not refer to low alcoholic strength but the absence of bitterness of hops. Mild has been produced in many forms from pale to dark in color, some fruity, others full-bodied and sweet, but never bitter in taste.

Pale ale

The term "pale ale" is not wholly inseparable from that of "bitter". The two types of ale overlap and are difficult to differentiate. Pale ales are often anything but pale in color, much more amber. The origins of pale ales lies in Burton-upon-Trent. Most draught pale ales are known as bitters and the term pale ale is mainly used for bottled beers. Pale ales are usually more rounded and less hoppy than draught bitter.

Sweet stout

Sweet stout is a British peculiarity (or specialty). One of the type is the milk stout made with the addition of lactose or milk sugars that has a pronounced sweet taste. Since the lactose is not fermented by the yeast it results in a much sweeter beer that is also lower in alcohol. These beers gained popularity in the early twentieth century among those who did not like the more bitter hop taste of other beers. The "milk" connotation led to these beers being promoted as a tonic for suckling mothers and a pick-me-up for those engaged in heavy labor.

ADNAMS & CO PLC, SOLE BAY BREWERY, SUFFOLK

Production in hectoliters: –
Founded: 1890

The history of this brewery dates back to 1872 when two brothers, George and Ernest Adnams, took over the brewery of the Old Swan Inn. They were joined in 1902 by Mr. P.C. Loftus who brought additional capital and expertise. The brewery's board of directors still consists of descendants of the two founders. Adnam's brewery is mainly aimed at the local market to which it still delivers to some pubs using a horse-drawn brewer's dray. The beer is sold throughout the UK by distributors. Bottled versions are filtered and pasteurized but this is omitted for the draught beer. The draughts are Adnams Bitter 3.7%, Old Ale 4.1%, Broadside 4.7%, and Tally Ho! Christmas beer at 6.4%. The bottled beers are Champion Pale Ale, Nut Brown Ale, and Broadside.

• • •

ARKELL'S BREWERY LTD, SWINDON, WILTSHIRE

Production in hectoliters: –
Founded: 1843

The term "family brewery" is perhaps nowhere else as appropriate as with Arkell's brewery. All the shares remain in the hands of the Arkell family and the company is currently run by the great great grandson of John Arkell who founded the brewery more than 150 years ago. Arkell's products include keg beer, bottled beer, soft drinks, wines and spirits in addition to draught real ale. The brewery's eighty-five tied houses all sell Adnam's beer together with some two hundred free houses. Their beers include 3B Best Bitter, Kingsdown Ale, Pale Ale, and North Star Keg.

• • •

ASH VINE BREWERY LTD, THE WHITE HART, TRUDOXHILL, SOMERSET

Production in hectoliters: –
Founded: 1987

The Ash Vine Brewery is a small brewery with three of its own pubs. The brewery is sited at one of these – The White Hart. Ash Vine also supplies beer to some fifty free houses. Their beers are Challenger, Black Bess Porter, Bitter, and different "guest ales" are also regularly brewed.

HOP & GLORY

TYPE: ALE
ALCOHOL: 5% VOL.
FERMENTATION: TOP

Special remarks: an amber-colored beer fermented in the bottle. Winter Ale has a bitter sweet taste and complex aroma of fruit, malt, and hops.

• • •

BALLARD'S BREWERY LTD, NYEWOOD PETERFIELD, HAMPSHIRE

Production in hectoliters: –
Founded: 1980

A small brewery without tied houses. Guided tours by appointment. A Christmas beer is brewed each year. Other beers include Wassail 6% with additional fermentation, Trotton Bitter 3.6%, Midhurst Mild 3.5%, Best Bitter 4.2%, and Golden Bine 4.2%.

DIVINE

TYPE: STRONG ALE
ALCOHOL: 9.6% VOL.
FERMENTATION: TOP

Special remarks: Divine is a strong winter ale brewed solely with natural ingredients. It has a strongly fruity aroma and is dark reddish brown in color. The taste is full sweet bitterness. This bottled beer ferments again in the bottle.

• • •

WOLVERHAMPTON AND DUDLEY BREWERIES PLC, BANKS'S, WOLVERHAMPTON, WEST MIDLANDS

Production in hectoliters: –
Founded: 1875

This is one of the larger independent breweries that came into being through the merger of three regional brewers. The company has almost one thousand tied houses.

BANKS'S

TYPE: MILD ALE
ALCOHOL: 3.5% VOL.
FERMENTATION: TOP

Special remarks: Banks's is one of this brewery's successes, which is perhaps why they have dropped the word "mild" from the former name of Banks's Mild. This is a reddish colored ale with a characteristic mild flavor. This is not a very full-bodied beer and the taste certainly is mild but with a aftertaste of short duration that is slightly bitter.

BANKS'S BITTER

TYPE: BITTER ALE
ALCOHOL: 3.8% VOL.
FERMENTATION: TOP

Special remarks: Banks's is a pale brown beer with a hoppy aroma and mildly malty taste with undertone of hops. The body is thin and there is a bittersweet aftertaste.

• • •

BASS BREWERS LTD, BURTON UPON TRENT, STAFFORDSHIRE

Production in hectoliters: 14,000,000
Founded: 1777

Part of Bass PLC of London. Burton upon Trent is the original home of Bass.

BASS PALE ALE

TYPE: PALE ALE
ALCOHOL: 5% VOL.
FERMENTATION: TOP

Special remarks: the Pale Ale with its red triangle label is undoubtedly the most successful of Bass's English ales. Originally this was an unfiltered beer with additional fermentation in the bottle that was not pasteurized. None of this is true of the bottled beer now on offer but this is no reason to turn this beer down. Bass brews this ale with pale ale malt and crystal malt using hops such as Challenger, Goldings, and Northdown, resulting in a fine fruity ale with a very malty and fruity taste.

BREAKER STRONG LAGER

TYPE: LAGER

ALCOHOL: 4.8% VOL.

FERMENTATION: BOTTOM

Special remarks: a pale lager with a reasonably full mouth sensation and neutral taste with a fairly sharp aroma of hops.

CAFFREY'S IRISH ALE

TYPE: ALE

ALCOHOL: 4.8% VOL.

FERMENTATION: TOP

Special remarks: this is an amber-colored ale with a "cream-flow" system that is soft and mild.

WORTHINGTON'S WHITE SHIELD

TYPE: ALE

ALCOHOL: 5.6% VOL.

FERMENTATION: TOP

Special remarks: this dark amber colored ale possesses a fine but compact head. The ale is slightly sweet but the taste is predominantly of hops with slightly dry undertones. The aroma has hints of roasted malt. Although Worthington is owned by Bass it is not actually brewed by them.

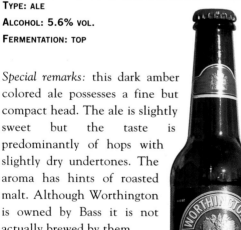

• • •

BASS PLC, LONDON

Production in hectoliters: –

Founded: 1967

Bass PLC was formed in 1967 by the merger of Bass, Mitchells & Butler Ltd, and Charrington UB Ltd. Bass has shares in the Czech Staropramen and also has distribution agreements for Dutch Grolsch, New Zealand Steinlager, and US Schlitz. Bass has a myriad of holdings and companies including breweries, soft drink manufacturers (Britvic), hotel chains, pub chains, restaurant chains, and even an insurance company (White Shield Insurance).

• • •

GEORGE BATEMAN & SON LTD, SALEM BRIDGE BREWERY, LINCOLNSHIRE

Production in hectoliters: –

Founded: 1874

This is an independent family brewery with around sixty outlets. The brewery today is headed by George Bateman, grandson of the founder. Their beers include Valiant, Victory Ale, Salem Porter, XB Bitter, and DM Mild. The Bateman company also owns Vine Hotel Ltd.

• • •

THE BLACK SHEEP BREWERY, MASHAM NORTH, YORKSHIRE

Production in hectoliters: –

Founded: 1992

This brewery was started by Paul Theakston of the Theakston Brewery family. Quite why he might be the "black sheep of the family" is unknown. Paul Theakston left the family firm when it was taken over by Scottish & Newcastle in 1988. Theakston now brews in the old Lightfoot maltings established in 1919 by his grandfather. The brewery has three different brews of which two are bottled.

BLACK SHEEP ALE

TYPE: ALE

ALCOHOL: 4.4% VOL.

FERMENTATION: TOP

Special remarks: the label of this dark amber ale suggests "serve chilled." Despite a not particularly high level of alcohol this ale conceals a pretty robust character. Well hopped, this Black Sheep has a mild bitter taste and leaves a dry sensation in the mouth. The ale is characterized by hops and dryness. This beer on draught is Best Bitter.

• • •

BODDINGTONS, STRANGEWAYS BREWERY, MANCHESTER

Production in hectoliters: –

Founded: 1778

Since 1990 Boddingtons has been part of Whitbread which is now aggressively marketing it throughout the UK.

BODDINGTON DRAUGHT

TYPE: ALE/BITTER

ALCOHOL: 3.8% VOL.

FERMENTATION: TOP

Special remarks: this "draught beer" in a can is fitted with a "draught-flow" system which injects gas when the can is opened to give the impression of a draught bitter. The pale and smooth beer is slightly malty in taste with an overtone of hops.

• • •

W.H. BRAKSPEAR AND SONS PLC, THE BREWERY, HENLEY-ON-THAMES OXFORDSHIRE

Production in hectoliters: –

Founded: 1779

Beer has been brewed at this site since 1700 but the later date marks the partnership between Robert Brakspear and Richard Hayward. The Brakspear brewery has some hundred of its own pubs and delivers to another three hundred free houses.

BRAKSPEAR STRONG ALE

TYPE: STRONG ALE

ALCOHOL: 5% VOL.

FERMENTATION: TOP

Special remarks: Brakspear's dark brown ale has a fruity and bitter taste with hints of dark malt, with dry palate and a prolonged bitter aftertaste.

• • •

BUFFY'S BREWERY, NORFOLK

Production in hectoliters: –

Founded: 1993

The two partners, Roger Abrahams and Julie Savory, brew some eight different ales which they supply to twenty local free houses. They also supply through wholesaler distributors. In addition to the ales described below they also brew Buffy's Bitter 3.9%, Polly's Folly 4.3%, Buffy's Strong Ale 6.5%, Festival 9X 9%, IPA 4.8%.

BUFFY'S ALE

TYPE: ALE

ALCOHOL: 5.5% VOL.

FERMENTATION: TOP

Special remarks: a light brown ale with a malty taste and bitter finish.

BUFFY'S MILD

TYPE: MILD ALE

ALCOHOL: 4.2% VOL.

FERMENTATION: TOP

Special remarks: a reddish-brown ale with malty aroma.

POLLY'S EXTRA FOLLY

TYPE: ALE

ALCOHOL: 4.9% VOL.

FERMENTATION: TOP

Special remarks: based on Polly's Folly, this ale is specifically brewed to create a more full sensation in the mouth.

• • •

BURTONWOOD BREWERY PLC, BURTONWOOD WARRINGTON CHESHIRE

Production in hectoliters: 130,000

Founded: 1867

James Forshaw established this family brewery in 1867 and members of his family can still be found in the company's management team. The Burtonwood Brewery has about five hundred pubs in its ownership. Several of its beers are James Forshaw Bitter, Top Hat, Burtonwood Bitter, and Burtonwood Mild.

• • •

ROBERT CAIN BREWERY, LIVERPOOL

Production in hectoliters: –

Founded: 1990

The brewery bearing the name of Robert Cain is part of the Danish Bryggerigruppen A/S (Danish Breweries

Group). The eponymous founder of the original Robert Cain Brewery was born in 1826 and gave up a sea-faring life at the age of eighteen to buy a small Liverpool pub where he quickly established a good reputation by brewing his own ales. He purchased the former brewery in Stanhope Street in 1858 that once again – after an absence of over seventy years – serves as the head office of the brewery. The brewery today produces their Dark Mild, Traditional Bitter, Formidable Ale, and three times per year their Superior Stout, with an eye to both tradition and quality.

Robert Cain, founder of the brewery.

CAIN'S FORMIDABLE ALE

TYPE: ALE

ALCOHOL: 5% VOL.

FERMENTATION: TOP

Special remarks: this darker pale ale of Cain's Brewery has a hoppy aroma and strongly bitter taste of hops with a prolonged dry finish. Formidable Ale is late hopped. It is available in 50 cl bottles and 1 liter cans.

CAIN'S SUPERIOR STOUT

TYPE: STOUT

ALCOHOL: 4.8% VOL.

FERMENTATION: TOP

Special remarks: this is not a year-round product from Cain's Brewery. The copper is made available three times each year to brew this special stout made with various types of English hops and dark burnt malt. The result is a mellow beer of medium body with a taste defined by burnt malt.

CAIN'S TRADITIONAL BITTER

TYPE: ALE/BITTER

ALCOHOL: 4% VOL.

FERMENTATION: TOP

Special remarks: this is an amber-colored bitter of medium body, with a hoppy aroma and taste. The palate is dry.

• • •

CARLSBERG-TETLEY PLC, BIRMINGHAM

Production in hectoliters: 10,000,000

Founded: 1992

This British giant brewery group was formed in 1992 when the British Allied-Domecq and the Danish Carlsberg joined forces to create the second largest British brewer. Allied-Domecq had resulted from a merger of Ansells, Ind Coope, and Tetley Walker in 1961, all of which had grown to their sizes through mergers and at the time of writing Carlsberg-Tetley was subject of a takeover bid by Bass. Carlsberg-Tetley control some four thousand pubs that are contracted to Allied-Domecq. Although the group brews many of its own products, it also brews a number of beers under license, including Löwenbrau, and the Australian Castelmaine, Swan, and Labatt.

• • •

CARLSBERG-TETLEY BURTON BREWERY LTD, BURTON UPON TRENT STAFFORDSHIRE

Production in hectoliters: 4,000,000

Founded: 1934

The brewery forms part of Carlsberg-Tetley PLC. This brewery resulted from the merger in 1934 of Allsopp's and Ind Coope. The Allsopp name has been brought to the fore again as a brand of special beers brewed to supply to pubs as guest beers.

JOHN BULL BITTER

TYPE: BITTER ALE

ALCOHOL: 4.5% VOL.

FERMENTATION: TOP

Special remarks: a light, malty, and fruity ale with a dry palate and a short aftertaste of slight bitterness.

TRIPLE DIAMOND

TYPE: STRONG ALE

ALCOHOL: 8.5% VOL.

FERMENTATION: TOP

Special remarks: this strong ale is brewed with a original gravity of 20 degrees. It is dark amber in color accompanied by a pale cream head. The aroma is of caramel and this is also found in the taste together with a mild but intense undertones of hops. The aftertaste is also slightly bitter, creating warmth in the mouth.

CASTLE EDEN BREWERY, DURHAM

Production in hectoliters: –
Founded: 1826

Castle Eden has been part of Whitbread since 1963. It has become the special beer brewer within the Whitbread group and it brews Higsons, Wethered Bitter, Castle Eden Ale and many of Whitbread's special editions.

FUGGLES IMPERIAL

TYPE: ALE
ALCOHOL: 5.5% VOL.
FERMENTATION: TOP

Special remarks: Fuggles Imperial is equipped with the so-called "draught-flow" system that ensures that the beer comes out of the bottle more-or-less in the same manner as a draught beer. This provides a fine but compact head which gives a creamy feeling in the mouth. The Fuggles name comes from Richard Fuggle whose Kentish hops became widespread in 1875. This brew is brewed exclusively with Fuggles hops that impart a bitter hop aroma and a mellow taste with a somewhat dry finish.

• • •

COTTAGE BREWING COMPANY, LITTLE ORCHARD, WEST LYDFORD SOMERSET

Production in hectoliters: –
Founded: 1993

The Cottage Brewing Company had such instant success with their Norman's Conquest that they were forced to expand significantly within their first year. The names of some of the beers are linked to the railways with names like Wheeltapper's Ale, Golden Arrow, and Our Ken. Beer is distributed locally from the Little Orchard Brewery by steam lorry and horse-drawn dray.

• • •

NORMAN'S CONQUEST

TYPE: ALE
ALCOHOL: 7% VOL.
FERMENTATION: TOP

Special remarks: within two years of its introduction this beer was named by CAMRA as "Champion Beer of Great Britain, 1995." This gave this dark and fruity ale of mildly hopped taste a great boost. Norman's Conquest continues to ferment in the bottle.

• • •

COURAGE LTD, ASHBY HOUSE, STAINES MIDDLESEX

Production in Hectoliters: 12,000,000
Founded: 1887

Courage is the part of Scottish Courage, that was acquired by Scottish & Newcastle from the Australian Carlton United Breweries, best-known for Fosters. Beers brewed by Courage include Fosters, Kronenbourg, Budweiser, Carlsberg, Holsten Pils, Miller, Beamish Stout, John Smith, and Courage Best Bitter.

BULLDOG

TYPE: STRONG ALE
ALCOHOL: 6.3% VOL.
FERMENTATION: TOP

Special remarks: Bulldog is a fruity and slightly sweet beer with a firm body and slightly dry palate. This strong ale was originally brewed for the Belgian market.

• • •

DALESIDE BREWERY, STARBECK NORTH YORKSHIRE

Production in hectoliters: –
Founded: 1988

The Daleside Brewery is owned by the Witty family who supply about two hundred local clients directly and many more elsewhere through wholesale distributors.

MONKEY WRENCH

TYPE: ALE

ALCOHOL: 5.3% VOL.

FERMENTATION: TOP

Special remarks: Monkey Wrench is a strong dark brown ale with a bittersweet taste and an aroma of roasted malt. The aftertaste is of pronounced bitterness.

MOROCCO ALE

TYPE: ALE

ALCOHOL: 5.5% VOL.

FERMENTATION: TOP

Special remarks: Morocco Ale creates a dry sensation in the mouth. Its taste is of muted roasted malt followed by a slightly bitter aftertaste of short duration.

ST. GEORGE ALE

TYPE: ALE

ALCOHOL: 4.1% VOL.

FERMENTATION: TOP

Special remarks: this is a mellow, fruity ale with a fine balance. It is medium-bodied with a slightly dry sensation in the mouth. The fruity and malty taste is set against a background bitterness of hops. The brewer advises to serve it chilled.

• • •

GOLDEN HILL BREWERY, EXMOOR ALES LTD, WIVELISCOMBE SOMERSET

Production in hectoliters: –
Founded: 1980

Exmoor Ales have been based in the former Hancock brewery where beer has been brewed since 1807. This was taken over in 1955 and closed in 1959. Exmoor Ales was established twenty years later. The most successful product is Exmoor Gold but the Golden Hill Brewery also brews Exmoor Stag, Exmoor Beast (a dark winter warmer), Exmoor Hart, and Exmoor Exmas (a Christmas beer).

EXMOOR GOLD

TYPE: ALE

ALCOHOL: 5% VOL.

FERMENTATION: TOP

Special remarks: Exmoor Gold was first brewed to celebrate the one thousandth brew of Exmoor Ale but this beer now has a firm place in the product range. As the name implies it is a golden ale brewed with a single type of malt, producing a malty aroma and sweet, rounded malty taste that is accompanied by a background bitterness of hops.

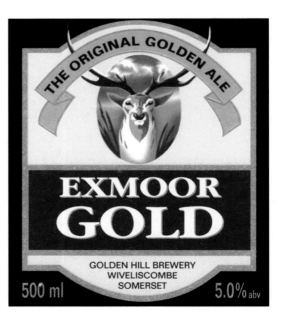

• • •

FREEDOM BREWING COMPANY LIMITED, LONDON

Production in hectoliters: –
Founded: 1995

The Freedom Brewery claims to be Britain's only micro-brewery for lager. Pilsener-type beer is produced using slow and methodical authentic craft processes without pasteurization.

FREEDOM PILSENER LAGER

TYPE: **PILSENER**
ALCOHOL: **5% VOL.**
FERMENTATION: **BOTTOM**

Special remarks: Freedom is a "blonde" Pilsener brewed using Maris Otter malt, Liberty and Saaz hops, water, and original lager yeast from the Bavarian Spaten brewery. Hence this Pilsener meets the German purity demands. The lager is matured for four weeks at -2°C. It is recommended that Freedom is drunk at a temperature of 4°C to get the best from its fruity and malty aroma with a slightly bitter hops finish.

• • •

FREEMINER BREWERY LTD, GLOUCESTERSHIRE

Production in hectoliters: –
Founded: 1992

The Freeminer Brewery is a small affair with just a single pub of its own and about fifty other clients. Freeminer brews private label beers for the wholesale trade and also has a number of bottled beers that continue to ferment in the bottle such as Shakemantle Ginger Ale, Slaughter Porter, and Deep Shaft Stout.

FREEMINER BITTER

TYPE: **BITTER ALE**
ALCOHOL: **4% VOL.**
FERMENTATION: **TOP**

Special remarks: Freeminer Bitter is an ale with definite bitterness of hops but somewhat floral and fruity hints can be detected in the aroma. The taste is full-blooded and quite bitter with a dry finish. This lively beer has a firm head that is extremely bitter.

SPECULATION ALE

TYPE: **BITTER ALE**
ALCOHOL: **4.7% VOL.**
FERMENTATION: **TOP**

Special remarks: Speculation Ale is a bottle-fermenting ale that is craft brewed using English malt, whole hops, a top fermenting ale yeast, and water from the brewery's own well. It is a rounded beer with a malty character and powerful finish of the bitterness of hops.

• • •

GRIFFIN BREWERY, FULLER, SMITH & TURNER PLC, CHISWICK, LONDON

Production in hectoliters: 200,000
Founded: 1845

The brewery bearing the Fuller, Smith & Turner name has a 325 year history. The Fuller name dates back to 1829 when John Bird Fuller was asked to come to the financial aid of an ailing brewery. The partnership of that time was broken in 1845 and Fuller merged with the Romford Brewery, bringing the names of Henry Smith and his son-in-law and brewer John Turner into the new joint company of Fuller, Smith & Turner. The partnership was replaced by a public company in 1929 but there are still Turners and Fullers to be found in the management of the present-day company and among the shareholders. Fuller's (as they are colloquially known) brew with English barley and hops from Kent and Worcestershire, mains water that is suitably treated, their own strain of yeast, and caramel. Among their brews are London Porter, London Cream (made as a nitrogen beer), Summer Ale, Mr. Harry, India Pale Ale, a pale ale, and a brown ale.

CHISWICK BITTER

TYPE: BITTER ALE
ALCOHOL: 3.5% VOL.
FERMENTATION: TOP

Special remarks: this amber ale with a hoppy and malty taste with slightly bitter overtones is available locally as a real ale (cask conditioned).

FULLER'S ESB

TYPE: ALE
ALCOHOL: 5.5% VOL.
FERMENTATION: TOP

Special remarks: a strong amber-colored ale that is aromatic with a clear malty flavor that gives way to an aftertaste of hops. Available on draught or bottled. The bottled form is ESB Export that is slightly stronger at 5.9% alc. vol.

FULLER'S 1845

TYPE: ALE
ALCOHOL: 6.3% VOL.
FERMENTATION: TOP

Special remarks: The Fuller, Smith & Turner partnership began in 1845. The descendants brewed this ale that is bottled with yeast 150 years later to commemorate the anniversary. It has a fruity aroma and the taste is malty, fruity, with a dry palate.

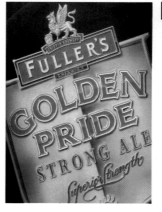

GOLDEN PRIDE

TYPE: STRONG ALE
ALCOHOL: 8.5% VOL.
FERMENTATION: TOP

HOCK DRAUGHT

TYPE: ALE

ALCOHOL: 3.2% VOL.

FERMENTATION: TOP

Special remarks: a darker ale brewed with plenty of malt. The taste is not overpoweringly of malt and there are hints of roasting. This ale has a very dry finish.

LONDON PRIDE

TYPE: ALE

ALCOHOL: 4.1% VOL.

FERMENTATION: TOP

Special remarks: London Pride is a well-balanced ale with a taste of malt and hops and a slightly fruity aroma. A true ale

OLD WINTER ALE

TYPE: ALE

ALCOHOL: 5.3% VOL.

FERMENTATION: TOP

Special remarks: Old Winter Ale is a seasonal beer with top fermentation.

• • •

GIBBS MEW PLC, ANCHOR BREWERY, SALISBURY, WILTSHIRE

Production in hectoliters: 30,000

Founded: 1898

Gibbs Mews results from a merger between Gibbs & Sons and Herbert Mew & Co in 1898. Gibbs Mew supply around four hundred pubs of which about three-quarters are tied houses. The brewery is family run with descendants of the founders among today's shareholders.

The Anchor Brewery brews real ales, bottled ales, and keg beers and the company also trades in wines, spirits, and imported beers. Its beers include Wiltshire Special Bitter, Wiltshire Traditional Bitter, Salisbury Best Bitter, Deacon, Overlord, Country Bitter, and Moonraker Brown Ale.

THE BISHOP'S TIPPLE

TYPE: STRONG ALE

ALCOHOL: 6.5% VOL.

FERMENTATION: TOP

Special remarks: The Bishop's Tipple (according to Gibb Mew's head brewer) was first brewed to mark the inauguration of George Reindorp as Bishop of Salisbury. It is an amber-colored ale with a full and rounded malty taste.

• • •

GREENE KING PLC, WESTGATE BREWERY, BURY ST. EDMUNDS, SUFFOLK

Production in hectoliters: –

Founded: 1799

Greene King is a substantial brewing firm that also has a lager brewery in Biggleswade, Bedfordshire, in addition to the special ales brewery at Bury St. Edmunds. The brewery owns almost nine hundred pubs and employees about two thousand people.

ABBOT ALE

TYPE: ALE

ALCOHOL: 5% VOL.

FERMENTATION: TOP

Special remarks: a sturdy ale that is fruity with a bittersweet aftertaste.

ST. EDMUNDS SPECIAL BREW

TYPE: SPECIAL ALE

ALCOHOL: 6.3% VOL.

FERMENTATION: TOP

Special remarks: this dark amber ale is robust and rounded in character. Brewed with crystal malt this well-balanced Special Brew has a slightly malty flavor with an outspoken but mild bitter aroma of hops. This ale has a strong dry sensation in the mouth.

STRONG SUFFOLK VINTAGE ALE

TYPE: STRONG SPECIAL ALE

ALCOHOL: 6% VOL.

FERMENTATION: TOP

Special remarks: a very dark ale with a fine, complex taste. Vintage Ale is mellow and very aromatic with suggestions of fruit and even of cherries. There is a slightly bitter aftertaste. Strong Suffolk Ale is a blend of two different beers that are mixed just before bottling. The old 5X is a strong ale that is matured for at least two years in sealed oak barrels. The lively new partner is a beer known as BPA. Limited amounts are made of this Vintage Ale and each bottle is numbered.

• • •

GUERNSEY BREWERY CO. (1920) LTD, GUERNSEY

Production in hectoliters: –

Founded: 1856/1920

This brewery is a subsidiary of the Ann Street Brewery in St. Helier, Jersey. This small brewery supplies about forty pubs with a continuously changing range of beers that include Braye Ale, Sunbeam Bitter, McGinty's Stout, Pony Original, and a wheat beer. The company was originally based in London but moved to the Channel Islands in 1920 for tax purposes.

• • •

GUINNESS BREWING GB, PARK ROYAL BREWERY, LONDON

Production in hectoliters: –

Founded: 1935/1952

Although Guinness is of Irish origin the brewing company created separate entities for its Irish and British operations in 1952. The Park Royal brewery is responsible for sales and distribution in the United Kingdom.

ENIGMA

TYPE: LAGER

ALCOHOL: 5% VOL.

FERMENTATION: BOTTOM

Special remarks: a "blonde" lager with a "widget": a combination that delivers a golden lager with malty sweetness in taste with a fresh and slightly dry palate. The feeling in the mouth is quite full but the aroma is less full.

• • •

HALL AND WOODHOUSE LTD, THE BADGER BREWERY, BLANDFORD ST. MARY, DORSET

Production in hectoliters: 150,000

Founded: 1777

This family brewery supplies more than 150 pubs with beers that include Tanglefooot, Badger Brewery Dorset Best, Dempsey's, and Badger Brewery IPA. The brewery exports to Russia, Europe, Africa, and almost half its production to South America.

• • •

KIMBERLEY BREWERY, HARDYS & HANSONS PLC, NOTTINGHAM

Production in hectoliters: –
Founded: 1832/1847/1931

This brewery results from the merging of the Hardy family brewery (since 1832) with that of the Hansons (since 1847). The merged company established a new brewery in 1932. There are still descendants of the family in the top management of the Kimberley Brewery, which was originally the brewery of the Hardy family. Hardys & Hansons supply beer to about three hundred outlets, most of which are supplied with real ale. The products include Kimberley Classic, Kimberley Best Mil, Kimberley Best, Kimberley Cool, and the Cellarman's Cask Range.

• • •

THOMAS HARDY BREWERY, ELDRIDGE, POPE & CO, DORCHESTER DORSET

Production in hectoliters: –
Founded: 1830

The brewery was originally established by the Eldridge family but Edwin and Alfred Pope then bought shares in the company. There are still Pope's running the company. The Thomas Hardy Brewery owns about two hundred pubs and also supplies its products nationally through distributors. Beers include Dorchester Bitter, Royal Oak, and Pope's Traditional.

ROYAL OAK

TYPE: ALE
ALCOHOL: 4.8% VOL.
FERMENTATION: TOP

Special remarks: an amber ale with a very fruity character. It has a firm body with ample maltiness and some hops. The aftertaste is sweetly fruity.

THOMAS HARDY'S ALE

TYPE: STRONG ALE
ALCOHOL: 12% VOL.
FERMENTATION: TOP

Special remarks: Thomas Hardy's Ale is a strong top fermenting ale that is allowed to ferment in the bottle. The brewery says that if stored at 12°C for twenty-five years the taste improves and suggest keeping the beer for at least five years before drinking it. The nineteenth century writer – for whom this beer and the brewery are named – described Dorchester's beer as "shining like a sunset in autumn." The bottle bears the year of its production on the label.

• • •

HARVEY'S & SONS LEWES LTD, THE BRIDGE WHARF BREWERY, LEWES, EAST SUSSEX

Production in hectoliters: 50,000
Founded: in the eighteenth century

This family brewery was established in the eighteenth century by John Harvey and is still a family brewery. The original Georgian brewery was rebuilt in Victorian gothic in 1881, with towers. Harvey's supplies about forty of its own pubs and six hundred other establishments. In addition to many specialty beers such as Tom Paine Ale it regularly brews Sussex Pale Ale, Sussex Best Bitter, and Sussex Old Ale.

HARVEYS TOM PAINE

TYPE: ALE
ALCOHOL: 5.5% VOL.
FERMENTATION: TOP

Special remarks: this slightly malty amber ale, with dry bitter overtones of hops, was first brewed to mark the bicentennial of Thomas Paine's The Rights of Man.

• • •

DERBY BREWERY, JOSEPH HOLT PLC, MANCHESTER, LANCASHIRE

Production in hectoliters: –
Founded: 1849

This small family brewery supplies real ale to about 220 establishments of which 120 are tied houses. Holt's beers include a 3.2% Mild, and quite hoppy 4% Bitter.

• • •

HOOK NORTON BREWERY CO. LTD, BANBURY, OXFORDSHIRE

Production in hectoliters: –
Founded: 1849

The Hook Norton Brewery was established in 1949 by John Harris and is still run by the Harris family. Much of the traditional brewing equipment is still used in the present-day Victorian tower brewery. The water for brewing is still pumped by an old steam engine. Hook Norton supply about three hundred pubs of which about thirty-five are tied houses. Apart from seasonal ales, Hook Norton brews a Best Bitter and a Mild.

OLD HOOKY

TYPE: ALE
ALCOHOL: 4.6% VOL.
FERMENTATION: TOP

Special remarks: Old Hooky is a tan-colored beer with a fruity taste and aroma of hops and malt, rounded off with a fruity and bitter hop aftertaste.

• • •

HOP BACK BREWERY PLC, SALISBURY, WILTSHIRE

Production in hectoliters: –
Founded: 1987

The Hop Back Brewery is a small brewery with five of its own pubs that also directly supplies almost another one hundred outlets. Its beers include a Mild, Special, Thunderstorm, and Powerhouse.

SUMMER LIGHTNING

TYPE: ALE
ALCOHOL: 5% VOL.
FERMENTATION: TOP

Special remarks: Summer Lightning is a top fermented beer that is allowed to ferment in the bottle. This "blonde" beer has a fresh aroma of hops and a malty taste with a dry and bitter aftertaste.

• • •

BEACON HOTEL, SARAH HUGHES BREWERY, SEDGLEY, DUDLEY, WEST MIDLANDS

Production in hectoliters: –
Founded: 1920/1987

Around 1920 Sarah Hughes first brewed her Dark Ruby Mild – that did not have a bitter hop taste – as a pick-me-up for those engaged in hard manual labor. Mild was generally much cheaper than other beers which made it popular with poorly paid workers. Dark Ruby is now brewed at the Beacon Hotel, a pub with its own brewery, by Sarah Hughes' grandson. This pub brewery can also serve its own Sedgley Surprise.

DARK RUBY MILD

TYPE: MILD ALE
ALCOHOL: 6% VOL.
FERMENTATION: TOP

Special remarks: Dark Ruby Mild continues to ferment in the bottle and needs a period of rest to allow the sediment to settle before serving. The intensely dark beer has a malt flavor with a very pronounced feeling in the mouth and possesses a richly fruity aroma.

• • •

HYDES' ANVIL BREWERY LTD, MANCHESTER, LANCASHIRE

Production in hectoliters: 35,000
Founded: 1863

Founded as a Crown brewery in 1863, the brewery became a company in 1912 and has been managed since by members of the Hyde family. About four hundred people are employed and real ale is supplied to about one hundred outlets of which sixty are tied houses. Hyde's Anvil's beers include Anvil Mild, Anvil Light, Anvil Bitter, and 4X. There are also a number of seasonal brews.

• • •

THE JERSEY BREWERY, ANN STREET BREWERY, ST. HELIER, JERSEY

Production in hectoliters: 45,000
Founded: 1905

This forms part of the Ann Street Brewery to which the Guernsey Brewery also belongs. There are fifty-two tied houses in Jersey and thirty-four in Guernsey, but not all of these are supplied with real ale. Besides their own beers they also brew Harp Lager under license. Their own beers include Mary Ann Best Bitter, Mary Ann Special Bitter, Ann's Treat, Old Jersey Ale, and several other ales and lagers under the Mary Ann brand name.

THE HORSHAM BREWERY, KING & BARNES LTD, HORSHAM, WEST SUSSEX

Production in hectoliters: 50,000
Founded: 1800/1850

The history of the King & Barnes brewery dates back to 1800. The breweries of the King and Barnes families that were united in 1906 had already been in existence for a hundred years at that time. The King family started brewing in 1850 when the great great grandfather of the present chairman started brewing in Horsham. He merged with another brewer in 1870 who he later bought out. The wholesale distribution business in wines and spirits of King & Barnes dates back to 1900 when the firm took it over from a certain Mr. Holden. The Barnes family bought shares in 1878 in a brewery that was founded in 1800 and changed its name to G.H. Barnes & Company. One hundred years on the brewery of these families brews both modern and traditional ales and lagers. The water used comes from the brewery's own well that was bored in 1947. King & Barnes has fifty-seven of its own pubs employing 150 people and another seventy work in the brewery.

CORN BEER

TYPE: ALE
ALCOHOL: 6.5% VOL.
FERMENTATION: TOP

Special remarks: most breweries that brew with corn (maize) do their best to hide the fact but not King & Barnes with their seasonal beer produced in April that uses 40% corn (maize). Corn Beer ferments in the bottle and is a pale-colored brew with a fruity and sweet aroma.

KING & BARNES FESTIVE ALE

TYPE: ALE
ALCOHOL: 5.3% VOL.
FERMENTATION: TOP

Special remarks: Festive Ale is bottled with yeast. It is a dark beer with a rosy glow and a fruity aroma. The taste is complex, containing malt, fruit, and hints of hops, with a malty aftertaste.

KING & BARNES HARVEST ALE

TYPE: ALE
ALCOHOL: 4.5% VOL.
FERMENTATION: TOP

Special remarks: King & Barnes brew this ale in September using the new harvest in a top fermented beer that also ferments in the bottle.

KING & BARNES MILLENNIUM ALE

TYPE: ALE
ALCOHOL: 9.5% VOL.
FERMENTATION: TOP

Special remarks: in common with many other brewers, King & Barnes produced a special brew to mark the Millennium. Their beer was bottled in 1996 so that the yeast bottled with it would be properly conditioned by the turn of the century, provided it was kept at cellar temperature. This ale is a limited edition provided with a number and a neck label. "Early Bird" Golding hops picked in Kent in 1995 were used for this special ale that were picked two days before brewing. The malt used was made from Maris Otter barley harvested in June 1966 and malted in the traditional manner on a floor by J.P. Simpsons. The yeast originates from two cultures that were in existence before Louis Pasteur's discoveries.

KING & BARNES OLD PORTER

TYPE: PORTER
ALCOHOL: 5.5% VOL.
FERMENTATION: TOP

Special remarks: a very dark beer that is sweet with the aroma and flavor of roasted malt.

KING & BARNES SUSSEX BITTER

TYPE: BITTER ALE
ALCOHOL: 3.5% VOL.
FERMENTATION: TOP

Special remarks: a brown-colored bitter with a malty taste and bitter aftertaste.

WHEAT MASH

TYPE: ALE/WHEAT BEER
ALCOHOL: 4.5% VOL.
FERMENTATION: TOP

Special remarks: Wheat Mash is a light-colored seasonal ale made around April. It is top fermented and also fermented in the bottle.

• • •

MASONS ARMS, LAKELAND BREWING CO, CARTMEL FELL CUMBRIA

Production in hectoliters: –
Founded: 1990

A pub brewery that is known for its wide assortment of bottled beers.

WINTER HOLIDAY

TYPE: ALE
ALCOHOL: 5% VOL.
FERMENTATION: TOP

Special remarks: Winter Holiday is tan in color and ferments in the bottle. The sediment must be kept in the bottle when serving. It is a lively beer with a dry and slightly fruity taste with hints of dark malt. The aftertaste is slightly bitter.

• • •

GREENGATE BREWERY, J.W. LEES & CO BREWERS, MANCHESTER

Production in hectoliters: 150,000
Founded: 1828

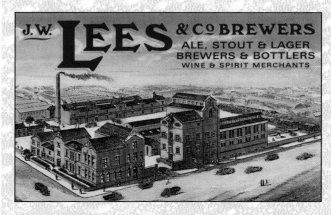

The J.W. Lees & Co brewery is one of a small number of family concerns surviving in Britain. The firm is justifiably proud of its heritage and tradition. The brewery's history began in 1828 when John Willie Lees – a retired weaver –

established a brewery where today's brewery also stands. Lees benefited from the growth of industrialization in the north of England and the increasing demand caused him to build a new "modern" tower brewery in 1876. Lees is still a family-run business with Richard Lees-Jones, a great great grandson of the founder heading today's craft-oriented brewery. Traditional methods are still used in brewing but supported by modern techniques. One third of the ales are supplied in wooden casks made and maintained by their own cooper. J.W. Lees of Manchester brew GB Mild, Moonraker, Golden Original, Edlebrau Strong Lager, Greengate, Bitter, Tulip Lager, and Lees Pilsener Lager.

• • •

MANSFIELD BREWERY PLC, MANSFIELD, NOTTINGHAMSHIRE

Production in hectoliters: was 700,000
(recently moved to Wolverhampton)
Founded: 1855

The Mansfield Brewery was one the UK's largest regional brewers which brewed Websters and several other beers for Scottish Courage beside its own local ales. Unfortunately the characteristic of the water from its own sandstone spring is lost with brewing moved to Wolverhampton and the brewery site to be redeveloped. Whether its local ales such as the Riding Mild and Bitter, Mansfield Bitter, Old Baily and the seasonal Deakins brews will survive the move is uncertain.

• • •

MARSTON, THOMPSON & EVERSED, PLC, THE BREWERY, BURTON-UPON-TRENT

Production in hectoliters: –
Founded: 1834

This English brewery of a variety of ales now holds a special place in brewing as the sole surviving user of a "union room" for initial start of the fermentation that was once widely used. In this union room the wort that has had yeast introduced is fermented in a row of interconnected oak barrels. An overflow from the barrels takes the wort to an open vat from where it returns to the barrels. The water used comes from the brewery's own well and is rainwater that is naturally filtered as it permeates through layers of chalk. Marston mainly uses Maris Otter malt and its hops are Goldings and Fuggles.

BURTON STRONG PALE ALE

TYPE: STRONG PALE ALE
ALCOHOL: 6.2% VOL.
FERMENTATION: TOP

Special remarks: the amber-colored ale has a fruity taste, and is sweet with a remarkably mild palate. Burton SPA is an amenable ale, which makes its 6.2% alcohol somewhat treacherous.

PEDIGREE BITTER

TYPE: BITTER ALE
ALCOHOL: 4.5% VOL.
FERMENTATION: TOP

Special remarks: Pedigree Bitter has definite overtones of malt and hops with a dry and slightly bitter aftertaste.

• • •

MOLES BREWERY & CASCADE DRINKS LTD, MELKSHAM, WILTSHIRE

Production in hectoliters: (capacity of 15,000)
Founded: 1982

The Moles Brewery ales are mainly sold on draught from pubs around the Bristol area. A small part of the production is sold nationally through distributors. Beers include Barley Mole Bitter, Best Bitter, Landlord's Choice, and Brew 97, not derived from a year but the ninety-seventh brewing.

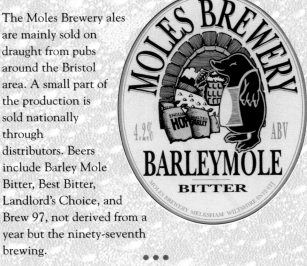

• • •

THE LION BREWERY, MORRELLS BREWERY LTD, OXFORD, OXFORDSHIRE

Production in hectoliters: 50,000
Founded: 1782

The history of the Lion Brewery predates 1782 for records show that the brewery already belonged in 1743 to a certain Richard Tawney. Brothers James and Mark Morrell originally worked for Tawney until they were able to buy him out in 1782. Since that time the brewery has been run by descendants of the Morrell brothers. Morrells is a local brewery and wishes to remain so. All the 130 tied houses are at no great distance from the brewery. In addition to its own ales, Morrells also brews Harp lager under license since 1987. Its own beers include Oxford Bitter, Oxford Mild, and Varsity. Morrells is keen to make a link between its ales and the university.

GRADUATE

TYPE: ALE

ALCOHOL: 5.2% VOL.

FERMENTATION: TOP

Special remarks: Graduate is a malty beer with an aroma of roasted malt and a bitter finish.

COLLEGE ALE

TYPE: ALE

ALCOHOL: 7.4% VOL.

FERMENTATION: TOP

Special remarks: a coppery ale brewed with some wheat. College ale is a caramel-like brew with caramel aroma and the sensation in the mouth of sweetness and alcohol with a body that is robust and drying. The aftertaste of this rounded ale is determined by the presence of alcohol.

• • •

MORLAND & CO PLC, THE BREWERY, ABINGDON, OXFORDSHIRE

Production in hectoliters: –

Founded: 1711

This medium-sized brewery has about 350 pubs and employs more than one thousand people. They brew Old Masters, Original Bitter, The Tanner's Jack, Independent IPA, Revival, and also Wilson's Original Mild for Scottish Courage. Morlands recently took over the larger Ruddles Brewery from Grolsch.

OLD SPECKLED HEN

TYPE: ALE

ALCOHOL: 5.2% VOL.

FERMENTATION: TOP

Special remarks: this is the flagship of one of the oldest independent breweries left in the UK. Old Speckled Hen is initially sweet but has a complex palate with caramel, roasted malt, and hops and its aftertaste is dry and slightly bitter.

• • •

OLD LUXTERS BREWERY, CHILTERN VALLEY, HAMBLEDEN HENLEY-ON-THAMES, OXFORDSHIRE

Production in hectoliters: –

Founded: 1984

In addition to its brewery, Chiltern Valley also has a vineyard and winery. Both are sited at an old farm and the single brew is named Barn Ale. It is an amber, fruity, bottle fermenting ale.

• • •

OLD MILL BREWERY LTD, SNAITH, GOOLE EAST YORKSHIRE

Production in hectoliters: –
Founded: 1983

The brewery has been set up in a two hundred years old corn mill. It has just over ten tied houses and also supplies some free houses as well. Brews include Bullion, Blackjack, Nellie Dene, Traditional Mild, and Old Curiosity.

BULLION
TYPE: BITTER ALE
ALCOHOL: 4.7% VOL.
FERMENTATION: TOP

Special remarks: a dark amber ale with a malty taste and overtones of fruit and hops and a hoppy aroma.

• • •

THE OLD BREWERY, J.C. & R.H. PALMER LTD, BRIDPORT, DORSET

Production in hectoliters: –
Founded: 1794

The initials are those of the founders, John Cleeves Palmer and Robert Henry Palmer. The great great grandsons of these gentlemen, A.J.C. Palmer and C.W.R. Palmer, are now at the helm of this small brewery that supplies cask conditioned real ale to around one hundred pubs. The beers include 200 in commemoration of the brewery's bicentennial, Palmer's Best Bitter, Bridport Bitter, and Tally Ho!

• • •

RCH BREWERY, WEST HEWISH, SOMERSET

Production in hectoliters: –
Founded: 1983

RCH stands for the Royal Clarence Hotel in which the brewery was first established. In 1993 it moved to new premises to cope with increasing demand for its products.

FIREBOX
TYPE: BITTER ALE
ALCOHOL: 6% VOL.
FERMENTATION: TOP

Special remarks: Firebox is a reddish bitter that ferments in the bottle.

OLD SLUG PORTER
TYPE: PORTER
ALCOHOL: 4.7% VOL.
FERMENTATION: TOP

Special remarks: a lively bottle-fermenting porter that ensures a very frothy head. This ale is dark black with a dry bitter taste and hints of roasting.

PITCHFORK
TYPE: BITTER ALE
ALCOHOL: 4.3% VOL.
FERMENTATION: TOP

Special remarks: bottled with yeast for further fermentation, this is a golden ale with a sharp and immediate dryness and bitterness. This is a robust beer with a marked mouth sensation.

• • •

REDRUTH BREWERY LTD, THE BREWERY, REDRUTH CORNWALL

Production in hectoliters: 50,000
Founded: 1742

After a succession of takeovers and mergers this brewery now belongs to the Dransfield Group of Hong Kong. There are no tied houses and the activities are solely those of brewing and bottling.

• • •

RINGWOOD BREWERY LTD, HAMPSHIRE

Production in hectoliters: –
Founded: 1978

Ringwood is a small brewery located in an old eighteenth century inn but with modern equipment. The brewery chiefly supplies its own pubs with brews such as True Glory, XXXX Porter, and Fortyniner.

OLD THUMPER

TYPE: ALE
ALCOHOL: 5.6% VOL.
FERMENTATION: TOP

Special remarks: an amber-colored ale with a rounded, sweet and fruity taste and dry hoppy overtones.

UNICORN BREWERY, FREDERIC ROBINSON LTD, STOCKPORT CHESHIRE

Production in hectoliters: –
Founded: 1838/1865

The Unicorn Brewery of the Robinson family is one of the UK's largest family breweries. Its history dates back to 1865 when Frederic Robinson began brewing at the Unicorn Inn, owned by his father William since 1838. Through extensions and acquisitions the brewery has managed to keep its head above

Frederic Robinson and his wife Emma.

water and is now managed by a fifth generation of the founder's descendants. The company is a modern multi-faceted concern that combines both family tradition and modern brewing methods. Hence the brewery has modern equipment alongside stables for Shire horses used to grace special occasions. In addition to brewing, Robinsons are bottlers and distributors of wines and spirits.

FREDERICS

TYPE: ALE
ALCOHOL: 5% VOL.
FERMENTATION: TOP

Special remarks: a pale golden amber ale named after the brewery's founder.

HATTERS MILD

TYPE: MILD ALE
ALCOHOL: 3.3% VOL.
FERMENTATION: TOP

Special remarks: a pale amber mild with slightly malt aroma. The body is thin, the taste slightly malty, with underlying dryness and a bitter aftertaste of short duration.

HARTLEYS XB BITTER

TYPE: BITTER ALE
ALCOHOL: 4% VOL.
FERMENTATION: TOP

Special remarks: an amber-colored ale originating from the Hartley Brewery that was taken-over in 1982. The taste is malty with a slightly hoppy undertone and dry palate.

OLD STOCKPORT BITTER

TYPE: BITTER ALE
ALCOHOL: 3.5% VOL.
FERMENTATION: TOP

Special remarks: a pale golden ale with a fruity aroma that does not have a firm body. There is some malt in the taste with fruit and hoppy overtones and a dry palate.

OLD TOM

TYPE: STRONG ALE

ALCOHOL: 8.5% VOL.

FERMENTATION: TOP

Special remarks: this is a very dark and strong ale. Old Tom is one of the old beers of the Unicorn Brewery that first appeared in the head brewer's handbook in 1899. Today this beer is brewed with a fruity aroma combined with a strong bittersweet taste of a vinous character. The aftertaste is also bitter.

ROBINSON'S BEST BITTER

TYPE: BITTER ALE

ALCOHOL: 4.3% VOL.

FERMENTATION: TOP

Special remarks: dark amber ale with malt and hops in its aroma and taste. The body is thin to medium and the aftertaste is bitter.

• • •

ROOSTER'S BREWERY, OUTLAW BREWING CO, HARROGATE, NORTH YORKSHIRE

Production in hectoliters: 3,000

Founded: 1993

Rooster's Brewery was started in 1993 by Sean and Alison Franklin. In addition to mainstays, a number of experimental brews are produced bearing the Outlaw Brewing name, such as Silver Lining, Desperado, and Silver Bullet.

NECTOR

TYPE: ALE

ALCOHOL: 5.8% VOL.

FERMENTATION: TOP

Special remarks: a slightly bitter ale with fruity aroma.

ROOSTER'S CREAM

TYPE: ALE

ALCOHOL: 4.7% VOL.

FERMENTATION: TOP

Special remarks: a pale amber beer with a fruity aroma and mildly bitter taste.

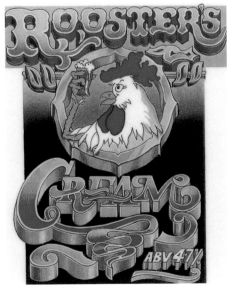

OUTLAW BREWING CO FIRST GOLD

TYPE: ALE

ALCOHOL: 3.9% VOL.

FERMENTATION: TOP

• • •

RUDDLES BREWERY LTD, LANGHAM, OAKHAM, RUTLANDSHIRE

Production in hectoliters: 200,000
Founded: 1858

Ruddles was a subsidiary of Grolsch from 1992 but was sold to Morland's Brewery. They still brew Webster's Green for Courage, who were also former owners. The brewery brews a 4.9% bitter, Ruddles County, 3.7% Ruddles Best Bitter, and Ruddles Independence.

BOB'S GOLD

TYPE: ALE
ALCOHOL: 4.7% VOL.
FERMENTATION: TOP

Special remarks: Bob's Gold is brewed with Golden Hops. This premium ale is slightly fruity with a dry finish.

• • •

SALOPIAN BREWING COMPANY LTD, SHREWBURY, SHROPSHIRE

Production in hectoliters: –
Founded: 1995

A small brewery that delivers directly to a mere twenty clients but also supplies through distributors. Beers include Iron Bridge Stout, Bitter, and Choir Porter.

JIGSAW

TYPE: WHEAT BEER
ALCOHOL: 4.8% VOL.
FERMENTATION: TOP

Special remarks: Jigsaw is a dark top-fermented wheat beer that ferments in the bottle and has a sweet coffee taste.

MINSTERLEY ALE

TYPE: BITTER ALE
ALCOHOL: 4.5% VOL.
FERMENTATION: TOP

Special remarks: amber bottle-fermenting bitter ale. Minsterley is only slightly bitter, is late hopped with an initial malty flavor and bitter finish with hints of fruit in the aroma.

SNAPDRAGON

TYPE: SPICED ALE
ALCOHOL: 4.5% VOL.
FERMENTATION: TOP

Special remarks: Snapdragon is bottled with yeast for further fermentation and enriched with Chinese five spice. The continued fermentation causes a somewhat cloudy amber appearance. The aroma is fruity and spicy with an unusual taste with dry overtones.

• • •

SCANLON'S FINE ALES, UXBRIDGE, MIDDLESEX

Production in hectoliters: –
Founded: 1996

Scanlon's Fine Ales no longer emerge from its own small brewery but are brewed for Jerry Scanlon by the Rebellion Brewery in Marlow. Scanlon started as an enthusiastic home brewer in 1981 and made determined efforts in 1994 to set up his own brewery. Initially he got his Spike brewed by the Rebellion Brewery and then opened his own brewery in 1996 but closed it in 1997. Since then the beers have been brewed by Rebellion.

The Scanlon ales include Brunel – a golden 4.8% bitter, Colne Valley Bitter – a 4.1% coppery bitter, Lord Ashford's S.R., Spike, and a number of seasonal brews including a wheat beer and a stout.

• • •

SCANLON'S MIDDLESEX GOLD

TYPE: BITTER ALE
ALCOHOL: 3.8% VOL.
FERMENTATION: TOP

Special remarks: golden ale.

• • •

FAVERSHAM BREWERY, SHEPERD NEAME LTD, FAVERSHAM, KENT

Production in hectoliters: 250,000
Founded: 1698

Shepherd Neame is the oldest still-surviving brewery in England. The company has about four hundred tied houses and delivers directly to another five hundred outlets. The brewery radiates considerable awareness of tradition. The beers include Original Porter, Master Brew Bitter, Best Bitter, India Pale Ale, and Borough Brown but lagers under license such as Kingfisher, Hürlimann, and Steinbock also come from the coppers.

BISHOP'S FINGER

TYPE: STRONG ALE
ALCOHOL: 5.4% VOL.
FERMENTATION: TOP

Special remarks: a dark amber ale with full pale malt and slightly bitter taste determined by the dry overtones of hops. Bishop's Finger is solely brewed with barley malted and grown in Kent and Kentish hops.

SPITFIRE

TYPE: ALE
ALCOHOL: 4.7% VOL.
FERMENTATION: TOP

Special remarks: a top fermented bottled amber ale that further ferments. The sediment from the hops must be kept in the bottle when pouring. Spitfire has a fruity aroma and a strong bitter aftertaste.

• • •

JOHN SMITH'S BREWERY, TADCASTER NORTH YORKSHIRE

Production in hectoliters: –
Founded: 1758

Forming part of Courage since 1970, this brewery was founded in 1758 and taken over by one John Smith in 1847 – not to be confused with the Samuel Smith Brewery also in Tadcaster, founded by a descendant of John Smith's brother.

IMPERIAL RUSSIAN STOUT

TYPE: IMPERIAL STOUT
ALCOHOL: 5% VOL.
FERMENTATION: TOP

Special remarks: Imperial Russian Stout is a very dark strong beer with a syrupy texture and burnt taste. The name probably derives from a time when the stout was exported to the Czarist Russia. Then as now the beer is neither filtered or pasteurized. The year of brewing is indicated on the label and the taste develops with age.

JOHN SMITH'S BITTER

TYPE: BITTER ALE
ALCOHOL: 4% VOL.
FERMENTATION: TOP

Special remarks: the dark amber bitter of John Smith is known throughout the British Isles as a major brand. It has a malty taste with aroma of hoppy bitterness and dry bitter aftertaste.

WEBSTER'S YORKSHIRE BITTER

TYPE: ALE
ALCOHOL: 3.5% VOL.
FERMENTATION: TOP

Special remarks: this is an amber-colored ale of medium body with a neutral taste developing into a fine bitter aftertaste.

• • •

SAMUEL SMITH OLD BREWERY, TADCASTER, NORTH YORKSHIRE

Production in hectoliters: –
Founded: 1758

A small independent brewery that still employees its own cooper to maintain the wooden casks. Samuel Smith was a brother of John Smith (Scottish Courage) but this brewery remains a family brewery to the present day. Some two hundred pubs are tied to this brewery.

IMPERIAL STOUT

TYPE: STOUT
ALCOHOL: 7% VOL.
FERMENTATION: TOP

Special remarks: this Imperial Stout is a dark black beer with a sweet roasted flavor and transparent presence of alcohol with quite dry palate with overtones that suggest cherry-like fruitiness.

OATMEAL STOUT

TYPE: STOUT
ALCOHOL: 5% VOL.
FERMENTATION: TOP

Special remarks: how fortunate that the UK does not have the German type purity laws or we would be denied such variety. Oatmeal is regarded as a healthy foodstuff and hence this stout is brewed with oatmeal. The proportion of oatmeal is limited because of the difficulty of brewing with oats. The result is a dark stout with a rounded full flavor with underlying sweetness of burnt malt. Samuel Smith has made a very drinkable beer with a mildly drying aftertaste and an aroma of bitter chocolate.

OLD BREWERY PALE ALE

TYPE: ALE
ALCOHOL: 5% VOL.
FERMENTATION: TOP

Special remarks: this pale ale is pale amber with a malty aroma and slight hints of roasting. The body is firm and rounded with a taste of roasted malt and hops. There is a hoppy aftertaste and dry palate. This ale uses water from the brewery's own well without any additives.

• • •

SMILES BREWING CO LTD, GLOUCESTERSHIRE

Production in hectoliters: 25,000
Founded: 1978

This small brewery has been owned since 1991 by Ian Williams. There are more than fifteen tied pubs and many other free outlets are also supplied. The beers brewed include Bristol Stout, Best Bitter, Brewery Bitter, and Heritage Bitter. Seasonal brews include Mayflower Summer Ale, Holly Hops Christmas Ale, Indian Summer, and March Hare.

• • •

ST. AUSTELL BREWERY CO LTD, ST. AUSTELL, CORNWALL

Production in hectoliters: –
Founded: 1851

Walter Hicks.

Walter Hicks, born in 1829, began his career as a maltster and wine trader. Around 1867 he bought the London Inn and on neighboring land built his steam brewery that later became known as Tregonissy House. Hicks brewed here from 1869. Because of the rapid growth of St Austell Hicks flourished as the town's only surviving brewery. A new brewery was built in 1893 that is still in use today. The St Austell brewery has remained an independent family brewery and descendants can be found today both among the shareholders and the brewery's workers. Perhaps because of this the tradition of supplying real ale was never lost and the brewery employs its own cooper to maintain more than five hundred wooden casks. The brewery uses its own water and Fuggles and Goldings hops. There are about 150 tied houses. Beside the brewing business, Walter Hicks & Co is a wine and spirits dealer. The brewery's beers include the light and somewhat sweet Bosun's Bitter, sweetly malt and fruity XXXX Mild, XXXX, Tinner's Ale, Hicks Special

Draught, Duchy Best Bitter, Wreckers Premium Bitter, Light Ale, Brown Ale, Duchy Ale, Smugglers Strong Ale, Prince's Ale, Special Barley Wine, and a lager, Export Gold.

Cooper at the St. Austell brewery.

CRIPPLE DICK

TYPE: BARLEY WINE (ALE)
ALCOHOL: 11.7% VOL.
FERMENTATION: TOP

Special remarks: Cripple Dick is a reddish brown barley wine with a sweet alcoholic aroma. The sweet rounded taste is accompanied by significant level of alcohol that ensures a warm sensation in the mouth.

• • •

ST. PETER'S BREWERY COMPANY, SUFFOLK

Production in hectoliters: (capacity) 6,000
Founded: 1996

The brewery is situated in an outbuilding of the Medieval St. Peter's Hall that now houses a bar and restaurant. The brewery is modern but manages to give its beers a craft appearance with striking packaging. The four different beers are all supplied in green oval half liter bottles with a small booklet on the neck telling the "story of..." The brewery draws water from its own well. In addition to Golden Ale there is also a fruit beer with elderberry juice, a very dark Honey Porter with a touch of Suffolk honey, and a wheat beer. All of them are 4.7% alcohol. Enormous growth has resulted from a major supermarket including the beers in its product range.

GOLDEN ALE

TYPE: ALE
ALCOHOL: 4.7% VOL.
FERMENTATION: TOP

Special remarks:
Golden Ale is brewed with Halcyon and lager malts together with Goldings hops. It is a darker "blonde" ale with a malty aroma and taste of malt and hops. The hop palate is not pronounced and the aftertaste is only briefly bitter.

• • •

SWALE BREWERY CO, MILTON REGIS, SITTINGBOURNE, KENT

Production in hectoliters: –
Founded: 1995

A small brewery established in 1995 by John Davison that delivers real ale to thirty free houses.

OLD DICK

TYPE: ALE
ALCOHOL: 5.2% VOL.
FERMENTATION: TOP

Special remarks:
a bottle-fermenting ale brewed with Maris Otter floor malted barley and Challenger hops. The darker ale has a mild hoppy taste and medium to rounded body. The aroma is slightly fruity with a slightly dry finish.

• • •

JOSHUA TETLEY & SON, THE BREWERY, LEEDS, WEST YORKSHIRE

Production in hectoliters: –
Founded: 1822

Forms part of Carlberg-Tetley PLC. The name is derived from Joshua Tetley who took the brewery over in 1822. Within the group it is the largest brewer of draught beer. There is a large museum and visitor's center at the brewery. Brews include Mild, Dark Mild, Wild Rover, and Imperial.

TETLEY'S BITTER

TYPE: BITTER ALE
ALCOHOL: 3.8% VOL.
FERMENTATION: TOP

Special remarks: this "draught bitter in a can" has a "widget" to imitate draught beer. This gives the beer a creamy head when the can is opened with a light brown beer beneath. It has a malty taste and bitter hoppy aroma with dry bitter aftertaste.

• • •

T & R THEAKSTON LTD, THE BREWERY, MASHAM, YORKSHIRE

Production in hectoliters: –
Founded: 1827

Theakston was swallowed-up in 1987 by Scottish Courage but has managed to retain its own position within the group although not all Theakston branded beers are now brewed at Masham.

THEAKSTON BEST BITTER

TYPE: BITTER ALE
ALCOHOL: 3.8% VOL.
FERMENTATION: TOP

Special remarks: Theakston Best Bitter is no heavyweight. It is light in color and character making it an excellent session ale. The neutral taste is combined with a certain hoppy aroma and a slightly bitter aftertaste.

LIGHTFOOT

TYPE: PALE ALE
ALCOHOL: 5.2% VOL.
FERMENTATION: TOP

Special remarks: this light-colored but full-bodied ale has a fine clear white head. The taste is malty with an aroma of hops.

OLD PECULIER

TYPE: OLD ALE
ALCOHOL: 5.6% VOL.
FERMENTATION: TOP

Special remarks: Old Peculiar is a very dark beer with full but mellow fruity sweet taste.

THEAKSTON XB

TYPE: ALE
ALCOHOL: 4.5% VOL.
FERMENTATION: TOP

Special remarks: XB is an attractive deep amber color. It is a fruity beer that is slightly sweet in flavor with a short bitter aftertaste. The dry palate of this ale is quite remarkable. It is astonishing how after half a liter of liquid you can experience such a dry mouth but this is no problem because this ale does make you want to drink more.

• • •

DANIEL THWAITES PLC, STAR BREWERY, BLACKBURN, LANCASHIRE

Production in hectoliters: 320,000
Founded: 1897

Daniel Thwaites is the name of the founder of this brewery that is still run by his direct descendants. Its beers include Big Ben, Bitter, Best Mild, and Craftsman.

LANCASHIRE STRONG BROWN ALE

TYPE: ALE
ALCOHOL: 5% VOL.
FERMENTATION: TOP

Special remarks: this Strong Brown Ale is a mellow beer with a rounded taste with slightly sweet overtones and suggestions of burnt malt in a very dark beer.

• • •

TIGERTOPS BREWERY, FOXFIELD BREWERY, WAKEFIELD YORKSHIRE

Production in hectoliters: –
Founded: 1995

A pair of micro-breweries set-up by Lynda and Stuart Johnson. The Foxfield Brewery is based at the Prince of Wales at Foxfield. In addition to brewing for the pub a small number of free houses are supplied. Stuart is more interested in developing new brews and brewing than marketing a single type of ale.

THE TITANIC BREWERY, BURSLEM STOKE-ON-TRENT, STAFFORDSHIRE

Production in hectoliters: –
Founded: 1985

A small brewery with two of its own pubs that also supplies some one hundred free outlets and supplies bottle fermenting beers through distributors. Other beers include Lifeboat Ale, White Star, Wreckage, and Captain Smith's. The names all relate to the Titanic, the captain of which came from Stoke-on-Trent.

TITANIC STOUT

TYPE: STOUT
ALCOHOL: 4.5% VOL.
FERMENTATION: TOP

Special remarks: this dark-colored stout is bottled with yeast. The flavor is of roasted malt.

• • •

TOLLEMACHE & COBBOLD BREWERY LTD, IPSWICH, SUFFOLK

Production in hectoliters: –
Founded: 1723

This brewery, with a history dating back to 1723, is better known as Tolly Cobbold. The first brewery was built by Thomas Cobbold in Harwich but because the water in Harwich was of inferior quality he fetched water from a clear family well in Ipswich. In 1746 he decided to move the brewery to the source of water in Ipswich. The Victorian tower brewery that is still in use today was built there. The merger between the Tollemache and Cobbold families was informally discussed between the two families for some years before it was finally realized in 1957. Until 1970 Tolly Cobbold was a family business but it was then taken over by the Ellerman Group. The Brent Walker property group bought the brewery and closed it in 1989, moving brewing to the Lion Brewery in Hartlepool. However the Tolly Cobbold management team re-opened the brewery in July 1990 so that the Cliff Brewery was able to celebrate 250 years of brewing in Ipswich in 1996. The beers include Tolly Mild, Cobbold's IPA, Tolly Bitter, Tolly Original Best Bitter, Tolly's Old Strong, Tollyshooter, Tolly Brown Ale, Tolly Light Ale, and Cobnut Brown Ale.

CARDINAL ALE

TYPE: ALE
ALCOHOL: 5.2% VOL.
FERMENTATION: TOP

Special remarks: Cardinal Ale is amber-colored with a striking flavor that is slightly malty. The body is medium to firm.

ST. GEORGE'S BEST

TYPE: ALE
ALCOHOL: 4.2% VOL.
FERMENTATION: TOP

Special remarks: this is a dry beer with bitter overtones of hops, a hoppy aroma, and strong bitter aftertaste.

•••

TYNE BREWERY, NEWCASTLE UPON TYNE

Production in hectoliters: –
Founded: 1890

Part of Scottish & Newcastle, Scottish Courage.

NEWCASTLE BROWN ALE

TYPE: ENGLISH BROWN ALE
ALCOHOL: 4.5% VOL.
FERMENTATION: TOP

Special remarks: in the local dialect the men of Newcastle tell their wives of an evening: "Am, just gan doon the road ta tak the dog for a walk." It is quite possible this is why this beer is nicknamed "the dog." In any event it is one of the best-selling bottled beers in the UK. This dark amber color and nutty taste result from a mixture of strong dark ale with a lighter ale.

•••

USHERS OF TROWBRIDGE PLC, TROWBRIDGE, WILTSHIRE

Production in hectoliters: 500,000
Founded: 1824/1991

Ushers was originally established in 1824 but was swallowed up by Courage from whose clutches it managed to escape in 1991 through a management buy-out. Ushers now owns more than five hundred pubs and in addition to its own brews also brews for third parties, such as Courage and an Indian brew called Lal Tofan. Its own beers include Founder's Ale, Ushers Best Bitter, and 1824 Particular. The company has since taken over Burt's Brewery on the Isle of Wight complete with its five pubs.

•••

VAUX BREWERIES LTD, NORTHUMBERLAND

Production in hectoliters: 800,000
Founded: 1837

The second largest independent British brewery was founded by Cuthbert Vaux, born in Sunderland in the north of England in 1813. After working as an office clerk for another brewery, Cuthbert started his own together with a partner, William Story. The partnership later split up with the partners going their own way and Vaux set-up Cuthbert Vaux & Sons in 1937. Today the brewery group employs some eight thousand people and in addition to its own brewing activities it brews beers under license and is a distributor for imported beers, soft drinks, wines and spirits, and manages some thousand pubs, restaurants, hotels, and inns. Ward's Brewery in Sheffield is also part of the Vaux Group. In addition to the beers described below, the company's beers include Ward's Best Bitter, Thorne Best Bitter, Darley's Dark Mild, Lorimer's Best Scotch, and Samson. The imported beers include Export Heineken (not the UK brewed variety), the US Budweiser, Holsten Pils, Beck's, Red Stripe, Sol, Stella Artois, Carlsberg, Labatt, Rolling Rock, Moretti, Guinness, and Murphy's.

WAGGLE DANCE

TYPE: ALE
ALCOHOL: 5% VOL.
FERMENTATION: TOP

Special remarks: this darker "blonde" ale is brewed with honey. The fully malty flavor with bitter overtones has a complex dry finish. Waggle Dance is hopped with a blend of Challenger, Fuggles, and Goldings.

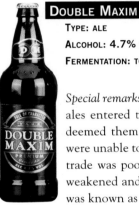

DOUBLE MAXIM

TYPE: ALE
ALCOHOL: 4.7% VOL.
FERMENTATION: TOP

Special remarks: when the first Maxim ales entered the trade the publicans deemed them too strong. Customers were unable to drink many of them so trade was poor. Hence the brew was weakened and in 1938 the brown ale was known as Double Maxim.

LAMBTON'S

TYPE: ALE
ALCOHOL: 3.8% VOL.
FERMENTATION: TOP

Special remarks: Lambton's is an unusually light ale that was introduced in 1996. Served chilled with the "draught-flow system" it is aimed at both ale and lager drinkers.

SCORPION

TYPE: ALE
ALCOHOL: 5% VOL.
FERMENTATION: BOTTOM

Special remarks: Scorpion is a neutral "blonde" lager intended to compete with imported lagers.

• • •

NORTHGATE BREWERY, WADWORTH & CO, DEVIZES WILTSHIRE

Production in hectoliters: —
Founded: 1875

Henry Alfred Wadworth was twenty-two years old when he took over the old Northgate Brewery in 1875 but already had six years experience as a brewer. His experience as a businessman was less sound and he started trading at a loss but was quick to learn and helped by the quality of his ales he moved into profit in his second year. Within ten years the brewery had outgrown its home and he developed one of the typical tower breweries. With no electricity the energy requirements of the brewery were provided by a steam engine and the tower also enabled the use of gravity for much of the process. Wadworth is the only brewery still using copper brewing vessels installed in 1885. The brewery maintains traditions and firmly believes that for beer to bear the Wadworth label it has to be brewed with the right ingredients, by the right method and with the necessary brewing skill. The character of the brewery too is considered to play its part. Not that the Wadworth brewery is solely rooted in tradition. Modern fermentation vessels and storage tanks have been introduced and even the brewing process amended to cope with increased demand. In essence though the brewing process that might take place twice each day is the same as when the brewery was founded. Since 1974 the brewery has returned to horse-drawn brewer's dray to deliver to local hostelries. Beside their daily toil the four Shire horses also make appearances at shows and other events in return for their daily feed and two pints of Best Bitter. The present head of the brewery is a grandson of the partner who was a brother-in-law of the founder and the brewery is still an independent family-run concern.

6X

TYPE: BITTER ALE
ALCOHOL: 4.3% VOL.
FERMENTATION: TOP

Special remarks: a dark amber ale with aromas of malt and fruit with a full fruity taste. It is medium-bodied with a bitter aftertaste.

FARMERS GLORY

TYPE: ALE
ALCOHOL: 4.5% VOL.
FERMENTATION: TOP

Special remarks: a darker beer with a light malty aroma and hoppy taste with a short hoppy bitter aftertaste. Farmer's Glory has a dry palate.

HENRY'S ORIGINAL IPA

TYPE: ALE

ALCOHOL: 3.8 % VOL.

FERMENTATION: TOP

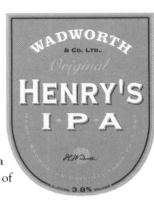

Special remarks: IPA means India Pale Ale, harking back to colonial days of the British Empire. This is a dark beer with a taste that is largely of malt.

OLD TIMER

TYPE: ALE

ALCOHOL: 5.8% VOL.

FERMENTATION: TOP

Special remarks: an amber-colored seasonal ale only available from October to March. It has a fruity and malty aroma with full rounded taste and malty but dry finish.

• • •

WARD'S BREWERY, SHEFFIELD, SOUTH YORKSHIRE

Production in hectoliters: 200,000

Founded: 1840

Ward's was established in 1840 by Josiah Kirby but has formed part of Vaux since 1972. Ward's has about two hundred tied houses and delivers to a further three hundred outlets. Its beers include Ward's Best Bitter, Thorne Best Bitter, and Darley's Dark Mild.

• • •

THE EAGLE BREWERY, CHARLES WELLS LTD, BEDFORD

Production in hectoliters: 800,000

Founded: 1876

The Eagle Brewery was founded by Charles Wells, born in Bedford in 1842. In order to marry his sweetheart Josephine Grimwade, Wells had to turn his back on a life at sea and so he set-up the family brewery in 1876. Today, more than 125 years on, the brewery is still managed by the same family and is one of the largest independent breweries in the UK. Wells brew with water from their own wells, once bored by the founder himself. In addition to Bombardier, Fargo, and Eagle IPA, the brewery also brews Red Stripe under license and distributes Bittburger and Kirin imported lager.

Charles Wells (1842–1914), founder of the Eagle Brewery.

BOMBARDIER PREMIUM BITTER

TYPE: BITTER ALE
ALCOHOL: 4.3% VOL.
FERMENTATION: TOP

Special remarks: Bombardier is amber in color with a malty aroma with hints of lemon. The taste is malty with a bitter finish and the aftertaste leaves a dry palate.

FARGO

TYPE: ALE
ALCOHOL: 5% VOL.
FERMENTATION: TOP

Special remarks: Fargo is Charles Wells' flagship introduced in the summer of 1994. It is equipped with a "draught-flow system" to produce a draught-type experience of a pub beer at home. It is a pale amber color with rich aroma and flavor with hops, fruit, and a certain maltiness. The bittersweet overtones vanish in the dry finish.

• • •

WHITBREAD PLC, LONDON

Production in hectoliters: 7,500,000
Founded: 1742

This is one of the big breweries of the UK with almost four thousand tied houses in various holding companies such as Whitbread Hotels Company, Whitbread Pub Partnership, and Whitbread Property. A consequence of the company's enormous growth is that it has swallowed up many breweries in the process. The assortment of Whitbread beers is enormous and it is not entirely transparent what Whitbread brews and where. Brand names include Campbell's, Boddington, Bentley, Flowers, Mackeson, Whitbread, Castle Eden, Wessex, Higsons, and Fuggles.

GOLD LABEL

TYPE: ALE/BARLEY WINE
ALCOHOL: 10.9% VOL.
FERMENTATION: TOP

Special remarks: Gold Label is a very strong beer supplied in a distinctive small bottle. This is not a wine but an ale (albeit with similar level of alcohol as wine). There is a fruity sweet aroma, the presence of alcohol is clearly apparent but accompanied with rounded sweetness and significant overtones of hops. The aftertaste is distinctively bitter.

MACKESON STOUT

TYPE: STOUT
ALCOHOL: 3% VOL.
FERMENTATION: TOP

Special remarks: the label depicts an old-fashioned milk churn, referring not to milk in this stout but lactose (milk sugar). Mackeson Stout is a very dark beer with an exceptionally pronounced and smooth sensation in the mouth. It is low in alcohol with a somewhat sweet underlying taste accompanied by roasted malt. The aroma reveals hints of chocolate and the aftertaste is dry and fresh. To achieve the fullness of body this beer is not filtered but it is pasteurized.

WHITBREAD BEST MILD

TYPE: ALE
ALCOHOL: 2.6% VOL.
FERMENTATION: TOP

Special remarks: this is a dark and almost entirely still ale that is slightly malty, mild in flavor with dry overtones.

WHITBREAD EXTRA STOUT

TYPE: STOUT

ALCOHOL: 5.1% VOL.

FERMENTATION: TOP

Special remarks: this very dark black stout has a pale brown head. The aroma is of roasted malt and the taste of bitter roasted malt, drying and quite full. The aftertaste is bitter and dry.

WHITBREAD PALE ALE

TYPE: ALE

ALCOHOL: 5.7% VOL.

FERMENTATION: TOP

• • •

THE WOOD BREWERY LTD, WISTANSTOW, CRAVEN ARMS, SHROPSHIRE

Production in hectoliters: –
Founded: 1980

The Wood family brothers Anthony and Edward started this brewery with their father in 1980 when they converted the stables attached to The Plough Inn into a brewery. Today they supply around two hundred independent outlets. Their ales include Wood's Wallop, Parish Bitter, Special Bitter, Wood's Wonderful, and Shropshire Lad that is one of the few bottled beers. The family also brew a number of seasonal and special occasion ales and have assumed the names of the former Sam Powell Brewery.

• • •

WORTH BREWERY, GREEN BOTTLE LTD, KEIGHLY, WEST YORKSHIRE

Production in hectoliters: –
Founded: 1992

This small brewery without its own pubs supplies about thirty independent pubs.

ALESMAN

TYPE: BITTER ALE

ALCOHOL: 3.7% VOL.

FERMENTATION: TOP

Special remarks: Alesman has a fruity aroma. This amber ale is light-bodied with a bitter taste and dry finish.

HI SUMMER

TYPE: ALE

ALCOHOL: 3.2% VOL.

FERMENTATION: TOP

Special remarks: this is one of the constantly changing special and seasonal ales with quite unusual names such as: Winter Blues 5.2%, Harvest Festival 4.5%, Ruggie's Russet Nectar 7.6%, Queen of May 3.2%, Owlcotes Special Ale 3.9%, and Santa's Toss 8.1%.

REFRESHING LIGHT ALE FROM

WORTH BEST BITTER

TYPE: BITTER ALE
ALCOHOL: 4.5% VOL.
FERMENTATION: TOP

Special remarks: amber ale with a fruity aroma and malty but bitter taste and extensive bitter-hop aftertaste.

• • •

WYCHWOOD BREWERY LTD, THE EAGLE MALTINGS, WITNEY, OXFORDSHIRE

Production in hectoliters: –
Founded: 1983

The brewery is set-up in a former maltings that was its original home but was sited elsewhere for some years. Wychwood has thirty of its own pubs and supplies a further eighty or so other pubs. The pubs are owned by a subsidiary company called Hobgoblin and most of them bear this name. The beer names include Black Wych Stout, Old Devil, and Hobgoblin.

DOGS BOLLOCKS

TYPE: ALE
ALCOHOL: 65% VOL.
FERMENTATION: TOP

Special remarks: a mellow rounded ale with a sweet malty taste that slips down easily with a warning on its label that it is "dangerously drinkable." The name despite its appearance is vernacular English roughly meaning "the very best."

HOBGOBLIN

TYPE: ALE
ALCOHOL: 5.5% VOL.
FERMENTATION: TOP

Special remarks: a coppery ale tending to reddish brown with a caramel aroma. The flavor is of roasted malt and mellow hoppy overtones and slight bitterness. The taste is partly defined by alcohol and this ale produces a strong dry sensation in the mouth. The aftertaste is hoppy and the body is medium.

OLD DEVIL

TYPE: ALE
ALCOHOL: 4.7% VOL.
FERMENTATION: TOP

Special remarks: a light amber-colored ale with bitter taste and dry palate and fruity aftertaste.

• • •

YORK BREWERY CO LTD, YORK, NORTH YORKSHIRE

Production in hectoliters: –
Founded: 1996

This brewery claims to be the first for forty years to brew within the walls of the City of York.

YORKSHIRE TERRIER

TYPE: ALE
ALCOHOL: 4.2% VOL.
FERMENTATION: TOP

YOUNG & CO, BREWERY PLC, THE RAM BREWERY, WANDSWORTH, LONDON

Production in hectoliters: 200,000
Founded: 1831

The Ram Brewery in south London's Wandsworth has a history that dates back to 1581 when a certain Humphrey Langridge brewed beer at The Ram Inn. The brewery came into the hands of the Draper family in 1786 who transferred it to Thomas Tritton in 1786 and his descendants in turn sold it to the partners Charles Allen Young and Anthony Fothergill Bainbridge. This

partnership was dissolved in 1883 and Young's son, Charles Florence Young continued the business on his own. Although the brewery is no longer a family business there is still a great great grandson of the founder heading the management. Young & Co maintain traditions but also embrace modern methods so that stainless steel and computer control work hand-in-hand with the oldest steam engine still in operation and twenty horses that daily deliver beer to London pubs.

OLD NICK

TYPE: BARLEY WINE (ALE)
ALCOHOL: 6.8% VOL.
FERMENTATION: TOP

Special remarks: Old Nick is predominantly an export product for Young & Co. This red-brown ale has a bittersweet taste and creates a warm sensation in the mouth. It has a rich fruity aroma.

SPECIAL LONDON ALE

TYPE: ALE
ALCOHOL: 6.4% VOL.
FERMENTATION: TOP

Special remarks: a pale amber ale with a fairly neutral underlying taste, mainly of hops. The rich aromas are finely fruity and hoppy with sweetness also present. The undertones are dry and the aftertaste is of short duration.

• • •

COUNTRY Scotland/The United Kingdom

The hills of northern England give way to the lowlands of Scotland and although there are no custom posts the borders between these two countries of the same kingdom are clearly marked. Although Scottish law has always been separate from that of the English, even before the Scots recently got their own parliament back after a long absence, the underlying laws and customs relating to beer are very similar. Scotland divides into the lowlands and the highlands with its mountains and extensive lochs that attracts many tourists, often in search of Scottish myths and legends. Scotland is a beautiful but largely rugged country that differs greatly from both England and Wales. The English prettiness as characterized by Laura Ashley wallpapers and drapes is not to be found in Scotland where buildings including the pubs and hotels are more down-to-earth in keeping with the character of the Scottish people, sometimes described as "dour." Many Scottish pubs are much more in keeping with their original character. A great deal of malting barley is grown in the thinly-populated lowlands and although our interest here is in malt for brewing, Scotland is the largest producer of distilled spirits from malted barley, better known as Scotch whisky. This competition with hard liquor and the distance between homes meant that the Scots

exchanged home brewing for commercial brewing much later than the English. Hops do not grow readily in the cold and wet of Scotland and with such high import costs the Scots therefore used hops sparingly. That is not to say that all Scottish beer is weakly hopped. The Scots have two manners for categorizing ales. One of these is derived from the price in the second half of the twentieth century of an entire cask. The stronger the beer, the higher its price expressed in the old money of shillings. Hence there was sixty shilling beer written 60/- and also 70/-, 80/- and 90/-. Another way was to describe the ale as Light, Heavy, Export, and Wee Heavy. Wee is a diminutive of weeny, Scots for a baby, from the sound a baby makes and hence "small." Strong ale was traditionally served in a small glass. Export is comparable with India Pale Ale, bearing in mind that many Scots left their land to seek their fortunes elsewhere, although it is generally less strong. Because of lower temperatures in Scotland the fermentation and conditioning times of ales is longer. Perhaps this is why Scottish beer is more full-bodied because it has not fully fermented. The Scottish brewers were not isolated from the round of mergers and acquisitions so that the number of breweries in the country has been significantly reduced.

BELHAVEN BREWERY COMPANY LTD, DUNBAR, EAST LOTHIAN

Production in hectoliters: 60,000
Founded: 1719

This more than 280 year old brewery is sited on the east coast of the Scottish lowlands, close to the smoke of Edinburgh. Following a management buy-out in 1993 the brewery made a new start and now has about sixty-five pubs under management. In former maltings on the coast the company brews 60/-, 70/-, 80/-, and occasionally 90/- ales. Belhaven also bottles Traquair House beers.

BELHAVEN BEST

TYPE: ALE
ALCOHOL: 3.5% VOL.
FERMENTATION: TOP

Special remarks: this is an amber-colored ale with a "draught-flow system". This gives this mellow-tasty ale a creamy head.

• • •

BROUGHTON ALES LTD, PEEBLESSHIRE

Production in hectoliters: –
Founded: 1980

A small brewery situated on the Scottish border.

BLACK DOUGLAS

TYPE: ALE
ALCOHOL: 3.5% VOL.
FERMENTATION: TOP

Special remarks: Black Douglas is a full-bodied and mellow malt ale with a dark ruby color named for Sir James Douglas, Chief of the Douglas clan who fought at the side of Robert the Bruce.

GREENMANTLE ALE

TYPE: ALE

ALCOHOL: 3.9% VOL.

FERMENTATION: TOP

Special remarks: Greenmantle Ale gets its name from a book by the author John Buchan from the Scottish borders. It has a fairly malty aroma with a fair degree of hops and fruit. The taste is slightly malty with a vague presence of hops and fruit in the overtones, and slightly dry palate.

MERLIN'S ALE

TYPE: ALE

ALCOHOL: 4.2% VOL.

FERMENTATION: TOP

Special remarks: a golden-blonde ale with malty taste and hoppy overtones. Merlin is named after the mythological figure at the court of King Arthur. Broughton hopes to have imparted a little of Merlin's magic in this ale.

SCOTTISCH OATMEAL STOUT

TYPE: OATMEAL STOUT

ALCOHOL: 4.2% VOL.

FERMENTATION: TOP

Special remarks: this very dark stout uses a small proportion of oats in its brewing. The taste is of burnt malt with fruity nuances with a drying bitter finish. The label depicts Robert Younger of whom David Younger, the founder of the brewery, is a descendant.

THE GHILLIE

TYPE: ALE

ALCOHOL: 4.5% VOL.

FERMENTATION: TOP

Special remarks: a firm hoppy ale with dry hoppy aftertaste. A ghillie is a sort of gamekeeper for fishing.

• • •

OLD JOCK

TYPE: ALE

ALCOHOL: 6.7% VOL.

FERMENTATION: TOP

Special remarks: this beer is named after the Scottish soldiers of the highland and lowland regiments that have been nicknamed "Jocks" since anyone can remember. This strong ale has a rounded sweet taste with fruity nuances and a sweet fruity aftertaste.

CALEDONIAN BREWING COMPANY LTD, EDINBURGH

Production in hectoliters: 50,000
Founded: 1869

This Scottish brewery was founded in 1869 by George Lorimer and Robert Clark who installed the first of three open coppers that was then heated by an open coal fire. In 1919 Vaux took over the brewery and brewed here until 1987. Threatened with closure, the brewery got new life following a management buy-out. Today the last three open coppers in Britain are heated by gas flames. Caledonian is regarded as one of the trend-setting Scottish breweries in the renaissance of Scottish ale with considerable care taken in use of traditional brewing methods. The brewery has none of its own pubs but delivers to around nine hundred free houses. Its beers include 60/-, 70/-, a porter, Merman XXX, and Golden Promise.

80/- EXPORT ALE

TYPE: ALE
ALCOHOL: 4.1% VOL.
FERMENTATION: TOP

Special remarks: this copper-colored ale bears both old type names for beers. In the days when there was little to choose from in a pub you indicated what strength of beer you wanted, knowing that all the ales came from the same brewer. This 80/- has a sweet malty flavor with a complex aroma of hops and fruit with a bitter aftertaste.

DEUCHARS IPA

TYPE: ALE (IPA)
ALCOHOL: 4.4% VOL.
FERMENTATION: TOP

Special remarks: this golden ale from Caledonian is full, fresh, and finely balanced. The taste of Deuchars IPA is malty, slight bitter from hops with background overtones of hoppy dryness.

• • •

HARVIESTOUN BREWERY LTD, DOLLAR, CLACKMANNANSHIRE

Production in hectoliters: 2,500
Founded: 1985

This small brewery was established in 1985 by two enthusiastic home brewers. Ken Brooker and Eric Harris turned their hobby into a business. Now craftsman-like beers emerge from an old creamery such as: Waverley 70/-, Old Manor, Montrose, Ptarmigan 85/-, and Original 90/-. The small brewery won a Gold Medal for its Schiehallion at one of the Great Britain Beer Festivals. Despite offers to merge with others Brooker prefers not to get any bigger because he would then lose contact with his customers.

SCHIEHALLION

TYPE: LAGER
ALCOHOL: 4.8% VOL.
FERMENTATION: BOTTOM

Special remarks: Schiehallion proves that it is not only ales that emerge from small Scottish breweries. This is a craft-brewed lager that is not filtered and hence has a slightly murky blonde coloring. The fruity aroma is succeeded by a malty and bitter taste and then by a bittersweet aftertaste.

• • •

HEATHER ALE LTD, GLASGOW

Production in hectoliters: –
Founded: 1992

Scotland is a land of myths and legends and this ale also has a wonderful story behind it. Heather Ale has probably been brewed for four thousand years. The story relates to a time when Scotland was inhabited by several different peoples and refers to a Pict chieftain. The Picts are renowned for their stone carvings that can be seen in many places and their knowledge of brewing. When the Picts were defeated by a Scottish king, the king demanded the secret of brewing from them. The Pict chieftain agreed on condition that the Scottish king kill his son, who had been taken captive, quickly. The king threw the chieftain's son off a cliff into the sea and turned to the chieftain, who swore that the secret of heather ale would die with him and he threw himself at the king to take them both over the cliff. The tale is related differently in Robert Louis Stephenson's poem. At the time that the British were conquering Scotland in the early eighteenth century, other ingredients than malt and hops in ale were forbidden. Since hops cannot be grown in Scotland, the English made the Scots dependent upon them for their beer. The Scots though were not given to such obedience towards their conquerors and happily

continued to brew heather ale. The recipe for this old brew re-emerged in 1986 when a women asked for help and advice in the home brew shop of Scott and Bruce Williams in making Leann Froach for which she had an old recipe. This recipe was written in old Scottish Gaelic and when she had translated it for him, Bruce explained it would take her seven hours to brew. The women decided instead to buy an ordinary home brew kit and left the recipe with Bruce who was intrigued by it and became determined to brew heather ale. He was surprised by the taste of it, tried it out on his friends, and launched it commercially in 1992. At first Heather Ale was brewed by the small West Highland Brewery in Argyll but demand meant it had to move in 1993 to the larger brewery of Maclay & Co in Alloa. It was no coincidence that both breweries were situated in what was once Pictland.

EBULUM ELDERBERRY BLACK ALE

TYPE: ALE
ALCOHOL: 6.5% VOL.
FERMENTATION: TOP

Special remarks: Elderberry Black Ale is a dark ale brewed with malted barley, oats, roasted barley, hops, and elderberries. It is brewed as a dark ale and fermented for one week. After this fresh elderberries are added and a further three weeks or so are allowed for further fermentation. The ale is black and has a predominantly fruity aroma with overtones of roasted bitterness. It is firm bodied, fairly well rounded, has a dry finish and slightly bitter aftertaste.

FRAOCH HEATHER ALE

TYPE: ALE
ALCOHOL: 5% VOL.
FERMENTATION: TOP

Special remarks: Fraoch (Gaelic for heather ale) is a pale top-fermenting ale that includes the use of heather flowers in its brewing according to traditions going back for thousands of years. It has a floral aroma with a strong herbal taste with suggestions of fruit followed by extensive dryness in the aftertaste.

GROZET GOOSEBERRY & WHEAT ALE

TYPE: ALE

ALCOHOL: 5% VOL.

FERMENTATION: TOP

Special remarks: Grozet is an old Scottish name for a gooseberry and this ale is brewed with gooseberries, malted barley, wheat, sweet gale (bog myrtle), meadowsweet, and hops.

• • •

MACLAY & CO, THE THISTLE BREWERY, ALLOA, CLACKMANNANSHIRE

Production in hectoliters: 25,000

Founded: 1830

MacLay brew in coppers above furnaces and the water is treated from the brewery's own well. Since 1869 this brewery has been established in a Victorian-style tower brewery. It remains a family brewery although there are none of the founder James MacLay's family still in the firm. MacLay's other beers include Kane's Amber Ale 4%, the golden Broadsword, St. Nicholas, Wallace IPA, Porter, and Oat Malt Stout. The main exports are to Canada with some exports to the USA, Spain, and France.

EIGHTY SHILLING EXPORT ALE

TYPE: ALE

ALCOHOL: 4% VOL.

FERMENTATION: TOP

Special remarks: MacLay's Eighty Shilling is an amber-colored pale ale with a full and creamy feeling in the mouth. The aroma is complex with maltiness and hops. The taste is bittersweet with a dry palate and slight bitterness in the aftertaste.

SCOTCH ALE

TYPE: ALE

ALCOHOL: 5% VOL.

FERMENTATION: TOP

Special remarks: this Scotch Ale is also brewed under license by the Swedish Spendrup brewery.

• • •

McEWAN'S FOUNTAIN BREWERY, EDINBURGH

Production in hectoliters: –

Founded: 1856

This brewery is part of Scottish Courage (S&N). The founder of this brewery was William McEwan who started brewing in Edinburgh in 1856. In 1931 McEwan's and Younger's breweries amalgamated to form Scottish Breweries Ltd. Some thirty years later they merged with Newcastle Breweries (of Newcastle Brown Ale) to form Scottish & Newcastle. In 1995 the group merged with Courage to form Scottish Courage.

GILLESPIE'S MALT STOUT

TYPE: STOUT

ALCOHOL: 4% VOL.

FERMENTATION: TOP

Special remarks: Gillespie's is a mild dark stout that is not particularly full-bodied. It is equipped with a "draught-flow system" that mixes carbon dioxide and oxygen when the can is opened for a very compact head.

GORDON FINEST GOLD

TYPE: ALE

ALCOHOL: 10% VOL.

FERMENTATION: TOP

Special remarks: this "blonde" Scottish ale is brewed in Scotland and bottled in Belgium by John Martin. The aroma of this robust Scot is of sweet malt with a hint of alcohol breaking through. There is malt in the taste too and alcohol also to the fore. This beer has a rounded firm body with a short sweet finish.

GORDON HIGHLAND SCOTCH ALE

TYPE: ALE

ALCOHOL: 8.6% VOL.

FERMENTATION: TOP

Special remarks: this brown ale hides beneath a firm cream-colored head. It is a full-bodied and sweet ale with hints of both fruit and roasted malt in both the aroma and taste. The aftertaste is sweetly malty. Gordon Highland Scotch Ale is bottled in Belgium by John Martin who changes the name to Douglas for the French market.

McEWAN'S 90/-

TYPE: ALE

ALCOHOL: 5.5% VOL.

FERMENTATION: TOP

Special remarks: this is a dark amber ale going on pale brown. The full-bodied and rounded ale has a strong taste of caramel and a fruity and hoppy aroma with hints of roasting. The finish is dry.

McEWAN'S LAGER

TYPE: LAGER

ALCOHOL: 4.1% VOL.

FERMENTATION: BOTTOM

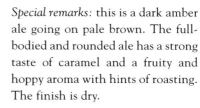

Special remarks: this is a strongly hopped lager, with more bite than many stronger versions. The dry undertones provide a good balance. This is a golden blonde lager with a fine bitter aftertaste.

McEWAN'S PALE ALE

TYPE: ALE

ALCOHOL: 3.2% VOL.

FERMENTATION: TOP

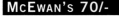

McEWAN'S 70/-

TYPE: ALE

ALCOHOL: 3.7% VOL.

FERMENTATION: TOP

YOUNGER'S KESTREL PILSNER

TYPE: PILSNER

ALCOHOL: 3.2% VOL.

FERMENTATION: BOTTOM

Special remarks: more is needed for a Pilsner than a scattering of Saaz hops and the use of lager brewing techniques. This version has a light body with a neutral taste and a somewhat bitter hop aftertaste.

YOUNGER'S KESTREL SUPER

TYPE: PILSNER
ALCOHOL: 9% VOL.
FERMENTATION: BOTTOM

Special remarks: this golden blonde lager fills the mouth with sweetness without going over the top within a robust body. The alcohol comes clearly through and the aroma is sharply hoppy.

TENNENT'S 80/-

TYPE: ALE
ALCOHOL: 4.2% VOL.
FERMENTATION: TOP

YOUNGER'S TARTAN SPECIAL

TYPE: ALE
ALCOHOL: 3.7% VOL.
FERMENTATION: TOP

Special remarks: a dark amber ale with slightly malty taste with vague hints of roasting and a touch of bitterness. The undertone is dry through to the finish.

• • •

TENNENT'S GOLD BEER

TYPE: PREMIUM LAGER
ALCOHOL: 5% VOL.
FERMENTATION: BOTTOM

Special remarks: a blonde slightly malty lager with a short bitter finish.

TENNENT-CALEDONIAN BREWERY, GLASGOW

Production in hectoliters: –
Founded: 1556

This brewery is part of Bass PLC. The Tennent Brewery or Wellpark Brewery has brewed lagers since 1885 but this Bass brewery now brews real ales for the Scottish market.

TENNENT'S LAGER

TYPE: LAGER
ALCOHOL: 4% VOL.
FERMENTATION: BOTTOM

Special remarks: a light blonde thin-bodied lager with neutral taste and no aftertaste.

TENNENT'S LOW ALCOHOL LAGER

TYPE: LOW ALCOHOL LAGER
ALCOHOL: 1.2% VOL.
FERMENTATION: BOTTOM

Special remarks: Tennent's LA is golden blonde and has a watery taste with a certain malty sweetness. There is no hoppiness or bitterness and the aftertaste is somewhat sweet. It is brewed with sugar and wheat flour.

TENNENT'S SUPER

TYPE: LAGER
ALCOHOL: 9% VOL.
FERMENTATION: BOTTOM

TENNENT'S VELVET 70/-

TYPE: ALE
ALCOHOL: 3.5% VOL.
FERMENTATION: TOP

Special remarks: this ale is equipped with a "draught-flow" system. It is amber-colored, light-bodied but tasty with a slightly bitter finish.

• • •

THE ORKNEY BREWERY, ORKNEY

Production in hectoliters: (capacity) 12,000
Founded: 1988

This most northerly brewery of the British Isles produces four different beers on this Scottish island. In addition to supplying local pubs the brews of Roger and Irene White are distributed nationally through wholesalers. In 1996 an extension was opened to increase production and improve quality. Future plans include increased national distribution and opening the brewery for guided tours.

DRAGONHEAD ORKNEY STOUT

TYPE: STOUT
ALCOHOL: 4% VOL.
FERMENTATION: TOP

Special remarks: this is a dark stout with a flavor of roasted malt with a medium body and complex aroma of hops.

ORKNEY DARK ISLAND

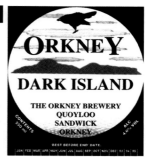

TYPE: ALE
ALCOHOL: 4.6% VOL.
FERMENTATION: TOP

Special remarks: the reddish-brown flagship of the Orkney Brewery is a typical Scottish ale in a slightly less sweet version. There is a rich fruity aroma with medium body and a good balance of malt and hops.

THE RED MACGREGOR

TYPE: ALE
ALCOHOL: 5% VOL.
FERMENTATION: TOP

SKULLSPLITTER

TYPE: ALE
ALCOHOL: 8.5% VOL.
FERMENTATION: TOP

Special remarks: a fearsome Viking on the label recalls that the Orkneys were ruled by the Vikings for six hundred years.

• • •

TRAQUAIR HOUSE BREWERY, THE BORDERS

Production in hectoliters: 1,000
Founded: 1965

Traquair House is situated in the valley of the River Tweed and is one of the oldest Scottish mansions still in occupation. The name means "house on the winding river", referring to the nearby Tweed. Many Scottish kings have been guest here and beer was being brewed here during the visit in 1566 of the Scottish Queen Mary Stuart. Now anyone can visit, as Traquair House is one of Scotland's many tourist attractions. In addition to the brewery there is an exhibition of old crafts. In 1739 a copper of 200 gallons capacity (approx. 900 liters) was installed beneath the chapel to brew beer for the house, servants, and laborers. The brewery fell into disuse around 1800 until rediscovered by the laird Peter Maxwell Stuart 150 years later. The equipment he found appeared in good condition and he was soon able to put it back into operation. Since his death in 1990 the brewery has been run by his daughter Catherine Maxwell Stuart. The beer is brewed with water from a spring in the Tweed valley, English malted barley, and Goldings hops from East Kent without

the addition of enzymes or preservatives. Today about half the production is exported (outside the UK) with the other half for domestic consumption or export to England. In addition to the ales described below there is also a Bear Ale and a number of special occasion brews such as Festival Ale, but these are not bottled.

TRAQUAIR HOUSE ALE

TYPE: ALE
ALCOHOL: 7.2% VOL.
FERMENTATION: TOP

Special remarks: the first ales were brewed with East Kent Goldings hops, own spring water, malted barley, and yeast. No artificial additives are used. This dark ale has a strong burnt taste with a somewhat bitter aroma.

TRAQUAIR JACOBITE ALE

TYPE: ALE
ALCOHOL: 8% VOL.
FERMENTATION: TOP

Special remarks: Jacobite Ale was first brewed in 1995 with malt, spring water, hops, and yeast with the addition of coriander. No preservatives are added to this sturdy dark brown ale but it can still be kept for at least ten years.

COUNTRY Wales / United Kingdom

As part of the United Kingdom, Wales does not differ in its beer culture from that of England and has the same structure with regard to its breweries and pubs. Here too the market is dominated by the giant breweries.

CROWN BUCKLEY LTD, PONTYCLUN, MID GLAMORGAN

Production in hectoliters: 200,000
Founded: 1767/1919

Crown Buckley is a fusion of the Crown Brewery of Pontyclun and the Buckley Brewery in Llanelli. The merger took place in 1989 and was financed by Harp, bringing the brewery within the Guinness group. Crown Buckley has been independent again since 1993 following a successful management buy-out. The Crown Brewery now bottles and fills the beer brewed at the former Buckley brewery. The brewery supplies about 450 outlets of which approx. seventy-five are tied houses. The beers include Buckley's Best Bitter, Buckley's Dark Mild, Crown Pale Ale, and Reverend James Original Ale.

● ● ●

THE OLD BREWERY S.A. BRAIN AND CO, LTD, CARDIFF

Production in hectoliters: 200,000
Founded: 1713/1882

The Old Brewery has been in the hands of the Brain family since 1882.

S.A. BEST BITTER

TYPE: ALE
ALCOHOL: 4.2% VOL.
FERMENTATION: TOP

Special remarks: a mild amber ale with well-balanced dry undertone and slight mellow bitterness in the finish.

Ireland / Eire

The Republic of Ireland lies alongside the United Kingdom in the British Isles and the country is riddled with British customs – even if the mainly Catholic Irish would prefer to be a million miles removed from the British. Ireland is a country with a very small population of just 3,500,000 and it is not easy to make a living in large parts of the hilly landscape. Many Irish men seek refuge in their local bar to make the troubles of the world seem a little less apparent. Whiskey (with an "e" as in the USA) is one popular means of escape but a few jars of Guinness are a more moderate alternative.

ARTHUR GUINNESS & SON, ST. JAMES'S GATE BREWERY, DUBLIN

Production in hectoliters: 11,000,000
Founded: 1756

Ireland is Guinness and Guinness is Ireland and the trade mark harp is also one of the country's national emblems. In spite of this it is a type of beer that originated in London. Arthur Guinness, son of the estate steward Richard Guinness, inherited £ 100 and used it to start his own small brewery in the hamlet of Lexlip in County Kildare. In 1979 he moved to Dublin where he rented a brewery that was no longer in use for £ 45 per annum. At that time the market for beer demanded ales, which were originally the only products that Guinness brewed. It was not until 1770 that Guinness first brewed porter but by 1799 he decided to switch solely to brewing porter. Porter was in vogue at that time in London and Guinness brought a brewer over from London for this new brew. Initially two porters were brewed, the X and XX. The second of these was later named Extra Stout Porter. There was also an export version to send to the colonies which was stronger and more heavily hopped to withstand a long voyage. This was known as Guinness Foreign Extra Stout. The taxation system in Ireland at that time, which was levied on the malt rather than the alcohol present in beer, led Arthur Guinness II to experiment with roasting rather than malting barley. This gave Guinness its roasted flavor, bitterness, and dryness that has made it so sought after throughout the world. The word porter eventually disappeared from the label and the around twenty versions of Guinness are known as stouts. There are a number of reasons that explain Guinness's phenomenal growth. Firstly of course the quality that shines out from this black beer but also the massive emigration of the Irish across the world has ensured widespread markets for it. World War I brought with it energy restrictions elsewhere in the British Isles that did not apply in Ireland. The roasting of malt was forbidden for English brewers and this opened the market for Ireland's black beer. The continued growth of Guinness – which immediately after World War I was the world's biggest brewer – ran into the era of Prohibition in the USA. Today the brewery is listed within the top twenty-five breweries in the world, which is quite remarkable for a brewery with its roots in a very small country and such a quirky style of beer as its main product.

GUINNESS BITTER

TYPE: BITTER ALE
ALCOHOL: 4.4% VOL.
FERMENTATION: TOP

Special remarks: an amber-colored bitter with the "draught-flow" system. It is fairly well hopped with medium body and a short bitter aftertaste.

DRAUGHT GUINNESS

TYPE: STOUT
ALCOHOL: 4.1% VOL.
FERMENTATION: TOP

Special remarks: Draught Guinness in a can is the closest form of Guinness to the true draught. The can contains a CO_2 capsule that is released when the can is opened. This results in the same creamy head that is produced by draught Guinness in pubs.

GUINNESS FOREIGN EXTRA STOUT

TYPE: STOUT
ALCOHOL: 7.5% VOL.
FERMENTATION: TOP

Special remarks: Foreign Extra Stout is a pasteurized beer that ferments in the bottle. The heavy beer was developed for shipment to the British colonies and hence has a higher level of alcohol.

GUINNESS SPECIAL EDITION

TYPE: STOUT
ALCOHOL: 5% VOL.
FERMENTATION: TOP

Special remarks: Special Edition is a version of the world-famous stout brewed for those winter evenings.

GUINNESS SPECIAL EXPORT STOUT

TYPE: STOUT
ALCOHOL: 8% VOL.
FERMENTATION: TOP

Special remarks: the Special Export Stout is a stronger version with great fruitiness and slight sweetness. Selected by John Martin for the Belgian market.

GUINNESS STOUT

TYPE: STOUT
ALCOHOL: 5% VOL.
FERMENTATION: TOP

Special remarks: this version is brewed for continental Europe in accordance with the German purity (Reinheitsgebot) rules. The roasted barley is replaced with roasted malt which rather changes the character of the beer.

HARP IRISH LAGER (UK)

TYPE: LAGER
ALCOHOL: 4.3% VOL.
FERMENTATION: BOTTOM

Special remarks: a golden-blonde lager that in its UK form is flat and neutral with little sensation in the mouth.

HARP IRISH LAGER (IRELAND)

TYPE: LAGER
ALCOHOL: 5% VOL.
FERMENTATION: BOTTOM

Special remarks: this lager is brewed by Guinness in Dundalk with an original gravity of 11.9°. Ingredients are water, malted barley, corn (maize), hops, anti-oxidants, and a stabilizing agent for the head.

• • •

BEAMISH & CRAWFORD PLC, THE BREWERY, CORK

Production in hectoliters: 500,000
Founded: 1792

Beamish & Crawford forms part of the British Scottish Courage group. Previously it was owned by Fosters and still brews the Australian lagers Carling and Fosters, but McEwans and Newcastle Brown Ale also come from the same lines as Bass and Tennents. Originally Beamish & Crawford was a Protestant brewery established by Messrs. Beamish and Crawford as the Cork Porter Brewery in 1792.

BEAMISH DRAUGHT IRISH STOUT

TYPE: STOUT
ALCOHOL: 4.2% VOL.
FERMENTATION: TOP

Special remarks: this Irish stout is soft and smooth with a dry roasted taste and bitter roasted aftertaste. Beamish Stout in a can is equipped with a "cask-pour-system" that injects oxygen into the beer on opening to form a creamy head. In addition to use of chocolate malt, malted wheat is used. The hops used are Challenger, Goldings, and Hersbruck.

• • •

CELTIC BREW, ENFIELD

Production in hectoliters: –
Founded: 1997

Celtic Brew was set up in 1997 by American Craft Brewing International. In addition to Finian's Irish Red Ale it also brews the original Finian's Original Gold.

FINIAN'S IRISH RED ALE

TYPE: ALE
ALCOHOL: 4.6% VOL.
FERMENTATION: TOP

Special remarks: this copper-colored ale has a small cream-colored head. Its aroma is hoppy, developing into quite significant bitterness. The body is medium; initially the taste of Red Ale is of an ale-type fruitiness with a mellow sensation in the mouth and little carbon dioxide.

•••

MURPHY BREWERY IRLAND, LADY'S WELL BREWERY, CORK

Production in hectoliters: 700,000
Founded: 1856

Since 1983 Murphy's has formed part of the Dutch Heineken group and has been thoroughly modernized. In addition to Murphy's it also brews original-style Heineken and Coors. Its most important local product is Murphy's Irish Stout.

MURPHY'S IRISH RED

TYPE: LAGER
ALCOHOL: 5% VOL.
FERMENTATION: BOTTOM

•••

GUINNESS IRELAND GROUP LTD, ST. FRANCIS ABBEY BREWERY, KILKENNY

Production in hectoliters: 1,200,000
Founded: 1710

This brewery was founded in 1710 by John Smithwick in the grounds of the St. Francis Abbey. The walls of this abbey are still standing at the heart of what is now a modern brewery run by Guinness. In addition to Kilkenny and Budweiser, Smithwick beers are also brewed here, including an ale, draught, export, and a bitter.

KILKENNY IRISH BEER

TYPE: LAGER
ALCOHOL: 5% VOL.
FERMENTATION: BOTTOM

Special remarks: Kilkenny is a robust beer with hoppy aroma and well-balanced flavor of hops and malt. It is amber going on red in color and is exported to some countries as Smithwick's Export.

•••

COUNTRY Belgium

Belgium is a country of a mere ten million or so people that makes no great mark on this world with the exception of its beers which are world famous. The Belgians have a great variety of beers of great quality: special ales, abbey and Trappist beers, lambic ales, and white beer that few other countries can match.

The Belgians are modest folk but do know how to look after their inheritance. Gastronomy is of great importance to the Belgians both in terms of their food and drink. The average Belgian likes to drink his "pint" but they are not excessive drinkers with an average consumption of 222 pints per head each year. Belgians have a relationship with their beer that is not really equaled anywhere else in the world. Belgian restaurants offer wine cards in addition to a menu and wine cards, and terms such as Grand Cru, Burgundy (Bourgogne), and Cuvée also apply in Belgium to beer. Many Belgian restaurants also serve dishes that are prepared with beer.

It is remarkable how ales have managed to hold their own against the Pilsener-type beers in Belgium. That is not to say that these ales have not come under pressure from Pilsener production and consumption for indeed they have. Many small craft brewers have had to give up because they either could not meet the scale of demands for Pilseners or did not wish to do so. The variety of ales though is much greater than in neighboring countries such as The Netherlands, France, and Germany.

Belgium has various types of beer that are specifically Belgian. One of these is *witbier* or "white beer" that has much in common with German wheat beer. The difference is in the use of Curacao orange peel and spices, in particular coriander. Both the German and Belgian beers of this type contain malted barley, wheat, and hops and the majority of these beers in both countries are not filtered or pasteurized. The Germans though, tied by their *Reinheitsgebot* do not use spices even if some of these German ales are spicier in taste than many Belgian white beers. Belgian white beer is best distinguished by the mild sourness that is fresh and well developed. White beer disappeared for a time in Belgium and its re-emergence is indissolubly linked with the small community of Hoegaarden and the local dairyman, Pieter Celis. White beer is most popular in summer as an ideal thirst quencher served chilled for outdoor drinking.

Another specifically Belgian type of beer is linked to the area around Brussels. This is *lambiek* or lambic ale derived from a village called Lembeek in the Zenne valley where the natural yeast in the air appears to be sufficient to cause exposed wort to ferment. Brewers of lambic ales transfer cooled wort to shallow open copper vessels in the attics of their brewery. These attics are often slightly open and left alone so as not to disturb the microorganisms present. A unique process known as spontaneous fermentation takes place. The beer is then stored in oak casks where

geuze. Geuze is always sour in taste but can also possess some sweetness. In addition to geuze brewers there are some who only blend lambic ales to make geuze without brewing themselves. Geuze needs to be conditioned for several months after blending. Another variety of lambic ale is *faro*. Faro is old lambic ale that is sweetened with sugar. Anybody can sweeten their own beer to personal taste in a bar with sugar. There are also bottled versions of faro where the lambic ale is sweetened.

Where the lambic is sweetened with fruit it is known as *vruchtenlambiek* or fruit lambic. These are flavored with peaches, raspberries, banana, cherries, and blackcurrants. These fruits can be added whole or as extracts. The resulting ales need a few months to condition before consumption. Fruit lambic ales can be produced using lambic ales or geuze, but also with top-fermenting ales that have often already been cask conditioned for quite some time.

A further type of beer widely found in Belgium is Trappist and related abbey beers. Trappes is the place in France where the Trappist monks first originated. Because of the French Revolution many monks were forced to seek safer refuges. There are still five Trappist breweries in Belgium and one in The Netherlands. Many Belgian beers are given abbey names. Sometimes these beers are related to an existing abbey and brewed under license by a brewery but some fine-sounding cloistered names have no evidence of a link with religious communities of any sort. The term Trappist may only be used for any of the six remaining genuine Trappist breweries and their ales.

it is allowed one to three years to mature. This conditioning process has a significant bearing on the characteristic taste of lambic brews. In the making of lambic ales brewers generally use one third wheat and year old hops to prevent the beer tasting too bitter.

Lambic ales have a sharp sour taste and are absolutely still. For this reason they are usually blended to make other beers. One of these is known as *geuze*. This is simply a blend of young and old lambic ales. The yeast still present in the young ale and unfermented sugar puts some life in the resulting blend. There is a great variation in the proportions of young and old ale used for

ABBAYE DE SCOURMONT, FORGES-LES-CHIMAY

Production in hectoliters: 105,000
Founded: 1862

Chimay and Westmalle are the largest producers of Trappist beers. Chimay is the best-known internationally. The abbey of Scourmont, situated close to the border with France, was established in 1850 and the brewery followed in 1862. Beers are brewed with water from their own well. In addition to blond or wit white beers and rouge or rood red beer the brewery also produces Chimay de Capsule Bleu. These colors relate to the caps used to seal the bottles. The 75 cl bottles with Champagne-type corks contain the same beers but with names such as Cinq Cent, Grande Réserve, and Première.

CHIMAY BLONDE

TYPE: TRIPLE TRAPPIST
ALCOHOL: 8% VOL.
FERMENTATION: TOP

Special remarks: the Blonde Triple – also called Capsule Blonde – brewed by the Trappist monks, continues fermenting in the bottle. It has a sweetish aroma with a hint of hops. The taste is bittersweet giving way to a bitter hoppy aftertaste. It is firm bodied and rounded.

CHIMAY RED

TYPE: DOUBLE TRAPPIST
ALCOHOL: 7% VOL.
FERMENTATION: TOP

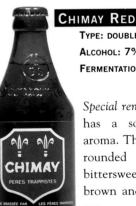

Special remarks: this Capsule Rouge has a somewhat sweet caramel aroma. The taste is sweet, firm, and rounded and the aftertaste is bittersweet. Chimay Red is reddish-brown and the taste develops with age.

• • •

ABBAYE NOTRE DAME DE ST. RÉMY, ROCHEFORT

Production in hectoliters: 15,600
Founded: 1899

The abbey of Notre Dame de St. Rémy was founded in 1230 and brewing started in 1595 but did not continue. The Trappist monks started brewing again in 1899. In addition to their 8 and 10, the monks also brew a 6. These figures relate to the original gravity that is expressed in the old Belgian manner.

TRAPPISTES ROCHEFORT 8

TYPE: TRAPPIST
ALCOHOL: 9.2% VOL.
FERMENTATION: TOP

Special remarks: this reddish-brown Trappist has a bittersweet taste. The aroma of this ale that ferments in the bottle is sweet and fruity and the body is full. Hops in the finish ensure a dry feeling in the mouth.

TRAPPISTES ROCHEFORT 10

TYPE: TRAPPIST
ALCOHOL: 11.3% VOL.
FERMENTATION: TOP

Special remarks: this Trappist 10 is a strong brown bottle-fermenting ale with a dark red glint. It is a strong beer of a lively nature. The aroma is fruity and malty, the taste is bittersweet with a range of nuances: fruit, coffee, malt, and hops are all apparent. The alcohol also ensures a warm feeling in the mouth and causes it to contract. Several of these nuances can be detected in the aftertaste.

• • •

THE TRAPPIST ABBEY OF WESTMALLE, MALLE, ANTWERP

Production in hectoliters: 128,000
Founded: 1836

The Trappist abbey of Westmalle is the largest of the six Trappist breweries, founded in the province of Antwerp in 1794. It brews double and triple and also an extra.

WESTMALLE DUBBEL (Double)

TYPE: TRAPPIST DOUBLE
ALCOHOL: 7% VOL.
FERMENTATION: TOP

Special remarks: this Trappist dubbel is a dark reddish-brown ale with a slightly fruity and malty aroma. The taste contains sweetness and roasted malt. The body is firm, rounded, and quite smooth. This double Trappist also ferments further in the bottle.

WESTMALLE TRIPEL (Triple)

TYPE: TRAPPIST TRIPLE
ALCOHOL: 9% VOL.
FERMENTATION: TOP

Special remarks: this blonde bottle-fermenting ale from Westmalle has a slightly hoppy and spicy aroma. The taste is of malt with overtones of hops and a somewhat bitter finish. This triple has a firm body.

• • •

ABBEY OF ST. SIXTUS, WESTVLETEREN

Production in hectoliters: 4,000
Founded: 1850

St. Sixtus is the smallest of the six Trappist abbey breweries. The monks brew mainly what is required for their own use and have a less commercial attitude than the other Trappist breweries. In addition to their 6, 8, and 12, the Benedictines also brew a 4 but only for their own consumption.

TRAPPIST WESTVLETEREN 6

TYPE: TRAPPIST
ALCOHOL: 6.2% VOL.
FERMENTATION: TOP

Special remarks: this very dark ale is full-bodied, rounded, and has a slightly dry palate. The taste is mildly bittersweet with hints of roasting and is very prolonged.

TRAPPIST WESTVLETEREN 8

TYPE: TRAPPIST
ALCOHOL: 8% VOL.
FERMENTATION: TOP

Special remarks: this extremely lively and dark ale has a red glint and dry, strongly burnt malty taste which is robust, starting with caramel and finishing with bitter chocolate.

TRAPPIST WESTVLETEREN 12

TYPE: TRAPPIST
ALCOHOL: 11% VOL.
FERMENTATION: TOP

Special remarks: this strong rounded ale is almost black and very lively. This beer has clear hints of roasted malt accompanied by toffee-like sweetness and a background haze of alcohol.

• • •

BRASSERIE D'ACHOUFFE, ACHOUFFE-WIBRIN

Production in hectoliters: 11,000
Founded: 1982

A small independent brewery set up by Chris Bauweraerts and Pierre Gobron. The brewery is established in a farm in Achouffe and was entirely renewed ten years after starting in order to cope with demand. The brewers plan to double capacity to 26,000 hectoliters so that they can meet the demand from the home and export markets. Most of the beer is bottled in 75 cl bottles. The main product is La Chouffe but there is also a darker version McChouffe. The brewery also produces four seasonal beers.

LA CHOUFFE

TYPE: SPECIAL BREW
ALCOHOL: 8% VOL.
FERMENTATION: TOP

Special remarks: this is the brewery's main product. It is an amber top-fermenting ale that continues to ferment in the bottle. It is brewed with water from an Ardennes spring and has a malty, somewhat spicy aroma and sweet malty taste with a finish of hops. The aftertaste is slightly bitter.

LA VIEILLE SALME

TYPE: SPECIAL BREW
ALCOHOL: 8.3% VOL.
FERMENTATION: TOP

Special remarks: this strong bottle-fermenting ale has a fruity aroma and slightly bittersweet taste. The aftertaste is bitter with a spirits like dryness.

• • •

ALKEN-MAES BREWERY N.V., WAARLOOS

Production in hectoliters: 2,300,000 (entire group)
Founded: 1880

The Alken-Maes brewery results from the fusion of a number of breweries. There are four different breweries still brewing: Alken in the town of that name, Maes in Waarloos, Union in Jumet, and Keersmaerker in Kobbegem. These united breweries in turn form part of the French BSN/Kronenbourg concern. The Ciney beers are marketed by Br. Demarche NV in Ciney.

CINEY BLONDE

TYPE: SPECIAL BREW

ALCOHOL: 7% VOL.

FERMENTATION: TOP

Special remarks: this golden top-fermenting ale has a fruity aroma. The taste is quite mild, of fruity malt but the body is firm. The aftertaste is of bitter hops.

CINEY SPECIALE

TYPE: SPECIAL BREW

ALCOHOL: 9% VOL.

FERMENTATION: TOP

Special remarks: this dark-brown top fermenting ale continues to ferment in the bottle. The taste is sweet with hints of roasted malt and caramel, the body is firm but fairly smooth and there is a slightly bittersweet aftertaste.

GOLDING CAMPINA

TYPE: PILSENER

ALCOHOL: 5% VOL.

FERMENTATION: BOTTOM

Special remarks: this beer originally came from the Campina brewery in Antwerp. This blonde Pilsener has a weak hoppy aroma and hoppy taste giving way to a bitter aftertaste. It has a medium body.

GRIMBERGEN BLOND

TYPE: SPECIAL BREW

ALCOHOL: 7% VOL.

FERMENTATION: TOP

Special remarks: the Grimberger ales are Alen-Maes abbey beers. It is brewed under license from the Norbertines of the Grimberger monastery. It is a mild golden blonde beer with malty taste and firm body.

GRIMBERGEN DUBBEL (Double)

TYPE: SPECIAL BREW

ALCOHOL: 6.5% VOL.

FERMENTATION: TOP

Special remarks: the Grimberger Dubbel is reddish-brown with an aroma of caramel. The taste too is of caramel, giving way to sweet and sour and finishing somewhat sour with a dry palate. There are hints of roasted malt and the body is firm and rounded. There is slight hint of roasting in the brief aftertaste.

GRIMBERGEN OPTIMO BRUNO

TYPE: SPECIAL BREW/BARLEY WINE

ALCOHOL: 10% VOL.

FERMENTATION: TOP

Special remarks: Optimo Bruno was originally brewed as an Easter beer but is now brewed year round. It is a strong brown ale with sweet aroma and taste. The alcohol creates a sensation in the mouth and there is a bitter hop aftertaste.

GRIMBERGEN TRIPEL (Triple)

TYPE: SPECIAL BREW

ALCOHOL: 9% VOL.

FERMENTATION: TOP

Special remarks: the Norbertine triple brew is a golden strong ale with sweet aroma of malt and a taste of malt and hops that is slightly sweet with a fair level of alcohol showing through. The aftertaste is also slightly sweet.

JUDAS

TYPE: SPECIAL BREW/DUVEL
ALCOHOL: 8.5% VOL.
FERMENTATION: TOP

Special remarks: this blonde top-fermenting ale ferments in the bottle. The beer must be served clear. Judas is a strong beer with a fairly malty taste and bitter hop aftertaste. It is fairly clear and not particularly rounded.

MORT SUBITE GUEUZE LAMBIC

TYPE: GEUZE LAMBIC ALE
ALCOHOL: 4.3% VOL.
FERMENTATION: SPONTANEOUS

Special remarks: the geuze variant of Mort Subite is a blend of old and young lambic ales. It is a sweet and sour beer brewed with water, barley malt, wheat, and hops. This geuze is amber in color.

MAES COOL

TYPE: ICE BEER
ALCOHOL: 5.7% VOL.
FERMENTATION: BOTTOM

Special remarks: as a consequence of the American trend for crystal filtered beers, Alken-Maes introduced this product. It is a light, thin beer with a vague hint of malty sweetness. The aroma is slightly reminiscent of alcohol in perfume. Served really cold it is a fine thirst quencher for those who do not like the taste of beer.

MORT SUBITE KRIEK LAMBIC

TYPE: CHERRY LAMBIC ALE
ALCOHOL: 4.3% VOL.
FERMENTATION: SPONTANEOUS

Special remarks: sweet and sour red cherry lambic.

MORT SUBITE PECHE LAMBIC

TYPE: PEACH LAMBIC ALE
ALCOHOL: 4.3% VOL.
FERMENTATION: SPONTANEOUS

Special remarks: this Pêche (peach) lambic ale is less sharp than the cherry version. It is fuller with the sourness balanced more by the sweetness of peaches.

MORT SUBITE CASSIS LAMBIC

TYPE: BLACKCURRANT LAMBIC ALE
ALCOHOL: 4% VOL.
FERMENTATION: SPONTANEOUS

Special remarks: this pale brown lambic ale is conditioned for a long time in wooden casks. Addition of blackcurrants gives this ale a sweet and sour fruity taste and aroma.

TOURTEL MALT

TYPE: ALCOHOL FREE BEER

ALCOHOL: NONE

FERMENTATION: NOT APPLICABLE

Special remarks: this "beer" is not fermented.

• • •

TOISON D'OR

TYPE: TRIPLE

ALCOHOL: 7% VOL.

FERMENTATION: TOP

Special remarks: this is a lively blonde triple ale with a slightly sweet and hoppy aroma. Hops predominate the taste but there are undertones of sweet malt. It has a firm body.

• • •

HET ANKER BREWERY, MECHELEN

Production in hectoliters: 4,000
Founded: 1873

The Anchor brewery has a history dating back to the fourteenth century.

ARTOIS BREWERY, LOUVAIN

Production in hectoliters: 4,000,000
Founded: 1366

The Artois brewery forms part of the huge Interbrew group. The name is that of Sebastiaan Artois, who took over De Horen brewery in 1717.

GOUDEN CAROLUS

TYPE: SPECIAL BREW

ALCOHOL: 7.5% VOL.

FERMENTATION: TOP

Special remarks: this is a reddish brown top fermenting ale with a taste that develops. The name of "Gouden Carolus" is a reference to the gold coins of Charles V, holy Roman emperor. The aroma is sweet with burnt malt and this is also found in the taste which is complex and rich. The sensation in the mouth is of slight warmth. This beer can be kept for a long time.

HERTOG JAN PILSENER

TYPE: PILSENER

ALCOHOL: 5% VOL.

FERMENTATION: BOTTOM

Special remarks: this blonde Pilsener is brewed with Saazer hops. It has a slight hoppy aroma and neutral taste with a dry palate and a slightly bitter aftertaste.

MECHELSCH BRUYNEN (Mechelen Brown)

TYPE: SPECIAL BREW

ALCOHOL: 6% VOL.

FERMENTATION: TOP

Special remarks: a beer selected by John Martin. It is copper-colored with a fruity and slightly sweet aroma and taste that also has a touch of sweetness with overtones of hops.

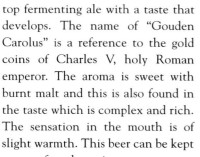

LOBURG

TYPE: DELUXE PILSENER
ALCOHOL: 5.7% VOL.
FERMENTATION: BOTTOM

Special remarks: Artois developed Loburg in response to the increasing popularity of Scandinavian lagers. They intentionally chose an unusual green bottle. The blonde Pilsener inside has a hoppy aroma and taste with a slightly bitter hop aftertaste. It is medium bodied.

STELLA ARTOIS

TYPE: PREMIUM LAGER
ALCOHOL: 5.2% VOL.
FERMENTATION: BOTTOM

Special remarks: Stella Artois is one of the leading brands of the Belgian lager market. It is brewed with the brewery's own floor-produced malt and Saazer hops. This golden lager is medium-bodied with a neutral to slightly hoppy taste and hoppy aroma. The aftertaste is of dry bitter hops. Stella Artois is Interbrew's leading brand that is exported as a premium lager.

VIEUX TEMPS

TYPE: BELGIAN ALE
ALCOHOL: 5% VOL.
FERMENTATION: TOP

Special remarks: this amber ale has a slightly fruity aroma. The taste is slightly sweet, the aftertaste is slightly fruity and hoppy.

• • •

BAVIK BREWERY, DE BRABANDERE, BAVIKHOVE

Production in hectoliters: 100,000
Founded: 1894

Bavik is a medium-sized brewery that brews several nationally-known special beers and some regional Pilseners.

DINNER BEER BLOND

TYPE: LIGHT BEER
ALCOHOL: 1.5% VOL.
FERMENTATION: BOTTOM

Special remarks: this light table beer has a vaguely wort-like aroma. The taste is honey sweet and a little wort like.

DINNER BEER FARO

TYPE: LIGHT BEER
ALCOHOL: 1.5% VOL.
FERMENTATION: BOTTOM

Special remarks: this black light beer has a slightly sweet aroma. The taste is as sweet as syrup but drying slightly towards the finish with a hint of caramel.

PETRUS TRIPLE

TYPE: TRIPLE SPECIAL BREW
ALCOHOL: 7.5% VOL.
FERMENTATION: TOP

Special remarks: this triple beer is blonde with an aroma of hops, present also in the taste with underlying malt. The body is robust and there is a prolonged bitter hop aftertaste.

WIT BIER (White Beer)

TYPE: WHEAT BEER

ALCOHOL: 5% VOL.

FERMENTATION: TOP

Special remarks: a lively bottle-fermenting wheat beer with murky blonde color and somewhat fruity aroma. The taste is fruity and spicy with a mellowness in the mouth. The aftertaste is somewhat sour and dry.

WITTE EZEL

TYPE: WHEAT BEER

ALCOHOL: 7% VOL.

FERMENTATION: TOP

Special remarks: this "white donkey" is a murky blonde wheat beer with slightly fruity aroma and mellow fruity taste.

• • •

BELLE VUE BREWERY, ST-JANS MOLENBEEK, BRUSSEL

Production in hectoliters: 200,000
Founded: 1913

The Belle-Vue brewery is part of the Interbrew group. Lambic ales have been produced here since the early days. There are several establishments related to this brewery in

which the lambic ales are housed at various stages. The Flemish-labeled bottles pay little respect to their content but do catch the eye.

BELLE-VUE FRAMBOISE

TYPE: RASPBERRY LAMBIC ALE

ALCOHOL: 5.2% VOL.

FERMENTATION: SPONTANEOUS

Special remarks: amber-colored spontaneously fermented raspberry beer. The lambic beer on which this is based is cask conditioned for a long period before use. This beer has a fresh sweet raspberry taste with a sharp finish. The aroma is of raspberry and the aftertaste is slightly bittersweet.

BELLE-VUE GUEUZE

TYPE: LAMBIC GEUZE

ALCOHOL: 5.2% VOL.

FERMENTATION: SPONTANEOUS

Special remarks: Belle-Vue's geuze is a blend of several lambic ales of one to three years old conditioned in oak casks. This spontaneous fermenting beer is golden blonde with sweet aroma and rounded sweet and sour taste. It is medium bodied.

BELLE-VUE KRIEK

TYPE: CHERRY LAMBIC ALE

ALCOHOL: 5.2% VOL.

FERMENTATION: SPONTANEOUS

Special remarks: a lambic ale flavored with cherries. It is dark red with an aroma and taste reminiscent of cherries.

• • •

DE BIE BREWERY, WATOU

Production in hectoliters: 1,000
Founded: 1992

An independent micro-brewery.

HELLEKAPELLE

TYPE: SPECIAL BREW
ALCOHOL: 5% VOL.
FERMENTATION: TOP

Special remarks: brewed with water, yeast, hops, and malt. It is a golden-blonde bottle fermenting ale that is not filtered. It is a lively ale with a somewhat thin mouth sensation and aroma of hops. The taste is mildly hoppy giving way to a long bitter aftertaste.

HELLEKETELBIER

TYPE: SPECIAL BREW
ALCOHOL: 7% VOL.
FERMENTATION: TOP

Special remarks: craft-brewed top fermenting ale that is not filtered, brewed with malt, hops, wheat, candy sugar, yeast, water, and spices. It is a cloudy amber in color and the taste if bittersweet, rounded, and somewhat full. The aftertaste is bitter.

ZATTE BIE

TYPE: SPECIAL BREW
ALCOHOL: 9% VOL.
FERMENTATION: TOP

Special remarks: a dark top-fermenting ale with a taste that develops. It is brewed with malt, hops, yeast, candy sugar, water, and spices. There is a richly sweet aroma with hints of spices and burnt malt. The taste is sweet with burnt malt giving way to a somewhat bitter aftertaste. The body is firm with a warm sensation in the mouth.

• • •

LA BINCHOISE BREWERY, BINCHE HENEGOUWEN

Production in hectoliters: 1,000
Founded: 1987

This small independent micro-brewery was set-up by André Graux and moved in 1989 to a former maltings.

BERENBIER

TYPE: SPECIAL BREW
ALCOHOL: 8.5% VOL.
FERMENTATION: TOP

Special remarks: this blonde top fermented ale continues to ferment in the bottle. In addition to hops and malt it also contains honey.

LA BINCHOISE BLONDE

TYPE: SPECIAL BREW
ALCOHOL: 6.5% VOL.
FERMENTATION: TOP

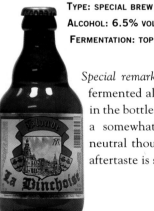

Special remarks: craft-brewed top fermented ale that also ferments in the bottle. This blonde ale has a somewhat fruity aroma and neutral though sharp taste. The aftertaste is slightly bitter.

• • •

BIOS VAN STEENBERGE BREWERY, ERTVELDE

Production in hectoliters: 40,000
Founded: 1785

A brewery that produces many special beers and exports almost a quarter of its production.

AUGUSTIJN GRAND CRU

TYPE: SPECIAL BREW

ALCOHOL: 9% VOL.

FERMENTATION: TOP

Special remarks: a robust top-fermented abbey ale that ferments in the bottle. It has a somewhat malty and faintly hoppy aroma with slightly sweet malty taste. The aftertaste has more pronounced hops. Rounded in body and warms the mouth.

CORSENDONK PATER

TYPE: SPECIAL BREW

ALCOHOL: 7.5% VOL.

FERMENTATION: TOP

Special remarks: dark brown bottle fermenting ale with a very mild sweet taste with aromas of burnt malt. It is rounded without a trace of bitterness.

DUBBEL BORNEM

TYPE: DOUBLE/SPECIAL BREW

ALCOHOL: 8% VOL.

FERMENTATION: TOP

Special remarks: a dark brown bottle fermenting ale with sweet caramel aroma and sweet taste of roasted malt. The aftertaste is sweet too with presence of alcohol. This beer is mellow in the mouth.

GULDEN DRAAK

TYPE: SPECIAL BREW/BARLEY WINE

ALCOHOL: 10.5% VOL.

FERMENTATION: TOP

Special remarks: this "golden dragon" is a strong top-fermented ale that ferments

in the bottle. The white bottle hides a dark beer with a somewhat sweet aroma. The taste is sweet and alcoholic with a slightly bitter aftertaste.

KEIZERSBERG

TYPE: SPECIAL BREW

ALCOHOL: 9% VOL.

FERMENTATION: TOP

Special remarks: a blonde triple ale with a sweet malty aroma. Hops can be detected in the underlying taste turning to slight bitterness in the aftertaste.

PIRAAT

TYPE: SPECIAL BREW

ALCOHOL: 10.5% VOL.

FERMENTATION: TOP

Special remarks: a very strong top-fermented blonde ale that ferments in the bottle. Alcohol is in the foreground of the aroma and taste that otherwise contains sweet maltiness, fruitiness, and some spiciness with a sharp finish. The aftertaste is more clearly bitter.

TRIPPEL BORNEM

TYPE: TRIPLE/SPECIAL BREW

ALCOHOL: 9% VOL.

FERMENTATION: TOP

Special remarks: a blonde triple with a sweet malty taste and bitter hop finish. The aftertaste is slightly bitter. Body is robust and warms the mouth.

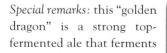

YERSEKES MOSSELBIER

TYPE: SPECIAL BREW
ALCOHOL: 5.2% VOL.
FERMENTATION: TOP

Special remarks: lively amber top-fermented ale that ferments in the bottle with neutral taste and slightly bitter aroma.

WILSON STOUT

TYPE: STOUT
ALCOHOL: 5.2% VOL.
FERMENTATION: TOP

Special remarks: black with a light brown head. The aroma is slightly sweet fruitiness and similar taste with hints of roasting and dry palate in the finish but dominantly rounded. Firm bodied with a sweet aftertaste.

• • •

DE BLOCK BREWERY, PEIZEGEM-MERCHTEM

Production in hectoliters: 10,000
Founded: 1887

Small family brewery.

SATAN GOLD

TYPE: SPECIAL BREW
ALCOHOL: 8% VOL.
FERMENTATION: TOP

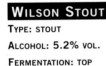

Special remarks: a pale amber top-fermented ale that ferments in the bottle. The taste is sweet, fruity, and with a slightly dry palate in the finish. Firm-bodied and rounded with a warm sensation of alcohol.

SATAN RED

TYPE: SPECIAL BREW
ALCOHOL: 8% VOL.
FERMENTATION: TOP

Special remarks: brown top-fermented ale that ferments in the bottle with a fruity aroma. A sweet malty taste finishes with sharp fruitiness. Firm bodied.

• • •

BRASSERIE DU BOCQ, PURNODE

Production in hectoliters: 60,000
Founded: 1858

Du Bocq is a small brewery with a wide assortment of beers and many private labels are also brewed.

CORSENDONK AGNUS

TYPE: SPECIAL BREW
ALCOHOL: 8% VOL.
FERMENTATION: TOP

Special remarks: the design on the bottle catches the eye. The contents are a strong triple blonde with malty aroma and taste, with underlying hops discernible and mildly bitter aftertaste. The "brother" Corsendonk Pater is brewed by Bios Van Steenberge.

LA GAULOISE AMBREE

TYPE: SPECIAL BREW
ALCOHOL: 6.5% VOL.
FERMENTATION: TOP

Special remarks: an amber-colored top-fermented ale that ferments in the bottle. The aroma is of sweet malt with hints of caramel. The taste is sweet with underlying hops and a mild bitter aftertaste.

LA GAULOISE BLONDE

TYPE: SPECIAL BREW

ALCOHOL: 7% VOL.

FERMENTATION: TOP

Special remarks: the blonde version of Gauloise ferments in the bottle and has an aroma of sweet malt, also found in the taste with a slightly bitter aftertaste.

LA GAULOISE BRUNE

TYPE: SPECIAL BREW

ALCOHOL: 9% VOL.

FERMENTATION: TOP

Special remarks: the brown version of Gauloise also ferments in the bottle. The aroma is sweeter with hints of candy and this is also found in the taste combined with a sensation of alcohol in the mouth. It is full-bodied with a bittersweet aftertaste.

RUBENS RED

TYPE: SPECIAL BREW

ALCOHOL: 4% VOL.

FERMENTATION: TOP

Special remarks:
amber bottle-fermenting ale with an orange glint. The aroma is slightly sweet, fruity, and spicy. The taste is mainly of sweet maltiness and the body is thin to medium.

ST. FEUILLIEN BLONDE

TYPE: SPECIAL BREW

ALCOHOL: 7.5% VOL.

FERMENTATION: TOP

Special remarks:
amber-colored abbey ale that ferments in the bottle. A slightly malty taste with underlying hops and a firm body.

TRIPLE MOINE

TYPE: SPECIAL BREW

ALCOHOL: 8% VOL.

FERMENTATION: TOP

Special remarks: Triple Moine is a blonde bottle-fermenting beer with a somewhat malty aroma and slightly sweet malty taste. The body is firm and the aftertaste contains a hint of hops.

• • •

FRANK BOON BREWERY, LEMBEEK

Production in hectoliters: 2,400
Founded: 1975

This small lambic ales brewery was started by Frank Boon.

KRIEK BOON

TYPE: CHERRY LAMBIC/GUEZE

ALCOHOL: 5% VOL.

FERMENTATION: SPONTANEOUS

Special remarks: a mellow red cherry lambic ale with a full taste of cherries. It is mild to quite sweet and sour. This cherry lambic is brewed with water, barley malt, wheat, sugar, hops, and 200 grams of cherries per liter. The beer is conditioned in wooden casks and the year of bottling is indicated on the label. The brewer suggests serving well chilled in a brandy glass or goblet but it is also fine at less cold temperatures.

• • •

VAN DEN BOSCHE BVBA BREWERY, HERZELE ST.-LIEVENS-ESSE

Production in hectoliters: 2,000
Founded: 1879

Small craft brewery.

BUFFALO

TYPE: SPECIAL BREW
ALCOHOL: 5.7% VOL.
FERMENTATION: TOP

Special remarks:
dark top-fermenting ale that ferments in the bottle. Brewed since 1907, the aroma and taste of this lively ale are somewhat sweet and sour.

LAMORAL TRIPEL

TYPE: SPECIAL BREW/TRIPLE
ALCOHOL: 8% VOL.
FERMENTATION: TOP

Special remarks: golden blonde top fermented ale. The aroma and taste are slightly sour and hoppy and this beer is full-bodied with a slightly drying aftertaste.

PATER LIEVEN

TYPE: SPECIAL BREW
ALCOHOL: 5.7% VOL.
FERMENTATION: TOP

Special remarks: dark brown ale with a slightly sweet and sour aroma and taste. There is a lively sensation in the mouth.

PATER LIEVEN BLOND

TYPE: SPECIAL BREW
ALCOHOL: 6.5% VOL.
FERMENTATION: TOP

Special remarks: a blonde abbey beer that ferments in the bottle. The aroma is sour and malty and the taste contains hops, malt, and is slightly sour. It is firm bodied but not rounded and light in the mouth with a tendency to contract the mouth in its finish.

● ● ●

BOSTEELS BREWERY, BUGGENHOUT

Production in hectoliters: 50,000
Founded: 1791

This family brewery was founded in 1791 by Josef Bosteels who was the first of six generations of brewers of whom the most recent is Antoine Bosteels. In addition to two ales, Prosit Pilsener is also brewed in the whitewashed brewery.

PAUWEL KWAK

TYPE: SPECIAL BREW
ALCOHOL: 8% VOL.
FERMENTATION: TOP

Special remarks: the amber-colored ale has a somewhat fruity aroma and malty taste. Its body is firm and the aftertaste is fruity with some presence of hops. The name Pawel Kwak comes from an eighteenth century innkeeper who provided food, refreshment, and a bed for the night for passing travelers, took care of the mail coaches, the coachmen, and their passengers. Because Napoleon ordained in his Codex that the coachmen were not permitted to drink with their passengers, Kwak had special glasses made that the coachmen could hang on the side of their coach in order not to lose any business and to increase consumption of his famous beer.

TRIPEL CARMELITE

TYPE: SPECIAL BREW

ALCOHOL: 8% VOL.

FERMENTATION: TOP

Special remarks: Bosteels brews this three grain beer (barley, oats, and wheat) using a recipe of 1679 from the Carmelite monastery of Dendermonde. In a blind tasting one could swear this was a German Weizen. The lively head also looks much like a German wheat beer and not surprisingly the taste is very similar, including hint of cloves in combination with sweetness. It is an intensely lively top-fermented ale that is a remarkable beer from a Belgian brewer.

• • •

BRASSERIE DE BRUNEHAUT, BRUNEHAUT

Production in hectoliters: 1,500
Founded: 1992

Small independent brewery.

BRUNEHAUT BLONDE

TYPE: SPECIAL BREW

ALCOHOL: 6.5% VOL.

FERMENTATION: TOP

Special remarks: traditionally brewed top-fermented ale that ferments in its bottle.

• • •

CANTILLON SPRL BREWERY, BRUSSELS

Production in hectoliters: 1,000
Founded: 1900

This brewer of lambic ales is situated in the center of Brussels. It is a craft type brewery that also serves as a museum.

CANTILLON GUEUZE LAMBIC

TYPE: GEUZE/LAMBIC ALE

ALCOHOL: 5% VOL.

FERMENTATION: SPONTANEOUS

Special remarks: a golden-blonde geuze with sour aroma and strong sour taste.

CANTILLON KRIEK LAMBIC

TYPE: CHERRY LAMBIC ALE

ALCOHOL: 5% VOL.

FERMENTATION: SPONTANEOUS

Special remarks: the color is bright red and the taste of sour cherries overpowers everything.

• • •

CROMBE BREWERY, ZOTTEGEM

Production in hectoliters: 2,000

Founded: 1798

Crombé is a small craft brewery.

CEZARKEN

TYPE: SPECIAL BREW

ALCOHOL: 5% VOL.

FERMENTATION: TOP

Special remarks: has a fruity aroma and somewhat fruity taste with bitter hop aftertaste.

EGMONT

TYPE: SPECIAL BREW

ALCOHOL: 6.8% VOL.

FERMENTATION: TOP

Special remarks: a blonde top-fermented ale that ferments in its bottle. This triple brew from Zottegem has a somewhat malty aroma and malty taste backed by hops. The aftertaste is of bitter hops and the body is firm.

OUD KRIEKENBIER CHERRY ALE

TYPE: SPECIAL BREW/CHERRY

ALCOHOL: 6.5% VOL.

FERMENTATION: TOP

Special remarks: an old-style cherry ale with an original gravity of 15°. This is a red beer with a cherry aroma and a mildly sour cherry taste. The aftertaste is sour.

OUD ZOTTEGEMS BIER

TYPE: FLEMISH BROWN

ALCOHOL: 6.5% VOL.

FERMENTATION: TOP

Special remarks: an amber top-fermented ale that has a taste that develops. The aroma is of hops and slightly sweet. The taste is bittersweet giving way to a bitter aftertaste. It is firm bodied.

ZOTTEGEMSE GRAND CRU

TYPE: SPECIAL BREW

ALCOHOL: 8.4% VOL.

FERMENTATION: TOP

Special remarks: dark strong beer with a sweet aroma and complex sweet taste and bittersweet aftertaste.

• • •

DECA SERVICES BREWERY, WOESTEN-VLETEREN

Production in hectoliters: 10,000
Founded: 1992

This brewery was set-up by the Isebaert brewery.

ANTIEK BLOND (Antique Blonde)

TYPE: SPECIAL BREW
ALCOHOL: 7% VOL.
FERMENTATION: TOP

Special remarks: a golden blonde beer that ferments in the bottle which is very aromatic and fruity. The taste is hoppy giving way to a bitter aftertaste. There is a hint of raspberry in both the aroma and flavor. Alcohol can be discerned through the dry mouth taste of the finish.

ANTIEK BRUIN (Antique Brown)

TYPE: SPECIAL BREW
ALCOHOL: 7% VOL.
FERMENTATION: TOP

Special remarks: this copper-colored ale that continues fermenting in the bottle has a somewhat fruity aroma. The taste is of hops with underlying sweetness and a slightly dry palate. The aftertaste is slightly bitter hoppiness and caramel. This is a very full and rounded ale.

• • •

DE DOLLE BROUWERS, ESEN-DIKSMUIDE

Production in hectoliters: 1,500
Founded: 1980

It is obvious from the name that the "idiot brewers" have a sense of humor and the term mud on some of their bottled beers needs to be regarded with a metaphoric wink of the eye. In Dutch and Flemish, mud was originally a unit of

volume (sack) for coriander but is also used for beers without coriander in its other meaning of abundance. It has become a metaphor for the great care taken with these brews. This micro-brewery is run by the three Herteleer brothers and in spite of their small production they export to the Netherlands and the USA.

BOSKEUN

TYPE: SPECIAL BREW
ALCOHOL: 7% VOL.
FERMENTATION: TOP

Special remarks: Boskeun is brewed for Easter celebrations. This top-fermented ale also ferments in the bottle. This amber colored ale is brewed with water, malt, hops, cane sugar, and mud. Boskeun has a hoppy aroma and taste giving way to a bitter aftertaste.

DULLE TEVE

TYPE: SPECIAL BREW
ALCOHOL: 10% VOL.
FERMENTATION: TOP

Special remarks: this beer is brewed with water, malt, hops, candy sugar, and mud. Dulle Teve is late hopped, is neither filtered or pasteurized and it has a warm malty aroma and bittersweet taste that gives way to a bitter aftertaste. The body is rounded and firm and there is a warm sensation in the mouth.

OERAL

TYPE: SPECIAL BREW
ALCOHOL: 6% VOL.
FERMENTATION: TOP

Special remarks: Oeral is made solely with malt, hops, water, and yeast. It is not filtered and allowed to ferment in the bottle. It has a hoppy aroma and strong bitter hops taste. The aftertaste is bitter.

OERBIER

TYPE: SPECIAL BREW

ALCOHOL: 7.5% VOL.

FERMENTATION: TOP

Special remarks: Oerbier is a dark top-fermenting ale with a somewhat sweet malty aroma with a slightly sour edge. The taste is sweet with a vaguely sour finish. It is firm in body and is brewed with water, malt, candy sugar, hops, yeast, and so-called mud, or great care. It is neither filtered or pasteurized and allowed to ferment in the bottle.

• • •

DE DOOL BREWERY, HOUTHALEN-HELCHTEREN

Production in hectoliters: 1,500

Founded: 1994

The label bears an invitation from the brewer to visit the brewery café for a beer-tasting and a chat. Guided tours are given daily for enthusiasts. Visitors can try the abbey beers for themselves on the terrace.

TER DOLEN

TYPE: SPECIAL BREW

ALCOHOL: 6% VOL.

FERMENTATION: TOP

Special remarks: this blonde abbey beer has a somewhat sweet malty aroma and taste. It is firm bodied but mellow.

• • •

DUBUISSON BREWERY, PIPAIX

Production in hectoliters: 20,000

Founded: 1769

The founder of this family brewery, Joseph Leroy, is an ancestor on the mother's side of the Dubuissons. He established the brewery on the family farm – and farm and brewery were synonymous with each other until 1933. In that year, Alfred Dubuisson and his brother decided to concentrate on the brewery and got rid of all their farming activities. There was considerable competition at that time from imported beers from England so the brothers decided to brew beers that both the English and Belgians would enjoy. The family name roughly translates into "bush" in English and hence this became the brewery's brand name. Today the brewery is managed by Vincent and Hugues Dubuisson who are carrying on the family brewing tradition into the eighth generation. The three beers from this brewery are top-fermented ales that are wholly natural and not pasteurized although they are filtered and hence do not ferment in the bottle.

BUSH 7%

TYPE: SPECIAL BREW

ALCOHOL: 7.5% VOL.

FERMENTATION: TOP

Special remarks: Hugues Dubuisson created this amber-colored ale in 1994 to mark the 225th anniversary of the family's brewing career. The taste is bittersweet with a fruity aroma due in part to Czech hops and coriander.

BUSH 12%

TYPE: SPECIAL BREW
ALCOHOL: 12% VOL.
FERMENTATION: TOP

Special remarks: this amber strong ale has a bittersweet taste and creates a considerably full and rounded sensation in the mouth. It has been brewed with water, yeast, hops, and sugar since 1933. Bush 12% is sold in some countries as Scaldis.

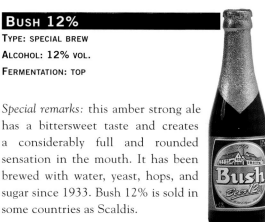

BUSH DE NOËL

TYPE: SPECIAL BREW
ALCOHOL: 12% VOL.
FERMENTATION: TOP

Special remarks: amber-colored sweet ale brewed for Christmas.

• • •

DUPONT BREWERY, TOURPES-LEUZE

Production in hectoliters: 6,000
Founded: 1850

This craft-style family brewery has been in the hands of the Dupont family since 1920.

MOINETTE BIOLOGIQUE

TYPE: SPECIAL BREW
ALCOHOL: 7.5% VOL.
FERMENTATION: TOP

Special remarks: a top-fermented ale that also ferments in its bottle. It is brewed with malt and hops of organic origin. Golden Moinette is robust, malty, and hoppy with a slightly buttery aroma.

MOINETTE BLONDE

TYPE: SPECIAL BREW
ALCOHOL: 8.5% VOL.
FERMENTATION: TOP

Special remarks: a strong, rounded ale with some presence of alcohol stamped on its taste.

MOINETTE BRUNE

TYPE: SPECIAL BREW
ALCOHOL: 8.5% VOL.
FERMENTATION: TOP

Special remarks: this unfiltered amber-colored top-fermented ale that ferments in the bottle is sweet with a warm sensation in the mouth and an aroma containing caramel.

SAISON DUPONT

TYPE: SEASONAL ALE
ALCOHOL: 6.5% VOL.
FERMENTATION: TOP

Special remarks: an unfiltered beer that ferments in its bottle and a has taste that develops. Golden Saison is lively with a hoppy aroma and sweet but also slightly sour taste. It provides a complex and rounded experience for the taste buds.

SAISON DUPONT BIOLOGIQUE

TYPE: SEASONAL ALE
ALCOHOL: 5.5% VOL.
FERMENTATION: TOP

Special remarks: an organic version of Dupont Saison that is lively, blonde, and sweet. This bottle-fermenting ale has little bitterness and is dry in its finish. It is brewed with malt and hops of organic origin.

• • •

VAN EECKE BREWERY, WATOU

Production in hectoliters: 10,000
Founded: 1862

The brewery's history goes back further than 1862, the year in which it came into the hands of the Van Eecke family. As early as 1629 there was a brewery associated with the château at Watou but this was destroyed by fire together with the chateau during the French Revolution. The brewery, then known as De Gouden Leeuw (The Golden Lion), was rebuilt following this.

HET KAPITTEL ABT

TYPE: SPECIAL BREW/ABBEY
ALCOHOL: 10% VOL.
FERMENTATION: TOP

Special remarks: the strongest of the Kapittel ales is amber-colored with slightly bitter taste. There is a full sensation in the mouth and extensively varied aromas.

HET KAPITTEL PATER

TYPE: SPECIAL
BREW/ABBEY
ALCOHOL: 6% VOL.
FERMENTATION: TOP

Special remarks: this sweet dark abbey beer has a slightly bitter aftertaste.

HET KAPITTEL DUBBEL

TYPE: SPECIAL BREW/ABBEY
ALCOHOL: 7.5% VOL.
FERMENTATION: TOP

Special remarks: this dark bottle-fermenting ale fills the gap in strength between Pater and Prior.

HET KAPITTEL PRIOR

TYPE: SPECIAL BREW/ABBEY
ALCOHOL: 9% VOL.
FERMENTATION: TOP

Special remarks: this strong bottle-fermenting ale has a rounded bittersweet taste. Prior is a dark abbey ale that is somewhat sour in its finish.

LIVINUS BLONDE

TYPE: SPECIAL BREW/ABBEY

ALCOHOL: 10% VOL.

FERMENTATION: TOP

Special remarks: a strong golden blonde bottle-fermenting ale. The aroma is sweet and the taste is hoppy with a bitter finish. This beer warms the mouth and has a prolonged dry alcohol palate.

POPERINGS HOMMELBIER

TYPE: SPECIAL BREW

ALCOHOL: 7.5% VOL.

FERMENTATION: TOP

Special remarks: despite the choice of three abbey ales this is still the beer that has become this brewery's outstanding product. Hops are grown around the town of Poperinge and hommel is the local dialect for hop. This dark blonde bottle-fermenting ale is brewed with aromatic pale malt and three varieties of Poperinge hops that enhance the aroma and provide a bitter flavor. Van Eecke advises slightly chilling this ale and pouring so that the yeast sediment is not disturbed.

WATOU'S WIT BIER

TYPE: WHEAT BEER

ALCOHOL: 5% VOL.

FERMENTATION: TOP

Special remarks: the wheat beer from this family brewery is brewed with pale barley malt, malted wheat, a mild dose of hops, and coriander. The slightly sour taste comes from the specific strain of yeast that is used. This top-fermenting ale is lightly filtered for its characteristic cloudy form.

• • •

GIRARDIN BREWERY, SINT-ULRIKS-KAPELLE-DILBEEK

Production in hectoliters: 4,000
Founded: 1882

An independent brewer of lambic ales.

FRAMBOISE GIRARDIN

TYPE: RASPBERRY LAMBIC ALE

ALCOHOL: 5% VOL.

FERMENTATION: SPONTANEOUS

Special remarks: this red raspberry lambic ale has an exceptional fruity taste which is sour and sharp.

GUEUZE GIRARDIN

TYPE: GEUZE LAMBIC ALE

ALCOHOL: 5% VOL.

FERMENTATION: SPONTANEOUS

Special remarks: this golden blonde geuze or gueuze in Francophone Belgium has a wine-like aroma and is sharply tart and dry.

KRIEK GIRARDIN

TYPE: CHERRY LAMBIC ALE

ALCOHOL: 5% VOL.

FERMENTATION: SPONTANEOUS

Special remarks: this red beer is initially very sour but this gives way to some sweetness. The underlying nature of this ale is dry and there is a strong taste of cherries.

• • •

DE GOUDEN BOOM BREWERY, BRUGES

Production in hectoliters: 32,000
Founded: 1983

Although "The golden tree" brewery was only established in 1983, this family of brewers has a much longer history. The present top man Vanneste has a name that goes back to his great grandfather Jules Vanneste who took over Het Hamerken distillery in 1872 and converted it into a brewery in 1889. Het Hamerken joined the trend for brewing lager in the early twentieth century but decided to put a halt to this in 1982 and determined to restart brewing of top-fermented ales. From that time the name was changed to De Gouden Boom. There is a small museum at the Bruges brewery and groups of fifteen people can have guided tours by appointment.

BRUGS BLOND
TYPE: SPECIAL BREW
ALCOHOL: 6% VOL.
FERMENTATION: TOP

BRUGSE TRIPEL
TYPE: TRIPLE ALE
ALCOHOL: 9.5% VOL.
FERMENTATION: TOP

Special remarks: this strong golden-blonde triple ale has a well-developed malty taste and alcoholic warmth in the mouth. This strong Bruges malt beer ferments in the bottle.

BRUGS TARWEBIER
TYPE: WHEAT BEER
ALCOHOL: 5% VOL.
FERMENTATION: TOP

Special remarks: Brugs Tarwebier (Bruges wheat beer) was the first beer to be launched by De Gouden Boom brewery when they switched to top-fermenting ales. It is a fresh and unfiltered beer brewed with barley, wheat, oats, spices including coriander, and orange peel. The murky blonde ale continues fermenting in the bottle. The aroma is of citrus fruit with spicy undertones. The taste is fruity and slightly sharp in the finish. It is a fairly full-bodied wheat beer.

STEENBRUGGE DUBBEL
TYPE: SPECIAL BREW/DOUBLE
ALCOHOL: 6.5% VOL.
FERMENTATION: TOP

Special remarks: this sweet dark abbey ale continues fermenting in the bottle. The taste of this double beer improves if kept for at least five years. St. Arnoldus, who founded the abbey of Steenbrugge, became patron saint of brewers because he got people to drink beer to protect them from disease.

STEENBRUGGE TRIPEL

TYPE: SPECIAL BREW/TRIPLE
ALCOHOL: 9% VOL.
FERMENTATION: TOP

Special remarks: the blonde version of the Steenbrugge abbey beer is a full-bodied triple beer with a neutral taste but a well-developed sensation in the mouth and bitter aftertaste. This bottle-fermenting beer can be kept for five years.

• • •

HAACHT BREWERY, BOORTMEERBEEK

Production in hectoliters: 900,000
Founded: 1898

The Haacht brewery is one of the larger Belgian brewers. Its principal product is Primus Pilsener.

CHARLES QUINT

TYPE: SPECIAL BREW
ALCOHOL: 7% VOL.
FERMENTATION: TOP

Special remarks: Charles Quint is mainly a local beer that is served in the French-speaking parts of Belgium in special mugs with four handles or "ears". It is a mellow and very dark ale with a malty aroma and sweet malty taste with hints of roasted malt. The aftertaste is also sweet and malty but there is a slightly bitter finish.

GILDENBIER

TYPE: SPECIAL BREW
ALCOHOL: 7% VOL.
FERMENTATION: TOP

Special remarks: Gildenbier was formerly brewed at the Cercel brewery in Diest that was absorbed into the Haacht brewery. This brown top-fermenting ale has a sweet taste with slight hints of roasting. There is a warming and dry mouth sensation throughout.

TONGERLO DUBBEL

TYPE: SPECIAL BREW/DOUBLE
ALCOHOL: 6% VOL.
FERMENTATION: TOP

Special remarks: this dark Tongerlo abbey beer has a sweet aroma. The taste is also sweet with a slight underlying bitterness and hints of roasted malt. The aftertaste is slightly bitter while the body is firm but quite mellow.

TONGERLO TRIPEL

TYPE: SPECIAL BREW/TRIPLE
ALCOHOL: 8% VOL.
FERMENTATION: TOP

Special remarks: this blonde bottle-fermenting ale has a somewhat sweet aroma of malt and a sweet taste that becomes hoppy in its finish. It is firm bodied.

• • •

VAN HONSEBROUCK BREWERY, INGELMUNSTER

Production in hectoliters: 80,000
Founded: 1902

The small family brewery was set up in 1902 by Emile van Honsebrouck. The company is now run by one of his descendants. Since 1960 the Van Honsebrouck brewery has only brewed special beers.

BACCHUS

TYPE: OLD FLEMISH BROWN
ALCOHOL: 4.5% VOL.
FERMENTATION: TOP

Special remarks:
Bacchus is conditioned in oak casks. This brown ale has a somewhat fruity aroma and a sweet taste that gives way to sourness in its finish. The aftertaste is slightly sweet.

BRIGAND

TYPE: SPECIAL BREW/TRIPLE
ALCOHOL: 9% VOL.
FERMENTATION: TOP

Special remarks: a strong top-fermenting ale of a lively nature. The aroma is somewhat sharp and the taste quite malty giving way to some bitterness at the end. The body is firm and the presence of alcohol is readily discernible.

KASTEELBIER INGELMUNSTER

TYPE: SPECIAL BREW
ALCOHOL: 11% VOL.
FERMENTATION: TOP

Special remarks: this dark bottle-fermenting ale has a sweet aroma with hints of roasted malt and a sweet taste that is combined with a warmth in the mouth. A very treacherous brew.

KASTEELBIER INGELMUNSTER TRIPLE GOLD

TYPE: SPECIAL BREW
ALCOHOL: 11% VOL.
FERMENTATION: TOP

Special remarks: the blonde version of the "castle" beer has greater alcohol discernible through its sweet malty taste.

ST. LOUIS GUEUZE LAMBIC

TYPE: GEUZE LAMBIC ALE
ALCOHOL: 4.5% VOL.
FERMENTATION: SPONTANEOUS

Special remarks: this geuze is amber in color with a somewhat sweet aroma and sweet and sour taste with a sweet aftertaste.

ST. LOUIS KRIEK LAMBIC

TYPE: CHERRY LAMBIC ALE
ALCOHOL: 4.5% VOL.
FERMENTATION: SPONTANEOUS

Special remarks: the contents are readily apparent because of the aroma of cherries once this ale is poured. The color is bright red and there is a pale pink head. The taste is dominated by sweet and sour cherries.

VLAAMSCH WIT (Flemish White)

TYPE: WHEAT BEER
ALCOHOL: 4.5% VOL.
FERMENTATION: TOP

Special remarks:
this fresh bottle-fermenting wheat beer is a murky blonde color. The taste is slightly sour and somewhat fruity while the aftertaste is a touch bitter and sour.

• • •

L. HUYGHE BREWERY, MELLE

Production in hectoliters: 50,000
Founded: 1906

In addition to a whole assortment of special brews, Huyghe also brews Golden Kenia Pilsener.

DELIRIUM TREMENS

TYPE: SPECIAL BREW
ALCOHOL: 9% VOL.
FERMENTATION: TOP

Special remarks: the appearance of this beer is striking. Pink elephants hide a golden-blonde ale that ferments in its bottle with an aroma of citrus fruit. The taste is malty, fruity, and spicy with underlying hops shining through a firm body. There is a warm sensation in the mouth.

LA GUILLOTINE

TYPE: SPECIAL BREW
ALCOHOL: 9.3% VOL.
FERMENTATION: TOP

Special remarks: another striking bottle from Huyghe. This strong bottle-fermenting ale with a malty taste has underlying hops. The aftertaste is slightly bitter. This beer also warms the mouth.

ST. IDESBALD BLOND

TYPE: SPECIAL BREW
ALCOHOL: 6.5% VOL.
FERMENTATION: TOP

Special remarks: a blond abbey ale that ferments in its bottle originating from the St Idesbald abbey in the dunes. The aroma is quite fruity and slightly malty. The taste is slightly sweet but gives way to hops in the finish. It has a firm body.

• • •

INTERBREW SA, LOUVAIN

Production in hectoliters: 36,000,000
Founded: 1988

The two old family breweries of Artois and Piedboeuf merged to form Interbrew. Sebastiaan Artois took over De Horen brewery in Louvain in 1717. This was already listed in the Duke of Brabant's books of 1366. The Piedboeuf branch traces back to the founding of a brewery in Liege in 1853. Both breweries merged in 1988 to form Interbrew and since that time other breweries have come under the concern's umbrella including the Dutch Dommelsch and Oranjeboom breweries, various Belgian breweries such as De Kluis, Belle-Vue, Jupiler, St. Guibert, and the Dinant brewery of Leffe abbey ale. Interbrew also owns breweries in France, Croatia, Romania, Hungary, Bulgaria, and China. In 1995 they took over John Labatt Ltd in Canada since when the company has entered the North American market. For South America, Labatt already owned twenty-two per cent of the Mexican company FEMSA that includes Cerveceria Cuauhtémoc Moctezuma. Interbrew now produces about 120 beers world wide.

JUPILER

TYPE: PILSENER
ALCOHOL: 5.2% VOL.
FERMENTATION: TOP

Special remarks: Jupiler is brewed in the former Piedboeuf brewery in Liege.

• • •

JOHN MARTIN, GENVAL, WAALS BRABANT

Production in hectoliters: –
Founded: 1993

This enterprise dates back to the start of the twentieth century when the brewer John Martin moved to Belgium because he felt the Belgians had a higher regard for his ales. The business is now run by his grandsons. The company is both an importer of specially-selected beers and owner of the Timmermans brewery in Itterbeek. Certain beers are brewed in the United Kingdom but bottled in Belgium.

JOHN MARTIN'S

TYPE: ALE
ALCOHOL: 5.8% VOL.
FERMENTATION: TOP

Special remarks: this amber ale is slightly fruity and sweet with a hoppy finish and slightly bitter aftertaste. It is medium-bodied.

● ● ●

KERKOM BREWERY, KERKOM-ST.TRUIDEN

Production in hectoliters: 500
Founded: 1987

This micro-brewery is based in an old brewery at a traditional Belgian rectangular farm.

BINK

TYPE: SPECIAL BREW
ALCOHOL: 5.5% VOL.
FERMENTATION: TOP

Special remarks: a golden-blonde bottle-fermenting ale with a taste that develops. The aroma is fruity while the taste is slightly sour and tartly drying. There is also a dry palate experience in the aftertaste.

● ● ●

DE KLUIS BREWERY, HOEGAARDEN

Production in hectoliters: 800,000
Founded: 1966

The brewery is part of Interbrew. There was once a large number of breweries in Hoegaarden brewing the local type of wheat beer. Most gave up in the struggle against clear Pilsener beers. The last closed down in 1957 and the mild Hoegaarden white beer appeared to be consigned to memories. Then in 1966 Pieter Celis decided to make a fresh start with "white beer." Previously he had worked at one of the breweries and knew the recipe. In 1979 an old lemonade plant was renamed as De Kluis brewery. After a period of explosive growth the brewery was taken over by Interbrew and Celis left to seek his fortune in the USA.

DE VERBODEN VRUCHT (The Forbidden Fruit)

TYPE: SPECIAL BREW
ALCOHOL: 8.8% VOL.
FERMENTATION: TOP

Special remarks: a dark red top fermenting ale which also ferments in its bottle. Both coriander and orange peel are used during brewing. This strong beer has a sweet fruity aroma and sweet taste. The body is firm. There is a warm sensation of alcohol and of dryness in the mouth towards the end and the aftertaste is of bitter hops.

HOEGAARDEN GRAND CRU

TYPE: SPECIAL BREW
ALCOHOL: 8.7% VOL.
FERMENTATION: TOP

Special remarks: a strong top-fermenting ale with a cloudy amber color. The taste is sweet but the aroma is more of fruit. Coriander and dried orange peel are among the ingredients used.

HOEGAARDEN SPECIALE

TYPE: WHEAT BEER
ALCOHOL: 5.6% VOL.
FERMENTATION: TOP

Special remarks: this is a golden-blonde wheat beer.

HOEGAARDEN WITBIER

TYPE: WHEAT BEER
ALCOHOL: 5% VOL.
FERMENTATION: TOP

Special remarks: this beer is brewed with the addition of coriander and Curacao orange peel. It is a fresh and remarkably mellow wheat beer. There is a slight cloudiness to its color. The draught version is clearly fresher and more mellow.

HOUGAERDSE DAS

TYPE: SPECIAL BREW
ALCOHOL: 5% VOL.
FERMENTATION: TOP

Special remarks: in addition to bringing about the rebirth of Hoegaarden "witbier", De Kluis brewery has also brought Das back from oblivion. The name comes from a colloquial Dutch/Flemish advertising slogan for this session beer that is back on the Belgian and Dutch market. Das is offered as an alternative to Pilsener, known as pils in The

Netherlands and Belgium but is a bit of an outsider in that territory with its slightly cloudy color. It is a dark blonde top-fermented ale which also ferments in the bottle. The misty color is a bit like crystallized honey. Today's Das is brewed by modern methods but using a recipe from 1931. The ingredients are water, burnt malted barley, hops, and spices. The brewers describe it as a mild beer that is fresh when drunk but there is more to this malted barley ale. There is a slightly sweet and sour aroma and the taste starts fresh but this gives way to spicy bitterness and the finish is sweet and sour. On the way one can detect hints of malt and spice in the aftertaste. The sediment on the bottom can be consumed, indeed it is recommended to first pour half the contents of the bottle in a clean straight glass and then to turn the bottle sharply upside down to empty the remaining beer with its sediment into the glass.

JULIUS

TYPE: SPECIAL BREW/DUVEL
ALCOHOL: 8.8% VOL.
FERMENTATION: TOP

Special remarks: this blonde top-fermented ale ferments in the bottle. This is a strong beer with a malty taste with an awareness of its alcohol. The aftertaste is more hoppy.

• • •

DE KONINCK BREWERY, ANTWERP

Production in hectoliters: 150,000
Founded: 1833

The founder of this Antwerp brewery was Joseph Henricus De Koninck who bought the De Plaisante Hof inn situated at the boundary between the communities of Antwerp and Berchem on 26 June, 1827. The hand depicted on the De Koninck label points to the boundary marker that once indicated the border between the two *gemeenten*. After a succession of direct inheritances the brewery was put into the hands of a manager Florent van Bauwel by Josephina Johanna De Koninck when she inherited it. He started working with one Modeste van den Bogaert, whose grandson was head of the company until recently. The great grandsons Bernard and Dominic are now the technical and commercial directors of this independent family concern. A new brewing hall with the latest technology was opened in 1995. The biggest difference between the old and new style of brewing is the manner in

which the mash and the wort are filtered in conical fermentation tanks in which both fermentation and storage take place.

CUVEE DE KONINCK

TYPE: SPECIAL BREW
ALCOHOL: 8% VOL.
FERMENTATION: TOP

Special remarks: this was originally brewed as Cuvée Antwerp '93 to mark the year in which Antwerp was European City of Culture. Following pleading by enthusiasts it is now retained as Cuvée de Koninck. It is a strong and sweet top-fermented ale with sweet and fruity aroma. It is amber colored and firm in body.

DE KONINCK

TYPE: BELGIAN ALE
ALCOHOL: 5% VOL.
FERMENTATION: TOP

Special remarks: this Belgian ale is a fine fruity variant on everyday beer. The brewer suggests serving in a small balloon glass (a bolleke) so that the aroma can be appreciated more fully. This amber-colored beer has a slightly malty taste with hints of spices. Hops are discernible in the background but do not predominate.

• • •

KLEINBROUWERIJ DE LANDTSHEER, BUGGENHOUT

Production in hectoliters: 5,000
Founded: 1997

It takes courage to start a micro-brewery in a country of specialty beers at the moment when beer consumption is actually going down. The man of courage is Manu De Landtsheer who started his brewery at Buggenhout in August 1997. De Landtsheer has an advantage as he heads a renowned drinks company with some 150 contracted inns and four of his own drinks retail outlets but this was still a challenge. The completely new brewery fitted out wholly with Belgian equipment is now in the hands of head brewer Luc Verhaegen formerly of the bankrupt Van Roy brewery of Wieze. The maximum potential capacity is 10,000 hectoliters. That De Landtsheer has surrounded himself with experience is pointed up by his choice of Jan van Gijsegem as an advisor. It was van Gijsegem who supported Pierre Celis when he established Hoegaarden in the USA. The brewer did extensive market research before deciding to brew Malheur, a session beer with more character than the run-of-the-mill Pilsener but mild-mannered enough for the public at large. De Landtsheer has plans to export, concentrating at first on The Netherlands, France, the UK, and Canada.

MALHEUR

TYPE: BELGIAN ALE

ALCOHOL: 4.5% VOL.

FERMENTATION: TOP

Special remarks: this ale is a lively blonde that ferments in its bottle. It has a hoppy aroma and a medium body. The mild taste tends towards sweet with underlying hops. Malheur uses Saazer hops in its brewing.

• • •

BARBAR WINTER BOK

TYPE: MALT BEER/BOCK

ALCOHOL: 8% VOL.

FERMENTATION: TOP

Special remarks: a lively dark brew that ferments in the bottle. The alcohol in the mouth is part of a rounded and sweet taste with a burnt aroma. It is brewed with honey from October to February.

BREWERY LEFEBVRE, QUENAST

Production in hectoliters: 15,000
Founded: 1876

This small family brewery has a wide assortment of special beers.

ABBAYE DE BONNE ESPERANCE

TYPE: SPECIAL BREW/ABBEY ALE

ALCOHOL: 8% VOL.

FERMENTATION: TOP

Special remarks: this strong bottle fermenting ale is bottled with candy sugar. The aroma of this golden-blonde brew is somewhat malty and there is a lively experience in the mouth that becomes dry towards the finish.

BRUSSELS WITTE
(Brussels White)

TYPE: WHEAT BEER

ALCOHOL: 4.5% VOL.

FERMENTATION: TOP

Special remarks: this cloudy blonde wheat beer has a fruity aroma. The taste is fruity and slightly sharp. There is brief slight bitterness in the aftertaste. It is medium-bodied.

FLOREFFE BLOND

TYPE: SPECIAL BREW

ALCOHOL: 6.5% VOL.

FERMENTATION: TOP

Special remarks: Floreffe Blond is a golden blonde abbey ale brewed with a nod in the direction of the beers of the monks of the abbey of Floreffe. It is a sweet top fermented ale with a slightly fruity and sweet aroma and slightly bittersweet aftertaste. Firm-bodied Floreffe continues fermenting in the bottle.

BARBAR

TYPE: SPECIAL BREW

ALCOHOL: 8% VOL.

FERMENTATION: TOP

Special remarks: this strong blonde bottle-fermenting ale is bottled with a little honey.

FLOREFFE DUBBEL

TYPE: SPECIAL BREW/DOUBLE

ALCOHOL: 7% VOL.

FERMENTATION: TOP

Special remarks: the double Floreffe is brown and has an aroma of caramel. The taste is sweet and the aftertaste is slightly bitter. The body is firm and rounded. This Floreffe also ferments in its bottle.

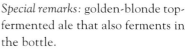

MOEDER OVERSTE

TYPE: SPECIAL BREW

ALCOHOL: 8% VOL.

FERMENTATION: TOP

Special remarks: golden-blonde top-fermented ale that also ferments in the bottle.

FLOREFFE LA MEILLEURE

TYPE: SPECIAL BREW

ALCOHOL: 8% VOL.

FERMENTATION: TOP

Special remarks:
"the best" Floreffe is a reddish-brown bottle-fermenting ale with a sweet taste and bittersweet aftertaste. The body is firm. There is a warm sensation of alcohol in the mouth.

NEWTON APPELBIER

TYPE: FRUIT BEER

ALCOHOL: 4.5% VOL.

FERMENTATION: TOP

Special remarks: Newton is a mix of a white beer and a cider. It is a slightly cloudy blonde color and has an aroma of apples and bananas. The taste is slightly fruity – apples and bananas again – and there is a sweet aftertaste.

• • •

FLOREFFE TRIPLE

TYPE: SPECIAL BREW/TRIPLE

ALCOHOL: 7.5% VOL.

FERMENTATION: TOP

Special remarks: the Floreffe triple is a blonde ale that ferments in the bottle with a sweet malty aroma, sweet taste with underlying hops and bittersweet aftertaste. It is firm bodied and has a lively but drying sensation in the mouth.

THE LEFFE ABBEY BREWERY, DINANT

Production in hectoliters: 350,000
Founded: —

Interbrew brews the Leffe abbey beers under license.

LEFFE BLOND

TYPE: ABBEY ALE

ALCOHOL: 6.6% VOL.

FERMENTATION: TOP

Special remarks: this top-fermenting golden ale has a slightly fruity aroma. The taste is neutral but finishes slightly drying and hoppy with a slightly bitter aftertaste.

LEFFE BRUIN (Brown)

TYPE: ABBEY ALE

ALCOHOL: 6.5% VOL.

FERMENTATION: TOP

Special remarks: this dark abbey ale is also known as Leffe Dubbel.

LEFFE RADIEUSE

TYPE: ABBEY ALE

ALCOHOL: 8.2% VOL.

FERMENTATION: TOP

Special remarks: this copper-colored abbey ale has an aroma of fruit and hops with similar taste that finishes drying with slight bitterness of hops. It is firm bodied.

• • •

LEROY BREWERY, BOEZINGE

Production in hectoliters: 35,000

Founded: 1720

In addition to the special beers listed below, Leroy also brew a number of Pilsners for their local market.

KATJE SPECIAL

TYPE: SPECIAL BREW

ALCOHOL: 6% VOL.

FERMENTATION: TOP

Special remarks: dark brown in color with a slightly sweet aroma. The taste is bittersweet with hints of roasted malt and the aftertaste is bitter. Body is thin to medium.

KERELSBIER

TYPE: LAGER

ALCOHOL: 6% VOL.

FERMENTATION: BOTTOM

Special remarks: this blonde lager (bottom fermented) has a well-balanced and fine malty taste with strong underlying bitterness of hops.

YPERMAN

TYPE: BELGIAN ALE

ALCOHOL: 5.5% VOL.

FERMENTATION: TOP

Special remarks: the aroma is slightly sharp and fruity. The taste is sweet with underlying hops becoming drying in the finish which is mildly bitter.

WEST PILS

TYPE: PILSENER

ALCOHOL: 5% VOL.

FERMENTATION: BOTTOM

Special remarks: this blonde pils has a slightly malty aroma. The taste starts malty but hoppiness develops. The aftertaste is quite bitter and the body is medium.

• • •

LIEFMANS BREWERY, OUDENAARDE

Production in hectoliters: 20,000
Founded: 1679

Since 1990 Liefmans have formed part of Riva of Dentergem. Liefmans beers are brewed by Riva and then conditioned at Oudenaarde.

GOUDENBAND (Gold Ribbon)

TYPE: FLEMISH BROWN

ALCOHOL: 8% VOL.

FERMENTATION: TOP

Special remarks: this strong ale that ferments in the bottle is dark brown with a red glint. The aroma is fruity while the taste is slightly sour with some sweetness and fruit, tending towards cherries. There is a lively sensation in the mouth from a firm bodied ale that is rich and complex.

JAN VAN GENT

TYPE: SPECIAL BREW

ALCOHOL: 5.5% VOL.

FERMENTATION: TOP

Special remarks: this blonde top-fermented ale also ferments in the bottle.

KRIEK

TYPE: CHERRY ALE/OLD FLEMISH ALE

ALCOHOL: 6.5% VOL.

FERMENTATION: TOP

Special remarks: the strong sweet and sour flavor of cherries makes a slow appearance in the foreground but then starts to strike you. This kriek or cherry ale has at least 120 grams of cherries added per liter.

• • •

LINDEMANS BREWERY, VLEZENBEEK

Production in hectoliters: 20,000
Founded: 1869

Lindemans are brewers of lambic ales, with emphasis on fruit beers.

FARO LAMBIC

TYPE: FARO LAMBIC

ALCOHOL: 4.5% VOL.

FERMENTATION: SPONTANEOUS

Special remarks: this faro is a spontaneously fermented lambic ale brewed with water, hops, malt, and wheat. The beer is conditioned

in oak casks and is sweetened with candy sugar just before bottling. It is copper-colored and has a sweet and sour aroma. The taste is mildly sweet and sour, fruity, with a slightly dry palate. It is a real treat of a drink.

PECHERESSE

TYPE: FRUIT LAMBIC
ALCOHOL: 2.5% VOL.
FERMENTATION: SPONTANEOUS

Special remarks: the lambic ale in this Pecheresse is brewed with water, malt, and wheat. It is then conditioned in oak casks and extended with sugar, peaches, and peach juice. This beer is amber in color with an aroma suggestive of peaches. The taste is sharply fruity from beginning to end. This lambic ale suggests cherries and yet it is milder and sweeter than actual cherry lambic ales. It is a beer that people either love or hate.

• • •

VANDER LINDEN BREWERY, HALLE

Production in hectoliters: 2,000
Founded: 1893

Within reach of Brussel's smoke haze the Vander Linden brewery produces six varieties of lambic ales. Beside a "plain" lambic there is a raspberry beer, a 4% faro, a geuze, and a kriek.

DUIVELS BIER

TYPE: BLENDED FARO
ALCOHOL: 6% VOL.
FERMENTATION: SPONTANEOUS/TOP

Special remarks: this is not a Duvel-type beer as the name might imply but a blend of

a spontaneous fermented ale with a top fermented one resulting in a strong amber colored beer with a sweet and sour taste.

VIEUX FOUDRE FARO

TYPE: FARO
ALCOHOL: 5.5% VOL.
FERMENTATION: SPONTANEOUS

Special remarks: this beer is bottled in a 3.75 liter bottle with both a cork and crown cap. This faro continues fermenting in the bottle and its taste develops. It is dark amber and the strong taste is clearly sweet and sour. The aroma is fruity with underlying dryness. Vieux Foudre "old vat" is an exceptional beer that is a million miles from an average Pilsener or lager.

VIEUX FOUDRE GUEUZE

TYPE: GEUZE
ALCOHOL: 6% VOL.
FERMENTATION: SPONTANEOUS

Special remarks: Vander Linden's geuze is a refreshing and dry beer with a definite sour yet fairly mild taste. It makes a good quick refreshment in its 25 cl bottle.

VIEUX FOUDRE KRIEK

TYPE: CHERRY LAMBIC ALE
ALCOHOL: 6% VOL.
FERMENTATION: SPONTANEOUS

Special remarks: this red cherry lambic ale is fairly mild with definite sweet and sour taste yet quite full and mellow cherry flavor.

• • •

LOUWAEGE BREWERY, KORTEMARK

Production in hectoliters: 25,000
Founded: 1877

The Louwaege brews are mainly consumed locally with the exception of Hapkin. In addition to special brews, Akila Pilsener is responsible for the majority of the output.

HAPKIN

TYPE: SPECIAL BREW/DUVEL
ALCOHOL: 8.5% VOL.
FERMENTATION: TOP

Special remarks: a strong blonde Duvel-type ale that ferments in the bottle. It has a slightly malty taste with underlying hops.

• • •

MARTENS BREWERY, BOCHOLT

Production in hectoliters: 700,000
Founded: 1758

This Limburg brewery was founded by Adriaan Geerkens who ran an inn where he brewed his own ales. Brewing traditions were handed down from generation to generation and the Martens name has been associated with the Bocholt brewery since 1823. The brewery exports most of its beer – mainly to Germany – with Limburg brewers having carefully heeded the German brewing regulations or Reinheitsgebot. Martens is also finding new markets in Eastern Europe. Martens has not lost touch with its past and has established a sizable museum at the brewery. The various sections of the museum include a maltings, brewery, bottling, and a general department where the coppers, heat exchangers, and compressors are sited. At the moment this is only open to parties by prior arrangement but plans are in hand to make individual visits possible.

MARTENS PILS

TYPE: PILSENER
ALCOHOL: 5% VOL.
FERMENTATION: BOTTOM

Special remarks: Martens pils is not some age old recipe but clearly a modern-day brew for today's market. This lager was introduced by Martens in 1987 after exhaustive consumer testing. This blonde Pilsener is particularly popular in Belgian Limburg. It has a neutral taste and short bitter aftertaste.

MISTY WHITE

TYPE: WHEAT BEER
ALCOHOL: 5% VOL.
FERMENTATION: TOP

Special remarks: according to the label this unfiltered Belgian wheat beer is *duo-brouw* or " duo-brewed". This does not refer to the two types of grain used but to cooperation between two breweries. Besides Martens brewery, Misty White is also brewed by Sint Jozef of Opitter where it is brewed without additives and without cutting any corners.

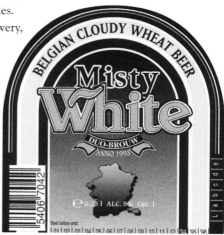

OPUS '97

TYPE: SPECIAL BEER

ALCOHOL: 6.5% VOL.

FERMENTATION: TOP

Special remarks: when the brewery museum was opened by Jean Martens the company felt this should be marked with a special beer. The result is a seasonal beer named Opus (work of art). Opus '97 is brewed for the first 111 days of the year using malted barley from the previous summer's harvest.

Opus '97 has fine development of its taste and can be kept for some time. This also makes it possible to compare different vintages.

SEZOENS BLOND (Season's Blonde)

TYPE: SPECIAL SEASONAL BEER

ALCOHOL: 6% VOL.

FERMENTATION: TOP

Special remarks: this is a top-fermented blonde ale of medium body with a slightly sweet and hoppy taste and short aftertaste of bitter hops. Martens uses late-hopping for Sezoens, with fresh hops being added at the start of the three months conditioning and again two weeks before the end. Sezoens is brewed in accordance with the German *Reinheitsgebot* and is best kept in a fridge.

SEZOENS QUATTRO

TYPE: SPECIAL SEASONAL BEER

ALCOHOL: 8% VOL.

FERMENTATION: TOP

Special remarks:
in addition to their blonde Sezoens, Martens also brew (since 1989) a darker and stronger Quattro version. This is a beer for the true connoisseur with strong and complex fruity aromas. Quattro is not late hopped.

• • •

HUISBROUWERIJ MEESTERS, GALMAARDEN

Production in hectoliters: –
Founded: 1994

This "home brewery" is a micro-brewery.

MEESTERS BIER GALMAARDEN KERST

TYPE: SPECIAL BEER
ALCOHOL: 9% VOL.
FERMENTATION: TOP

Special remarks:
this craft-brewed Christmas beer
includes coriander and seaweed
in addition to water, barley, and
hops. It is almost black in color.
The taste is slightly sweet with
roasted malt and the body is
firm and rounded. There is a dry
palate sensation in the finish
and a malty aftertaste.

• • •

MOORTGAT BREWERY, BREENDONK-PUURS

Production in hectoliters: 250,000
Founded: 1871

The best-known brew from the Moortgat brewery is the
renowned Duvel. This brewery remains a family-run
concern. In addition to the mighty top-fermented ales
there is also some attention given to brewing their Bel Pils.

DUVEL

TYPE: DUVEL
ALCOHOL: 8.5% VOL.
FERMENTATION: TOP

Special remarks: this red and
unfiltered Duvel from the
Moortgat brewery is regarded as
the original version of this type.
This strong top-fermented ale is
conditioned for a further two months after bottling
at cellar temperature. The yeast sediments must
remain in the bottle when pouring. There are
special Duvel glasses into which an experienced
hand can serve this lively beer in one movement.
Duvel does not initially appear to be a strong ale.
This blonde beer has a malty and fruity aroma with
malty taste with underlying hops. The aftertaste is
of bitter hops. It is medium bodied and there is a
slight sensation of alcoholic warmth in the mouth.

DUVEL GROEN (Green)

TYPE: DUVEL
ALCOHOL: 7.5% VOL.
FERMENTATION: TOP

Special remarks: the green label
version of Duvel comes in 25 cl
bottles and is filtered unlike the
original. It is a blonde-color and
has a vaguely hoppy aroma. The
taste starts slightly malty and
develops into a hoppy flavor
in the finish and there is a
prolonged bitter aftertaste. It is
fairly full-bodied and quite full.

MAREDSOUS 8

TYPE: SPECIAL BEER/DOUBLE
ALCOHOL: 8% VOL.
FERMENTATION: TOP

Special remarks: this Maredsous 8 is
a sweet-tasting brown double ale with a
sweet aroma. Roasted malt is apparent
in both aroma and flavor. The
aftertaste continues the main taste.
Maredsous is a small place with
a Benedictine monastery for which
Moortgat brews their beer. In
addition to this "8" there are also
a "6", "9", and "10".

• • •

BRASSERIE D'ORVAL, VILLERS-DEVANT-ORVAL

Production in hectoliters: 38,000
Founded: 1931

Orval is one of the five Belgian Trappist breweries. In terms of output it sits in the middle of the range. The brewery itself has always been run by laity although it is housed within the grounds of a Trappist abbey which also produces honey, bread, and cheese. The Cistercian abbey is open for visitors at certain times. Unlike the other Trappist breweries, Orval produces just one beer. To provide connoisseurs with different ways to enjoy this beer the abbey has a book of recipes using its beer from starters through to desserts. The water used in brewing comes from the Mathilde well, named for a former Countess of Tuscany, who legend has it lost her wedding ring in the well. A trout is said to have sprung from the well with the ring in its mouth. This trout with the ring is now the emblem of the Orval Trappist beer.

The history of the abbey situated in its golden valley is quite moving. The community of Trappist monks regularly went their separate ways as a result of wars and despoliation and then was then rebuilt. The history starts in 1070 when it was founded by two Benedictines. The present abbey's roots date back to 1926 when work was started to restore it with money donated by a Mrs Charles-Albert de Harenne. This work continued from 1927 to 1948 and the abbey functioned again from 1931. An abbot, Father Marie-Albert van der Cruysen, first proposed the notion of starting a brewery within the walls of the cloisters in 1931. This was not so much to keep themselves occupied for the monks were busily engaged baking bread and making cheese but with an eye to establishing a business that could help to maintain the abbey for the future. The brewery was set-up with financial help and was manned by laity right from the start. The shares of the company that was formed were then handed over to the religious order. Orval brews its beer with four or five different types of malted barley and two to three types of hops, its own strain of yeast, and candy sugar. The main fermentation takes six days and the second fermentation in tanks takes three weeks. Orval uses the English method of late hopping. Orval needs to be allowed to rest in its bottle for about six weeks in cool storage at 15°C (59°F)

ORVAL

TYPE: TRAPPIST
ALCOHOL: 6.2% VOL.
FERMENTATION: –

Special remarks: Orval continues fermenting in the bottle for eight to nine months. The bottling date is five years prior to the consume by date. This amber-colored beer has a hoppy and fruity aroma and well-developed hoppy flavor with underlying sweetness. There is some apparent warmth of alcohol and the aftertaste is of bitter hops and drying.

• • •

PALM BREWERY, STEENHUFFEL

Production in hectoliters: 700,000
Founded: 1747

The main export market for this medium-sized independent brewery is The Netherlands. Its leading product is Palm Speciale.

AERTS 1900

TYPE: SPECIAL BREW
ALCOHOL: 7.5% VOL.
FERMENTATION: TOP

Special remarks: an amber-colored ale that ferments in the bottle. It has a malty aroma and slightly bittersweet taste. Malt and a firm body characterize the background and there is a prolonged bitter aftertaste.

PALM SPECIALE

TYPE: BELGIAN ALE
ALCOHOL: 5.1% VOL.
FERMENTATION: TOP

Special remarks: an amber-colored ale with slightly sweet aroma. The taste is also on the sweet side with hints of caramel. The finish to the taste is a dry palate and the aftertaste contains more hops without really being bitter. Palm is a mild and quite full-bodied ale that has a great deal of character alongside an ordinary Pilsener. It is a suitable session ale for a full evening's drinking, ideal with a meal, or on its own as a beer to savor.

STEENDONK BRABANTS WITBIER

TYPE: WHEAT BEER
ALCOHOL: 4.5% VOL.
FERMENTATION: TOP

Special remarks: this unfiltered wheat beer has an aroma of spices and citrus fruit. The fresh taste also contains these same elements. It is brewed with the addition of coriander and Curacao orange peel. Steendonk results from cooperation between the Palm brewery in Steenhuffel and the Moortgat brewery in Breendonk from which the name has been extracted: Steen(huffel) (Breen)donk.

• • •

DE RANKE BVBA BREWERY, WEVELGEM

Production in hectoliters: 300
Founded: 1994

This is a small craft-operated brewery resulting from a fusion of the activities of the one-person's brewery of Nino Bacelle and the home brewery of Guido Devos who jointly set up De Ranke in 1996.

GULDENBERG

TYPE: SPECIAL BREW/TRIPLE
ALCOHOL: 8.5% VOL.
FERMENTATION: TOP

Special remarks: this blonde abbey beer is a post-bottling fermenting ale. The label bears an illustration of the Guldenberg Abbey destroyed in the seventeenth century. Guldenberg is brewed by craft means with whole hops and is also late hopped. The aroma is hoppy and the taste is of sweet fruit with underlying hops. The aftertaste is quite significantly bitter and there is a lively sensation in the mouth from the firm-bodied ale.

PERE NOEL

TYPE: SPECIAL BREW

ALCOHOL: 7% VOL.

FERMENTATION: TOP

Special remarks: Père Noël (Father Christmas) is a dark Christmas ale brewed with whole hops and spices. It is a bitter and spicy beer with underlying sweetness and bitter aftertaste.

XX BITTER

TYPE: SPECIAL BREW

ALCOHOL: 6.2% VOL.

FERMENTATION: TOP

Special remarks: XX Bitter is a post-bottling fermenting ale that is neither filtered or pasteurized. It is brewed with whole hops from Poperinge.

• • •

DE REGENBOOG (The Rainbow) BREWERY, ASSEBROEK-BRUGGE

Production in hectoliters: –
Founded: 1997

The brewer claims this is the smallest brewery in Flanders. The Regenboog indicates on the labels of its beers how long each beer can be kept and when it was bottled.

'T SMISJE BANANENBIER

TYPE: SPECIAL BREW/FRUIT BEER

ALCOHOL: 6% VOL.

FERMENTATION: TOP

Special remarks: in addition to pale malt, Hersbrücker hops, water, and top-fermenting yeast, this beer uses fresh bananas in its brewing. It is not filtered and continues fermenting in the bottle. It is blonde in color, has a fruity aroma, and a quite markedly sour and sharp taste with considerable dryness.

'T SMISJE HONEY BEER

TYPE: SPECIAL BREW

ALCOHOL: 6% VOL.

FERMENTATION: TOP

Special remarks: an amber post-fermenting beer that has a taste that develops. It is brewed with water, yeast, pale malt, Munich malt, caramel malt, Hersbrücker hops, and honey. The aroma is malty, the taste is sweet caramel, and the body is firm. There is nothing new in the aftertaste.

'T SMISJE BROWN HONEY BEER

TYPE: SPECIAL BREW

ALCOHOL: 6% VOL.

FERMENTATION: TOP

Special remarks: brewed with pale malt, Munich malt, caramel malt, black malt, Hersbrücker hops, honey, candy sugar, yeast, and water. It is not filtered and continues fermenting in the bottle. It is a rounded sweet ale with no bitterness but does have a dry palate to its finish.

• • •

RIVA BREWERY, DENTERGEM

Production in hectoliters: 100,000
Founded: 1896

Riva is owned by Liefmans brewery and it brews a number of Pilseners and Dentergem Witbier.

LUCIFER

TYPE: SPECIAL BREW/DUVEL
ALCOHOL: 8% VOL.
FERMENTATION: TOP

Special remarks: Riva's blonde duvel combines a fruity aroma with alcoholic sweetness. The taste is slightly hoppy with underlying malt and there is a warming sensation in the mouth. It is firm-bodied.

VONDEL

TYPE: SPECIAL BREW
ALCOHOL: 8.5% VOL.
FERMENTATION: TOP

Special remarks: this brown top-fermented ale continues fermenting in the bottle. It has a firm, rounded body and slightly sweet aroma. The taste is of sweet malt with underlying hops.

• • •

RODENBACH BREWERY, ROESELARE

Production in hectoliters: 150,000
Founded: 1836

Roeslare in the western part of Flemish-speaking Belgium is home to a remarkable brewery with three specialty beers that have gained it considerable renown. The brewery came into the hands of the Rodenbach family in 1836 when Alexander Rodenbach bought it. One of the great assets of this brewery must surely be its vats. There are 294 large oak vats in the cellars where beers can spend a long time conditioning. These vats have a capacity of 10,000–65,000 hectoliters and are not horizontal as is customary but are upright. The brewery's own cooper maintains these vats without the use of a single nail. Contact with the oak and the microorganisms it contains is an essential part of developing the taste of the beer. After the main fermentation the beer then ferments for about six weeks in metal tanks. After this it is

transferred to the oak vats to condition for at least twenty months. Hence there is more than seven million liters of beer conditioning in oak vats in the brewery. The forming maltings now serves as a small museum.

ALEXANDER RODENBACH

TYPE: CHERRY ALE

ALCOHOL: 6% VOL.

FERMENTATION: TOP

Special remarks: Rodenbach's kriek (cherry ale) is freshly sweet and sour with a fruity aroma.

RODENBACH

TYPE: WEST FLEMISH BROWN

ALCOHOL: 5% VOL.

FERMENTATION: TOP

Special remarks:

a blend of six-weeks-old and almost two-years-old beer is conditioned in oak vats. The color is reddish-brown, in part through the use of Viennese malt. There is a fresh sweet aroma and a complex sweet and sour taste. The body is medium firm and rounded and the aftertaste is somewhat sweet.

RODENBACH GRAND CRU

TYPE: WEST FLEMISH BROWN

ALCOHOL: 6% VOL.

FERMENTATION: TOP

Special remarks: the Grand Cru version is cask-matured in oak for two years giving it a stronger and more intense sour taste. It is a fine, complex, and strong ale.

• • •

ROMAN BREWERY, OUDENAARDE-MATER

Production in hectoliters: 95,000

Founded: 1545

The Roman brewery is a family concern situated in the Flemish part of the Ardennes. The 110 personnel are headed by Louis Roman and include other members of the family. In addition to brewing beer the company also produces soft drinks using water from a renowned spring. Besides special beers Roman also brew several Pilseners including Romy Pils, which is probably the best known. They also brew beers by John Smith Tadcaster of the UK under license (Scottish Courage) such as Pale Ale and Scotch Ale.

ALFRI

TYPE: ALCOHOL FREE

ALCOHOL: 0.5% VOL.

FERMENTATION: BOTTOM

Special remarks:
this is a low calorie and alcohol free beer.

ENAME DUBBEL

TYPE: SPECIAL BREW/DOUBLE

ALCOHOL: 6.5% VOL.

FERMENTATION: TOP

Special remarks: this abbey beer is brewed according to the style of the Benedictine abbey of Sint Salvator in Ename. Dubbel is reddish-brown with a rich aroma combined with a somewhat sweet malty taste. It continues fermenting in the bottle and is best kept at cellar temperature until serving.

DOBBELEN BRUINEN

TYPE: OLD FLEMISH BRAWN

ALCOHOL: 8% VOL.

FERMENTATION: TOP

Special remarks: the label declaims that this strong ale with a sweet malty aroma is free from all artificiality. The taste of this brown ale is of burnt malt, sweetness, and a hint of bitterness. It is fairly full-bodied and reveals sweet alcohol in its finish. The aftertaste is of bitter roasted flavor.

ENAME TRIPEL

TYPE: SPECIAL BREW/TRIPEL

ALCOHOL: 9% VOL.

FERMENTATION: TOP

Special remarks: this golden-blonde version of the abbey beer is a strong and sweet triple that ferments in the bottle. The beer is best kept at a temperature of 10–12°C (50–53.6°F) until served.

MATER WIT BIER

TYPE: WHEAT BEER

ALCOHOL: 5% VOL.

FERMENTATION: TOP

Special remarks:
this fresh and slightly cloudy wheat beer has a spicy taste turning a little sharp at the end. The aroma has hints of fruit and some spice. The aftertaste is briefly sour. It is medium-bodied and in general this is a mellow ale.

SLOEBER

TYPE: DUVEL

ALCOHOL: 7.5% VOL.

FERMENTATION: TOP

Special remarks: this Sloeber or "wretch" is a pale amber duvel with a neutral malty taste and bitter aftertaste of hops. It ferments in the bottle and has a firm and rounded body.

SPECIAL ROMAN

TYPE: OLD FLEMISH BROWN

ALCOHOL: 5.5% VOL.

FERMENTATION: TOP

Special remarks: this dark ale has a sweet taste and bitter aftertaste.

• • •

BRASSERIE DE SILLY, SILLY

Production in hectoliters: 11,000
Founded: 1854

Silly is a small family brewery that brews both bottom and top fermenting beers.

LA DIVINE

TYPE: SPECIAL BREW

ALCOHOL: 9.5% VOL.

FERMENTATION: TOP

Special remarks: this amber ale has a rich fruity aroma with a little hoppiness. The taste is of hops, becoming bitter in the finish. The mouth experiences a warm sensation.

DOUBLE ENGHIEN BLONDE

TYPE: SPECIAL BREW

ALCOHOL: 7.5% VOL.

FERMENTATION: TOP

Special remarks: this blonde top-fermenting ale ferments in the bottle. It has a somewhat malty aroma and sweet taste. The aftertaste of this strong, rounded beer is slightly bitter.

SAISON

TYPE: SEASONAL BREW

ALCOHOL: 5% VOL.

FERMENTATION: TOP

Special remarks: this copper-colored ale has a slightly sweet, fruity aroma. Saison is a fairly mellow beer with a hint of hops in a drying taste.

SUPER 64

TYPE: BELGIAN ALE

ALCOHOL: 5.2% VOL.

FERMENTATION: TOP

Special remarks: this amber top-fermented ale has been brewed since 1964. The aroma is slightly sweet and malty while the taste is mildly of hops, quite drying, and has a fairly bitter hop finish. This beer displays quite some character.

TITJE

TYPE: WHEAT BEER

ALCOHOL: 5% VOL.

FERMENTATION: TOP

Special remarks: this cloudy blonde wheat beer has a slightly fruity aroma and mildly spicy taste. The aftertaste is somewhat drying but reveals nothing new.

• • •

SLAGHMUYLDER BREWERY, NINOVE

Production in hectoliters: 8,000

Founded: 1860

This small family brewery employs about fifteen people. They not only brew for the Belgian market but also for export to The Netherlands, and the USA. Their regional beer is sold as Slag Lager.

WITKAP PATER DUBBELE PATER

TYPE: SPECIAL BREW/DOUBLE

ALCOHOL: 7% VOL.

FERMENTATION: TOP

Special remarks: this dark brown abbey ale has a somewhat sweet aroma and a slightly malty taste with hints of roasted malt. The aftertaste is slightly bitter.

WITKAP PATER STIMULO

TYPE: SPECIAL BREW

ALCOHOL: 6% VOL.

FERMENTATION: TOP

Special remarks: this is a blonde ale that continues fermenting in the bottle with a slightly fruity and malty aroma and mild malt taste. The aftertaste is slightly of hop bitterness.

WITKAP PATER TRIPEL

TYPE: SPECIAL BREW/TRIPLE

ALCOHOL: 7.5% VOL.

FERMENTATION: TOP

Special remarks: this blonde triple has a lively nature. This bottle- -fermenting ale has a slightly fruity aroma and a malty taste. There is a warm sensation in the mouth towards the end. It is firm bodied.

• • •

DE SMEDT BREWERY, OPWIJK

Production in hectoliters: 50,000

Founded: 1790

De Smedt is a medium-sized independent brewery that solely brews top fermenting ales, and particularly abbey beers. About a quarter of the production is exported.

ABBAYE D'AULNE 6

TYPE: SPECIAL BREW

ALCOHOL: 6% VOL.

FERMENTATION: TOP

Special remarks: this bottle-fermenting ale is marketed by Les Ets. Leveau in Charleroi. The misty brown ale has a reddish glint. The aroma is fruity and sweet with a hint of sourness while the taste is sweet with a hint of apple and drying sourness in the finish. It is firm bodied. The aftertaste yields up further hints of burnt malt.

ABBAYE D'AULNE 8

TYPE: SPECIAL BREW

ALCOHOL: 8% VOL.

FERMENTATION: TOP

Special remarks: this brown ale has a warm sweet aroma. The taste combines sweetness and roasted malt with sweet alcohol in the finish and aftertaste. It is firm bodied and rounded.

Special remarks: this Affligem double is a dark ale that ferments in the bottle. The yeast sediment must be left in the bottle. The aroma is of sweet malt, somewhat fruity, and betrays alcohol. The taste is rich and complex with underlying sweetness and a bittersweet aftertaste. It is firm bodied and warms the mouth with alcohol.

ABBAYE D'AULNE 10

TYPE: SPECIAL BREW

ALCOHOL: 10% VOL.

FERMENTATION: TOP

AFFLIGEM PATERS VAT

TYPE: SPECIAL BREW/ABBEY BEER

ALCOHOL: 7% VOL.

FERMENTATION: TOP

Special remarks: Affligem Paters Vat is brewed once each year in late summer. It is made with Affligem hops and is then available as a blonde Christmas ale. This strong full-bodied ale is quite neutral in taste and it has a slightly hoppy aroma and warms the mouth with alcohol.

AFFLIGEM BLOND

TYPE: SPECIAL BREW

ALCOHOL: 7% VOL.

FERMENTATION: TOP

Special remarks: this blonde ale is brewed to a recipe of the Benedictine monks of the abbey of Affligem. The aroma is somewhat hoppy and likewise the taste with a hint of spice. The taste is balanced and the aftertaste is mildly bitter hoppiness. There is a lively and dry sensation in the mouth. It is medium in body.

AFFLIGEM DUBBEL

TYPE: SPECIAL BREW/DOUBLE

ALCOHOL: 7% VOL.

FERMENTATION: TOP

AFFLIGEM TRIPEL

TYPE: SPECIAL BREW/TRIPEL

ALCOHOL: 8.5% VOL.

FERMENTATION: TOP

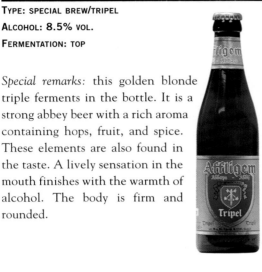

Special remarks: this golden blonde triple ferments in the bottle. It is a strong abbey beer with a rich aroma containing hops, fruit, and spice. These elements are also found in the taste. A lively sensation in the mouth finishes with the warmth of alcohol. The body is firm and rounded.

NE FLIEREFLUITER

TYPE: SPECIAL BREW

ALCOHOL: 7% VOL.

FERMENTATION: TOP

Special remarks: this beer is marketed by Fisser NV of Zammel.

DIKKENEK (Thick Neck)

TYPE: SPECIAL BREW

ALCOHOL: 5.1% VOL.

FERMENTATION: TOP

Special remarks: this amber top-fermenting ale has a sweet and spicy aroma. The taste is sweet with a bitter aftertaste. It has a medium-full body. Dikkenek (thick neck) refers to a traditional "thick beer" that was brewed with three different grains in Hasselt around 1600.

OP-ALE SPECIALE

TYPE: BELGIAN ALE

ALCOHOL: 5% VOL.

FERMENTATION: TOP

Special remarks: this amber ale has a fruity aroma. The taste is of hops and fruit with a dry finish. The aftertaste is bitter. The body is medium. Speciale is a simple ale but it is full of character.

NAPOLEON

TYPE: SPECIAL BREW

ALCOHOL: 8% VOL.

FERMENTATION: TOP

Special remarks:
strong top-fermented ale that ferments in the bottle. Taste and aroma are sweet with a finish of bitter hops.

POSTEL DOBBEL

TYPE: SPECIAL BREW/DOUBLE

ALCOHOL: 7% VOL.

FERMENTATION: TOP

Special remarks: a dark abbey ale that is not filtered and that ferments in the bottle. The aroma is fruity with hints of apple. The taste is sweet apple with underlying roasted malt. There is slight warmth and some bitterness in the finish. A well-balanced beer.

POSTEL TRIPEL

TYPE: SPECIAL BREW/DOUBLE
ALCOHOL: 8.5% VOL.
FERMENTATION: TOP

Special remarks: this unfiltered abbey ale ferments in the bottle. The gold-blonde triple has a sweet and hoppy aroma with sweet taste with alcoholic warmth in the finish. The aftertaste is of hops but predominantly sweet alcohol. There is a prolonged shriveling of the mouth.

• • •

ST. BERNARDUS BREWERY, WATOU

Production in hectoliters: 15,000
Founded: 1946

This small independent brewery is situated on the Trappistenweg (Trappist Way). Once brewed St. Sixtus abbey beer to a genuine Trappist recipe but this has been considerably altered over the years.

ST. BERNARDUS ABT 12

TYPE: SPECIAL BREW
ALCOHOL: 10% VOL.
FERMENTATION: TOP

Special remarks: the pale brown Abt 12 is a strong ale that ferments in the bottle with a sweet malt taste. There are hints of roasting and caramel that become less sweet with age. The aroma is sweet with a hint of fruit and there is a warm sensation in the mouth. It is firm bodied.

ST. BERNARDUS PATER 6

TYPE: SPECIAL BREW
ALCOHOL: 6.7% VOL.
FERMENTATION: TOP

Special remarks: this brown top-fermenting ale has a sweet aroma. The taste is sweet with underlying hint of sweet and sour. There are more hops in the finish and a bittersweet aftertaste.

ST. BERNARDUS PRIOR 8

TYPE: SPECIAL BREW/DOUBLE
ALCOHOL: 8% VOL.
FERMENTATION: TOP

Special remarks:
a brown ale with a somewhat sweet malt aroma and sweet and sour taste with underlying dark malt. The aftertaste is somewhat sweet with a touch of hops.

ST. BERNARDUS TRIPEL

TYPE: SPECIAL BREW/TRIPLE
ALCOHOL: 7.5% VOL.
FERMENTATION: TOP

Special remarks: the blonde triple St. Bernardus is a lively sweet malty ale which ferments in the bottle.

TRIPLE WATOU

TYPE: SPECIAL BREW/TRIPLE
ALCOHOL: 7% VOL.
FERMENTATION: TOP

Special remarks: this golden-blonde bottle-fermenting ale has a slightly fruity aroma. The taste is quite sharply bitter but the aftertaste is only brief and mildly bitter. It is firm bodied.

• • •

ST. JOZEF BVBA BREWERY, BREE-OPITTER

Production in hectoliters: 75,000
Founded: 1955

This small brewery is best known locally. Its leading products are Pax Pils and the most sumptuous Ops Ale.

BOSBIER

TYPE: FRUIT BEER
ALCOHOL: 4.5% VOL.
FERMENTATION: TOP

Special remarks: this regional brew made with blueberries is red in color. The aroma is fruity and if you did not know you would swear this was blackcurrant liqueur not beer. The taste is of blueberries with underlying malt.

• • •

STERKENS BREWERY, MEER

Production in hectoliters: 10,000
Founded: 1650

Sterkens is a small family brewery that only brews top-fermented ales.

ST. PAUL BLOND

TYPE: SPECIAL BREW
ALCOHOL: 5.3% VOL.
FERMENTATION: TOP

Special remarks: this Blond is a craft-brewed abbey ale that is brewed using Oregon hops. It has a hoppy aroma and taste with underlying malt and a slightly sour finish. The aftertaste is of dry-mouthed hops.

ST. PAUL DOUBLE

TYPE: SPECIAL BREW/DOUBLE
ALCOHOL: 6.9% VOL.
FERMENTATION: TOP

Special remarks: the double version of this abbey ale is brown and has a sweet aroma. The taste is slightly bitter with hints of dark malt and the aftertaste is also slightly bitter.

ST. PAUL SPECIAL

TYPE: SPECIAL BREW
ALCOHOL: 5.5% VOL.
FERMENTATION: TOP

Special remarks: this Special is an amber top-fermented special brew. It has a somewhat fruity and slightly sweet aroma and a sweet taste.

ST. PAUL TRIPLE

TYPE: SPECIAL BREW/TRIPLE
ALCOHOL: 7.6% VOL.
FERMENTATION: TOP

Special remarks: this blonde triple has an aroma of hops and malt and there are hops too in the taste with underlying malt. The aftertaste is a dry-mouthed hoppy bitterness.

TREMELOOS DAMIAANBIER

TYPE: SPECIAL BREW
ALCOHOL: 6.5% VOL.
FERMENTATION: TOP

Special remarks: this dark ale has a somewhat sweet aroma and a bittersweet taste. The aftertaste is of bitter hops.

• • •

STRAFFE HENDRIK BREWERY, BRUGES

Production in hectoliters: 5,000
Founded: 1989

Straffe Hendrik was a family brewery dating back to 1856, formerly known as the Halve Maen brewery. It is now operated by RIVA of Dentergem.

BRUGSE STRAFFE HENDRIK

TYPE: SPECIAL BREW
ALCOHOL: 6% VOL.
FERMENTATION: TOP

Special remarks: Straffe Hendrik has a somewhat hoppy aroma and fairly malty taste with a

prolonged bitter hop finish. The hops used are Goldings, Styrian, and Fuggles. This is a golden-blonde top-fermented ale that continues fermenting in the bottle.

• • •

167

STRUBBE BREWERY, ICHTEGEM

Production in hectoliters: 15,000
Founded: 1830

The Strubbe brewery is a small family concern that brews specialty beers and a Pilsener of regional character in its range.

DIKKE MATHILE

TYPE: SPECIAL BREW
ALCOHOL: 6% VOL.
FERMENTATION: TOP

Special remarks: Dikke Mathile is an amber ale with a slightly fruity sweet aroma and slightly sweet taste with some hops in the finish. The aftertaste is of mild bitterness over a medium body.

VLASKOP

TYPE: SPECIAL BREW
ALCOHOL: 5.5% VOL.
FERMENTATION: TOP

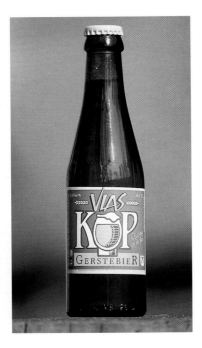

Special remarks:
this lively blonde ale has secondary fermentation. Its aroma is somewhat hoppy with butter. The taste is neutral with a hint of spice. The finish is slightly drying.

• • •

TIMMERMANS BREWERY, ITTERBEEK

Production in hectoliters: 10,000
Founded: 1781

This lambic ale brewery is part of the John Martin concern.

BOURGOGNE DES FLANDRES

TYPE: OLD BROWN/LAMBIC
ALCOHOL: 5% VOL.
FERMENTATION: TOP/SPONTANEOUS

Special remarks: this brown beer is a blend of old brown and lambic and it has a sweet and sour taste.

TIMMERMANS CASSIS

TYPE: BLACKCURRANT LAMBIC
ALCOHOL: 4% VOL.
FERMENTATION: SPONTANEOUS

Special remarks: the blackcurrant (cassis) Timmermans' lambic is a spontaneously fermented wheat beer conditioned in oak casks and flavored with blackcurrants. The aroma of this brown beer is predominated by blackcurrant like the sweet and sour taste.

TIMMERMANS FRAMBOISE

TYPE: RASBERRY LAMBIC
ALCOHOL: 4% VOL.
FERMENTATION: SPONTANEOUS

Special remarks: the color of this raspberry beer is amber with a red glint. Raspberries are clearly present in the aroma and also underlie the sweet and sour taste.

TIMMERMANS GUEUZE

TYPE: GEUZE LAMBIC

ALCOHOL: 5% VOL.

FERMENTATION: SPONTANEOUS

Special remarks: this amber-colored geuze is conditioned in oak casks. The aroma is quite sweet and the taste is sweet and sour.

CHAPEAU GUEUZE LAMBIC

TYPE: GEUZE LAMBIC

ALCOHOL: 5.5% VOL.

FERMENTATION: SPONTANEOUS

Special remarks: this geuze lambic has a sharp sourness.

TIMMERMANS KRIEK

TYPE: CHERRY LAMBIC

ALCOHOL: 5% VOL.

FERMENTATION: SPONTANEOUS

Special remarks: this kriek is red with aroma and taste of cherries. It is extremely sweet and sour.

CHAPEAU TROPICAL LAMBIC

TYPE: FRUIT LAMBIC

ALCOHOL: 3% VOL.

FERMENTATION: SPONTANEOUS

Special remarks: this amber-colored lambic is sweetened with bananas. It is a craft-made fruit beer with the aroma of banana and a mainly sour taste.

• • •

TIMMERMANS PECHE

TYPE: PEACH LAMBIC

ALCOHOL: 4% VOL.

FERMENTATION: SPONTANEOUS

Special remarks: the Pêche lambic of Timmermans is amber in color with a peach aroma. The sweet and sour taste is not sharp.

• • •

VERHAEGHE BREWERY, VICHTE

Production in hectoliters: 7,500
Founded: 1892

Verhaeghe is a small brewery with a wide assortment of special beers and a regional Pilsener in its range.

CAMBRINUS

TYPE: BELGIAN ALE

ALCOHOL: 5.1% VOL.

FERMENTATION: TOP

Special remarks: amber-colored ale with a slightly fruity and typically ale type aroma. The taste is also fruity, slightly sweet, with fresh dryness. The aftertaste is dry and somewhat hoppy.

DE TROCH BREWERY, TERNAT-WAMBEEK

Production in hectoliters: 4,000
Founded: 1830

This small independent lambic brewer offers a wide assortment of lambic ales.

CAVES

TYPE: SPECIAL BREW
ALCOHOL: 5.8% VOL.
FERMENTATION: TOP

Special remarks: this amber ale has an aroma of caramel. The taste is sweet and sour, very mild, and extremely fruity. It is a rich and complex flavor that is also dry mouthed. Although the brewer's name does not appear on the label, they have nothing to be ashamed of, on the contrary.

DUCHESSE DE BOURGOGNE

TYPE: OLD FLEMISH BROWN
ALCOHOL: 6.2% VOL.
FERMENTATION: TOP

Special remarks: Duchesse de Bourgogne is an old ale that is conditioned in oak casks. It has a sweet aroma and sweet and sour taste.

ECHTE KRIEK (Real Kriek)

TYPE: OLD BROWN/CHERRY ALE
ALCOHOL: 6.8% VOL.
FERMENTATION: TOP

Special remarks: this red cherry ale is made using old Flemish brown. There is a sweet and sour cherry taste.

GAPERS BIER ANSOLD

TYPE: SPECIAL BREW
ALCOHOL: 7% VOL.
FERMENTATION: TOP

Special remarks: no alcohol content is indicated on the label. The aroma is somewhat sour with underlying alcohol sweetness that is clearly detected in the mouth. It is amber in color, the taste is sweet but with a dry palate towards the end.

KERSTMIS

TYPE: SPECIAL BREW
ALCOHOL: 7.2% VOL.
FERMENTATION: TOP

Special remarks: this blonde top-fermented ale has a sweet taste. It is brewed specially for Christmas.

• • •

VILLERS BREWERY, LIEZELE-PUURS

Production in hectoliters: 1,500
Founded: 1993

This small brewery was previously Vielle Villers, and before that was known as Van Assche.

LOTELING BLOND

TYPE: SPECIAL BREW
ALCOHOL: 8.5% VOL.
FERMENTATION: TOP

Special remarks: this golden-blonde ale has a sweet and slightly fruity aroma. The taste is also sweet with underlying hops and the body is firm and rounded. There is the warmth of alcohol in the finish.

LOTELING BRUIN (Brown)

TYPE: SPECIAL BREW
ALCOHOL: 7% VOL.
FERMENTATION: TOP

Special remarks: this dark brown bottle-fermenting ale has a somewhat sour aroma with hints of roasting. Roasted malt is also found in the taste which finishes slightly sour before return of sweetness in the aftertaste.

VILLERS TRIPPEL (Triple)

TYPE: SPECIAL BREW/TRIPLE
ALCOHOL: 8.5% VOL.
FERMENTATION: TOP

Special remarks: this full-bodied and rounded blonde triple ale holds malt and hops in balance.

● ● ●

PARANOIA GROEN

TYPE: SPECIAL BREW
ALCOHOL: 6.2% VOL.
FERMENTATION: TOP

Special remarks: there are pink elephants on the bottle of this beer which is also wrapped in foil representing bricks.

PARANOIA ROZE (Pink)

TYPE: SPECIAL BREW
ALCOHOL: 7% VOL.
FERMENTATION: TOP

Special remarks: like its compatriot Paranoia Green this beer has a very unusual bottle.

The Germans are among the biggest beer drinkers in the world. With an average consumption of 140 liters, more than eighty million Germans drink about 112 million hectoliters (29,590,000 gallons) of beer each year. This makes Germany one of the biggest beer consuming and producing nations and yet there is not a single German brewing concern in the top twenty brewery companies and despite the enormous market the giant world brewers are not strongly active in the German market.

These remarkable facts are due to the traditional attitude of the Germans. The purity regulations known as the *Reinheitsgebot* has had an enormous influence on this and many Germans have a marked preference for their regional beers. This has much to do with the quality that most of Germany's 1,300 breweries deliver. Because of the *Reinheitsgebot* they brew exclusively with natural ingredients that impart higher than average quality to Germany's enormous variety of different beers. The demand

for imported beers is hence not great and with the help of the *Reinheitsgebot* it not stimulated either. A German happily drinks a Budweiser but chooses a Czech original brewed according to the *Reinheitsgebot*. The American Budweiser on the other hand – known in Germany as a *Bud* – will never be hugely popular with Germans because of the high proportion of rice used, regardless of how well brewed it is.

On the other hand the huge home market has meant little stimulus for German brewers to seek export markets, except some Bavarian beers. Despite this German-style beer can be found throughout the world. This is due to large numbers of German emigrants who took their brewing techniques with them so that they could drink reines beer in their new world. For this reason the term Reinheitsgebot 1516 can be encountered from Africa to North America.

The drinking customs of the Germans are not uniform throughout the country. In general blonde lagers lead the way but around Cologne for instance Kölsch beer has the upper hand and around Düsseldorf they prefer Alt. Wheat beer or white beer accounts for about a quarter of the total market but is at its strongest in Southern Germany. These Southern Germans, and particularly the Bavarians, play a very major role and indeed more than half the German breweries are to be found in this part of the country. The average Bavarian beer consumption is higher than the national average at 240 liters per annum. This takes the Bavarians to the top of the beer drinking league.

The fall of the wall in 1989 is an extremely important time in German history and development. All the neglected former East German companies, including breweries, that belonged to the East German state (DDR) were offered for sale. Many of those breweries became part of former West German breweries, making it possible to modernize through injection of much-needed capital. The brewers of East Germany did not brew according to the Reinheitsgebot and this did not change following reunification.

Germany has a unique position in the world of brewers with its many small regional breweries but there are some big German brewers.

OKTOBERFEST

Nothing is so typically German (well Southern German) as Oktoberfest: huge beer halls, giant marquees, a million Bratwurst, just as many roasted chickens, pig's trotters, noise-making oompah-bands, and above all oceans of beer. This is the manner in which a million people celebrate the Munich beer festival or Münchener Oktoberfest each year. And not just Germans for many tourists, including Japanese and Americans help to swallow the five million liters that is brewed by six Munich brewers. The only breweries permitted to serve their beers at the Oktoberfest are Paulaner and its affiliate Hacker-Pschorr, Höfbrau, Augustiner, Spaten, and Löwenbrau. These brewers have brewed a special Oktoberfest brew since 1872. This is brewed in the Viennese style that is also known as Märzen. It is known as "Viennese style" because it was developed jointly by the Spaten brewery with the Viennese brewer Anton Dreher. The name Märzen refers to the time when the beer was brewed in the days before refrigeration was commonplace, immediately before the warm days of summer.

The reason for the original Oktoberfest was the wedding of King Ludwig I of Bavaria to Princess Theresa in 1810. This day was originally commemorated with a horse race but the Bavarian love of beer has proven stronger than

The people of Munich celebrate Oktoberfest from September on.

their love or horses. The Oktoberfest concludes on the first Sunday in October. Sixteen days earlier the burgomaster of Munich strikes a brass tap into the first barrel with traditional words. There is a procession with decorated floats of the six brewers drawn by horses on the first day. Then there are sixteen days of day and night festivities, food, dancing, and music, and fun fairs...and a lot of beer.

REINHEITSGEBOT

Those wanting to brew and sell beer in Germany are bound by German law. One set of legal rules governing them is the Reinheitsgebot made law by the Bavarian Duke Wilhelm IV in 1516. In Medieval Bavaria beer was brewed with every imaginable ingredient and this led to some concoctions that tasted dreadful or worse, could make you seriously ill. In addition to spices and plants all manner of animal additives were included in efforts to flavor beer. The many small breweries which already existed in Germany did use barley, wheat, and rye but also gleanings, peas, and beans.

The monarchs decided to regulate the brewing and sale of beer for a variety of reasons, not least of which were financial motives. Brewers were obliged to brew using malted barley and hops. These ingredients were taxed to provide revenue for the monarch's treasury. Such laws were enforced for Munich by Duke Albert IV in 1487. No other ingredients were permitted other than water, hops, and barley. The working of yeast was unknown at the time and hence not regulated. No other additives could be added to the beer by either the brewer or innkeeper. The brewer had to seek a permit to brew from the Duke's steward and of course such a permit had to be paid for. The brewers of Munich were also told how much they could charge for their summer and winter beer. For a given unit of winter beer they could charge one pfennig and twice that for summer beer.

Other cities took Munich's lead in the years that followed and then in 1516 Wilhem IV introduced rules that applied more or less throughout Bavaria. This ensured Bavarians of good quality beer since brewing other than in accordance with these rules could be severely punished. There were various methods for checking the brews, one of which is still used for festive occasions, although the reliability of the method is dubious. A glass of beer is poured onto a wooden bench. Three men clad in lederhosen then sit on the wet bench. After one hour the three men stand up together. If the bench remains stuck to the men's rear ends then the beer was approved. Despite changing times and advances in techniques, this legislation continued to be respected in Bavaria.

When the German Federal Republic (FDR) was established after World War II the Reinheitsgebot became applicable throughout Germany. The former East Germany (DDR) that disappeared behind the so-called "Iron Curtain" did not adopt this law. This presented brewers in the eastern part of the country with an additional problem following reunification. They also had very ancient equipment and were unable to comply with the Reinheitsgebot and hence unable to compete with brewers in the western part of the country because consumers there considered East German beer to be inferior, with additives. Brewers in the former East Germany now comply with the Reinheitsgebot – in so far as they are still applicable.

It was not been possible for a considerable time to import foreign beer that did not comply with the Reinheitsgebot. French brewers, led by Michel Debus, challenged this at the European Court in 1987. The French complained that the law was a protective measure which prevented a free market between European countries. The Germans maintained the measure merely protects the German consumer – who slakes his thirst daily with barley brew – against dangerous chemical additives. The European Court decided in favor of the French. The German government can no longer use the Reinheitsgebot to block imports. This has not led to a huge culture shock since the German consumer is quite skeptical about foreign beer. There are few imported beers to be found in the German market. Guinness is certainly sold in Germany but it is a Guinness brewed specially for the German market in accordance with the Reinheitsgebot.

These are fundamentally the rules that Germans still adhere to:

Diebels are brewers of alt.

– in brewing a bottom-fermenting beer only barley malt, hops, water, and yeast may be used;
– in brewing a top-fermenting beer it is permissible in addition to barley malt, hops, water, and yeast to use other forms of malt and certain sugars. This enables the brewing of wheat beers etc.;

– hop pellets, powdered hops. or hops extract may be used in place of whole hops provided these are prepared from pure hops;

– beers may only be filtered by means that leave no trace in the beer and may only be by mechanical means or through absorption.

The term Reinheitsgebot is used throughout the world. Results of this German influence can be found throughout the world of beer, in the USA, South Africa, and Austria. It is regarded as a mark of quality by brewers and this is entirely appropriate. Surely no-one can object to brewing beer of good quality at competitive prices, without the use of chemical additives. The Germans have managed within these rules to create great diversity in lagers and ales, which almost every beer enthusiast enjoys.

Despite this the restrictions of the Reinheitsgebot are too severe to permit their passage into European legislation. Such a law does not, for instance, permit the brewing of such excellent beers as the Belgian kriek (cherry) lambic ales, restricts the use of wheat that is not malted, and completely excludes the use of spices and herbs. Suitably adapted though, the Reinheitsgebot could form the basis for protection of European consumers against less careful brewers who try to speed up the brewing process by the use of chemicals.

TYPES OF BEER

There are very diverse types of beer in Germany including both top and bottom fermenting kinds in both pale and dark versions.

ALT

Alt or old beer (not to be confused with the Anglo-Saxon word alt for "ale", although German alt is an ale) is one of the types of beer that has survived the great popularity of the bottom-fermenting beers. This type is very popular around Dusseldorf. It is a top-fermenting beer that is conditioned under temperatures of 0–8°C (32–46.4°F) for three to eight weeks. This combination of ale yeasts with lager-type conditioning is also known by some as hybrid brewed beer.

If you order a "beer" at a bar in the old town of Dusseldorf then the chances are high that you will be served an "alt" for this dark beer of lightly less than 5% alcohol by volume is the everyday beer here accounting for about 30% of the market. Alt is still brewed in the old town in breweries within the hostelries themselves, where fresh beer is often served by draught by means of gravity. Alt is a reserved type of beer that contains many elements such as bitterness, maltiness, and fruitiness but none of these dominate.

Many places throughout the world have imitated alt to a greater or lesser extent. It is a style of beer that micro-brewers in the USA like to differentiate themselves with. Certain Belgian ales of a similar alcohol content are very similar in both taste and experience. Color is similar, although an alt tends to be darker than amber Belgian beers, but this is often a matter of degrees.

first time of the beer brewed the previous autumn that had been conditioning in cellars during the winter. This robust beer had greater potential to survive longer journeys because of its greater use of hops and long cask conditioning. With Einbeck astride a trade route that linked the important cities of the Hanseatic League, Einbeck's beer became more widely known in various parts of Europe.

The original bock beers were darker and there still are some dark forms to which blonde and amber-colored types have been added.

With a few exceptions bock is a bottom-fermented beer that needs long conditioning under cool temperatures (lagern) and substantial density. The alcohol content varies from 6–8% but there are also stronger versions. Maltiness is often accompanied in the darker versions with roasted malt but these beers are always sweetly malty (hence their name in English). The extent of the hops varies widely from weak to strong. There are simple bock beers but also special versions for the start of summer (May), autumn, and "double bock", such as those of Paulaner regarded as their savior (Salvator) and originator. Many breweries add "-ator" to the name of their double bock beers.

BOCK/MALT BEER

The name bock beer results from a bastardization of the name of the place in Bavaria where this type of beer originated. The Bavarians asked for this beer from Einbeck by demanding "einpock Bier", which became further modified to "ein bock bier". There are other stories explaining the origins of this name but these are more sensational and less believable.

Einbeck is a small place near Hanover. The town already had brewing rights in the fourteenth century and was known for the good quality of its beer. The burghers of Einbeck had a sort of interchange system for the use of the brewing copper. During the spring celebrations the use of the copper for that years was decided by drawing lots. This celebration was marked with consumption for the

DIET BEER/ DIATBIER

Although the attitude of many Bavarians is that a man without a beer belly is like a man with only one leg, there are increasing numbers of Germans who are concerned about their weight. This means there is a demand for a daily thirst quencher that is suitable for those on a diet (and usually also for diabetics). These are run-of-the-mill lagers that have their sugar entirely fermented. Some cover their thinness with good doses of hops. These beers are similar in style to Japanese dry beers which also ensure total fermentation of the sugar.

DORTMUNDER

Dortmund is Germany's largest producer of beer. The city has had brewing rights since 1293. The Dortmunder beer was originally brewed by the Dortmunder Union brewery soon after the arrival of blonde Pilseners. The city gets its name from the River Dort that joins the Ruhr near the city. The city was a major coal and steel producing center with large numbers of workers which provided a good market for the Dortmund brewers and strong background against which to develop their beers. The city became the largest beer producer in Germany. Once Dortmunder had become known throughout Germany and even in some other countries this beer became known as Export and the local interest in Dortmunder fell away. This type of beer did not appear to be so popular with the white collar workers who replaced the blue collar workers after the reduction in size of the coal and steel industries. The big Dortmund breweries still brew this type of beer but add "export" to the name. This type can be found in The Netherlands, Japan, and the USA (where it was very popular before prohibition), often known simply as "Dort" but these are not always true to the original.

A true Dortmunder Export is a blonde bottom-fermented beer that is darker in color than a Pilsener with greater density and alcohol above 5%. The true Dortmunder must be strong, malty, with modest carbon dioxide and must certainly not be strongly hopped.

DUNKEL (Dark)

Dunkel or dark beer is a specialty of Southern Germany. This is a brown to dark brown beer that is opposite of a Helles, Münchener, or Pilsener. These are bottom fermenting brews that are generally quite dry and possess a variety of tastes including some spice and roasted malt flavors. Dunkel provides greater variation through its use of darker malt but it is not so highly regarded in Bavaria.

Gabriel Sedlmayer II is considered to be the first person to brew this type of lager. He developed the lager that was later used in Pilzen to brew the first blonde lagers. Before World War II dunkel was the most popular form of lager in Southern Germany but since then it has had to make room for the more popular blonde lagers but dunkel is still widely brewed in Germany and it is also still brewed elsewhere, including the Czech Republic and the USA.

HELL/HELLES

To a Bavarian an ordinary lager is Helles. Just as all bottom fermenting blonde beers are known as lager in English, so a Bavarian asks for a Helles for his everyday beer. This type of beer is also generally known as Münchener or Munich beer. They are straightforward blonde lagers that are slightly more malty than a Pilsener with less hops.

KELLERBIER

This is the type of beer that can be drunk in the cellars of breweries, hence the name "cellar beer". This is unfiltered lager also known as gekräusend. It is blonde and also slightly cloudy due to the presence of yeast. These beers are generally well hopped. It is not a great beer and is most popular in Southern Germany.

KÖLSCH

While many brewers freely use the name of the Czech town of Pilzen for their bottom-fermented blonde lagers, the brewers of Cologne have found

Kölsch not only has its own style of brewing but a special serving tray.

diminutive of Jakobus, which is what the waiters in the hostelries of Cologne are called. The kobus serve the small undecorated straight glasses on a special tray with a hand grip and a special slot for the glasses. Kölsch is not just easily drunk but can also soothe the stomach, although too much of course can have the opposite effect.

RAUCHBIER/SMOKED BEER

Drying malt over a fire of beech wood was common throughout Central Europe in the mid nineteenth century. There was an abundance of timber and the process had not been industrialized. This gave beer a smoky flavor but this type of beer almost disappeared when modern methods of malting were adopted that did not create this taste.

Today Rauchbier is a specialty that has survived virtually only in Franconian Bamberg. A few brewers continue to use this method of drying their malt and to make beers from such malt although these beers are now brewed with bottom-fermenting yeasts. The smoky taste is now a specialty that some praise and others revile. The color of today's smoked beers vary from dark brown to black.

WHEAT BEER/WEISSBIER/WEIẞBIER/WEIZEN

One type of beer that has seen enormous growth in popularity in recent times in Germany is wheat beer. Quite different from the Belgian equivalent, wheat beer in Germany is brewed using 50% barley malt and 50% wheat malt, hops, and water. Despite the often quite spicy taste no spices are added. The popularity of this type of beer started in the USA where many small brewers imitate it although they do not use genuine wheat malt that provides the taste of cloves. The Americans brew their wheat beer with ale yeast. This type of beer is also popular in Austria and Switzerland but finds much less favor in other countries bordering Germany such as Belgium, the Czech Republic, France, The Netherlands, and Poland. In Germany both Weizen (wheat

ways to keep their city's name for themselves. Kölsch (from Cologne or Köln in German) may only be used in respect of beer brewed by a small group of Cologne breweries.

In 1985 twenty-four German brewers set-up the Kölsch convention which laid down precise rules regarding the brewing of Kölsch. This paid particular attention to forging the link between the beer and its city of origin and banned the use of adjectives such as Super, Original, or Rheinisches (of the Rhine or Rhineland) in order to prevent confusion and also any attempts by individual brewers to gain an advantage. These conventions were written on parchment, decorated with twenty-four red ribbons, and signed by the twenty-four brewers.

Kölsch is a top-fermented beer that can ferment within a matter of days at warm temperatures. It is then stored close to freezing. The color is always pale blonde from which the saying "the lighter the Kölsch, the better the taste." Alcohol by volume is about 5%. The taste is malty and hops are required to be present but not to dominate. Kölsch is a readily drinkable beer and this happens in Cologne in great volume.

It is a Kölsch that the average man or woman in Cologne will order on every occasion as the standard thirst quencher. Ordering a 20 cl glass – that is indelibly linked to this blonde top-fermented beer – can be done through Kobus, a

beer) and Weissbier/Weißbier (white beer) are interchangeable. Although both pale and dark varieties of these beers are brewed the odd-sounding Weissbier Dunkel (dark white beer) is used without raising an eyelid.

There is a long and noble history behind Weizen. In the fifteenth century the aristocrats who ruled reserved the right for themselves to use wheat for brewing. These dukes set up court breweries to produce wheat beer and sales were guaranteed since the innkeepers were required to buy it. It was not until the nineteenth century that the dukes relinquished their exclusive rights. The public lost interest in wheat beer for a long time and by the beginning of the twentieth century there were only a handful of brewers still making it. Brewers like Schneider and Maisel's injected new life into wheat beer and it has become widely popular in the past twenty years among younger people who drink it with a slice of lemon. Wheat beers are top-fermented and generally bottled with some new yeast and a little wort (gekräusend) in order to create a new fermentation in the bottle which ensures the characteristic lively ale. There are versions without this second fermentation. Those that do are known on the label as Hefe Weiss or Hefe Weizen while the non-second fermentation kind generally bears Kristall on the bottle. Around the onset of winter there is also a stronger wheat beer, weizenbok available on draught although the bottled version is more popular, and according to some has greater character.

Schneiders old brewery for wheat beer in Kelheim.

ADLER BREWERY GÖTZ GMBH & CO., GEISLINGEN

Production in hectoliters: –
Founded: 1686

This small brewery is in the hands of the Götz family.

ALPIRSBACHER GLAUNER, CLOISTER BREWERY, ALPIRSBACH

Production in hectoliters: 350,000
Founded: 1880

The beer is brewed with untreated water from the brewery's own well.

ADLER-GOLD

TYPE: PILSENER
ALCOHOL: 4.8% VOL.
FERMENTATION: BOTTOM

Special remarks: this beer is brewed with an original gravity of 11°. It is a golden, mellow, and full-bodied lager with a fine compact head. The aroma and taste are somewhat malty with dryness and mild hops in the finish. The aftertaste is briefly slightly bitter.

ALPIRSBACHER KLOSTER-WEISSE

TYPE: WHEAT BEER
ALCOHOL: 5.2% VOL.
FERMENTATION: TOP

Special remarks: this fresh and cloudy blonde wheat beer has an aroma of wheat. The malty fresh taste has a prolonged drying finish.

ADLER FILSTAL PILS

TYPE: PILSENER
ALCOHOL: 4.8% VOL.
FERMENTATION: BOTTOM

Special remarks: this blonde Pilsener is brewed with an original gravity of 11°. Filstal Pils has a slightly hoppy aroma and both malt and hops can be found in the taste. The aftertaste is slightly drying and hoppy to bitter but not intensely so. It is medium bodied.

• • •

ALPIRSBACHER PILS

TYPE: PILSENER
ALCOHOL: 4.9% VOL.
FERMENTATION: BOTTOM

Special remarks: this yellow blonde Pilsener has a somewhat malty aroma. It is medium-bodied with a dry sensation in the mouth and more hoppy and drying aftertaste.

ALPIRSBACHER SPEZIAL

TYPE: EXPORT LAGER
ALCOHOL: 5.2% VOL.
FERMENTATION: BOTTOM

Special remarks: this blonde lager has a malty aroma and malty taste with vague hoppiness in its finish. The aftertaste is somewhat bitter.

• • •

ANDECHSER CLOISTER BREWERY, ANDECHS

Production in hectoliters: 85,000
Founded: 1445

It is not only in Belgium and The Netherlands that the Benedictines assiduously brew beer. The St. Boniface (St. Bonefatius) Benedictines of the Andechs monastery brew a number of fine beers that are tasted by large numbers of visitors. Andechs brews a Spezial Hell and Export Dunkel among its beers.

ANDECHS DOPPELBOCK DUNKEL

TYPE: MALT LAGER/BOCK
ALCOHOL: 7.1% VOL.
FERMENTATION: BOTTOM

Special remarks: this dark double bock has a rich aroma of burnt malt. The taste is complex, with fruitiness, sweetness, and hints of roasting with dryness near the finish. The aftertaste has somewhat dry bittersweet notes.

ANDECHSER WEISSBIER

TYPE: WHEAT BEER
ALCOHOL: 5.1% VOL.
FERMENTATION: TOP

Special remarks: this amber-colored wheat beer has a spicy and fruity aroma. The taste is spicy and there is both spice and malt in the aftertaste. It is medium bodied and lively.

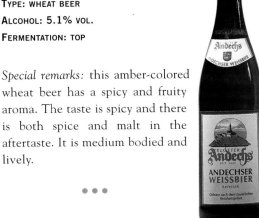

• • •

AUERBRÄU AG, ROSENHEIM

Production in hectoliters: 150,000
Founded: 1889

The main shareholder in Auerbräu is the Munich Paulaner brewery.

ROSENHEIMER EXPORT

TYPE: EXPORT LAGER
ALCOHOL: 5.5% VOL.
FERMENTATION: BOTTOM

Special remarks: this robust golden-blonde lager has quite a hoppy aroma and this is found in the taste also with underlying dryness. The aftertaste is dry and hoppy.

ROSENHEIMER HEFE WEISSBIER

TYPE: WHEAT BEER
ALCOHOL: 5.5% VOL.
FERMENTATION: TOP

Special remarks: this is a post-fermenting wheat beer with a cloudy amber color and spicy aroma. The taste is spicy with a sharply sour finish and dry and spicy aftertaste. There is a lively sensation in the mouth.

ROSENHEIMER HELLES

TYPE: HELLES LAGER
ALCOHOL: 5% VOL.
FERMENTATION: BOTTOM

Special remarks: this blonde lager has a somewhat hoppy and lightly malty aroma. The taste is slightly of sweet malt, found also in the aftertaste. It has a medium body.

ROSENHEIMER LEICHTE WEIßE

TYPE: LIGHT WHEAT BEER

ALCOHOL: 2.9% VOL.

FERMENTATION: TOP

Special remarks: this light version of Rosenheimer's wheat beer is lively from fermentation in the bottle. It is golden blonde and has a slightly spicy aroma with a sharp edge with hints of clove in the taste. It is thin-bodied but lively.

• • •

AUGUSTINER BRAU WAGNER, MUNICH

Production in hectoliters: –

Founded: 1328

Began as a monastery brewery in 1328. The company is listed as the oldest brewery of Munich and it produces its own malt.

LAGERBIER HELL

TYPE: HELLES LAGER

ALCOHOL: 5.2% VOL.

FERMENTATION: BOTTOM

Special remarks: this yellow blonde lager has quite a firm body. The taste is slightly bitter rather than sweet and there is a bitter aftertaste.

• • •

AYINGER BREWERY, AYING

Production in hectoliters: 100,000

Founded: 1878

The small twelve hundred years old village of Aying lies about 15 miles southeast of Munich. The local church tower is found on the label of this more than hundred years-old brewery. The great grandfather of the present head Franz Inselkammer, Johann Liebhard founded the brewery. The Aylinger brewery has won many prizes for its assortment of fifteen beers. Naturally they are all brewed in accordance with the Reinheitsgebot. Ayinger uses aromatic Hallertau and Spalt hops, its own yeast culture, own well water, and Bavarian barley. The local distribution takes place within a radius of sixty miles or so and about ten per cent of production is exported to Italy, the USA, Spain, and Scandinavia. Aylinger lager is brewed under license by the Samuel Smith Old Brewery of Tadcaster. There is an inn, restaurant, and small museum attached to the brewery. In addition to the beers described below, Ayinger brews Bräu Hell 4.8%, Pils 5%, Kellerbier 5.8%, Heller Bock 6.8%, Frühlingsbier 4.9%, Kirtsbier 5.8%, and Leichte Bräu-Weisse 3.2%.

ALTBAIRISCH DUNKEL

TYPE: DUNKEL/DARK BEER

ALCOHOL: 5% VOL.

FERMENTATION: BOTTOM

Special remarks: this dark lager from Ayinger has a light malty taste with medium fullness and an aroma with hints of coffee. This dunkel is recommended as accompaniment for pasta, potato dishes, and freshly-baked bread. The serving temperature is 7–9°C (44.6–48.2°F).

BRÄU WEISSE

TYPE: WHEAT BEER

ALCOHOL: 5.1% VOL.

FERMENTATION: TOP

Special remarks: this pale wheat beer with sediment has a fresh sour taste and an effervescent character.

CELEBRATOR

TYPE: MALT LAGER/DOUBLE BOCK

ALCOHOL: 6.7% VOL.

FERMENTATION: BOTTOM

Special remarks: an original gravity of 18.5° gives this double bock a firm character. The dark beer has a rather sweet initial taste and slightly smoky suggestions in its aroma.

FEST-MÄRZEN

TYPE: MÄRZEN

ALCOHOL: 5.8% VOL.

FERMENTATION: BOTTOM

Special remarks: this beer is brewed in March in time to be served to celebrate the harvest in September and the Oktoberfest. Its original gravity of 13.5° and the long conditioning results in a slightly sweet and malty beer with slight dryness that combines well with Wiener Schnitzel and Bockwurst.

JAHRHUNDERT-BIER

TYPE: DORTMUNDER

ALCOHOL: 5.5% VOL.

FERMENTATION: BOTTOM

Special remarks: this beer is brewed with a slightly higher level of alcohol and is more mildly hopped.

With an original gravity of 12.8° this is a medium-bodied golden export lager that can happily accompany a wide range of food. The recommended serving temperature is 7–9°C (44.6–48.2°F).

MAIBOCK

TYPE: MALT LAGER/BOCK

ALCOHOL: 7.2% VOL.

FERMENTATION: BOTTOM

Special remarks: brewed for spring this May malt lager is golden in color and has a sturdy malt taste.

UR-WEISSE

TYPE: WHEAT BEER

ALCOHOL: 5.8% VOL.

FERMENTATION: BOTTOM

Special remarks: this amber wheat beer has an original gravity of 13.3°. This lively wheat beer has underlying dryness with fruity aromas.

WEIHNACHTS-BOCK

TYPE: MALT LAGER/DOUBLE BOCK

ALCOHOL: 7% VOL.

FERMENTATION: BOTTOM

Special remarks:
this dark double bock malt lager is brewed specially for Christmas.

• • •

BECK & CO BREWERY, BREMEN

Production in hectoliters: 5,500,000
Founded: 1873

The foundations of the Bremen brewery were laid by contractor Luder Rutenberg, merchant Thomas May, and brewer Heinrich Beck. The first beer was brewed at their newly-constructed Kaiserbrauerei Beck & Co in May of 1873. In addition to his brewing knowledge Beck also brought ten years experience in the USA to the new venture and as early as 1876 Beck's Pilsener won its first award as Best Continental Beer at the World Exhibition in Philadelphia. Beck's is still the biggest selling imported beer in the USA. Becks exported right from the early days and now more than half their production is exported to more than one hundred different countries. In 1921 Beck & Co merged with the C.H. Haake Brauerei AG and Becks has taken over a number of other since that time, including the Rostcoker Brauerei in 1991. Becks has its own glass works and also produces around three million hectoliters of soft drinks and mineral waters each year.

BECK'S

TYPE: PILSENER
ALCOHOL: 5% VOL.
FERMENTATION: BOTTOM

Special remarks: this Pilsener from the Bremen brewery is found all over the world. It has a malty aroma and a clean light malty taste as becomes a world-class beer.

BECK'S ALKOHOL FREE

TYPE: NON ALCOHOLIC LAGER
ALCOHOL: –
FERMENTATION: BOTTOM

Special remarks: Beck's non-alcoholic Pilsener is brewed like other Pilseners and stored as with lagers before the alcohol is removed. The aroma is both malty and slightly sharply hoppy. The taste gives a rather thin sensation in the mouth but quite good presence of hops and a short bitter aftertaste.

BELLHEIMER BREWERY K. SIBERNAGEL AG, BELLHEIM

Production in hectoliters: 300,000
Founded: 1865

Since 1995 the Bellheimer brewery has formed part of Park Brewery AG of Pirmasens. It is a medium-sized brewery that also produces soft drinks and mineral waters. In addition to wheat beer this brewery also produces Bellheimer Lord, Bellheimer Silber Pils, Bellheimer Silber Bock, and Bellheimer Silber Doppelbock.

BELLHEIMER WEIZ'N BRÄU HEFE-WEIZEN

TYPE: WHEAT BEER
ALCOHOL: 5.4% VOL.
FERMENTATION: TOP

Special remarks: a lively, slightly cloudy post-fermenting beer.

BELLHEIMER WEIZ'N BRÄU KRISTALL

TYPE: WHEAT BEER
ALCOHOL: 4.9% VOL.
FERMENTATION: TOP

Special remarks: clear filtered wheat beer.

• • •

BERGISCHE LÖWEN BREWERY, COLOGNE

Production in hectoliters: –
Founded: 1869

Bergische Löwen Brauerei in Cologne is part of Dortmundse Brau und Brunnen. Various brands of Kölsch are brewed here that are sold under names such as Sester, Gilden, Fels, Krone, Kurfürsten, and Sion.

D-PILS

TYPE: DIET LAGER
ALCOHOL: 4.9% VOL.
FERMENTATION: BOTTOM

Special remarks: D-Pils is a proper Pilsener with a reduced level of carbohydrate. It is brewed in accordance with the Reinheitsgebot and is suitable for diabetics. It is marketed under the Wicküler brand name.

GILDEN KÖLSCH

TYPE: KÖLSCH
ALCOHOL: 4.8% VOL.
FERMENTATION: TOP

Special remarks:
as is required of a Kölsch, this is a light blonde top fermented ale. It has a mild neutral taste with fine underlying presence of hop bitterness moving on to a slightly bitter and drying aftertaste.

SION KÖLSCH

TYPE: KÖLSCH
ALCOHOL: 4.8% VOL.
FERMENTATION: TOP

Special remarks: the Sion version of Kölsch top fermented ale has a floral and hoppy aroma.

WICKÜLER PILSENER

TYPE: PILSENER
ALCOHOL: 4.9% VOL.
FERMENTATION: BOTTOM

Special remarks: this blonde Pilsener is happily consumer in Cologne's bars alongside Kölsch. It is a hoppy Pilsener with dry bitter aftertaste.

• • •

BINDING BREWERY, FRANKFURT AM MAIN

Production in hectoliters: 9,000,000
Founded: 1870

Conrad Binding founded the Binding brewery when he took over the small Ehrenfried Glock brewery in Frankfurt in 1870. Binding had just completed his training as a brewer and acquired the brewery behind the cathedral for around $40,000. Eleven years later he had increased production from 1,500 hectoliters to 46,000 hectoliters. The tiny brewery was bursting at the seams and a new brewery was built in 1884 financed by issuing shares. In 1895 Conrad Binding stepped down from the day-to-day management and became Chairman of the board of directors on which he remained until 1921. Quite how important a figure Conrad Binding was deemed in Frankfurt life is demonstrated by his sculpture in stone at the entrance to Frankfurt's town hall. The brewery became much weaker following World War I and it merged with Hofbrauerei Schöfferhof and with it also the Johan Jacob Jong brewery. After World War II Binding once again found times hard. Under the management of Conrad Binding II (son of Conrad's brother Carl), Binding reached the astonishing level of 1,000,000 hectoliters in 1961. Conrad Binding laid the basis for the present-day company. He was one of the first to promote his beer directly to the consumer. He stepped down in 1967, breaking the last family link with the company. Today the Binding group has taken a whole collection of breweries and soft drinks and mineral water companies under its umbrella. There are around twenty-five companies in the group including the Dortmunder-Aktien brewery, the Erbacher brewery, Berlin's Kindl brewery, the Krostitzer brewery, and Krušovice in the Czech Republic. These breweries have their own management but with overall group objectives. The total turnover is of the order of $2.7 billion.

Binding is notable for a large assortment of beers of many different types including diet beers, alcohol-free, bock, several wheat beers, an alt, Pilseners, lagers, an ice beer, beer and lemonade mix, and an Irish-style stout. The brewery seeks to serve all tastes.

Conrad Binding was the founder.

BINDING DIESEL

TYPE: BEER MIX
ALCOHOL: 2.5% VOL.
FERMENTATION: BOTTOM

Special remarks: this Diesel is a mix of 50% lager and 50% cola. It takes all sorts!

BINDING EXPORT

TYPE: EXPORT LAGER
ALCOHOL: 5.3% VOL.
FERMENTATION: BOTTOM

Special remarks: this export or Dortmunder from the Binding brewery is a blonde malty lager with underlying brief bitterness. It is medium bodied with a brief bitter hop aftertaste.

BINDING LAGER

TYPE: LAGER
ALCOHOL: 4.5% VOL.
FERMENTATION: BOTTOM

Special remarks: "the International taste" it says on the can. Nothing exciting in other words and true to form the metallic-colored can contains a blonde lager with fresh but neutral taste with a hint of malt but ideal as a thirst quencher.

BINDING RÖMER PILS

TYPE: PILSENER
ALCOHOL: 4.9% VOL.
FERMENTATION: BOTTOM

Special remarks: pale blonde and well-balanced Pilsener with hoppy aroma. It has a strong bitter hop taste with sufficient underlying malt. The aftertaste is bitter.

CLAUSTHALER PREMIUM ALCOHOL FREE

TYPE: ALCOHOL FREE LAGER
ALCOHOL: 0.4% VOL.
FERMENTATION: BOTTOM

Special remarks: Bindings had no idea in 1979 when they introduced this alcohol-free lager of the success that this product would enjoy. It is responsible for one third of the German market for alcohol-free beer. It has a sweet malty aroma with malty taste. The aftertaste is briefly hoppy and slightly bitter.

SCHÖFFERHOFER DUNKLES

TYPE: WHEAT BEER
ALCOHOL: 5% VOL.
FERMENTATION: TOP

Special remarks: this dark brown wheat beer is brewed by Binding's brewery in Kassel. The aroma of cloves is intense and the taste is also mainly of cloves. There is a hard dry sensation in the mouth that ends with sharpness. The aftertaste is spicy with hints of roasting.

SCHÖFFERHOFER KRISTALLWEIZEN

TYPE: WHEAT BEER
ALCOHOL: 5% VOL.
FERMENTATION: TOP

Special remarks: a blonde filtered wheat beer with mild aroma of cloves, spicy taste with a little sourness at the finish and somewhat spicy, dry, and sharp aftertaste. It has medium body. It is remarkably intense in its make up for a filtered wheat beer.

BITBURGER BREWERY THEO SIMON, BITBURG

Production in hectoliters: 4,130,000
Founded: 1817

Johan Peter Wallenborn founded the Bitburger brewery when he was 33 years old. When he died in 1839 his wife took over as brewer and when Wallenborn's daughter married Ludwig Bertrand Simon in 1842 the brewery passed into his hands. That same year Joseph Groll brewed his first bottom fermented blonde lager in Pilzen. When the next in line of the Simon family, Theobald took control in 1876, the brewery produced around one thousand hectoliters each year. Theobald was fascinated by the Czech development of the new blonde lager and brewed his first Pilsener in 1883. The use of the name "Simonbräu Deutsch Pilsener" was hotly disputed by Pilsener Urquell but the German high court dismissed the Czech claim to the sole rights of the term "Pilsener", so that the link between the term and the town of Pilzen was from that time on greatly diluted throughout the world.

Theobald Simon made the brewery into a truly commercial undertaking and in 1891 the Bitburger Dampfbrauerei (steam brewery) produced 10,000 hectoliters. The brewery was almost totally destroyed at the end of World War II and much hard work was needed to start brewing again in 1945. Shortage of ingredients in the immediate post-war years meant that adapted beers had to be brewed until 1949, that became known as Dünnbier or "thin beer". In 1955 the brewery introduced a slogan "Bitte ein Bit" ("a Bit please") and forty years on this slogan is still known by around ninety percent of beer drinkers. In 1971 the brewery turned its full attention to brewing Bitburger Pils and the brewery crossed the one million hectoliters line in 1973. In 1979 Bitburger took over Gerolsteiner Brunnen, in 1991 the Köstritzer Zwartbier brewery, in 1993 the Schultheis brewery in Weissenthurm (not to be confused with Schultheiss in Berlin), and in 1997 they took over Browar Szcecin in Poland, In 1995 the Bitburger brewery produced more than four million hectoliters of beer and remains in the management of descendants of the founder. Bitburger is sold in some thirty-four countries and is one of Germany biggest brewers.

BITBURGER PREMIUM PILS

TYPE: PILSENER
ALCOHOL: 4.6% VOL.
FERMENTATION: BOTTOM

Special remarks:
Bitburger's Pils is one of the best-selling Pilseners in Germany and it is the top draught beer. Premium is brewed with an original gravity of 11.3° that is pretty well average for a Pilsener. The yeast culture used ensures more or less complete fermentation which makes the Pilsener thin but very clear. The water used to brew Bit comes from the brewery's own three hundred meter deep well. Bitburger use German barley, a third of which is from Rheinland-Pfalz. The most northerly cultivated hops in Germany are grown at Holstum close to Bitburg and these hops are kept exclusively for Bitburger. In addition to some other varieties, the majority of the hops used are of the Hallertau variety. Bitburger is one of the bitter Pilseners with a slightly dry mouth sensation without loss of the malty character.

BITBURGER DRIVE

TYPE: ALCOHOL FREE
ALCOHOL: 0.5% VOL.
FERMENTATION: BOTTOM

Special remarks: the alcohol-free version of Bitburger's Pilsener is named Drive. It is brewed with a normal higher original gravity and then heated before the alcohol is removed by dialysis.

BOLTEN BREWERY CARL BOLTEN GMBH & CO

Production in hectoliters: 40,000
Founded: 1266/1764

The Bolten brewery claims to be the oldest in the world having been granted its brewing rights in 1266. The brewery has been in the hands of the family of the present owner Hans Otto Bolten since 1764. Bolten brew alt and several wheat beers.

BITBURGER LIGHT

TYPE: LIGHT BEER
ALCOHOL: 2.8% VOL.
FERMENTATION: BOTTOM

Special remarks: after years of only brewing Pilsener they decided the time had come to introduce low alcohol and alcohol-free beers. The Bitburger Light was launched in 1992 with an original gravity of 7.8° and low calories.

BOLTEN ALT

TYPE: ALT
ALCOHOL: 4.7% VOL.
FERMENTATION: TOP

Special remarks: Bolten Alt is a brown, rather thin-bodied top-fermented beer with a malty taste with slight hints of roasting and slight underlying bitterness. The ale is found beneath a small and compact head. There is fruitiness in the aroma.

NIEDERRHEIN ALT

TYPE: ALT

ALCOHOL: 4.7% VOL.

FERMENTATION: TOP

• • •

BORBECKER DAMPF (Steam Brewery) ESSEN

Production in hectoliters: –
Founded: 1896

BORBECKER HELLES DAMPFBIER

TYPE: STEAM BEER

ALCOHOL: 4.8% VOL.

FERMENTATION: TOP

Special remarks: a clear blonde steam beer with mild malty aroma and slightly sweet taste.

• • •

DIEBELS BREWERY ISSUM

Production in hectoliters: 1,620,000
Founded: 1878

The founder of the brewery in Issum was Josef Diebels who established his own brewery at the age of thirty-two. The brewery got off to a good start and by the turn of the nineteenth/twentieth centuries was brewing around 11,000 hectoliters of beer. By the time it celebrated its fiftieth anniversary twenty-eight years later Diebels produced 25,000 hectoliters. Diebels growth was steady and sure and it came through the two World Wars fairly

Jozef Diebel (1845–1922), founder of Diebels brewery.

unscathed with the family firmly in charge. Diebels was an innovator in 1968 in the installation of vertical fermentation tanks. It is worth noting that this brewery's growth has not resulted from large-scale take-overs but from concentration on its specialties to the exclusion of other activities. Evidence that this strategy has proven successful is witnessed in the alt beer market sector. Of every ten alt beers served in Germany six come from this family brewery to the tune of 1,5 million hectoliters. By far the majority of their output is alt. Of the 1.6 million hectoliters that Diebels brew only 60,000 hectoliters is light beer, alcohol-free, and private label. Of the 1.5 million hectoliters of alt more than one million is bottled. More than 120 year old Diebels puts no effort at all into creating an historic image but just happens to be a modern business that has a high regard for an older type of beer.

DIEBELS ALT

TYPE: ALT

ALCOHOL: 4.8% VOL.

FERMENTATION: TOP

Special remarks: this old-style alt has a pleasing fruity aroma with a fresh neutral taste that is slightly malty and vaguely spicy. The aftertaste is dry and hoppy.

DIEBELS LIGHT

TYPE: LIGHT ALT

ALCOHOL: 2.7% VOL.

FERMENTATION: TOP

Special remarks: Diebels introduced this Light version of their alt in 1992 to meet the increasing demand for low alcohol beer.

DINKELACKER CD-PILS

TYPE: PILSENER

ALCOHOL: 4.9% VOL.

FERMENTATION: BOTTOM

Special remarks: in order that the consumer can see how fresh their beer is Dinkelacker indicate both the drink by date and the date the beer was brewed on the label. The blonde Pilsener appears to have a shelf life of six months. The name is derived from the initials of Carl Dinkelacker who founded the brewery. This Pilsener has a malty aroma and taste with underlying hops in the flavor.

· · ·

DINKELACKER-SCHWABEN BRÄU AG, STUTTGART

Production in hectoliters: –

Founded: 1996

The result of a merger between the breweries of Dinkelacker and Schwaben Bräu Rob. Leicht AG in 1996. The original breweries were founded in 1888 and 1878. The new company also owns all the shares in the Mauritius brewery in Zwickau and the monastery brewery at Metzingen. The majority shareholders of Dinkelacker-Schwaben Bräu are Spanten-Franziskaner-Bräu of Munich.

DINKELACKER DIÄT PILSENER

TYPE: DIET PILSENER

ALCOHOL: 4.5% VOL.

FERMENTATION: BOTTOM

Special remarks: this thin-bodied blonde diet Pilsener has a fresh and slightly malty aroma. There is mild sweet malt in the taste too giving way to hops. The aftertaste is mildly bitter.

DINKELACKER ALKOHOL FREE

TYPE: ALCOHOL-FREE BEER

ALCOHOL: –

FERMENTATION: BOTTOM

DINKELACKER PRIVAT

TYPE: LAGER

ALCOHOL: 5.1% VOL.

FERMENTATION: BOTTOM

Special remarks: because the brewer recommends drinking this beer as young as possible they indicate both the consume by and brewing dates on the label. Privat is a blonde lager with mellow hoppy aroma with hops too in the taste, drying with a slightly bitter finish. The aftertaste is of dry hop bitterness. This is a medium-bodied and well-balanced to slightly full-flavored lager.

SANWALD WEIZEN DUNKEL

TYPE: WHEAT BEER

ALCOHOL: 4.9% VOL.

FERMENTATION: TOP

Special remarks: unfiltered wheat beer of 11.5° original gravity. Weizen Dunkel is dark brown and has an aroma of spices. The flavor is also spicy – mainly of cloves – although this is pushed to the background by the lively character of this beer and there is dryness in the finish. It is thin to medium-bodied.

SANWALD HEFEWEIZEN

TYPE: WHEAT BEER

ALCOHOL: 4.9% VOL.

FERMENTATION: TOP

Special remarks: this version of the Sanwald unfiltered wheat beer of 11.5° original gravity is a cloudy blonde with a slightly spicy aroma and there is spice too, mainly in the form of cloves in the taste which is slightly sour and then somewhat drying. It is lively.

SANWALD KRISTALL WEIZEN

TYPE: WHEAT BEER

ALCOHOL: 4.9% VOL.

FERMENTATION: TOP

Special remarks: the Kristallweizen is the filtered version of the Sanwald wheat beer. This clear blonde beer has an aroma of cloves and a taste that is mainly spicy with a lively but slightly drying sensation in the mouth. This is a thin to medium-bodied beer with an original gravity of 11.5°.

SCHWABEN BRÄU MÄRZEN

TYPE: MÄRZEN

ALCOHOL: 5.5% VOL.

FERMENTATION: BOTTOM

Special remarks: a golden-blonde Märzen with a malty aroma with medium to firm body. There is malt too in the taste that is slightly sharp and drying.

SCHWABEN BRÄU MEISTER PILS

TYPE: PILSENER

ALCOHOL: 4.9% VOL.

FERMENTATION: BOTTOM

Special remarks: a blonde Pilsener with a hoppy aroma and taste and slightly drying and bitter aftertaste of medium body. Meister Pils includes Tettnanger hops and barley from the brewery's own land.

SCHWABEN BRÄU MEISTER WEIZEN

TYPE: WHEAT BEER

ALCOHOL: 5% VOL.

FERMENTATION: TOP

Special remarks: a post-fermenting cloudy blonde wheat beer.

SCHWABEN BRÄU URTYP EXPORT

TYPE: EXPORT

ALCOHOL: 5.1% VOL.

FERMENTATION: TOP

Special remarks: blonde export lager with a hoppy aroma and good medium body. The taste starts slightly sweet and malty quickly followed by hops and then finishing with bitterness. The aftertaste is prolonged bitterness.

• • •

DOM (Cathedral) BREWERY, COLOGNE

Production in hectoliters: –

Founded: –

Part of Stern Brauerei Carl Funke AG of Essen which in turn is owned by Jacob Stauder of Essen.

DOM KÖLSCH

TYPE: KÖLSCH

ALCOHOL: 4.8% VOL.

FERMENTATION: TOP

Special remarks: this golden-blonde top-fermented beer has an aroma in which both malt and hops are present. The body is not especially firm but the beer has a lot of carbon dioxide gas. The taste is mainly malty with underlying hops. The aftertaste is briefly bitter.

• • •

DAB (Dortmunder Aktien Brauerei), DORTMUND

Production in hectoliters: 3,000,000

Founded: 1867

Dortmunder Aktien Brauerei is generally known as DAB. It is part of the Binding Group but recently took over the Dortmund Kronen brewery. DAB has exported since 1879 when it supplied beer to African countries, Japan, and India. The popularity of their beer – which is mainly export lager – was built on this strength.

DAB DIÄT PILS

TYPE: DIET PILSENER

ALCOHOL: 4.8% VOL.

FERMENTATION: BOTTOM

Special remarks: a diet beer brewed according to the Reinheitsgebot, intended mainly for calorie counters.

DAB EXPORT

TYPE: DORTMUNDER/EXPORT LAGER

ALCOHOL: 5.1% VOL.

FERMENTATION: BOTTOM

Special remarks: in Dortmund they ask for an "Export" when they want a Dortmunder. It is a sweet, malty lager of medium body. Hops surface towards the end of the taste in this well-balanced beer.

DAB ORIGINAL

TYPE: DORTMUNDER

ALCOHOL: 5% VOL.

FERMENTATION: BOTTOM

Special remarks: blonde medium-bodied lager with slightly hoppy aroma. The taste is somewhat malty with underlying hops.

DAB PILSENER

TYPE: PILSENER
ALCOHOL: **4.8%** VOL.
FERMENTATION: BOTTOM

Special remarks: DAB's Pilsener is pale blonde with malty aroma and hoppy taste plus dry bitter aftertaste.

REGENTEN PILS

TYPE: PILSENER
ALCOHOL: **4.8%** VOL.
FERMENTATION: BOTTOM

DAB STRONG

TYPE: PILSENER
ALCOHOL: **4.8%** VOL.
FERMENTATION: BOTTOM

Special remarks:
DAB's "Strong" Pilsener has a slightly sharper taste than the standard one. The brewers ascribe this to the use of Australian hops.

STADES LEICHT

TYPE: LIGHT LAGER
ALCOHOL: **2.8%** VOL.
FERMENTATION: BOTTOM

Special remarks:
a blond Pilsener-type lager with reduced alcohol and calories. The thin body remains masked by the quite reasonable hoppiness.

• • •

FELS KRONE ALT

TYPE: ALT
ALCOHOL: **4.8%** VOL.
FERMENTATION: TOP

Special remarks: the alt of Fels Krone is amber-colored. It has a fresh mild malty taste and is thin to medium-bodied.

DORTMUNDER STIFTS BRAUEREI AG, DORTMUND

Production in hectoliters: 150,000
Founded: 1900

The Stifts brewery is owned by Kronen which in turn is owned by DAB, which is part of the Binding Group.

HANSA PILS

TYPE: PILSENER
ALCOHOL: **4.8%** VOL.
FERMENTATION: BOTTOM

Special remarks: a light and neutral Pilsener. Hansa is one of the breweries taken-over in mergers in 1971. DAB decided to re-introduce the Hansa brand in 1992 with the slogan "hauptsache Hansa, alles andere ist euer Bier," which loosely means "the main thing about Hansa is your beer." The brand is marketed by a separate organization in Bad Sassenhof.

STIFTS PILS

TYPE: PILSENER
ALCOHOL: **4.9%** VOL.
FERMENTATION: BOTTOM

Special remarks: a blonde Pilsener.

• • •

DORTMUNDER UNION BRAUEREI AG, BRAU & BRUNNEN, DORTMUND

Production in hectoliters: 10,000,000
Founded: 1873

The Dortmund arm of Brau & Brunnen is a fusion of about ten small breweries. Many other breweries were also merged following the initial merger to form DUB and in 1973 DUB merged with Schultheiss of Berlin. The brewery thus formed of Dortmunder Union-Schultheiss was given the new name of Brau & Brunnen in 1988. Those with a knowledge of German will have guessed that this company is also a soft drinks and mineral water concern in addition to brewing. In addition to the breweries of the Schultheiss fusion, breweries such as Küppers, Gilden Kölsch, Johan Sion (all of Cologne), St. Pauli of Bavaria, Friesische Jever, Dortmund Ritter, and Einbecker Brauhaus of Einbeck belong to the group.

BRINKHOFF'S No1

TYPE: PILSENER
ALCOHOL: 5% VOL.
FERMENTATION: BOTTOM

Special remarks: when the Dortmund breweries merged to form the Dortmunder Union they selected Fritz Brinkhoff as head brewer. This Pilsener is brewed to his recipe in his honor. It is a mild and lively Pilsener with gentle aroma of hops and a dry finish.

DORTMUNDER UNION EXPORT

TYPE: DORTMUNDER/EXPORT LAGER
ALCOHOL: 5.3% VOL.
FERMENTATION: BOTTOM

Special remarks: pale blonde Dortmunder with a malty aroma and taste accompanied by some hoppiness. It is medium to firm-bodied with a dry and hoppy aftertaste.

RITTER EXPORT

TYPE: DORTMUNDER/EXPORT LAGER
ALCOHOL: 5.3% VOL.
FERMENTATION: BOTTOM

Special remarks: the blonde Export of the Ritter label is a reasonably full-bodied malty lager with some hoppiness, especially in the drying aftertaste.

RITTER FIRST PREMIUM PILS

TYPE: PILSENER
ALCOHOL: 4.8% VOL.
FERMENTATION: BOTTOM

Special remarks: this premium Pilsener is blonde in color and has a sharply hoppy aroma. The slightly malt taste combines with the same sharp hoppiness that extends into bitterness. The aftertaste is drying. The body is thin to medium and fitting for the taste.

SIEGEL PILS

TYPE: PILSENER
ALCOHOL: 4.8% VOL.
FERMENTATION: BOTTOM

Special remarks: a blonde Pilsener with fine compact head. It is a typical bitter Pilsener.

EDER'S FAMILY BREWERY, GROSSOSTHEIM

Production in hectoliters: 300,000
Founded: 1779/1872

The first signs of existence of this brewery are found in books that indicate that the Zum Ochsen inn already possessed brewing rights in 1779. The inn with its small brewery was taken over in 1872 by Friedrich Eder, forefather of the Eder family that now runs the brewery. In 1901 the brewery was separated from the inn and a new brewery was built on a site where brewing still takes place. Today Eder's is a modern brewery employing some 120 people that serves both the domestic German and export markets. In addition to the beers described below Eder" also brew Eder's Leicht 2.9% ABV, Eder's Schwarzes 4.9% ABV, Sport Malz, and a number of beer and lemonade mixes.

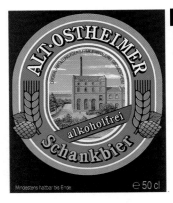

ALT-OSTHEIMER

TYPE: ALCOHOL FREE BEER
ALCOHOL: –
FERMENTATION: BOTTOM

Special remarks: original gravity is 7.3°.

BAVARIA DUNKLES STARKBIER

TYPE: STRONG DARK LAGER
ALCOHOL: 7.5% VOL.
FERMENTATION: BOTTOM

Special remarks: brewed with an original gravity of 19° and dark malt. This dark specialty brewed with burnt malt is available year round.

BAVARIA BAYRISCH MÄRZEN

TYPE: MÄRZEN
ALCOHOL: 5.8% VOL.
FERMENTATION: BOTTOM

Special remarks: brewed with an original gravity of 13.5° with Münchener malt that ensures the characteristic pale brown color and malty taste.

BAVARIA HEFE WEIZEN

TYPE: WHEAT BEER
ALCOHOL: 5.3% VOL.
FERMENTATION: TOP

Special remarks: cloudy blonde and lively wheat beer.

BAVARIA KRISTALL WEIZEN

TYPE: WHEAT BEER
ALCOHOL: 5.3% VOL.
FERMENTATION: TOP

Special remarks: clear blonde wheat beer with neutral taste and high carbon dioxide level.

EDER'S PILSENER

TYPE: PILSENER
ALCOHOL: 4.8% VOL.
FERMENTATION: BOTTOM

Special remarks: a blonde Pilsener with original gravity of 11.3° and reasonable bitterness of hops.

• • •

BAVARIA WEITZ

TYPE: WHEAT BEER
ALCOHOL: 5.3% VOL.
FERMENTATION: TOP

Special remarks: while most wheat beers contain 30–50% barley malt this is brewed solely with wheat malt. The original gravity is 12.3°. Eder's claim to be the first to sell a wheat beer brewed with 100% wheat malt.

EICHBAUM BREWERY, MANNHEIM

Production in hectoliters: 1,200,000
Founded: 1679

The precise history of the Eichbaum brewery is unknown but local authority papers show that Jean de Chain sought permission from the local council in 1679 to hang a board with the text "zum Eichbaum" on the facade of his building. This is where tasting takes place today although the brewery moved elsewhere in 1850. Today around 350 people work for the brewery that produces a wide variety of beers. Frankfurtse Henniger owns three-quarters of the shares in this brewery.

EDER'S ALT

TYPE: ALT
ALCOHOL: 4.9% VOL.
FERMENTATION: TOP

Special remarks: copper-colored alt with bitter hop flavor and original gravity of 11.3°.

EDER'S EXPORT

TYPE: EXPORT LAGER
ALCOHOL: 5.4% VOL.
FERMENTATION: BOTTOM

Special remarks: a malty and mild export lager that is rounded with little hop bitterness. Original gravity of 12.5°.

EICHBAUM APOSTULATOR

TYPE: MALT LAGER/DOUBLE BOCK
ALCOHOL: 7.5% VOL.
FERMENTATION: BOTTOM

Special remarks: this is a dark strong "double bock" malt lager. The color is brown tinged with a red glint. Roasted malt is found both in the aroma and taste.

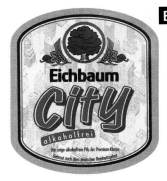

EICHBAUM CITY

TYPE: ALCOHOL-FREE LAGER

ALCOHOL: 0% VOL.

FERMENTATION: BOTTOM

Special remarks: City is brewed as other lagers and then has its alcohol removed so that it complies with the Reinheitsgebot.

EICHBAUM KRISTALL WEIZEN

TYPE: WHEAT BEER

ALCOHOL: 5% VOL.

FERMENTATION: TOP

Special remarks: a lively filtered wheat beer with a fruity aroma. The clear golden beer has the aroma and taste of cloves.

EICHBAUM DUNKLES WEIZEN

TYPE: WHEAT BEER

ALCOHOL: 5% VOL.

FERMENTATION: TOP

Special remarks: a dark wheat beer with a slightly spicy and malty aroma and taste, with cloves dominating.

EICHBAUM LEICHTER TYP

TYPE: LIGHT LAGER

ALCOHOL: 2.2% VOL.

FERMENTATION: BOTTOM

Special remarks: this blonde beer has a sharp aroma of hops. The taste is somewhat thin with underlying hops giving way to mild bitterness.

EICHBAUM EXPORT

TYPE: DORTMUNDER/EXPORT LAGER

ALCOHOL: 5.5% VOL.

FERMENTATION: BOTTOM

Special remarks:
a blonde premium lager that is rounded with a malty taste.

EICHBAUM PILSENER

TYPE: PILSENER

ALCOHOL: 4.9% VOL.

FERMENTATION: BOTTOM

Special remarks: blonde, mild Pilsener with hoppy aroma and hops in the finish of the taste.

EICHBAUM HEFE WEIZEN

TYPE: WHEAT BEER

ALCOHOL: 5% VOL.

FERMENTATION: TOP

Special remarks: a cloudy blonde wheat beer with a mild taste of hops and spices.

EICHBAUM UREICH

TYPE: PILSENER

ALCOHOL: 4.8% VOL.

FERMENTATION: BOTTOM

Special remarks: this blonde Pilsener is Eichbaum's leading product. Ureich means "original", indicating the strongly hopped nature of this Pilsener.

EICHBAUM SCHWARZBIER

TYPE: BLACK BEER

ALCOHOL: 4.9% VOL.

FERMENTATION: BOTTOM

Special remarks: this is a dark and unfiltered black beer brewed with dark malt and September hops.

• • •

EINBECKER BRAUHAUS, EINBECK

Production in hectoliters: 500,000

Founded: 1794

The Einbecker Brauhaus dates back to 1794 when it was the civic brewery but there is evidence pointing to a history as far back as the late fourteenth century. The majority shareholder now is Brau & Brunnen. In addition to malted lager "bock" beers the brewery produces Brouwherren Pils, a dunkel, and a Spezial.

EINBECKER MAI-UR-BOCK

TYPE: MALT LAGER/BOCK

ALCOHOL: 6.5% VOL.

FERMENTATION: BOTTOM

Special remarks: this is a light amber-colored seasonal bock. It has a fine aroma of malt and flavor of sweet malt with underlying hops. It is firm-bodied and reveals its alcohol in the mouth.

• • •

LICHER BREWERY, JHRING-MELCHIOR GMBH & CO KG, LICH

Production in hectoliters: 1,500,000

Founded: 1854

This brewery arose from a merger in 1922 between the Jhring brewery founded in Lich in 1845 and the Melchoir brewery, founded in Butzbach in 1858. In addition to Pilsener and ice beer the Licher brewery also brews and export lager and an alcohol-free lager. The shares are still in the hands of descendants of the founders.

LICHER ICE BEER

TYPE: ICE BEER

ALCOHOL: 5.1% VOL.

FERMENTATION: –

Special remarks: this is a blonde and slightly malty lager.

LICHER PILSNER PREMIUM

TYPE: PILSENER

ALCOHOL: 4.9% VOL.

FERMENTATION: BOTTOM

Special remarks: this blonde Pilsener has a slightly hoppy aroma. The taste is a balance between hops and malt. It is thin to medium in body and has a slightly hoppy aftertaste.

• • •

LÖWENBRÄU AG, MUNICH

Production in hectoliters: 1,200,000
Founded: 1383

Löwenbräu is one of Munich's major breweries with an enormous bierhalle. This beer can be sampled in many places throughout the world as many licenses have been granted for foreign brewing.

LÖWENBRÄU ICE BEER

TYPE: ICE BEER
ALCOHOL: 4.9% VOL.
FERMENTATION: BOTTOM

Special remarks: this lager that is filtered over ice is neutral in taste, slightly malty and a touch sweet.

LÖWENBRÄU ALKOHOLFREI

TYPE: ALCOHOL-FREE LAGER
ALCOHOL: –
FERMENTATION: BOTTOM

Special remarks: a blonde non alcoholic lager with a carrot-like aroma. The taste is quite malty, not balanced and there is no sign of hops or bitterness.

LÖWENBRÄU KRISTALLWEIZEN

TYPE: WHEAT BEER
ALCOHOL: 4.9% VOL.
FERMENTATION: TOP

Special remarks: golden filtered wheat beer with fresh and fruity aroma. The taste is slightly sweet, drying, with a fresh slightly sour finish. It is thin to medium-bodied.

LÖWENBRÄU EXPORT

TYPE: EXPORT LAGER
ALCOHOL: 5.6% VOL.
FERMENTATION: BOTTOM

Special remarks:
this is a blonde malty lager that is lightly hopped.

LÖWENBRÄU ORIGINAL MÜNCHNER HELL

TYPE: HELLES
ALCOHOL: 5.2% VOL.
FERMENTATION: BOTTOM

Special remarks: this Helles has an original gravity of 11.8°. It is neutral with few surprises. This blonde beer has a vague somewhat malty aroma with hints of hops. The aftertaste is quite drying.

LÖWENBRÄU HEFE WEISSBIER

TYPE: WHEAT BEER
ALCOHOL: 5.1% VOL.
FERMENTATION: TOP

Special remarks: a honey blonde wheat beer that continues fermenting in the bottle. It is lively and has a sweet malty taste with underlying dry sourness. The aroma is lightly malty with hint of vanilla.

LÖWENBRÄU PREMIUM PILS

TYPE: PILSENER
ALCOHOL: 5.2% VOL.
FERMENTATION: BOTTOM

Special remarks: this premium Pils is brewed with an original gravity of 11.8°. It is a pale blonde Pilsener with hoppy aroma and lively head. It is thin to medium in body and has a taste that starts malty but is increasingly of hops ending in a prolonged dry bitter aftertaste.

LÖWENBRÄU SCHWARZE WEISSE

TYPE: WHEAT BEER

ALCOHOL: 5.2% VOL.

FERMENTATION: TOP

Special remarks: this "black white" beer by the Bavarian brewery is quite sedentary for a wheat beer. Its original gravity is 11.8°. It is a dark amber wheat beer with a neutral taste with faint suggestion of banana and underlying dryness.

• • •

BRAUEREI GEBRÜDER MAISEL, BAYREUTH

Production in hectoliters: 480,000
Founded: 1887

This brewery in Bayreuth was founded in 1887 by brothers Hans and Eberhardt Maisel. Where they first started is now the site of a small museum of the brewery's history. The red-brick building is alongside the present brewery that is visited by thousands each year. They can admire an old steam engine from which the Dampfbier gets its name. The brewery is now run by Hans and Oscar Maisel. The most important product for Maisel is their wheat beer. They pioneered the brew at a time when it was not common currency. Today Maisel's Weisse is one of Germany's most popular wheat beers.

KRITZENTHALER ALKOHOLFREIES PILS

TYPE: ALCOHOL-FREE LAGER

ALCOHOL: –

FERMENTATION: BOTTOM

Special remarks: brewed as a Pilsener before the alcohol is removed. This blond lager has a malty aroma that starts wort-like and the same applies to the taste. Dry hops become apparent in the aftertaste. A medium-bodied lager.

MAISEL'S DAMPFBIER

TYPE: STEAM BEER

ALCOHOL: 4.9% VOL.

FERMENTATION: TOP

Special remarks: fine robust yet mildly hopped taste. Dry with slightly malty and fruity aromas. This top-fermenting beer is reminiscent of Belgian ales of similar strength but clearly has different hops. This pale amber specialty is an ideal session beer. The name "steam beer" is a pointer to Maisel's old steam engines.

MAISEL'S EDELHOPFEN

TYPE: DIET BEER

ALCOHOL: 4.9% VOL.

FERMENTATION: BOTTOM

Special remarks: low calorie diet beer that may be suitable on doctor's advice for diabetics. It is brewed in compliance with the Reinheitsgebot.

MAISEL'S WEISSE DUNKEL

TYPE: WHEAT BEER
ALCOHOL: 5.4% VOL.
FERMENTATION: TOP

Special remarks: this "dark white" wheat beer is dark brown with a tan colored head. It ferments in its bottle. It is quite dark for a wheat beer and there are hints of roasted malt. The banana and clove notes are only faintly apparent. Maisel's Weisse Dunkel is a fresh and fine full ale with a slightly sweet aftertaste. The wheat beer is apparent in the lively head but otherwise this has nothing in common with other dark wheat beers but there is nothing wrong in that.

MAISEL'S WEISZEN BOCK

TYPE: WHEAT BOCK
ALCOHOL: 7.2% VOL.
FERMENTATION: TOP

Special remarks: even those skilled at pouring beer need patience before drinking this beer because of its lively head that endures for some time. The fine sweet pleasing aroma of banana can be detected straight away. This dark cloudy beer has a full sensation in the mouth, remains lively, and is slight sweet with a hint of bitterness in the finish. The underlying notes are tart and finely balanced.

• • •

MAISEL'S WEISSE HEFE-WEIZENBIER

TYPE: WHEAT BEER
ALCOHOL: 5.7% VOL.
FERMENTATION: TOP

Special remarks: a post-bottling fermenting pale amber wheat beer that is cloudy and has aromas of malt and fruit. The taste is slight sour and sharp with pleasing hints of banana. Drying.

MAISEL'S WEISSE KRISTALLKLAR

TYPE: WHEAT BEER
ALCOHOL: 5.2% VOL.
FERMENTATION: TOP

Special remarks: a golden blonde clear and lively wheat beer with initially sharp wheat aroma. The taste is somewhat spicy but dry and slightly malt towards the finish.

MAURITIUS BRAUEREI GMBH, ZWICKAU

Production in hectoliters: –
Founded: 1991

A subsidiary of Dinkelacker-Schwaben Bräu of Stuttgart.

MAURITIUS BOCK DUNKEL

TYPE: MALTED LAGER/BOCK
ALCOHOL: 7.1% VOL.
FERMENTATION: BOTTOM

Special remarks: this is a black bock that is astoundingly smooth. It is rounded and sweet with aroma of burnt malt and caramel. It is medium bodied.

• • •

SCHLOSSBRAUEREI MAXLRAIN – LEO, GRAF VON HOHENTHAL BERGEN, TUNTENHAUSEN

Production in hectoliters: –
Founded: 1636

A small "castle" brewery of Count von Hohenthal, employing about thirty people.

MAXLRAINER SCHLOSS GOLD

TYPE: EXPORT LAGER
ALCOHOL: 5.1% VOL.
FERMENTATION: BOTTOM

Special remarks: a blonde lager that is sweet and malty with no bitterness and medium body.

• • •

MONINGER BREWERY, KARLSRUHE

Production in hectoliters: –
Founded: 1856

Majority shareholder is Stuttgarter Hofbräu AG.

MONINGER EXPORT

TYPE: EXPORT LAGER
ALCOHOL: 5.2% VOL.
FERMENTATION: BOTTOM

Special remarks: this export is a pale blonde lager with fine compact head. The aroma is malty with vague hoppiness. The taste is mildly malty with a finish of dry hop bitterness. The aftertaste is slightly bitter. Medium-bodied Moninger Export is brewed with water from the brewery's own well.

• • •

GRÄFLICH VON MOY'SCHES HOFBRAUHAUS, FREISING

Production in hectoliters: 200,000
Founded: –

Under the management of Count von Moy this brewery sells is beers under the name of Hofbrauhaus Freising. These include Urferlder, Pils, and Jägerbier

HUBER WEISSES

TYPE: WHEAT BEER
ALCOHOL: 5.3% VOL.
FERMENTATION: TOP

Special remarks: a lively blonde wheat beer that is slightly cloudy and rounded. The taste is slightly sweet and malty.

KLARES EDELWEIZEN

TYPE: WHEAT BEER
ALCOHOL: 5.4% VOL.
FERMENTATION: TOP

Special remarks: a clear, fresh wheat beer that is blonde in color. The aroma is very fresh with a mix of banana and floral notes. These are also found in the taste but accompanied by suggestions of cloves. The body is thin to medium. Although the head is large and firm this Edelweizen does not have an exaggerated sensation in the mouth.

• • •

BRAUHAUS OETTINGEN, OETTINGEN

Production in hectoliters: 1,200,000
Founded: 1731

Besides Oettingen there is a brewery in Gotha.

ORIGINAL OETTINGER ALT

TYPE: ALT
ALCOHOL: 4.9% VOL.
FERMENTATION: TOP

Special remarks: this brown top-fermenting alt has a fresh taste with mainly malty and slightly burnt nuances.

ORIGINAL OETTINGER EXPORT

TYPE: EXPORT LAGER
ALCOHOL: 5.4% VOL.
FERMENTATION: BOTTOM

Special remarks: a blonde export with a malty aroma with hops also apparent. The taste is sweetly malty finishing drying with vague hoppiness. It is medium bodied.

ORIGINAL OETTINGER DUNKLES HEFEWEIZEN

TYPE: WHEAT BEER
ALCOHOL: 4.9% VOL.
FERMENTATION: TOP

Special remarks: this is a cloudy mid-brown ("dark white") wheat beer with a lively head, a somewhat tart wheat aroma and wheat-like taste of cloves. The aftertaste is dry and slightly sharp.

ORIGINAL OETTINGER HEFEWEIßBIER

TYPE: WHEAT BEER
ALCOHOL: 4.9% VOL.
FERMENTATION: TOP

Special remarks: a cloudy golden wheat beer with post-bottling fermentation. The aroma is quite malty with hints too of cloves. The taste is more clearly malt and cloves and the aftertaste is drying. The body is thin to medium.

ORIGINAL OETTINGER KRISTALL WEIZEN

TYPE: WHEAT BEER
ALCOHOL: 4.9% VOL.
FERMENTATION: TOP

Special remarks: a filtered version of the wheat beer. A blonde with a somewhat malty aroma and slightly malty taste.

ORIGINAL OETTINGER HELL

TYPE: LAGER/HELLES
ALCOHOL: 4.7% VOL.
FERMENTATION: BOTTOM

Special remarks: a blonde lager with a sharp aroma of hops. The taste is briefly of hops and the body medium. There is underlying dryness and a dry aftertaste.

ORIGINAL OETTINGER LEICHT

TYPE: LIGHT LAGER

ALCOHOL: 2.8% VOL.

FERMENTATION: BOTTOM

Special remarks: a light blonde lager with low alcohol and few calories. This light is also thin in body but this is kept in the background by the robust hops. The taste is slightly bitter and drying towards the finish when vague maltiness makes an appearance.

ORIGINAL OETTINGER LEICHTE WEIßE

TYPE: LIGHT WHEAT BEER

ALCOHOL: 2.8% VOL.

FERMENTATION: TOP

Special remarks: a cloudy blonde wheat beer with low alcohol and few calories.

ORIGINAL OETTINGER PILS

TYPE: PILSENER

ALCOHOL: 4.7% VOL.

FERMENTATION: BOTTOM

Special remarks: a gold-blonde Pilsener with a hoppy aroma. The taste is hoppy and has prolonged bitterness. This Pils is thin to medium bodied with a drying finish but the taste is dominated by the robust character of the hops.

ORIGINAL OETTINGER SCHWARZBIER

TYPE: BLACK BEER

ALCOHOL: 4.9% VOL.

FERMENTATION: BOTTOM

Special remarks: this dark lager has a malty aroma and fresh taste with hints of roasted malt. It is slightly drying.

•••

PADERBORNER HAUS CRAMER BREWERY, PADERBORN

Production in hectoliters: –

Founded: 1990

This brewery results from a merger of the Paderborn, Isenbeck, and Weissenburg breweries whose names are still used for its beers. It belongs to Albert Cramer who also owns the Warnsteiner brewery.

PADERBORNER PILSENER

TYPE: PILSENER

ALCOHOL: 4.9% VOL.

FERMENTATION: BOTTOM

Special remarks: a golden blonde Pilsener with mild aroma containing a little malt and hops. Hops are more readily apparent in the taste and drying hoppy aftertaste.

•••

PAULANER BRAUEREI AG, MUNICH

Production in hectoliters: 2,000,000

Founded: 1634

The holding company of this brewery also incorporates the Fürstliche Brauerei Thurn und Taxis, and the Hacker-Pschorr brewery of Munich.

ORIGINAL MÜNCHNER

TYPE: PREMIUM LAGER

ALCOHOL: 4.9% VOL.

FERMENTATION: BOTTOM

Special remarks: a pale blonde lager with a malty aroma. The taste is slightly sweet with slight underlying dryness. There is little evidence of hops in this lager of 11.5° original gravity

ORIGINAL MÜNCHNER DUNKEL

TYPE: DUNKEL

ALCOHOL: 5% VOL.

FERMENTATION: BOTTOM

Special remarks: this dark lager has an aroma with hops and fruity malt. The taste continues this followed by a drying slightly bitter aftertaste.

PAULANER PREMIUM LEICHT

TYPE: LIGHT LAGER

ALCOHOL: 3.2% VOL.

FERMENTATION: BOTTOM

Special remarks: this light lager is brewed with an original gravity of 7.7°. This blonde lager has a thin body. Its taste is slightly hoppy and there is a brief and slightly bitter aftertaste.

PAULANER HEFE-WEIßBIER

TYPE: WHEAT BEER

ALCOHOL: 5.5% VOL.

FERMENTATION: TOP

Special remarks: a lively cloudy blonde wheat beer with mild aroma of cloves. In addition to cloves the taste also has sweet malt but drying towards the finish.

PAULANER PREMIUM PILS

TYPE: LIGHT LAGER

ALCOHOL: 4.9% VOL.

FERMENTATION: BOTTOM

Special remarks: brewed with an original gravity of 11.5°. This premium Pilsener has a hoppy aroma. The taste is initially malty but gradually is replaced by a mild bitterness. The aftertaste is quite prolonged bitterness. It is medium-bodied.

PAULANER HEFE-WEIßBIER DUNKEL

TYPE: WHEAT BEER

ALCOHOL: 5.3% VOL.

FERMENTATION: TOP

Special remarks: a dark version of this post-bottling fermenting wheat beer. The aroma is of spices with a hint of banana and the taste concurs with the aroma but finishes both somewhat tart and drying.

PAULANER WEISSBIER KRISTALLKLAR

TYPE: WHEAT BEER

ALCOHOL: 5.5% VOL.

FERMENTATION: TOP

Special remarks: a blond and filtered wheat beer. This lively beer has a somewhat spicy aroma and malty and slightly spicy taste that is drying. It is medium in body.

SALVATOR

TYPE: MALT LAGER/DOUBLE BOCK
ALCOHOL: 7.5% VOL.
FERMENTATION: BOTTOM

Special remarks: Paulaner brew their Salvator double bock with an original gravity of 18.3°. It is a ruby-red malt lager with a cream-colored head. The aroma is of caramel and burnt malt while the taste is malty, very mellow with sweet nuances of burnt malt. The mouth sensation is slightly of alcohol and of dryness. The taste is rounded and full. This is unquestionably a complex and rich double bock.

THURN UND TAXIS ROGGEN

TYPE: SPECIAL RYE BREW
ALCOHOL: 4.7% VOL.
FERMENTATION: TOP

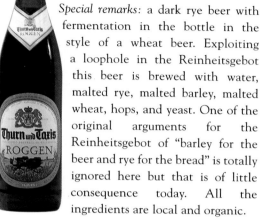

Special remarks: a dark rye beer with fermentation in the bottle in the style of a wheat beer. Exploiting a loophole in the Reinheitsgebot this beer is brewed with water, malted rye, malted barley, malted wheat, hops, and yeast. One of the original arguments for the Reinheitsgebot of "barley for the beer and rye for the bread" is totally ignored here but that is of little consequence today. All the ingredients are local and organic.

THOMAS BRÄU ALKOHOLFREI

TYPE: ALCOHOL-FREE LAGER
ALCOHOL: –
FERMENTATION:

THURN UND TAXIS WEISSBIER

TYPE: WHEAT BEER
ALCOHOL: 5.3% VOL.
FERMENTATION: TOP

Special remarks: a cloudy amber wheat beer with somewhat sweet and slightly spicy aroma. The taste is spicy and also sweet finishing with drying sweet and sour.

THURN UND TAXIS PILSENER

TYPE: PILSENER
ALCOHOL: 4.9% VOL.
FERMENTATION: BOTTOM

Special remarks: a blond Pilsener brewed with an original gravity of 11.6°. It is a strongly hoppy Pilsener but of the mellow and fulsome kind. The body is firm and full and well balanced. There is the bitter hops of a Pilsener but fuller and even slightly fruity. The aroma also conveys maltiness.

BAYERISCHE BRAUHAUS PFORZHEIM, PFORZHEIM

Production in hectoliters: 40–50,000
Founded: 1889

This is a small regional brewery.

GOLDSTADT EXPORT

TYPE: EXPORT LAGER
ALCOHOL: 5% VOL.
FERMENTATION: BOTTOM

Special remarks: this is a blonde export lager with a malty aroma and sweet malty taste. The aftertaste is drying and slightly hoppy. It is medium bodied.

GOLDSTADT PILSENER

TYPE: PILSENER
ALCOHOL: 4.9% VOL.
FERMENTATION: BOTTOM

Special remarks: a blonde mildly sweet Pilsener that gives way to slight bitterness of hops.

GOLDSTADT PREMIUM

TYPE: LIGHT LAGER
ALCOHOL: 2.2% VOL.
FERMENTATION: BOTTOM

Special remarks: this light lager has been given a strange choice of name considering that Premium is generally reserved for stronger lagers. This lager is brewed in accordance with the Reinheitsgebot with low alcohol and few calories.

GOLDSTADT SPEZIAL EXPORT HELL

TYPE: EXPORT LAGER/HELLES
ALCOHOL: 5% VOL.
FERMENTATION: BOTTOM

Special remarks: a blonde export lager with a malty aroma through which a certain hoppiness is apparent. It has a medium body. The taste is mellow sweet with slightly hoppy undertones. It is well-balanced and has a brief slightly bitter aftertaste.

RATSKELLER PILS

TYPE: PILSENER
ALCOHOL: 4.9% VOL.
FERMENTATION: BOTTOM

Special remarks: an unfiltered Pilsener which gives the blonde beer a cloudy appearance. It has a fine compact head with a slightly hoppy aroma. The taste is also of hops with bitterness. The body is thin to medium and dry. Bitterness continues into the aftertaste. This is a Pilsener of some character.

● ● ●

PINKUS MÜLLER BREWERY, MUNSTER

Production in hectoliters: 21,000
Founded: 1816

The founder of this family brewery was Johannes Müller who moved to Munster in 1816. He married Friederika Cramer and established a bakery and brewery at 10 Kreuzstrasse. Four generations later the company is run by Hans Müller who acquired his nickname of Pinkus from his father. The brewery's seven beers are all brewed using

organic malt from strictly organic farming and also organically-grown hops. Müller's beers include Pinkus Alt 5%, Pinkus Spezial 5.1%, Pinkus Hefe-Weizen 5.2%, Pinkus Leicht 2.8%, Müller's Malz, and Pinkus Honey Malt.

PINKUS PILS

TYPE: PILSENER
ALCOHOL: 5% VOL.
FERMENTATION: BOTTOM

Special remarks:
a completely organic Pilsener with cold conditioning of three months.

•••

POTT'S BREWERY, OELDE

Production in hectoliters: 100,000
Founded: 1769

The brewery is owned by Rainer Pott. Pott's beers are bottled in dumpy bottles with neck brackets and include Pott's Paddy.

POTT'S LANDBIER

TYPE: LAGER
ALCOHOL: 4.8% VOL.
FERMENTATION: BOTTOM

Special remarks: an amber lager with a mild sweet malt aroma. It is a mellow beer with a neutral, slightly malty taste. The gentle nature of this beer is in part die to a low level of carbon dioxide.

POTT'S PILSENER

TYPE: PILSENER
ALCOHOL: 5.5% VOL.
FERMENTATION: BOTTOM

Special remarks: a fairly robust blonde Pilsener with a mild hoppy character.

•••

RADEBERGER EXPORT BEER BREWERY, RADEBERG

Production in hectoliters: 1,500,000
Founded: 1872

The Radeberger Brewery is part of the Binding Group of Frankfurt.

RADEBERGER PILSENER

TYPE: PILSENER
ALCOHOL: 4.8% VOL.
FERMENTATION: BOTTOM

Special remarks: this blonde Pilsener has a fresh hoppy aroma and quite pronounced hoppy taste. The aftertaste is drying bitterness. This Pilsener was nominated by royal decree in 1905 as the table beer of King Friedrich August of Saxony.

• • •

BÜRGERLICHES BRAUHAUS RAVENSBURG-LINDAU, RAVENSBURG

Production in hectoliters: –
Founded: 1817

A medium-sized brewery resulting from the merger of a number of regional breweries. In addition to their Weisse they brew a Pilsener, Senator, Export, and Urtype (original).

BÜRGER WEISSE

TYPE: WHEAT BEER
ALCOHOL: 5.5% VOL.
FERMENTATION: TOP

Special remarks: a golden-blonde wheat beer that ferments in the bottle. It has a fresh and spicy aroma and a spicy taste with underlying sourness. It is drying and lively in the mouth but there is nothing new in the aftertaste.

• • •

HEINRICH REISSDORF BREWERY, COLOGNE

Production in hectoliters: –
Founded: 1894

Reissdorf is one of the twenty-four brewers of Kölsch. It is a small family concern that solely brews the Kölsch specialty.

REISSDORF KÖLSCH

TYPE: KÖLSCH
ALCOHOL: 4.8% VOL.
FERMENTATION: TOP

Special remarks: a pale blonde top-fermented ale with a vaguely malty aroma. Mild malt is also in the taste balanced by underlying hops. The aftertaste is hoppy and drying.

• • •

RHENANIA BREWERY, ROBERT WIRICHS, KREFELD-KÖNIGSHOF

Production in hectoliters: –
Founded: 1838

The history of the Krefeld brewery dates back to before Herman Josef Wirichs took it over in 1838 and the family is still present. In addition to Rhenania Alt there is also a Wirichs Leicht.

RHENANIA ALT

TYPE: ALT
ALCOHOL: 4.8% VOL.
FERMENTATION: TOP

Special remarks: the coppery Rhenania has a malty aroma and quite firm body. The first impression is of a much stronger beer. The mellow malt taste is slowly replaced by increased hoppiness. This alt is more bitter in the drying aftertaste.

• • •

RIEDENBURGER BRAUHAUS, MICHAEL KRIEGER KG, RIEDENBURG/ALTMÜHLTAL

Production in hectoliters: –
Founded: 1866

The Riedenberg brewery brews mainly wheat beers, all using organically-grown ingredients.

RIEDENBURGER MICHAELI DUNKEL

TYPE: WHEAT BEER
ALCOHOL: 5.2% VOL.
FERMENTATION: TOP

Special remarks: this beer is brewed with an original gravity of 12°. The cloudy copper-colored wheat beer is very lively. The taste is sharply malty, spicy, with closely underlying bitter sourness. It is medium bodied.

• • •

S. RIEGELE BREWERY, AUGSBURG

Production in hectoliters: 200,000
Founded: 1600/1884

The history of this family brewery begins around 1600. The brewery known as Zum Goldenen Rofl was taken over in 1884 by Sebastiaan Riegele. Today this medium-sized brewery uses its own water to produce their Feines Urhell, Würziges Export, Commercienrat Riegele Privat, Augsburger Herren Pils, Aechtes Dunkel, Kräusen Weisse, Speziator, and an alcohol-free lager. The company also produces soft drinks and mineral waters.

• • •

GEBR. RÖHRL BREWERY, STRAUBING

Production in hectoliters: 100,000
Founded: 1431

The brewery has been in the Röhr family's ownership since 1881.

STRAUBINGER WEISSE

TYPE: WHEAT BEER
ALCOHOL: 5.2% VOL.
FERMENTATION: TOP

Special remarks: this wheat beer is brewed with an original gravity of 12.6°. It is a cloudy copper color and has a very rich aroma of fresh banana with sweetness and a hint of vanilla. The taste is more spicy, quite mellow, and drying in the finish which is accompanied by sourness.

• • •

A. ROLINCK BREWERY, STEINFURT NORDRHEIN-WESTFALEN

Production in hectoliters: 300,000
Founded: 1820

In addition to Pilsener, Rolinck also brew an Alt, Spezial, Light, and an alcohol-free lager.

ROLINCK PILSENER PREMIUM

TYPE: PILSENER
ALCOHOL: 4.7% VOL.
FERMENTATION: BOTTOM

Special remarks: a blonde Pilsener with a lively and hoppy character.

• • •

BADISCHE STAATSBRAUEREI ROTHAUS AG, ROTHAUS

Production in hectoliters: 500,000
Founded: 1791

The Baden state Rothaus brewery is situated in the Upper Black Forest where it gets its water from seven different wells. The brewery was originally established by Benedictine monks.

FRANZ JOSEPH SAILER, MARKTOBERDORF

Production in hectoliters: –
Founded: –

This small family brewery is owned by the Borges family and employs about 120 people. Besides this brewery the family have since 1978 also owned the Altenmünster brewery that was founded in 1648 by Capuchin friars.

ROTHAUS MÄRZEN EXPORT

TYPE: MÄRZEN
ALCOHOL: 5.6% VOL.
FERMENTATION: BOTTOM

Special remarks: a medium-bodied blonde with a sweet taste that becomes bitter and finishes dry.

ALTENMÜNSTER BRAUER BIER URIG WURZIG

TYPE: LAGER
ALCOHOL: 4.9% VOL.
FERMENTATION: BOTTOM

Special remarks: this is a blonde lager with a malty and hoppy aroma. Against underlying dryness, the taste is hoppy with a little malt. It is medium-bodied.

TANNEN ZÄPFLE

TYPE: PILSENER
ALCOHOL: 5.1% VOL.
FERMENTATION: BOTTOM

Special remarks: this pale blonde Pilsener has a fine compact head. It is a fairly full-bodied lager with an aroma that is both slightly malty and hoppy. The taste is bitter extending into a drying aftertaste.

• • •

ALTENMÜNSTER BRAUER BIER HERB

TYPE: LAGER
ALCOHOL: 4.9% VOL.
FERMENTATION: BOTTOM

Special remarks: the aroma of this blonde lager is malty and hoppy. The taste is malty with a dry hop flavor. There is prolonged bitterness in the aftertaste.

FRANZ JOSEPH JUBELBIER

TYPE: DUNKEL
ALCOHOL: 5.5% VOL.
FERMENTATION: BOTTOM

Special remarks: this amber-colored dunkel has slight hints of roasting. The bottle is of very

original design with a sort of hand grip at the rear. The bottles are distributed in wooden crates.

SCHÄFFBRÄU RUDOLF SCHÄFF TREUCHTLINGEN, TREUCHTLINGEN

Production in hectoliters: –
Founded: –

A small brewery that produces its own malt and various soft drinks and mineral waters.

SCHÄFF'S HELLE WEISSE

TYPE: WHEAT BEER
ALCOHOL: 5.4% VOL.
FERMENTATION: TOP

Special remarks: a blonde wheat beer from the Altmuhltal nature park.

OBERDORFER WEISSBIER DUNKEL

TYPE: WHEAT BEER
ALCOHOL: 4.8% VOL.
FERMENTATION: TOP

Special remarks: this is a dark "white" beer or wheat beer that ferments in the bottle. It has a spicy aroma with a malty taste with hints of roasting.

• • •

SCHLÖSSER BREWERY, DUSSELDORF

Production in hectoliters: 1,000,000
Founded: 1873

A large brewery that specializes in alt.

OBERDORFER WEISSBIER HELLES

TYPE: WHEAT BEER
ALCOHOL: 4.8% VOL.
FERMENTATION: TOP

SCHLÖSSER ALT

TYPE: ALT
ALCOHOL: 4.8% VOL.
FERMENTATION: TOP

Special remarks: this blonde version of their wheat beer has a lively character and a fruity aroma and taste. The finish is drying and slightly tart.

• • •

Special remarks: this tan-colored alt has a somewhat hoppy aroma and a taste of malt with underlying dryness of hops. There are vague hints of roasted malt. The body is thin to medium.

• • •

ADOLF SCHMID BREWERY, USTERSBACH

Production in hectoliters: –
Founded: 1605

The small place of Usterbach lies in the Augsburg Western Forest national park. Thirteen generations of the Schmid family has brewed here since 1605. One of the family's proudest possessions is the inn next to the brewery built in 1720 and still in its original condition. Ustbacher beer is served here together with Southern German specialties. The Schmid brewery also produces soft drinks in addition to beer and has its own maltings.

Most of the grain to be malted is grown organically under contract by local farmers. The hops used are Hallertau and the water comes from within the national park. No additives are used and the beer is not pasteurized. Cold fermentation takes more than a week and a further six are needed for conditioning of the beer. Of course the beer is brewed in accordance with the Reinheitsgebot.

The old Gasthof or inn of the Adolf Schmid brewery.

ALTBAYERISCH DUNKEL

TYPE: DUNKEL
ALCOHOL: 5.3% VOL.
FERMENTATION: BOTTOM

Special remarks: a reddish brown lager.

BRAUHERREN-BIER

TYPE: LAGER
ALCOHOL: 5.5% VOL.
FERMENTATION: BOTTOM

Special remarks: the brewer regards this more full-bodied beer as one of his specialties.

BAYERISCHE HEFE-WEIZEN

TYPE: WHEAT BEER
ALCOHOL: 5.5% VOL.
FERMENTATION: TOP

Special remarks: a cloudy blonde wheat beer.

DUNKLE WEISSE

TYPE: WHEAT BEER
ALCOHOL: 5.3% VOL.
FERMENTATION: TOP

Special remarks: this is a dark and slightly cloudy amber-colored wheat beer with post-fermentation.

EDEL-EXPORT

TYPE: LAGER

ALCOHOL: 5.5% VOL.

FERMENTATION: BOTTOM

Special remarks: Edel Export at an original gravity of 12.6° is one of the more robust Usterbach brews.

PILSENER

TYPE: PILSENER

ALCOHOL: 4.9% VOL.

FERMENTATION: BOTTOM

KRISTALL WEIZEN

TYPE: WHEAT BEER

ALCOHOL: 5.3% VOL.

FERMENTATION: TOP

Special remarks: a filtered golden-blonde wheat beer.

PRIVAT-PILSENER

TYPE: PILSENER

ALCOHOL: 4.9% VOL.

FERMENTATION: BOTTOM

LEICHTE HELLE

TYPE: LIGHT (HELLES) BEER

ALCOHOL: 3.2% VOL.

FERMENTATION: BOTTOM

URHELL

TYPE: LAGER/HELLES

ALCOHOL: 4.9% VOL.

FERMENTATION: BOTTOM

Special remarks: a pale blonde lager.

LEICHTE WEISSE

TYPE: LIGHT WHEAT BEER

ALCOHOL: 3.3% VOL.

FERMENTATION: TOP

Special remarks: a light unfiltered wheat beer.

WEIHNACHTSBIER

TYPE: MALTED LAGER/BOCK

ALCOHOL: 5.8% VOL.

FERMENTATION: BOTTOM

Special remarks: Christmas special.

• • •

SCHMUCKER OBER-MOSSAU BREWERY, MOSSAUTAL-ODENWALD, HESSE

Production in hectoliters: 200,000
Founded: 1780

A small family brewery.

SCHMUCKER HEFE WEIZEN DUNKEL

TYPE: WHEAT BEER
ALCOHOL: 5% VOL.
FERMENTATION: TOP

Special remarks: a cloudy amber wheat beer with post-fermentation in the bottle. The aroma is somewhat sweet with a hint of spice. The taste is sweet caramel with underlying spice, becoming dry towards the finish. It is a medium-bodied and lively beer.

• • •

G. SCHNEIDER & SOHN BREWERY, KELHEIM

Production in hectoliters: –
Founded: 1607/1872

The Schneider family brewery once began in Munich and would probably still be there but for bombing during World War II which forced them to move the copper to Kelheim. Georg Schneider I was brewer in 1855 at the Münchener Weisses Hohbräuhaus am Pltazl, where the present Staatliches Hofbräuhaus is now sited. He rented the brewery from King Max II who then had the sole rights for brewing wheat beer. Once the popularity of wheat beer had virtually vanished the King rid himself of this right. King Ludwig II gave his rights to Georg I in 1872 who started the Schneider brewery in Munich at Im Tal 10. This grew to become one of the most important breweries for wheat beer. Schneider & Sohn took advantage of the growing popularity of wheat beer and bought up other wheat beer breweries

Weisses Bräuhaus, München, Thal.

around the Munich area, including the Kelheim brewery in 1927. This is Bavaria's oldest wheat beer brewery, founded in 1607 by Maximiliaan I. This brewery is now the head office for Schneider & Sohn although they still consider themselves Münchener. The brewery Im Tal has been extensively restored and is now used as a restaurant and meeting room. The brewery is still run by a Georg Schneider, as the first sons are named. The only exception to this was in the period 1905–1927 when Mathilde, the widow of Georg Schneider III, successfully ran the brewery. At present it is run by Georg V and his son Georg VI is preparing to take over the reins. George VI maintained family tradition in 1995 when he not unsurprisingly named his new-born son Georg VII.

Schneiders current brewery in Kelheim.

AVENTINUS

TYPE: WHEAT BOCK

ALCOHOL: 8% VOL.

FERMENTATION: TOP

Special remarks: this dark ruby-red wheat bock beer of Schneider is brewed according to the Reinheitsgebot to an original gravity of 18.5° is a post-bottling fermenting beer. Schneider claim to be the first Bavarian brewer of such a beer and points to a history of brewing this beer since 1907. The Munich brewery was sited on the Aventinusstrasse, name for a Bavarian sixteenth century poet. Aventinus is a slightly cloudy And lively beer with a firm head and strong smell of wheat with a hint of spice. The taste is full, sharp, and spicy. The aftertaste is prolonged and somewhat tart.

calories on the low side. This wheat beer is neither filtered or pasteurized, ferments after bottling, and has an original gravity of 7.8°.

SCHNEIDER WEISSE ORIGINAL

TYPE: WHEAT BEER

ALCOHOL: 5.4% VOL.

FERMENTATION: TOP

Special remarks: the brewers say this beer has been brewed without change from a recipe of Georg Schneider – the founder – since 1872. It is an amber-colored wheat beer of 12.8° original gravity. It is neither filtered or pasteurized and ferments further in its bottle. It has a sharp wheaten aroma with hints of spice while the taste is mild and slightly sweet, with a drying sour finish with further spice. The aftertaste is dominated by a dry sour sensation in the mouth.

SCHNEIDER WEISSE KRISTALL

TYPE: WHEAT BEER

ALCOHOL: 5.3% VOL.

FERMENTATION: TOP

Special remarks: Schneider's Kristall is a filtered wheat beer with an original gravity of 12.3°. It is a fresh wheat beer with spicy notes and a drying slightly tart finish.

SCHNEIDER WEISSE WEIZENHELL

TYPE: WHEAT BEER

ALCOHOL: 5.4% VOL.

FERMENTATION: TOP

Special remarks: Schneider has brewed its Weizenhell since 1994 for those who like a blonde wheat beer. It has an original gravity of 11.5°, making it lighter then their Original. The taste is less sweet and somewhat fresher. It is a lively post-bottling fermenting beer of course.

SCHNEIDER WEISSE LIGHT

TYPE: LIGHT WHEAT BEER

ALCOHOL: 3.3% VOL.

FERMENTATION: TOP

Special remarks: Schneider's light wheat beer is for the enthusiast who wishes to keep both alcohol and

• • •

SCHULTHEISS-BRAUEREI VERBUND, BERLIN

Production in hectoliters: 3,000,000
Founded: 1821

The Berlin arm of Dortmunder Brau & Brunnen is this Schultheiss united brewery. Dortmunder Union Brauerie AG and the West Berlin Schultheiss brewery jointly formed Dortmunder Union-Schultheiss Brauerei AG in 1972. This was changed in 1988 to Brau und Brunnen AG.

The Schultheiss Group was formed by merging the two former East German breweries of Berliner Pilsener Brauerei and the Oderland Brauerei of Frankfurt an der Oder close to the Polish border.

The Berliner Pilsener brewery was established in 1902 as the Gabriel & Richter brewery with a capacity of 120,000 hectoliters. After World War II the Communist government created a union of East Berlin breweries and the Pilsener brewery became the most modern East Berlin brewery with a capacity of 1,200,000 hectoliters. After the Berlin wall came down the Treuhand merged the brewery with two other breweries and a distillery to form Brau und Erfrishchungsgetränke AG (BEAG). Brau Und Brunnen took BEAG over at the end of 1990. Brau und Brunnen divested itself of the other activities of BEAG and renamed the brewery as Berliner Pilsener Brauerei GmbH in 1992, invested in modernization, and brought the company within the Schultheiss Group. The Berliner Pilsener Brauerei has a yearly beer output of around 2,000,000 hectoliters.

The Oderland Brauerei GmbH is a relatively new brewery. In 1984 there was bottling plant there and soft drinks were produced too. A brewery was added to this in 1988 and in 1989 this produced 750,000 hectoliters of beer. The following year though the drinks combine could only sell about seven percent of its capacity. Brau und Brunnen took control in 1991 and merged the business with the Schultheiss Group. They invested around one million Deutschmarks in the brewery which is now producing in excess of one million hectoliters. The brand name of the Oderland brewery is Spitzkrug.

The Schultheiss brewery that forms the West Berlin arm of the group was founded in 1842 by an Berlin chemist, August Heinrich Prell as a small brewery with its own maltings in central Berlin. This was taken over eleven year later by Jobst Schultheiss and renamed. Another eleven years on the brewery came into the hands of Richard Roesicke who turned it from a craft brewery into a major concern without changing the name. Through a succession of take-overs Schultheiss grew to the one million hectoliter mark and a decade later it was the biggest brewery in Germany. Schultheiss's production in 1938 was 2,800,000 hectoliters. The brewery lost a large part of its market following World War II and also its establishments and was forced by West Berlin's isolation to rely solely on West Berlin for its market. When the Berlin wall came down the brewery produced 1.1 million hectoliters each year.

Before the Schultheiss Group was formed in 1992 Brau und Brunnen had invested heavily in the antiquated brewery. Through a process of modernization, adapting, painful closures, and down-sizing it is now an up-to-date operation

producing three million hectoliters but badly in need of investment since no investment was made in the former East Bloc zone after 1976. In order to continue as German companies the former East Bloc breweries had as minimum requirement the need to brew in accordance with the Reinheitsgebot and badly needed

technical improvements. Schultheiss's main market is the area immediately surrounding the brewery. The group beers include top fermented Schultheiss Original Berliner Weisse, Diät Schankbier, Pilsener, Schwarz Lager, Aecht Patzenhofer Premium Pilsener, Spitzkrug Märkisches Pils, and Berliner Pilsener.

BERLINER PILSNER

TYPE: PILSENER

ALCOHOL: 5% VOL.

FERMENTATION: BOTTOM

Special remarks: Berliner Pilsener is a slightly hoppy beer with lively level of carbon dioxide.

SCHULTHEISS LAGER

TYPE: LAGER

ALCOHOL: 5% VOL.

FERMENTATION: BOTTOM

Special remarks: this lager was introduced in 1998. The mild taste combined with blonde color and medium body must attract people to the beer for any bitterness has been omitted.

SCHULTHEISS DIÄT

TYPE: DIET PILSENER

ALCOHOL: 3.8% VOL.

FERMENTATION: BOTTOM

Special remarks: brewed with an original gravity of 7.5° for calorie counters.

SCHULTHEISS LAGER SCHWARZ

TYPE: LAGER

ALCOHOL: 5% VOL.

FERMENTATION: BOTTOM

Special remarks: a very dark lager that is mildly hopped with a malty taste with slightly burnt notes.

SCHULTHEISS MIX

TYPE: BEER/SYRUP MIX
ALCOHOL: 3.7% VOL.
FERMENTATION: TOP

Special remarks: although the German beer brewers and drinkers hold the banner high for the Reinheitsgebot mixer drinks have found a place in the German market. Schultheis has adapted an old practice of mixing white beer and fruit syrup with this drink aimed at a young market.

SCHULTHEISS ORIGINAL BERLINER WEISSE

TYPE: WHEAT BEER
ALCOHOL: 3.7% VOL.
FERMENTATION: TOP

Special remarks: with its original gravity of 7.5° this wheat beer is a light beer. It has a fresh and slightly sour taste. It is slightly cloudy from not wholly fermented yeast which dominates the taste. It is lively.

SCHULTHEISS PILSENER

TYPE: PILSENER
ALCOHOL: 5% VOL.
FERMENTATION: BOTTOM

Special remarks: this Pilsener is Schultheiss' regional trump card. This blonde pils is quite malty, dry, and finishes hoppy.

SCHWEIGER BREWERY, MARKT SCHWABEN

Production in hectoliters: –
Founded: 1934

A small family brewery.

SCHWEIGER SCHMANKERL WEISSE

TYPE: WHEAT BEER
ALCOHOL: 5.1% VOL.
FERMENTATION: TOP

Special remarks: an original gravity of 12.3°. A golden-blonde misty wheat beer with slightly spicy aroma. The taste is fresh and slightly spicy. Drying and somewhat tart in the aftertaste.

SPATEN-FRANZISKANER-BRÄU, MUNICH

Production in hectoliters: 1,100,000
Founded: 1397

The history of the Spaten brewery dates back to 1397 but it has had the present name since George Spaeth became the owner in 1622. The Franciscan brewery was founded in 1363 and it was taken over in 1807 by the royal brewer Gabriel Sedlmayer. His son, Gabriel II, was regarded as the great innovator in the field of lagers. Joseph Sedlmayer, brother of Gabriel II took the brewery over in due course and introduced a copper-colored brew for the Oktoberfest. This Viennese style lager resulted from cooperation between the Sedlmayers and Anton Dreher. The brothers' descendants united the breweries in 1922 to form Spaten-Franziskaner-Bräu and the biggest shareholders are members of the Sedlmayer family.

FRANZISKANER HEFE WEISSBIER

TYPE: WHEAT BEER
ALCOHOL: 5% VOL.
FERMENTATION: TOP

Special remarks: a cloudy blonde wheat beer with a fairly malty and grainy aroma. The taste is slightly sharp and hoppy. It is thin to medium in body.

FRANZISKANER HEFE WEISSBIER DUNKEL

TYPE: WHEAT BEER
ALCOHOL: 5% VOL.
FERMENTATION: TOP

Special remarks:
a dark post-fermenting beer with a spicy aroma and taste. Lively, and drying towards the end.

FRANZISKANER WEISSBIER KRISTALLKLAR

TYPE: WHEAT BEER
ALCOHOL: 5% VOL.
FERMENTATION: TOP

Special remarks: a filtered wheat beer. Kristallklar is a pale blonde beer with mild wheaten aroma with cloves. The taste is freshly spicy and slightly drying and tart.

MÜNCHNER HELL

TYPE: HELLES
ALCOHOL: 5.2% VOL.
FERMENTATION: BOTTOM

Special remarks: a pale blonde lager with a neutral basic taste. There is no aftertaste and is has a high level of carbon dioxide. Hops and malt come to the fore in the aroma but not strongly.

SPATEN ALKOHOLFREI

TYPE: ALCOHOL-FREE BEER
ALCOHOL: –
FERMENTATION: BOTTOM

Special remarks: this beer is brewed as a normal lager according to the Reinheitsgebot with an original gravity of 11.2°. The alcohol is then removed and this also reduces the calories by two-fifths.

SPATEN DIÄT-PILS

TYPE: DIET LAGER
ALCOHOL: 4.9% VOL.
FERMENTATION: BOTTOM

Special remarks: this diet beer has a pale blonde color and slightly malty aroma. The taste is of hops with a slightly bitter finish. The body is medium. Because of its robust body and slightly drying hoppiness it is difficult to be aware that this is a reduced calorie beer.

• • •

STAATLICHES HOFBRÄUHAUS IN MÜNCHEN, MUNICH

Production in hectoliters: 250,000
Founded: 1859

This is certainly not one of the biggest breweries in Germany but it is well known. The reference to Staatliches in the name refers to the state of Bavaria which has owned the brewery since 1935. Prior to this the brewery was the Königliches or royal Hofbrauhaus, owned by the Bavarian royal family. During the period of royal ownership the brand mark "HB" with a crown above was registered in the trade registers of Munich. The court brewery was first established in 1589 by William V, Duke of Bavaria who did not want to depend on the Einbeckers for good quality beer. Today the state-owned brewery brews on the edge of the city and the former brewery of 1897 am Platz is now a function room, restaurant, and beer garden and has become popular with tourists to sample everything Munich is famous for, including Bratwurst, Lederhozen, many large liter tankards filled with beer, and ear-deafening oompah bands.

ALT MÜNCHENER DUNKELGOLD

TYPE: MÜNCHENER
ALCOHOL: 5.5% VOL.
FERMENTATION: BOTTOM

Special remarks: before blonde bottom-fermented beers became all the rage there were darker beers of this type. HB brews this Alt Münchener in accordance with the Reinheitsgebot. The mid-brown beer has a full malty taste with suggestions of roasting. It is medium-bodied and a good balance of mild hops that are drying in the finish.

MÜNCHENER KINDL WEISSBIER

TYPE: WHEAT BEER
ALCOHOL: 5.1% VOL.
FERMENTATION: TOP

Special remarks: this is an unfiltered cloudy wheat beer with a fairly malty aroma. It is lively with a sweet malty and somewhat fruity taste that becomes slightly tart and drying towards the end.

ORIGINAL HB MÜNCHEN

TYPE: MÜNCHENER
ALCOHOL: 5.1% VOL.
FERMENTATION: BOTTOM

Special remarks: a blonde lager with a hoppy aroma, brewed with an original gravity of 12.1°. Original is medium bodied with a rich taste of both hops and malt. The prolonged aftertaste is of drying hops.

SCHWARZE WEISSE

TYPE: WHEAT BEER
ALCOHOL: 5.1% VOL.
FERMENTATION: TOP

Special remarks: this "black white" is a dark wheat beer with a lively nature and fruity/malty aroma. The taste is similar with roasted notes. This post-fermenting beer is drying towards the finish.

• • •

JACOB STAUDER BREWERY, ESSEN

Production in hectoliters: –
Founded: 1867

This brewery's slogan to promote its beer is "the small personal kindness." Stauder is a small family brewery in which modern technology assists craft techniques. It takes patience, according to the brewer, to produce Pilsener the way they choose to. How much of that patience is in the family's "secret recipe".

Theodor Stauder

Jacob Stauder

Caspar Stauder

Hans Jacob Stauder

STAUDER PREMIUM PILS

TYPE: PILSENER
ALCOHOL: 4.6% VOL.
FERMENTATION: BOTTOM

Special remarks: a blonde premium Pilsener brewed according to the Reinheitsgebot. This light Pilsener has a rich aroma of hops.

• • •

STUTTGARTER HOFBRÄU, STUTTGART

Production in hectoliters: 1,000,000
Founded: 1872

A big brewery that in addition to Pilseners includes alcohol-free and several wheat beers in its range. It also owns the Moniger and Sinner breweries, both in Karlsruhe.

STUTTGARTER HOFBRÄU HERREN

TYPE: PILSENER
ALCOHOL: 4.6% VOL.
FERMENTATION: BOTTOM

Special remarks: a golden-blonde Pilsener with a quite hoppy aroma. There are hops in the taste too with underlying malt and it is medium-bodied. The aftertaste is of hops and is slightly drying.

STUTTGARTER HOFBRÄU PILSNER

TYPE: PILSENER
ALCOHOL: 4.9% VOL.
FERMENTATION: BOTTOM

Special remarks: a light-blonde Pilsener with sharply hoppy aroma. The taste is initially of malt but quickly becomes fairly bitter. The aftertaste is bitter but not drying.

• • •

TUCHER BRÄU, NUREMBERG

Production in hectoliters: 1,500,000
Founded: 1672

In addition to Tucher beers they also produce Ledere, Patrizier, Grüner, Zirndorfer, Humbser, and Hürner.

TUCHER BAJUVATOR

TYPE: MALT LAGER/DOUBLE BOCK
ALCOHOL: 7% VOL.
FERMENTATION: BOTTOM

Special remarks: a red-brown double bock malt beer with roasted aroma of malt. The taste is rounded and sweetly malty with hints of roasted malt. The robust Bajuvator has a malty finish that is slightly drying with roasted notes.

TUCHER HELLES HEFE

TYPE: WHEAT BEER
ALCOHOL: 5.3% VOL.
FERMENTATION: TOP

Special remarks: a lively cloudy blonde wheat beer with an aroma of spices. The taste is spicy with drying malt in the finish.

• • •

OBERGARIGE HAUSBRAUEREI ZUM UERIGE, DUSSELDORF

Production in hectoliters:–
Founded: 1862

Zum Uerige is a small "home" brewery with its own bar that is run by Josef and Christina Schnitzler. It was set-up in 1862 by Wilhelm Cürten and has brewed top fermented ales since that time. The alt is served here in characteristic squat straight glasses.

UERIGE

TYPE: ALE/ALT
ALCOHOL: 4.6% VOL.
FERMENTATION: TOP

Special remarks: a mid-brown ale with a rich aroma of malt and hops. The taste is malty, dry, and then quite strongly hoppy, giving way to a slightly delayed bitter aftertaste.

• • •

C. & A. VELTINS BREWERY, MESCHEDE-GREVENSTEIN

Production in hectoliters: 2,000,000
Founded 1824

A medium-sized brewery run by the Veltins family.

VELTINS LEICHT

TYPE: LIGHT BEER
ALCOHOL: 2.4% VOL.
FERMENTATION: BOTTOM

Special remarks:
Brewed in the same way as their Pilsener before the alcohol and calories are reduced by 40%.

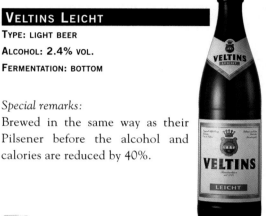

VELTINS PILSENER

TYPE: PILSENER
ALCOHOL: 4.8% VOL.
FERMENTATION: BOTTOM

Special remarks: the Pilsener is Veltins' major product. It is a pale blonde beer with mild bitterness and underlying malt. The aroma has some hops. The aftertaste is briefly bitter.

• • •

FÜRSTLICHE BRAUEREI SCHLOSS WÄCHTERSBACH, WÄCHTERSBACH, HESSEN

Production in hectoliters: approx. 50,000
Founded: 1578

A small brewery of aristocratic (Fürst = prince) background that brews a double bock, Edel Classic, Fürsten Pils Premium, and Jubiläums (special occasion) beer.

WÄCHTERBACHER DOPPEL BOCK

TYPE: MALT LAGER/DOUBLE BOCK
ALCOHOL: 7.1% VOL.
FERMENTATION: BOTTOM

Special remarks: this double bock is a strong dark malt lager with slight sweetness of malt and a firm body.

• • •

WARSTEINER BREWERY, HAUS CRAMER GMBH & CO KG, WARSTEIN

Production in hectoliters: 6,000,000
Founded: 1753

The Warsteiner brewery is one of the largest and most modern in Germany and Warstein beer is known throughout the country. The brewery's origins stem from a small brewery founded by Konrad Cramer that is one of a number run by today's company which grew slowly to its present size.

WARSTEINER PREMIUM LIGHT

TYPE: LIGHT BEER
ALCOHOL: 2.4% VOL.
FERMENTATION: BOTTOM

Special remarks: this pale blonde light beer has a slightly hoppy aroma and drying hoppy taste. The aftertaste is dry and slightly bitter. It is thin in body but quite reasonable hoppiness is found behind this. With some tongue in cheek (and losing subtlety in translation) the brewer describes this as "half the pleasure". It has half the calories and alcohol of their Premium Verum.

WARSTEINER PREMIUM VERUM

TYPE: PILSENER

ALCOHOL: 4.8% VOL.

FERMENTATION: BOTTOM

Special remarks: Warsteiner describe this as "a queen among beers." It is one of Germany's best-selling Pilseners. The pale blonde lager has a fairly hoppy aroma and a well-balanced flavor of malt and hops giving way to a drying bitter finish. The prolonged aftertaste is drying and of bitter hops.

• • •

BAVARIAN STATE BREWERY WEIHENSTEPHAN, FREISING-WEIHENSTEPHAN

Production in hectoliters: 200,000
Founded: 1040

The Bavarian State brewery in Freising is part of beer's history. It is the world's oldest brewery and linked to one of the most respected training institutes for studying beer in the world. The brewing began in 1040 under the abbot, Arnold, of the abbey founded by the order of St. Stephen in 1021. Following repeated plundering and rebuilding, the brewery was secularized in 1803 in the ownership of the Bavarian monarchs. Subsequently it

passed into the hands of the Bavarian State which is still the owner. The Königlich or royal of the former title was dropped at that time but the royal arms still appear on the label. The yeast bank established here supplies breweries throughout the world who then hang their marketing on this feature. The beers brewed here include Original, Edel Pils, Export Dunkel, Festbier, Korbinian, Kristallweissbier, Hefeweissbier Dunkel, and Hefeweissbier Leicht.

WEIHENSTEPHANER HEFE WEISSBIER

TYPE: WHEAT BEER

ALCOHOL: 5.4% VOL.

FERMENTATION: TOP

Special remarks: a golden-blonde wheat beer with aroma and taste of cloves. The taste is also tart and drying in its finish. The aftertaste is somewhat spicier.

• • •

WEISS RÖSSL BRÄU, E. WAGER, ELTMANN BAVARIA

Production in hectoliters: approx. 100,000
Founded: 1744

A small brewery with a range that includes a Pilsener, Export Lager, Oktoberfest beer, Keller, Ratsherren Dunkel, and a Märzen.

WEISS RÖSSL LEONHARDI BOCK

TYPE: MALT LAGER/BOCK

ALCOHOL: 6.6% VOL.

FERMENTATION: BOTTOM

Special remarks: a brown bock with a slightly roasted malt aroma. The taste is malty, robust, has a malty finish with some roasted bitterness.

• • •

WELTENBURG ABBEY BREWERY, KELHEIM

Production in hectoliters: – / Founded 1050

It is probably that the Weltenburg abbey brewery predates 1050 but their is written evidence of brewing at these cloisters beside the Danube since that time. The abbey works closely with the Bischofshof brewery and maltings in Egenburg.

WELTENBURG KLOSTER ASAM-BOCK

TYPE: MALT LAGER/BOCK
ALCOHOL: 6.5% VOL.
FERMENTATION: BOTTOM

Special remarks: this is a dark bock with a dark red glint. It is a full-bodied and rich beer with a roasted malt aroma. The taste is complex malt and hops drying slightly in the finish and an aftertaste of hops.

• • •

WERNESGRÜNER BREWERY, WERNESGRÜN, SAXONY

Production in hectoliters: 800,000/ Founded 1436

The brewery in Wernesgrün takes 1436 as its founding year because this is when the two Schor brothers were granted brewing rights. This former East German brewer mainly produces Pils Legende.

WERNESGRÜNER PILS LEGENDE

TYPE: PILSENER
ALCOHOL: 4.9% VOL.
FERMENTATION: BOTTOM

Special remarks: this pale blonde Pilsener has an aroma and flavor of hops, becoming bitter and dry in the finish before a dry and prolonged bitter aftertaste.

• • •

M.C. WIENINGER BREWERY, TEISENDORF

Production in hectoliters: – / Founded 1666

This brewery has been in the hands of the Wieninger family that still runs it since 1813. It brews with water from its own wells. In addition to the Hell there is a blonde bock and dark robust Impulsator.

WIENINGER HELL

TYPE: HELLES
ALCOHOL: 4.9% VOL.
FERMENTATION: BOTTOM

Special remarks: brewed with an original gravity of 11.5°. It is a blonde, slightly sweet malty lager with an aroma of malt and medium in body. It dries towards its finish and has an aftertaste of hops.

• • •

ZOLLER-HOFF BREWERY, GRAF-FLEISCHHUT, SIGMARINGEN

Production in hectoliters:– / Founded 1845

Family brewery founded and run since 1845 by descendants of Count Fidelis.

FIDELIS HEFE WEIZEN

TYPE: WHEAT BEER
ALCOHOL: 4.9% VOL.
FERMENTATION: TOP

Special remarks: an amber wheat beer named after the founder of the family brewery. It has a slight aroma of banana and a dry and malty taste with hints of spice. It is tart and lively.

SPEZIAL-EXPORT

TYPE: EXPORT LAGER
ALCOHOL: 5.5% VOL.
FERMENTATION: BOTTOM

Special remarks: this is a blonde lager with an aroma of hops and mildly hoppy taste, with some sweet malt and a prolonged aftertaste of hops.

COUNTRY The Netherlands

The Netherlands is a relatively small country which consequently does not really have a national type of beer, having adopted beers from the countries almost surrounding it. Pilsener or pils accounts by far for most beer consumption and this comes mainly from large breweries. The various brands of Pilsener are supplied to bars and for home consumption by Heineken, Bavaria, Grolsch, and the Belgian Interbrew. Being neighbors in the south with Belgium, The Netherlands have adopted a number of Belgian beers and some Dutch brewers have added these to the product range. Hence companies like Interbrew provide kriek (cherry lambic), abbey beers, witbier (white beer/wheat beer) and Palm de Belgische ale has gained a firm foothold in the country. The average Dutch person drinks about eighty-five liters and can choose them from a fairly broad range in specialist outlets which may provide a selection of one to six hundred different beers. Alongside the big brewers there is a minor role for a few smaller breweries that often supply first-class specialty beers, although generally they concentrate on their locality.

3 HORNE, KAATSHEUVEL

Production in hectoliters: 400
Founded: **1991**

Close to the largest Dutch amusement park there is another source of pleasure: not least for the brewer himself, who – only constrained by the limitations of time – brews an enormous selection of different beers. Sjef Groothuizen brews his beer more or less single-handedly, receives guests in his tasting rooms alongside, and keeps himself active with his other love of trying to find ways to improve and simplify brewing. Few breweries of this size will possess a closed cooling circuit to cool the wort. This is environmentally friendly and saves time. Other expensive possessions are the three brewing coppers of 3 Horne. They were recovered from a soft drinks producer and Groothuizen has converted them from steam to gas-fired heating. For fermentation he uses plastic containers because he finds they are less susceptible to infection and are easier to clean. The crushing of the malt is done with an ancient roller mill. Groothuizen uses a brewing copper for the creating the mash and the wort is them pumped to a clarification tank. The clarified wort is subsequently pumped back to the brewing copper so that the process of brewing can start. The discarded malt goes for animal feed, and the remaining yeast goes to a pigeon breeders' association. The 3 Horne brews its beers as private labels in small batches for drinks supply companies and bars. Due to its owner's enormous passion and enthusiasm, the 3 Horne can find a niche in the market in which the big boys cannot make any money.

BOCKAAR TRIPLE BOCK

TYPE: MALT BEER/BOCK
ALCOHOL: 9% VOL.
FERMENTATION: TOP

Special remarks:
a dark top-fermented triple bock with secondary fermentation. This full and sweet beer is brewed with Pilsener malt, amber malt, Munich malt, and caramel malt.

DRAKENBLOED (Dragon's Blood)

TYPE: SPECIAL TRIPLE BREW
ALCOHOL: 9% VOL.
FERMENTATION: TOP

Special remarks: Drakenbloed is brewed to order for Bockaar. It is a strong post-fermenting beer that needs to be served slowly and carefully in a spacious balloon glass so that the sediment stays in the bottle. The same patience is required for drinking. The taste is rounded and slightly sweet with spicy notes and the aroma is of coriander.

HORN'S WIT

TYPE: WHEAT BEER
ALCOHOL: 7% VOL.
FERMENTATION: TOP

Special remarks: a cloudy amber wheat beer brewed in Belgian style with orange peel and coriander. It immediately provides a mouth filled with rounded and sweet and very fruity aromas, dominated by oranges, from which the only slight hint of bitterness also seems to originate.

HORN'S BOCK

TYPE: MALT BEER/BOCK
ALCOHOL: 7% VOL.
FERMENTATION: TOP

Special remarks: a very dark unfiltered bock beer with sweet caramel taste and an aroma of roasted malt. There is virtually no aftertaste and it is best described as mellow, full, and rounded. The beer is brewed with water, hops, yeast, and Pilsener, amber, caramel, Munich, and crystal malt.

KAAT'S WITJE

TYPE: WHEAT BEER

ALCOHOL: 6% VOL.

FERMENTATION: TOP

Special remarks: a white wheat beer brewed with Pilsener malt, wheat flakes, and a mixture of fruit.

'T LEMPKE

TYPE: SPECIAL BREW

ALCOHOL: 6% VOL.

FERMENTATION: TOP

Special remarks: amber-colored special brew that ferments in its bottle. 't Lempke (the little lamp) is a sweet and fruity beer that has a taste that develops. It is brewed with water, Pilsener malt, caramel malt, hops, yeast, and oranges.

LIEMPD'S GILDEBIER ANTONIUS ABT

TYPE: SPECIAL BREW

ALCOHOL: 6% VOL.

FERMENTATION: TOP

Special remarks: brewed to order for the Guild of St. Antonius Abt of Liempd. It is a top-fermented beer with secondary fermentation that is brewed using water, Pilsener and caramel malt, and Saaz and Northern Brewer hops. The yeast sediment can be poured out. The dark amber ale has a robust full taste and is medium bodied. The taste is sweet caramel.

TRIPPELAER

TYPE: SPECIAL BREW

ALCOHOL: 8.5% VOL.

FERMENTATION: TOP

Special remarks: this robust, rounded, and sweet special brew has an aroma of malt with coriander and oranges. It is brewed using water, hops, yeast, Pilsener, Munich, and caramel malt, oranges, and coriander. The cloudy amber and mellow sweet Trippelaer gives no hint of its 8.5% alcohol.

WIEGELEIR

TYPE: SPECIAL BREW

ALCOHOL: 8.7% VOL.

FERMENTATION: TOP

Special remarks: this beer is specially brewed for the Zomerlust Café in Tilburg. It contains orange peel and apricots in its ingredients.

WOLLUK BIER

TYPE: SPECIAL BREW

ALCOHOL: 6.5% VOL.

FERMENTATION: TOP

Special remarks: a robust and somewhat sweet post-fermenting beer brewed for Bockaar.

ZONDEBOCK

TYPE: MALT BEER/BOCK

ALCOHOL: 7% VOL.

FERMENTATION: TOP

Special remarks: this blonde top-fermented bock is brewed with water, hops, yeast, and Pilsener malt.

• • •

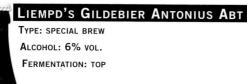

ALFA, SCHINNEN

Production in hectoliters: 60,000
Founded: **1870**

The Netherlands is almost entirely flat except for the very southern tip of the country. Here lies the province of Limburg with its rolling hills and modest valleys. The independent Alfa brewery of the Meens family lies in one of these valleys. A natural spring was found on the farm of Josef Meens and in 1870 it was decided to use the clear water to brew beer. At first this was just for the surroundings bars but in 1960 the brewery

The spring from which water is drawn for brewing Alfa's beer.

decided to enter the take home market through its own shop. Alfa is now a modern brewery that retains traditional values. It is managed by a fourth generation of the Meens family, Harry Meens, who was responsible for the technological improvements. Storage and filling of the beer is now fully automated and in order to number each bottle that leaves the brewery there is advanced laser technology. The numbering underlines that the quantity of beer produced from the natural spring water is limited. The spring is now officially recognized. The water is no longer taken from the surface as previously but is pumped from a depth of 152 meters (498 ft). This water fell on the Eiffel as rain about six thousand years ago and eventually came to rest in the thick layer of chalk from which it is now pumped. This water is protected from pollution by a thick and impenetrable layer of soil. The water is checked every six months by government scientists to maintain its recognition as an official natural spring. Alfa is only permitted to remove a limited volume of water each year to brew its beer. Alfa is the only Dutch brewer to use natural spring water. The water is not treated in any way. Since its 125th anniversary Alfa have been the first in Limburg to be suppliers to the Dutch royal family.

ALFA BOKBIER

TYPE: MALT LAGER/BOCK

ALCOHOL: 6.5% VOL.

FERMENTATION: BOTTOM

Special remarks: Alfa's bock is brewed in fall with their own spring water in limited volume, ready for the winter. The color is ruby red and the taste is sweet, giving way to a mild bitter aftertaste. It has a robust body.

ALFA EDEL PILS

TYPE: PILSENER

ALCOHOL: 5% VOL.

FERMENTATION: BOTTOM

Special remarks: Alfa's Edel Pils is a very clear Pilsener with a pure light body. The taste is hoppy, giving way to a slightly bitter aftertaste.

• • •

ARCENSE BREWERY, ARCEN

Production in hectoliters: 40,000
Founded: 1981

Part of Interbrew. The Arcense brewery brews special top-fermented beers.

ARCENER PILSENER BIER

TYPE: PILSENER

ALCOHOL: 5% VOL.

FERMENTATION: BOTTOM

Special remarks: brewed with water, hops, barley malt, and wheat malt. This golden blonde Pilsener has a firm white head. The taste combines malt and hops. The body is fairly firm. There is mild and drying bitterness towards the finish.

HET ELFDE GEBOD

TYPE: SPECIAL BREW

ALCOHOL: 7% VOL.

FERMENTATION: TOP

Special remarks: this golden-blonde top-fermented beer has a somewhat sweet aroma. The taste is also sweet, the body is firm, and the aftertaste is of bitter hops. A well-balanced beer with a sensation of warm alcohol in the mouth.

HERTOG JAN BOCKBIER

TYPE: MALT BEER/BOCK

ALCOHOL: 6.5% VOL.

FERMENTATION: TOP

Special remarks: this fall-time bock is a ruby-red top-fermenting beer with ingredients including water, barley malt, hops, and caramel. It has a slightly fruity and sweet aroma of caramel and the taste is sweet caramel with a somewhat bitter aftertaste. The body is firm and rounded.

HERTOG JAN DUBBEL

TYPE: SPECIAL BREW

ALCOHOL: 7% VOL.

FERMENTATION: TOP

Special remarks: this "double" is a firm-bodied brown top-fermented beer with secondary fermentation. The aroma is sweet and the taste too is sweet with underlying malt. The aftertaste is quite bittersweet. Brewed with water, barley malt, yeast, hops, candy sugar, and caramel. The sediment must remain in the bottle when pouring.

HERTOG JAN GRAND PRESTIGE

TYPE: BARLEY WINE

ALCOHOL: 10% VOL.

FERMENTATION: TOP

Special remarks: the brewery claims this is the strongest beer brewed in The Netherlands. At 10% there are a number of other claimants for the title and I think it better to strive for the title "The Netherland's best beer." Sweet alcohol comes to the fore in both the aroma and taste. The aftertaste is quite bittersweet.

JANNEKE

TYPE: BELGIAN ALE

ALCOHOL: 5.4% VOL.

FERMENTATION: TOP

Special remarks: named for the reddish love of Duke Jan I of Brabant and Limburg, Janneke Pijlijser. It is brewed using water, barley malt, unmalted grain, yeast. and hops. It has a quite fruity aroma and slightly sweet fruity taste with underlying hops.

HERTOG JAN MEIBOCK

TYPE: MALT BEER/BOCK

ALCOHOL: 7% VOL.

FERMENTATION: TOP

Special remarks: a golden blond spring beer with a sweet malty aroma. The body is firm and the aftertaste is sweet with some hoppiness.

LIEVE ROYALE

TYPE: SPECIAL BREW

ALCOHOL: 6% VOL.

FERMENTATION: TOP

Special remarks: a darker blonde top-fermented beer of a robust nature. The taste is mildly malty and a touch tart fruity with underlying hops.

HERTOG JAN TRIPEL

TYPE: TRIPLE SPECIAL BREW

ALCOHOL: 8.5% VOL.

FERMENTATION: TOP

Special remarks: this strong "triple" is a top-fermented beer with secondary fermentation. The golden-blonde beer has a sweet and slightly fruity aroma with a slightly sweet taste. The alcohol warms the mouth in the finish.

WITTE RAAF

TYPE: WHEAT BEER

ALCOHOL: 5% VOL.

FERMENTATION: TOP

Special remarks: reproduction of the white beer of the former Raaf brewery of Heumen in Gelderland. It is a fresh and tart wheat beer with a cloudy pale blonde color.

• • •

BAVARIA, LIESHOUT

Production in hectoliters: 4,000,000
Founded: 1719

The Bavaria brewery lies in the center of eastern Brabant, in the village of Lieshout – or perhaps given the relative sizes it is a matter that Lieshout lies next to the Bavaria brewery. Bavaria is an independent family-run business in which the Swinkels are firmly involved in the management. The original brewery was founded by Laurentius Morees in 1719. This is a big brewery that shows signs of further growth. At the brewery site there is a mixture of efficient modern buildings and historic ones. The brewery lies alongside a canal and its barley is shipped via Aachen. The brewery has its own maltings and a further one at Wageningen. All the Bavaria beer that is sold is brewed at Lieshout, regardless of whether it is sold in Russia or to the home market. The Pilsener is the leading product but specialty beers are also brewed, a great deal of "own brand", other brands under license, and some soft drinks. While Heineken and Grolsch – the only two Dutch brewers who present any real competition for Bavaria in terms of size – mainly attempt to use atmosphere and style in their advertising, Bavaria uses humor, film stars, and footballers. Bavaria is positioned as the common man's pils and has established a strong position in its domestic market of cyclists with half crates of a dozen 33 cl bottles that are easily carried home by hand or on the back of a bike. They maintain quality but compete ferociously through pricing.

View of the exterior of the Bavaria brewery.

BAVARIA 8.6

TYPE: SPECIAL BREW

ALCOHOL: 8.6% VOL.

FERMENTATION: BOTTOM

Special remarks: a golden-blonde lager brewed with an original gravity of 17°, with crystal malt, and a small proportion of corn (maize). It has a slightly sweet aroma and taste that is rounded and firm with hints of caramel. The taste dries towards the end and becomes more hoppy. The aftertaste is bittersweet. Alcohol is readily apparent. Half liter cans are consumed in volume on the streets of Paris.

BAVARIA MALT

TYPE: ALCOHOL FREE

ALCOHOL: 0.1% VOL.

FERMENTATION: –

Special remarks: not surprisingly the taste is of malt (with wort), with a slightly bitter aftertaste.

BAVARIA MILLENIUM BREW

TYPE: PILSENER

ALCOHOL: 5% VOL.

FERMENTATION: BOTTOM

BAVARIA PILSENER

TYPE: PILSENER

ALCOHOL: 5% VOL.

FERMENTATION: BOTTOM

Special remarks: Bavaria's Pilsener has a vaguely malt aroma with mild maltiness too in the taste with very delicate hoppy finish. A very mild and neutral Pilsener.

BAVARIA TARWEBOK

TYPE: WHEAT MALT LAGER/BOCK

ALCOHOL: 6.5% VOL.

FERMENTATION: BOTTOM

Special remarks: brewed with barley malt, wheat malt, and dark crystal malt. The taste is of burnt malt. There is alcoholic sweetness, depending on temperature. It is a fairly dry bock.

MOREEKE

TYPE: SPECIAL BREW

ALCOHOL: 5% VOL.

FERMENTATION: TOP

Special remarks: name after the brewery's founder, Laurentius Morees. An pale amber top-fermented beer with a quite fruity aroma and mild sweet taste of malt. The drying aftertaste is of bitter hops with a touch of fruit. The body is thin to medium.

• • •

DE GANS BREWERY, GOES

Production in hectoliters: 100
Founded: 1988

A microbrewer situated in the Goes recreation park "De Hallands Hoeve" in which a number of old crafts are performed within reproduction "historical" buildings. The beers are brewed by craft means and continue to ferment in the bottle which can generally be kept for some years if kept cool and dark.

GANZE BIER

TYPE: ALE
ALCOHOL: 5.5% VOL.
FERMENTATION: TOP

Special remarks: a pale amber ale with secondary fermentation. The yeast sediment has to be left in the bottle when pouring. The label indicates the date of bottling and that this developing beer can be kept for at least one year. It has a quite sweet taste with hints of spice and an aftertaste of bitter hops. The aroma is spicy.

GANZE BOKBIER

TYPE: MALT BEER/BOCK
ALCOHOL: 7.5% VOL.
FERMENTATION: TOP

Special remarks: a robust dark top-fermented bock with secondary fermentation. The yeast sediment must not be poured out. The taste is mainly of caramel sweetness with hints of burnt malt and there is a warm sensation in the mouth.

KERSTBIER

TYPE: SPECIAL BREW
ALCOHOL: 10% VOL.
FERMENTATION: TOP

Special remarks: De Gans brews this Christmas beer that undergoes secondary fermentation for the colder days. Ingredients are tap water, Pilsener, amber, and caramel malt, unmalted wheat, rice, corn (maize), oats, brown sugar, whole hops, coriander, grains of Paradise, Curacao peel, and beer yeast.

MANEBLUSSERTJE
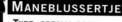

TYPE: SPECIAL BREW
ALCOHOL: 6.5% VOL.
FERMENTATION: TOP

Special remarks:
a beer with secondary fermentation in its bottle and a taste that develops. Pour carefully to leave the sediment behind.

ZOMER BOKBIER

TYPE: MALT BEER/BOCK
ALCOHOL: 7% VOL.
FERMENTATION: TOP

Special remarks: summer bock is an amber top-fermented beer with secondary fermentation. Taste is mainly sweet caramel with firm and rounded body.

ZOT MANNEKE

TYPE: SPECIAL BREW
ALCOHOL: 10% VOL.
FERMENTATION: TOP

Special remarks:
a robust top fermented beer with a taste that improves with age.

DE HALVE MAAN, HULST

Production in hectoliters: –
Founded: 1990

This small microbrewery in Zeeland is sited in a former granary. The Halve Maan is a typical of home brewing that has got out of hand. A former copper from Artois of Louvain is used for brewing. The beers include Zeeuwsche Witte (white beer), Dobbele Java, Zeeuws Vlegelbier, Zondebock, and Grof Geschut.

SINT CHRISTOFFEL, ROERMOND

Production in hectoliters: 4,000
Founded: 1986

St. Christoffel is one of the Dutch microbreweries that prefers to produce small batches of high quality beer rather than large volume. The two beers from this small brewery are both bottom fermented and are neither sterilized or pasteurized. The owner and brewer Leo Brand brews according to the Reinheitsgebot.

CHRISTOFFEL BLOND

TYPE: PILSENER
ALCOHOL: 5% VOL.
FERMENTATION: BOTTOM

Special remarks: this blonde Pilsener has a robust taste of bitter hops that is prolonged. The beer's character changes over time through the yeast sediment that remains through not filtering.

CHRISTOFFEL ROBERTUS

TYPE: DUNKEL
ALCOHOL: 6% VOL.
FERMENTATION: BOTTOM

Special remarks:
a red/amber lager brewed in the Münchener style. Firm bodied with taste of sweet malt and slightly bitter aftertaste.

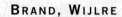

BRAND, WIJLRE

Production in hectoliters: 500,000
Founded: 1340

This brewery has a long history dating back to 1340. The Brand family only became associated in 1871 when former railroad builder Egmond Brand took over the brewery in Wijlre. The brewery has been owned by Heineken since 1989 but the Brand brewery has been allowed considerable independence and a descendant of the Brand family, Thijs Brand is still a director. Brand has the advantage of its own Limburg water that is pumped up from beneath the brewery. Brand uses Saaz, Tettnang, Hersbrucker, and Spalt hops. The beers are not pasteurized and can easily pass through the hoops of the Reinheitsgebot. The beers include Imperator, Meibock, Dubbelbock, and Oud Bruin.

BRAND PILSENER

TYPE: PILSENER
ALCOHOL: 5% VOL.
FERMENTATION: BOTTOM

Special remarks: a mild and neutral blonde Pilsener with slightly hoppy aroma and medium body. The aftertaste is of bitter hops.

BRAND SYLVESTER

TYPE: SPECIAL BREW

ALCOHOL: 7.5% VOL.

FERMENTATION: TOP

Special remarks:
copper-colored top fermented beer with secondary fermentation in its bottle with a sweet and slightly fruity aroma and sweet taste. Firm and rounded in body it has a fairly bitter aftertaste. Brewed with water, barley malt, hops, and yeast.

BRAND UP

TYPE: PILSENER

ALCOHOL: 5.5% VOL.

FERMENTATION: BOTTOM

Special remarks: UP stands for urtyp Pilsner or original Pilsener. The robust hops recall the original type of Pilsener. This blonde pils has a medium body and aroma of hops. The taste is initially of malt but becomes mildly bitter and then bitter and the bitterness endures.

• • •

'T IJ BREWERY, AMSTERDAM

Production in hectoliters: 1,500
Founded: 1984

A small microbrewery with a place for tasting its brews, named after Amsterdam's main waterway.

BOCKBIER

TYPE: MALT BEER/BOCK

ALCOHOL: 6.5% VOL.

FERMENTATION: TOP

Special remarks: the dark brown bock from this Amsterdam brewer has a somewhat sweet fruity aroma and slightly bittersweet taste. The aftertaste

is bittersweet. It is neither filtered or pasteurized and ferments in its bottle.

COLUMBUS

TYPE: SPECIAL BREW

ALCOHOL: 9% VOL.

FERMENTATION: TOP

Special remarks: a top-fermented beer with secondary fermentation. A strong unpasteurized and unfiltered light brown beer with a sweet fruity aroma and ditto taste. The aftertaste is slightly bitter.

NATTE

TYPE: SPECIAL BREW

ALCOHOL: 6.5% VOL.

FERMENTATION: TOP

Special remarks:
a post-bottling fermenting top-fermented dark brown beer with a sweet taste of caramel and roasting. The aftertaste is bitter.

PLZEŇ

TYPE: PILSENER

ALCOHOL: 5% VOL.

FERMENTATION: BOTTOM

Special remarks: a blonde bottom-fermented Pilsener with secondary fermentation in its bottle. It has a quite fruity/malty aroma and bitter taste and aftertaste. Medium-bodied; the sediment must be left in the bottle when pouring.

STRUIS

TYPE: SPECIAL BREW

ALCOHOL: 9% VOL.

FERMENTATION: TOP

Special remarks: this robust and dark post-fermenting beer is neither filtered or pasteurized. Struis has a quite fruity aroma and a sweet taste. The firm body is combined with a warm sensation in the mouth.

VLO SPECIALE

TYPE: SPECIAL BREW

ALCOHOL: 7% VOL.

FERMENTATION: TOP

Special remarks: a secondary fermentation top-fermented beer brewed for Bierkoning of Amsterdam. It has a bittersweet taste and bitter aftertaste. The aroma is of sweet fruit.

ZATTE

TYPE: SPECIAL TRIPLE BREW

ALCOHOL: 8% VOL.

FERMENTATION: TOP

Special remarks: a robust secondary fermentation golden-blonde beer. An aroma of fruit and malt and malty taste. The aftertaste is of bitter hops.

• • •

BUDELSE BEER BREWERY, BUDEL

Production in hectoliters: 20,000
Founded: 1870

A small independent brewery with the Aarts family as management and brewer.

BATAVIER

TYPE: BELGIAN ALE

ALCOHOL: 5% VOL.

FERMENTATION: TOP

Special remarks: an amber ale that is slightly fruity and sweet with some hops in the finish.

BUDELS BOCK

TYPE: MALT LAGER/BOCK

ALCOHOL: 6.5% VOL.

FERMENTATION: BOTTOM

Special remarks: a ruby-red seasonal beer with a sweet aroma. The taste is bittersweet and succeeded by a fairly bitter aftertaste. Firm bodied.

BUDELS PILS

TYPE: PILSENER

ALCOHOL: 5% VOL.

FERMENTATION: BOTTOM

Special remarks: a mild and slightly sweet malty Pilsener with modest hops that has been brewed for around 125 years.

CAPUCIJN

TYPE: SPECIAL BREW

ALCOHOL: 6.5% VOL.

FERMENTATION: TOP

Special remarks: a ruby-red abbey beer with a sour fruity aroma and bitter taste and prolonged bitter aftertaste; firm bodied.

DE DRIE RINGEN BREWERY, AMERSFOORT

Production in hectoliters: 1,500

Founded: 1989

Independent microbrewery.

PAREL

TYPE: SPECIAL BREW

ALCOHOL: 6% VOL.

FERMENTATION: TOP

Special remarks: this "pearl" is a blonde top-fermented ale with a slightly malty aroma and vaguely malty taste. The aftertaste is slightly bitter.

• • •

BOKBIER

TYPE: MALT BEER/BOCK

ALCOHOL: 6.5% VOL.

FERMENTATION: TOP

Special remarks: this dark fall bock has a secondary fermentation in its bottle. It has a sweet aroma and sweet caramel taste becoming more bitter in the finish with a prolonged aftertaste. It is firm bodied and rounded.

DE DRIE KRUIZEN BREWERY, WESTMAAS

Production in hectoliters: 1,000

Founded: 1991

The brewer rents this brewery.

MEIBOK

TYPE: MALT BEER/BOCK

ALCOHOL: 6.5% VOL.

FERMENTATION: TOP

Special remarks: this top-fermented secondary fermentation bock is brewed for spring consumption.

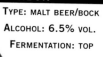
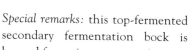

KARTHUIZER DUBBEL

TYPE: SPECIAL BREW

ALCOHOL: 6.5% VOL.

FERMENTATION: TOP

Special remarks: this "Carthusian" abbey-style beer is a brown top-fermented ale with secondary fermentation. Brewed with caramel malt and candy sugar. There is sweet caramel in both the aroma and taste. Firm and rounded in body.

• • •

VEENS NAT

TYPE: SPECIAL BREW

ALCOHOL: 5% VOL.

FERMENTATION: TOP

Special remarks: golden-blonde top-fermented beer with slightly fruity aroma and taste.

• • •

DE KROON BREWERY, OIRSCHOT

Production in hectoliters: 15,000
Founded: 1627

In the heart of the Brabant countryside lies the old village of Oirschot. When De Kroon brewery opened its doors there were some thirteen breweries in the village but this old family business is now the sole survivor, still partly housed in historic buildings. The gasthaus in particular from which tours begin, radiates ancient atmosphere. The brewery itself is a mixture of modern technique and craftsman-like ambiance. De Kroon still uses a copper "kettle" and the water comes from the breweries own well from rainwater won from the sandy soil. Fermentation takes place in tall open vessels which the brewer insists imparts much of the character to his beer. The storing or lagern is done in huge horizontal steel tanks. The brewery has a modern filling line for the casks but for bottling the beer is taken to Lieshout where part-owner Bavaria completes the task.

Bavaria has held a fifty percent interest since 1997 and has invested in both management and organization. The family concern takes advantage of the Bavaria connection and will probably do so further but continues to be an independent brewery. One advantage of the change has been the improved image to go with national awareness and availability. New labels and crates are part of this process. The brewery concentrates on just five beers. In addition to a Pilsener, there is Kroon Bokbier, Lentebock, Oirschots Witbier, and Oud Bruin.

KROON PILSENER

TYPE: PILSENER
ALCOHOL: 5% VOL.
FERMENTATION: BOTTOM

Special remarks: a deep golden-blonde Pilsener with fresh aroma of grain. The sensation in the mouth is quite full with mildly bitter taste and delicate hints of malt. The aftertaste is prolonged and robust bitterness.

• • •

DE LEEUW BREWERY, VALKENBURG, LIMBURG

Production in hectoliters: 150,000
Founded: 1886

One of the still independent breweries of Limburg is De Leeuw of southern Limburg's Valkenburg. The brewery has over 110 years experience. The founder was a German, Wilhelm Dittman who was sent out by the Aachner Export Brauerei to find a suitable place to set up a new brewery. This was found in a former gunpowder works with its ancient waterwheel that is still in existence. He established the Valkenburgsche Leeuwenbrouwerij Dittman & Sauerländer Actien Maatschappij. Leeuwenbrouwerij is the Dutch equivalent of the German Löwenbräu, which is a prominent name in Germany. The brewery passed into Dutch ownership in 1920 and changed its name to Bierbrouwerij de Leeuw. The beers produced are mainly drunk locally but are available throughout The Netherlands. The water comes from their own well at a depth of 140 meters.

JUBILEEUW

TYPE: LAGER
ALCOHOL: 5% VOL.
FERMENTATION: BOTTOM

Special remarks: brewed to commemorate the centennial of the brewery in 1986. It is a pale amber lager with aroma of malt and slightly bitter finish. It is not pasteurized and is best drunk from a balloon glass,

LEEUW BOCKBIER

TYPE: MALT LAGER/BOCK
ALCOHOL: 6.5% VOL.
FERMENTATION: BOTTOM

Special remarks: this ruby-red bock is not pasteurized and is best enjoyed in a special bock

glass at a temperature of 7–9°C (44.6–48.2°F). This rounded and slightly sweet beer is produced from dark malt with the brewery's own well water. it has a bitter aftertaste.

LEEUW DORTMUNDER

TYPE: EXPORT LAGER/DORTMUNDER
ALCOHOL: 6.5% VOL.
FERMENTATION: BOTTOM

LEEUW MEIBOCK

TYPE: MALT BEER/BOCK
ALCOHOL: **6.5% VOL.**
FERMENTATION: BOTTOM

Special remarks: an unpasteurized spring bock.

LEEUW OUD BRUIN

TYPE: OLD BROWN
ALCOHOL: **3.5% VOL.**
FERMENTATION: BOTTOM

LEEUW PILSENER

TYPE: PILSENER
ALCOHOL: **5% VOL.**
FERMENTATION: BOTTOM

Special remarks: Leeuw Pilsener is not pasteurized and has a neutral, slightly sweet taste. It is brewed with water from the brewery's well and has a long period of conditioning.

LEEUW VALKENBURG WITBIER

TYPE: WHEAT BEER
ALCOHOL: **4.8% VOL.**
FERMENTATION: TOP

Special remarks: brewed with the brewery's own water. It is bottled without filtering and retains its natural cloudiness. The brewer advises holding the bottle upside down before pouring so that the sediment is spread throughout the beer. Valkenburg's Wit is fruity tasting with a slightly bitter aftertaste. It is brewed with various types of wheat, barley malt, and spices. There is no secondary fermentation.

LEEUW WINTER WITBIER

TYPE: WHEAT BEER
ALCOHOL: **5.8% VOL.**
FERMENTATION: TOP

Special remarks: this more robust wheat beer is brewed specially for cold winter evenings. The pale amber top-fermented beer is unfiltered and hence slightly cloudy. This brew of barley malt, wheat, and spices is best drunk at 7–9°C (44.6–48.2°F). Hold the bottle upside down before pouring.

VENLOOSCH ALT

TYPE: ALT
ALCOHOL: **4.5% VOL.**
FERMENTATION: BOTTOM

Special remarks: the brewer claims "the only bottom-fermented alt in The Netherlands" for this mid-brown specialty. It was first brewed to mark the 150th anniversary of a bar in Venlo in 1983. It has since become a firm part of the product range. The taste is of slightly sweet malt with hints of roasted malt. The aroma is somewhat sweet caramel and the aftertaste is slightly bitter. This alt is a mild and fairly full beer.

• • •

DE LINDEBOOM BREWERY, NEER

Production in hectoliters: 50,000
Founded: 1869

A small independent family brewery.

GOUVERNEUR

TYPE: PILSENER
ALCOHOL: 5% VOL.
FERMENTATION: BOTTOM

Special remarks: Gouveneur or governor is the title used in Limburg for the Queen's Commissioner. This is a golden-blonde Pilsener with slightly sweet and quite hoppy aroma. The taste is initially slightly of malt giving way to a drying bitter hops finish. The body is medium.

LINDEBOOM LENTE BOCK

TYPE: MALT LAGER/BOCK
ALCOHOL: 6,5% VOL.
FERMENTATION: BOOTOM

Special remarks: an amber-colored bock with a full malty aroma and sturdy, somewhat rounded body. The taste starts malty but increasingly becomes bitter and there is a warmth in the mouth.

• • •

STADSBROUWERIJ DE RIDDER, MAASTRICHT

Production in hectoliters: 90,000
Founded: 1857

De Ridder was originally founded by the van Aubel brothers in the center of Maastricht on the banks of the river Maas. This ready supply of water (from which the brewing water is still drawn) was one of the reasons for the brewery's location. De Ridder is now a subsidiary of Heineken and has hence lost some of its regional character. The white beer and Vos are marketed nationally.

RIDDER MALTEZER

TYPE: EXPORT LAGER/DORTMUNDER
ALCOHOL: 6.5% VOL.
FERMENTATION: BOTTOM

Special remarks: this beer is dark gold and has a rich aroma of malt with underlying hops. The taste is modestly of malt with underlying hops, giving way to dryness. The sensation in the mouth is quite rounded with a hint of alcohol.

RIDDER PILSENER BIER

TYPE: PILSENER
ALCOHOL: 5% VOL.
FERMENTATION: BOTTOM

Special remarks: this Pilsener is not pasteurized and is popular in southern Limburg. It is blonde with a slight aroma of hops with a clean and neutral taste, giving way to a bitter aftertaste.

VOS

TYPE: BELGIAN ALE

ALCOHOL: 5% VOL.

FERMENTATION: TOP

Special remarks: Heineken developed Vos in response to the growing demand in the Dutch market for Belgian ales. Marketed with the slogan "try something different for a change, try a Vos" they aimed at the pils drinker who might like trying something "foreign" occasionally. Vos is a session beer with rather more character than the average Pilsener. It has a slightly fruity aroma with mellow, slightly sweet taste. The aftertaste reminds of bitter hops.

WIECKSE WITTE

TYPE: WHEAT BEER

ALCOHOL: 5% VOL.

FERMENTATION: TOP

Special remarks: De Ridder brews this wheat beer with water, barley malt, wheat malt, non-malted grain, hops, spices, yeast, and orange peel. The original gravity is 12.5°. Because it is not filtered its blonde color is cloudy. The name is derived from the local dialect name for the part of the city in which the brewery is situated.

• • •

TRAPPIST BREWERY DE SCHAAPSKOOI, BERKEL-ENSCHOT, TILBURG

Production in hectoliters: 40,000

Founded: 1884

"They are truly monks if they live by their own labor." This motto was the motivation for the Trappist Cistercian/Benedictine monks brewing beer. Because of the age of the monks and their other work, the beer is now brewed by lay persons but still under supervision of the monks and within the cloistered walls. The beer from De Schaapskooi is the only beer brewed in The Netherlands permitted to use the term Trappist. De Schaapskooi is the name of the brewery, the beers are sold as La Trappe, and the Benedictine abbey is Onze Lieve Vrouwe Koningshoeven (dedicated to Our Lady) near Tilburg. The brewery was taken over in 1998 by the family brewery of Bavaria of Lieshout within the rules laid down by the Belgian Trappist brewers.

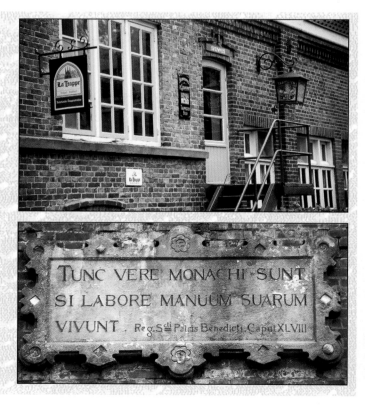

LA TRAPPE DUBBEL

TYPE: DOUBLE TRAPPIST
ALCOHOL: 6.5% VOL.
FERMENTATION: TOP

Special remarks: the "double" La Trappe is a mellow rounded top-fermented ale with secondary fermentation. The taste is bittersweet with roasted notes and the aftertaste is prolonged bitterness.

LA TRAPPE ENKEL

TYPE: SINGLE TRAPPIST
ALCOHOL: 5.5% VOL.
FERMENTATION: TOP

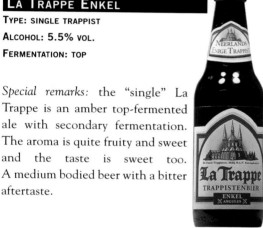

Special remarks: the "single" La Trappe is an amber top-fermented ale with secondary fermentation. The aroma is quite fruity and sweet and the taste is sweet too. A medium bodied beer with a bitter aftertaste.

LA TRAPPE QUADRUPEL

TYPE: QUADRUPLE TRAPPIST
ALCOHOL: 10% VOL.
FERMENTATION: TOP

Special remarks: one of the strongest Dutch beers. It is a very dark top-fermented ale with secondary fermentation. The aroma is sweet, the taste is bittersweet with underlying alcohol, and the aftertaste is bitter.

• • •

DOMMELSCHE BREWERY, DOMMELEN

Production in hectoliters: 650,000
Founded: 1744

Dommelsch forms part of Belgian Interbrew. The foundation year is taken as 1744 when a farmer, Willem Snieders started brewing on his farm. In addition to providing for his family's needs he also supplied local establishments and it remained like this until another Willem Snieders built a modern brewery to cope with the growing demand. As a sign that church and brewery can happily coexist, the brewery's steam engine also provided electricity for the Dommelen church. Up to the 1980s Dommelsche was predominantly a regional brewery but since that time has marketed itself nationally. Today the brewery is a modern industry employing about three hundred people.

DOMMELSCH DOMINATOR

TYPE: MALT LAGER/BOCK
ALCOHOL: 6% VOL.
FERMENTATION: BOTTOM

DOMMELSCH MALT

TYPE: ALCOHOL-FREE

ALCOHOL: 0.1% VOL.

FERMENTATION: –

Special remarks:
non-alcoholic blonde beer that is
malty and somewhat wort-like.

DOMMELSCH OUD BRUIN

TYPE: OLD BROWN

ALCOHOL: 2% VOL.

FERMENTATION: BOTTOM

Special remarks: brewed with water
from the brewery's own well, barley
malt, sugar, hops, nutritative acid,
lactic acid, and caramel. It is a dark
sweet but light-bodied beer. Its aroma
is slight sweet.

DOMMELSCH PILSENER

TYPE: PILSENER

ALCOHOL: 5% VOL.

FERMENTATION: BOTTOM

Special remarks: this blonde Pilsener
is brewed with water, barley malt,
non-malted grain, hops, and yeast.

HERTOG JAN OUD BRUIN

TYPE: OLD BROWN

ALCOHOL: 2% VOL.

FERMENTATION: BOTTOM

Special remarks: a dark but light lager
with sweet aroma and taste brewed
with water, barley malt, sugar, hops,
caramel, and lactic acid.

HERTOG JAN PRIMATOR

TYPE: PILSENER

ALCOHOL: 6% VOL.

FERMENTATION: BOTTOM

Special remarks:
a slightly stronger Pilsener with
substantially more maltiness which
increases the body. Hops are there too
but discreetly.

• • •

FRIESCHE BIERBROUWERIJ, SNEEK

Production in hectoliters: 1,000
Founded: 1985

An independent microbrewery.

US HEIT TWELS PILSNER

TYPE: PILSENER

ALCOHOL: 5% VOL.

FERMENTATION: BOTTOM

Special remarks: a blonde Pilsener with
a quite hoppy taste and bitter aftertaste
with thin to medium body.

US HEIT TWELS

TYPE: MALT BEER/BOCK

ALCOHOL: 6% VOL.

FERMENTATION: TOP

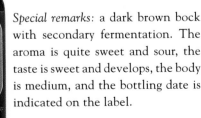

Special remarks: a dark brown bock
with secondary fermentation. The
aroma is quite sweet and sour, the
taste is sweet and develops, the body
is medium, and the bottling date is
indicated on the label.

• • •

GROLSCHE BREWERY NEDERLAND, GROENLO

Production in hectoliters: 4,500,000
Founded: 1615

The history of brewing in Groenlo dates back to 1615. The brewery did not pass into the Groen family's hands though until the late nineteenth century. In their hands it grew into a large national concern and has gained wide prominence because of its bracket-top bottles. Although expensive to produce and to bottle Grolsch maintains the century-old tradition. Grolsch beer is conditioned for six to eight weeks and is not pasteurized. The brewery supplies northern Europe and some other export markets and has allowed its brews to be brewed under license in certain countries. Since 1996 there has been a partnership with Gulpener for special beers. The name Grolsch means "from Grolle", which is the old name for Groenlo. Grolsch also brews in Enschede.

AMBER

TYPE: AMBER ALE
ALCOHOL: 5% VOL.
FERMENTATION: TOP

Special remarks: this amber top-fermented ale is not pasteurized. The aroma is of sweet malt and the taste is mildly bittersweet. Light-bodied Amber is fresh in the mouth, becoming fuller as it warms.

GROLSCH BARITON

TYPE: SPECIAL BREW
ALCOHOL: 6.5% VOL.
FERMENTATION: TOP

Special remarks: test marketed in 1998, this amber ale has a sweet malty aroma and sweet taste with hints of spices. The body is full and rounded. It is brewed with water, barley malt, hops, sugars, and sweetwood.

GROLSCH 2.5

TYPE: LIGHT BEER
ALCOHOL: 2.5% VOL.
FERMENTATION: BOTTOM

Special remarks: a golden-blonde light beer with vague aroma of hops. Mellow hops are distant in the taste. Body is thin to medium. This is a mild beer in taste and alcohol but finely balanced.

GROLSCH HET KANON

TYPE: SPECIAL BREW
ALCOHOL: 11.6% VOL.
FERMENTATION: BOTTOM

Special remarks: a golden-blonde lager with sweet alcoholic aroma. The taste is of robust apple-like sweetness. The aftertaste is also dominated by sweetness and alcohol. Het Kanon is the most of special beers produced to celebrate the centennial of the bracket-top bottle. It certainly meets demands for a strong lager.

GROLSCH OUD BRUIN

TYPE: OLD BROWN
ALCOHOL: 2.5% VOL.
FERMENTATION: BOTTOM

Special remarks: a dark-colored light beer with a sweet aroma and taste. The taste becomes bitter towards the finish.

GROLSCH PREMIUM PILSNER

TYPE: PILSENER
ALCOHOL: 5% VOL.
FERMENTATION: BOTTOM

Special remarks: this beer became well-known in part because of its 45 cl bracket-top bottles. The contents have significantly more hop character than most international lagers and has a drying finish. The aftertaste is prolonged and bitter. Medium-bodied, this Grolsch is a true Pilsener, brewed according to the original style without too many concessions to taste.

GROLSCH SPECIAL MALT

TYPE: ALCOHOL FREE
ALCOHOL: 0.1% VOL.
FERMENTATION: –

Special remarks: a golden blonde non-alcoholic beer. The aroma is of malt with a hint of carrot. The taste is malty, slightly sweet, with some bitterness in the finish.

• • •

GULPENER BREWERY, GULPEN

Production in hectoliters: 130,000
Founded: 1825

Gulpener leaves brewing for the masses to Grolsch. This brewery at the southern tip of The Netherlands started "exporting" in 1985 when it first sent beer above the great rivers that divide The Netherlands. Until then it had been just a regional brewer. This Limburg brewery now concentrates on producing special beers for niche markets. The brewery was founded on its present site in 1825 by Laurens Smeets. It is still family owned but the Smeets name has vanished through marriage to be

replaced by that of Rutten. Paul Rutten is the seventh generation at the top of the company.

CHATEAU NEUBOURG

TYPE: PILSENER
ALCOHOL: 5% VOL.
FERMENTATION: BOTTOM

Special remarks: this premium Pilsener is named after the local castle or château. It is bottled in a fine slim blue bottle with relief molding to depict its "aristocratic" heritage. The contents are a Pilsener of character with strong hoppy aroma. It is blonde in color and has a compact and firm head. The taste is of hops, finishing bitter. Medium-bodied and well-balanced, this Pilsener has a bitter aftertaste. The hoppiness of this Premium beer is strongly spicy.

GULPENER BRUNETTE

TYPE: BROWN BEER
ALCOHOL: 3% VOL.
FERMENTATION: BOTTOM

Special remarks: a dark brown beer with a light brown head and aroma of sweet caramel found also in the very rounded and mellow taste. The aftertaste is also sweet. The pretty girl on the label is not aimed at attracting men for the beer is targeted at Dutch women with its mellow sweetness.

GULPENER DORT

TYPE: EXPORT LAGER/DORTMUNDER
ALCOHOL: 6.5% VOL.
FERMENTATION: BOTTOM

Special remarks: the Gulpener interpretation of a Dortmunder is more alcoholic than the original. A higher original gravity gives this dark blonde beer a full malty taste with a finish of bitter hops. It combines really well with sweet and sour Chinese dishes.

GULPENER GIGANTEN GALLIUS

TYPE: SPECIAL BREW
ALCOHOL: 8% VOL.
FERMENTATION: BOTTOM

Special remarks: Gallius is a pale brown beer brewed with herbs and spices. There is a rich palette of an aroma with distinct hints of banana. The sensation in the mouth is of a medium body and it is an easily drunk beer despite the 8% alcohol which remains in the background. It is a well-balanced beer without dominant sweet or bitter flavor.

GULPENER GIGANTEN GLADIATOR

TYPE: SPECIAL BREW
ALCOHOL: 8% VOL.
FERMENTATION: BOTTOM

Special remarks: a pale amber beer that is rounded and sweet with alcohol more up the foreground initially but this is masked by the firm body. The aroma is of fruit and caramel and caramel is found in the taste with malt.

GULPENER KORENWOLF

TYPE: WHEAT BEER

ALCOHOL: 5% VOL.

FERMENTATION: TOP

Special remarks: the harvest mouse – known locally as korenwolf – lays in supplies of summer grain for the winter in the marl hills of southern Limburg. Gulpener has translated this into the name for a wheat beer that is brewed with four types of cereal grain grown locally and spices, elderflowers, and water from their own well. This is neither filtered or pasteurized. The result is a cloudy "white" beer with a sweet taste with hints of spice. The aroma bears the tartness of wheat and spice too. The aftertaste is dry and sharply bitter.

GULPENER PILSNER

TYPE: PILSENER

ALCOHOL: 5% VOL.

FERMENTATION: BOTTOM

Special remarks: brewed with locally-grown spring barley that is grown specially for the brewery. It is an unpasteurized Pilsener with a slightly malty taste and hint of bitterness in the aftertaste.

MESTREECHS AAJT

TYPE: BLENDED BEER

ALCOHOL: 3.5% VOL.

FERMENTATION: BOTTOM

Special remarks: this beer mix is brewed by Gulpener under the flag of the "black knight." It is a blend of lager and brown beer and has a ruby-red color and sharp apple aroma. The taste is sweet and sour.

SJOES

TYPE: SPECIAL BREW

ALCOHOL: 4.5% VOL.

FERMENTATION: BOTTOM

Special remarks: this is a blend of Pilsener and old brown to create a brown beer with a quite sweet caramel aroma. The taste is slightly sweet and that aftertaste is lightly bitter.

● ● ●

HEINEKEN NEDERLAND BV, ZOETERWOUDE

Production in hectoliters: 75,000,000

Founded: 1864

Heineken no longer brews in Amsterdam itself but the old brewery is a busy visitor's center. Today Heineken brews in Zoeterwoude, Rotterdam, and 's-Hertogenbosch, and also at its subsidiaries De Ridder and Brand in Maastricht and Wijlre. In addition to this Heineken brews in almost sixty countries at about 120 breweries. This makes Heineken second only to the US giant Budweiser in the world league. There is almost no country where you cannot drink

Heineken and it is the biggest international brand. Among its foreign subsidiaries are names like BT Multi Bintang in Indonesia, Zlat-Bazant of Slovakia, the Fischer group in France, El Aguila of Spain, Heineken, Dreher, and Moretti in Italy, Murphy's of Ireland, Calanda Haldengut in Switzerland, Zwiec of Poland, and breweries in other countries including Rwanda, the Congo, and Burundi. In addition to this Heineken has minority stakes in many other foreign breweries in virtually every part of the world. One of their great prides is Heineken Technical Services, a group of technicians who ensure that wherever Heineken is brewed (except for the one license in the UK) it is the same. They also oversee the installation of new breweries and equipment.

The Heineken story starts on December 16, 1864 when Gerard Adriaan Heineken took over Amsterdam's de Hooiberg brewery. In 1869 he employed a German brewer who knew all about brewing bottom-fermenting beer and established a laboratory to ensure quality. In 1886 a student of Louis Pasteur, named Elion, isolated a pure yeast culture which from then on became known as Heineken A yeast. This culture is still sent from The Netherlands to Heineken breweries throughout the world. Heineken was the first to land a shipload of beer after the end of prohibition in the USA which gave the brand enormous positive publicity and helped it become the best-selling imported beer. In the meantime Heineken finished off the Amstel brewery and used the brand to compete on price and to enter new markets.

AMSTEL GOLD

TYPE: SPECIAL BREW

ALCOHOL: 7% VOL.

FERMENTATION: BOTTOM

Special remarks: the strong golden-blonde Amstel lager is brewed with water, barley malt, hops, and no additives. The original gravity is 16°. Amstel Gold has created its place in the Dutch market since 1956. The aroma is hoppy and slightly fruity. The full flavor is of mellow hops giving way to bitterness. The body is robust and in balance with the taste experience. The aftertaste is of bitter hops.

AMSTEL HERFSTBOCK

TYPE: MALT LAGER/BOCK

ALCOHOL: 7% VOL.

FERMENTATION: BOTTOM

Special remarks: the ruby-red "fall" bock is sold in that season. It has an original gravity of 16.5° and is brewed with barley malts, hops, and water. The taste is above all sweet with hints of roasted malt with underlying hops found also in the aftertaste. It has a firm body and is well-rounded.

AMSTEL LENTEBOCK

TYPE: MALT LAGER/BOCK
ALCOHOL: 7% VOL.
FERMENTATION: BOTTOM

Special remarks: this amber spring bock is very much a sweet lager with a firm rounded body. It is brewed with water, barley malt, hops, and sugar. The original gravity is 16°. The aftertaste is slightly and briefly bitter.

AMSTEL OUD BRUIN

TYPE: OLD BROWN
ALCOHOL: 2.5% VOL.
FERMENTATION: BOTTOM

Special remarks: brewed with water, barley malt, sugar, caramel, and hops. The original gravity is 9.5°. The taste of this light beer is predominately that of sweet caramel.

AMSTEL LIGHT

TYPE: LIGHT BEER
ALCOHOL: 3.5% VOL.
FERMENTATION: BOTTOM

Special remarks: this pale blonde lager with a third less calories than normal Pilseners has an original gravity of 7.5°. The aroma is briefly and faintly of carrot. The taste is neutral with a hint of sweet malt.

AMSTEL PILSENER 1870

TYPE: PILSENER
ALCOHOL: 5% VOL.
FERMENTATION: BOTTOM

Special remarks: 1870 is the year the Amstel brewery was founded. Amstel brought out this more robust version of their Pilsener to commemorate this. Its original gravity is 12.5° and the bitterness units are 29 EBE instead of 21 EBE of the ordinary Amstel pils. The

aroma of this golden-blonde Pilsener is of malt with a taste of bitter hops and underlying malt. It is medium-bodied and the aftertaste is prolonged bitterness.

AMSTEL MALT

TYPE: ALCOHOL-FREE
ALCOHOL: 0.1% VOL.
FERMENTATION: –

Special remarks: this Amstel Light is brewed with an original gravity of 7°. The brewing process aims to create as little alcohol as possible. The aroma of malt has an undertone of carrot. The taste is similar. Virtually no sign of hops can be detected.

AMSTEL PILSENER

TYPE: PILSENER
ALCOHOL: 5% VOL.
FERMENTATION: BOTTOM

Special remarks: brewed with water, malted barley, and hops to an original gravity of 11.5°. Heineken regards Amstel mainly as a marketing instrument. While the Heineken brand must remain unsullied, Amstel is used to take on the competition,

although it is certainly not a Beta brand. Amstel is a blonde, neutral Pilsener with thin to medium body. Its aftertaste is briefly slightly bitter.

HEINEKEN PILSENER

TYPE: PILSENER
ALCOHOL: 5% VOL.
FERMENTATION: BOTTOM

Special remarks: the leading product of Heineken's empire. Available almost everywhere in the world and therefore the world's most international beer. It is brewed with an original gravity of 11.5°, with malted barley, water, and hops. It is fermented with Heineken A yeast, which has been in use for many years. Taste and aroma are suited to the international character. There is a vague, slightly fresh aroma and the taste is neutral, while the aftertaste is only slightly bitter and not at all intense. It is medium in body and yet Heineken is a true Pilsener with far more character than say an ice beer from which anything to which anyone might object has been removed.

HEINEKEN OUD BRUIN

TYPE: OLD BROWN
ALCOHOL: 2.5% VOL.
FERMENTATION: BOTTOM

Special remarks: brewed with an original gravity of 9.5° with malted barley, hops, water, sugar, and caramel. The taste is above all sweet.

HEINEKEN WHEAT BOCK

TYPE: MALT LAGER/WHEAT BOCK
ALCOHOL: 6.5% VOL.
FERMENTATION: BOTTOM

Special remarks: brewed with malted barley and wheat, hops, and sugar. The original gravity is 16.5° and the color is ruby-red. The taste is sweet and the aftertaste slightly bitter.

KYLIAN

TYPE: SPECIAL BREW
ALCOHOL: 6.5% VOL.
FERMENTATION: TOP

Special remarks: this originally Irish ale entered the Dutch market from Heineken's Pelforth subsidiary. The coppery top-fermented ale still has a touch of Irish about it. The aroma is soft and fruity and the taste is initially of sweet malt giving way to dry hops. The aftertaste is slightly bitter. It is brewed with an original gravity of 16.5°, malted barley, with the red color provided by Viennese malt, water, and hops.

LINGEN'S BLOND

TYPE: LIGHT BEER
ALCOHOL: 2% VOL.
FERMENTATION: BOTTOM

Special remarks: a light beer for those finding the gap between an alcohol-free beer and an ordinary Pilsener too big. It is brewed with water, malted barley, unmalted grain, yeast, and hops.

SLEUTEL BOCKBIER

TYPE: MALT LAGER/BOCK
ALCOHOL: 6.5% VOL.
FERMENTATION: BOTTOM

Special remarks: a ruby-red bock with a quite sweet aroma and taste. It has a medium and fairly rounded body.

• • •

JANTJES BREWERY, UDEN

Production in hectoliters: –
Founded: 1994

Microbrewery.

BEDAFSE VREUGDE

TYPE: SPECIAL BREW
ALCOHOL: 5.5% VOL.
FERMENTATION: TOP

Special remarks: a top fermented beer with secondary fermentation and a taste that matures.

JANTJES ZOMER BIER

TYPE: SPECIAL BREW
ALCOHOL: 5% VOL.
FERMENTATION: TOP

Special remarks: "summer beer" is top-fermented with secondary fermentation and a taste that matures.

UDENS KERSENBIER

TYPE: SPECIAL (CHERRY) BREW
ALCOHOL: 5.5% VOL.
FERMENTATION: TOP

Special remarks: this cherry beer is red and has secondary fermentation. It has a fruity aroma and a slightly sour taste with a slightly bitter aftertaste. Udens Kersenbier develops its taste with age.

• • •

MAASLAND BREWERY, OSS

Production in hectoliters: 500
Founded: 1990

This microbrewery in Oss in Brabant brews a number of top-fermented beers of fine quality. None of these beers is either pasteurized or filtered and the ingredients often include in addition to barley, yeast, hop, and water, also coriander, sweetwood, honey, and caramel. Chemical additives are entirely out of the question in the small brewery. The "Schele Os" (different ox) featured on the label of one of the beers is also mounted on a wall as a shooting trophy.

THE OLDTIMER

TYPE: SPECIAL BREW/TRIPLE
ALCOHOL: 7.5% VOL.
FERMENTATION: TOP

Special remarks: this beer is brewed with barley and wheat malt, hops, yeast, and spices. It is neither filtered or pasteurized and has a sweet taste. It is firm and rounded in body and has a somewhat bitter aftertaste.

D'N SCHELE OS

TYPE: SPECIAL BREW (TRIPLE)
ALCOHOL: 7.5% VOL.
FERMENTATION: TOP

Special remarks: this top-fermented beer is neither filtered or pasteurized and has a secondary fermentation. It is a strong triple with quite sweet malty aroma with a hint of spice and a rounded sweet taste with more hops in the finish and a bittersweet aftertaste.

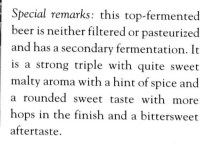

WITTE WIEVEN WITBIER

TYPE: WHEAT BEER
ALCOHOL: 5.5% VOL.
FERMENTATION: TOP

Special remarks: a cloudy blonde wheat beer with a fruity aroma. The taste is quite spicy with a sour finish and the aftertaste is bitter.

• • •

MOERENBURG, TILBURG

Production in hectoliters: –
Founded: –

A small independent microbrewery.

MEIBOK MOERENBURG

TYPE: MALT BEER/BOCK
ALCOHOL: 5.8% VOL.
FERMENTATION: TOP

Special remarks: a sweetish top-fermented spring bock with secondary fermentation.

• • •

QUIST BREWERY, EZINGE

Production capacity in hectoliters: –
Founded: 1993

This small microbrewery invites one on the label to visit them in the far north of The Netherlands by appointment. In addition to their Borgenbier they also brew a wheat beer.

BORGENBIER

TYPE: SPECIAL BREW
ALCOHOL: 5% VOL.
FERMENTATION: TOP

Special remarks:
a reddish-brown top fermented beer with secondary fermentation. It is best to leave the sediment behind when pouring. The aroma is of sweet caramel notes and the taste likewise. The aftertaste yields more hops and is slightly bitter.

• • •

SCHELDEBROUWERIJ, 'S GRAVENPOLDER

Production in hectoliters: –
Founded: 1993

A small microbrewery with a craftsman-like approach.

DE DRAAK

TYPE: SPECIAL BREW
ALCOHOL: 5% VOL.
FERMENTATION: TOP

Special remarks: "the dragon" was first brewed to commemorate six hundred years of the Hotel De Draak in Bergen op Zoom. It is brewed with water, pale malt, caramel malt, Hallertau and Saaz hops, coriander, candy sugar, and a top-fermenting yeast. The label indicates the date of bottling. This beer is not pasteurized and develops its flavor in the bottle. The sediment is best left behind when pouring. There is also an 8% version of this beer.

LAMME GOEDZAK

TYPE: SPECIAL BREW

ALCOHOL: 6.5% VOL.

FERMENTATION: TOP

Special remarks:
a beer with secondary fermentation for which it is best to leave the sediment in the bottle. The taste develops with time. It is brewed with water, pale caramel malt, Hallertau and Spalt hops, candy sugar, and a top fermenting yeast. The taste is of sweet caramel followed by a bitter finish.

MERCK TOCH HOE STERCK

TYPE: SPECIAL BREW

ALCOHOL: 8.5% VOL.

FERMENTATION: TOP

Special remarks: this strong ale from this brewery has secondary fermentation and a taste that matures. The sediment must be left in the bottle. It is brewed with water, Pilsener, amber, crystal, and caramel malt, Hallertau and Hersbrücker hops, spices, dark candy sugar, and top-fermenting yeast. The label indicates the date of bottling and drink by date. This is this brewery's strongest beer.

DE ZEEZUIPER

TYPE: SPECIAL BREW

ALCOHOL: 7.5% VOL.

FERMENTATION: TOP

Special remarks: a robust and rounded top-fermented beer with overtones of sweet malt, spice, and fruit. It is brewed with water, pale and amber malt, hops, sweet woodruff, Curacao orange peel, sugar, and top-fermenting yeast. The label indicates bottling and drink by dates.

• • •

TESSELSE BREWERY, OUDESCHILD

Production in hectoliters: –
Founded: 1994

A small independent microbrewery.

LICHT VAN TROOST

TYPE: SPECIAL BREW

ALCOHOL: 8.5% VOL.

FERMENTATION: TOP

Special remarks: Troost is the name of a Texel family that were lighthouse keepers for three generations. The beacon at the Mok bay is name after them. The beer of the same name (light of Troost) is a blonde triple with secondary fermentation.

• • •

ORANJEBOOM BREWERY, BREDA

Production in hectoliters: 2,000,000
Founded: 1538

This Breda brewery (the orange tree) is now part of Belgian Interbrew. Previously it was owned by the British Allied

Breweries. At that time it consisted of the Oranjeboom brewery in Rotterdam and the United Breweries of Breda. Previous to this the company was Skol. The Dutch offices of Interbrew are also situated in Breda.

ORANJEBOOM PREMIUM MALT

TYPE: ALCOHOL-FREE BEER
ALCOHOL: 0.1% VOL.
FERMENTATION: –

Special remarks:
a blonde non alcoholic beer with malty taste and aroma with a hint of carrot in both.

ORANJEBOOM PREMIUM PILSENER

TYPE: PILSENER
ALCOHOL: 5% VOL.
FERMENTATION: BOTTOM

Special remarks: a lightly hopped Pilsener with a neutral taste but both the aroma and taste reveal presence of hops. The draught is much milder and fuller than the bottled form with greater malt in the middle of the taste.

• • •

CLASSE ROYALE

TYPE: PILSENER
ALCOHOL: 5% VOL.
FERMENTATION: BOTTOM

Special remarks: this Pilsener is sold as the beer of De Vriendenkring brewery of Breda. It is a neutral Pilsener with brief bitter finish.

BROUWERIJ DE VAETE, LEWEDORP

Production in hectoliters: –
Founded: 1993

De Vaete is a small microbrewery created as a hobby by two home brewers. The beers include Bruin's Ale, Polderblondje, Tripel, Meibock, and Winterbier.

ORANJEBOOM OUD BRUIN

TYPE: OLD BROWN
ALCOHOL: 2.5% VOL.
FERMENTATION: BOTTOM

Special remarks: this old brown is a sweet light beer.

BOCKBIER

TYPE: MALT BEER/BOCK
ALCOHOL: 8% VOL.
FERMENTATION: TOP

Special remarks:
a robust, ruby-red top fermented beer with secondary fermentation. The taste is of sweet caramel and it matures.

• • •

Luxemburg / Luxembourg

Luxembourg is a small but wealthy country of about 400,000 people. The bilingual Luxembourgers generally drink Pilsener type beer.

With a consumption of almost one hundred liters per head their consumption places them between the Dutch and the Belgians.

BRASSERIE BATTIN, ESCH SUR ALZETTE

Production in hectoliters: 15,000
Founded: 1937

A small family-run brewery.

BATTIN EDELPILS

TYPE: PILSENER
ALCOHOL: 4.8% VOL.
FERMENTATION: BOTTOM

Special remarks: a blonde Pilsener with light to medium body. It has a neutral taste with prolonged slightly bitter aftertaste.

BATTIN GAMBRINUS

TYPE: LAGER
ALCOHOL: 5.2% VOL.
FERMENTATION: BOTTOM

Special remarks: a blonde lager with a bright white head. It is a mellow beer with a neutral to sweet taste and underlying bitterness of hops. It is lightly drying.

• • •

BRASSERIE DE DIEKIRCH, DIEKIRCH

Production in hectoliters: 160,000
Founded: 1871

Interbrew owns forty-five percent of the shares of this small Luxembourg brewery. It exports to Belgium, Germany, France, Italy, Spain, and the United Kingdom.

DIEKIRCH EXCLUSIVE

TYPE: LAGER

ALCOHOL: 5.1% VOL.

FERMENTATION: BOTTOM

Special remarks: this golden lager has a malty aroma and taste which is fairly full. The underlying taste and aftertaste are of bitter hops.

DIEKIRCH GRANDE RESERVE

TYPE: SPECIAL BREW

ALCOHOL: 6.9% VOL.

FERMENTATION: BOTTOM

Special remarks: an amber-colored beer with an orange glint. The taste is neutral going on sweet malt with some alcohol in the foreground. Caramel sweetness is modestly present in the aroma with a slightly bitter finish.

DIEKIRCH PREMIUM

TYPE: LAGER

ALCOHOL: 4.8% VOL.

FERMENTATION: BOTTOM

Special remarks: a thin-bodied golden premium lager with a vaguely hoppy aroma. The taste is slightly hoppy an balanced on the edge between sweetness and bitterness without either being in the foreground, The aftertaste is slightly malty.

• • •

BRASSERIE NATIONALE, BASCHARAGE

Production in hectoliters: 190,000
Founded: 1764

The Brasserie Nationale – also known as Bofferding – results from a merger between La Brasserie Bofferding and La Brasserie Funck-Bricher in 1975.

BOFFERDING HAUSBEIER

TYPE: LAGER

ALCOHOL: 5% VOL.

FERMENTATION: BOTTOM

Special remarks: a brewer's special that is not pasteurized. Mellow golden lager with medium body and neutral taste.

BOFFERDING LAGER PILS

TYPE: PILSENER

ALCOHOL: 4.8% VOL.

FERMENTATION: BOTTOM

Special remarks: a medium-bodied blonde Pilsener that is clear and fairly neutral with slight aroma of hops and malt. The aftertaste is slightly bitter. Brewed with some corn (maize) and conditioned for four weeks.

• • •

BRASSERIE REUNIES DE LUXEMBOURG MOUSEL & CLAUSEN, LUXEMBOURG

Production in hectoliters: 176,000
Founded: 1825

The Mousel brewery is one of the oldest in Luxembourg. It is a medium-sized brewery employing almost one hundred people in the neighborhood of Clausen. The brewery has its own water supply for its lagers. Beers for the domestic market are only filtered but those for export are also pasteurized. The lagers are conditioned for two months.

DONKLE BEER

TYPE: LAGER
ALCOHOL: 7% VOL.
FERMENTATION: BOTTOM

Special remarks:
original gravity of 17°.

HENRI FUNCK

TYPE: PILSENER
ALCOHOL: 4.8% VOL.
FERMENTATION: BOTTOM

LUXEMBOURG BLACK LAGER

TYPE: LAGER
ALCOHOL: 4.8% VOL.
FERMENTATION: BOTTOM

Special remarks: this amber lager was brewed in 1995 when Luxembourg was cultural city of Europe. It is a mild and mellow lager with a neutral to slightly caramel-malt taste. There are underlying hints of roasted malt and Black Lager is slightly dry.

ALTMUNSTER

TYPE: EXPORT LAGER/DORTMUNDER
ALCOHOL: 5.5% VOL.
FERMENTATION: BOTTOM

Special remarks: a robust full malt lager with an original gravity of 13.2°. It is golden, initially malty, slowly becoming hoppy and with a prolonged bitter hop aftertaste.

CLAUSEN

TYPE: ALCOHOL-FREE
ALCOHOL: 0.4% VOL.
FERMENTATION: BOTTOM

LUXEMBOURG EXPORT

TYPE: LAGER
ALCOHOL: 4% VOL.
FERMENTATION: BOTTOM

LUXEMBOURG LAGER

TYPE: LAGER

ALCOHOL: 3% VOL.

FERMENTATION: BOTTOM

MANSFELD

TYPE: PILSENER

ALCOHOL: 4.8% VOL.

FERMENTATION: BOTTOM

BRASSERIE SIMON, WILTZ

Production in hectoliters: 23,000

Founded: 1824

This small lager brewery was founded by Georg Pauly in 1824. It was taken-over in 1901 by Jules Simon and his partner Charles Mathieu, who left five years later. The great grandson of Jules Simon, Jacques Fontaine now keeps the fire burning beneath the coppers. The Simon brewery uses Halletau hops, well water, and barley malt and does not pasteurize its beer. For Christmas they also brew Simon Noel.

MOUSEL PREMIUM-PILS

TYPE: PILSENER

ALCOHOL: 4.8% VOL.

FERMENTATION: BOTTOM

Special remarks: the original gravity is 11.6°. This blonde Pilsener is named after the founder's family. A small proportion of rice is used in brewing plus Saaz and Hallertau hops. It is a fresh-tasting and clear beer with slightly malty taste and aroma, with some hops in the finish.

SIMON PILS

TYPE: PILSENER

ALCOHOL: 4.8% VOL.

FERMENTATION: BOTTOM

Special remarks: full malt Pilsener.

O'SCHTERBEIER

TYPE: LAGER

ALCOHOL: 5.5% VOL.

FERMENTATION: BOTTOM

Special remarks: this mellow malty golden lager is fairly full without any bitterness. It has no aftertaste and is brewed as an Easter beer.

• • •

SIMON REGAL

TYPE: EXPORT LAGER/DORTMUNDER

ALCOHOL: 5.5% VOL.

FERMENTATION: BOTTOM

Special remarks: this golden lager has a slightly malty aroma and a medium body. It is mildly hopped with a short bitter aftertaste.

• • •

COUNTRY **France**

When one thinks of France one thinks of wine. The French have made a name for their wines throughout the world. Wine is always a competing product with beer. Where wine is popular beer tends to play a lesser role and vice-versa. France once had many small breweries but with the coming of industrialization the majority of these have disappeared and only a small number of big players remain. Today there are about forty breweries, concentrated in the north and in Alsace. It is not that the French drink little beer, on the contrary. The French beer market is equal to that of the Dutch and Belgians combined. The French consume little more than forty liters per person but there are sixty million French...Only Heineken and some Belgian beers are likely to be found alongside the French Kronenbourg. The main beer drinkers are in the north and particularly in the cities. The tourists in France of course also account for some of the consumption.

A trend towards special beers is apparent and small microbreweries are on the increase, brewing

many specialties in the Belgian style and also biãre de garde. The heart of the French beer market though is Alsace. This region with its city of Strasbourg fell under German governance for a long period of time and this influence is still apparent. Names like Fischer, Adelshoffen, and Schutzenberger are perhaps unexpected in France but are to be encountered. The brewers of Alsace mainly produce Pilsener-type beer with the Reinheitsgebot having been adopted from their German neighbors.

A typical French style of beer is biãre de garde – or beer for keeping. There were many small breweries in the north of France close to the Belgian border that brewed their summer stocks of beer in the spring. Brewing in the summer was virtually impossible in the past because of the higher temperatures. With the arrival of lagers and industrialized brewing this style virtually disappeared along with the breweries but a few breweries have managed to breathe new life into this type of beer.

BRASSERIE DES 2 RIVIERES, MORLAIX

Production in hectoliters: 3,500
Founded: 1985

Small craftsman-like brewery that was originally a brewery attached to a bar.

COREFF AMBREE

TYPE: SPECIAL BREW
ALCOHOL: 6.5% VOL.
FERMENTATION: TOP

Special remarks: the amber Coreff is a top-fermented beer with secondary fermentation that is not pasteurized.

COREFF BRUNE

TYPE: SPECIAL BREW
ALCOHOL: 6.5% VOL.
FERMENTATION: TOP

Special remarks: the darker "brown" – designated as étiquette noir – also undergoes secondary fermentation. It has a fairly fruity aroma with a sweet fruit taste combined with hints of roasted malt.

• • •

GRANDE BRASSERIE ALSACIENNE D'ADELSHOFFEN SA, SCHILTIGHEIM

Production in hectoliters: 700,000
Founded: 1864

Part of the Heineken group that produces Rheingold, Tradition Adelshoffen, and Munsterbrau.

ADELSCOTT

TYPE: SMOKE BEER
ALCOHOL: 6.6% VOL.
FERMENTATION: BOTTOM

Special remarks: an amber-colored beer brewed with malt dried above a peat fire in the manner malt for Scotch whisky gets its color and flavor. The aroma is somewhat of caramel and reveals a little of the smoke. The taste is of smoked malt, not strong but distinctly present. Body is thin to medium and the mouth sensation reveals alcohol. The balance is good. This is undoubtedly a remarkable beer with a character of its own.

ADELSCOTT NOIR

TYPE: SMOKE BEER

ALCOHOL: 6.6% VOL.

FERMENTATION: BOTTOM

Special remarks: this darker version of the smoke beer has a grubby cream head. It is a mild beer with little carbon dioxide. The aroma is of smoked malt, found in the taste too. The aftertaste is slightly bitter.

• • •

Special remarks: the brewer takes six weeks over brewing this dark blonde ale. It is not pasteurized and possesses a sweet taste with sweet and fruity aroma and slightly bitter aftertaste. It is brewed solely with barley malt. The recommended serving temperature is 6–7°C (42.8–44.6°F).

• • •

BRASSERIE D'ANNOEULLIN, ANNOEULLIN

Production capacity in hectoliters: 4,000
Founded: 1905

The present head of the brewery in Annoeullin is Bertrand Lepers, a fifth generation brewer who brews two beers with much passion with help of six employees.

BRASSERIE CASTELAIN, BENIFONTAINE

Production in hectoliters: 30,000
Founded: 1926

A small craft brewery run by Yves Castelain. The biãre de garde is brewed with bottom-fermenting strains of yeast at a relatively high temperature. There are also brown and amber version of the Ch'ti and an organic beer named Jade.

L'ANGELUS

TYPE: BIERE DE GARDE

ALCOHOL: 7% VOL.

FERMENTATION: TOP

Special remarks:
blonde L'Angelus has 30% wheat. It is brewed by craft methods and is not pasteurized. The squat bottle with foil neck contains a full-bodied beer with a rounded taste and fruity aroma.

CH'TI BLONDE

TYPE: BIERE DE GARDE

ALCOHOL: 6.4% VOL.

FERMENTATION: BOTTOM

Special remarks: a blonde fruity beer with full and sweet malty taste. The aroma is sweet and fruity.

PASTOR ALE

TYPE: BIERE DE GARDE

ALCOHOL: 6.4% VOL.

FERMENTATION: TOP

CH'TI SAINT PATRON

TYPE: BIERE DE GARDE

ALCOHOL: 7.5% VOL.

FERMENTATION: BOTTOM

Special remarks: this blond beer that undergoes secondary fermentation is dedicated to the patron saint of beer, St. Arnoldus. The contents of the bottle are golden with an ivory head. The aroma is of sweet malt and the taste is sweet with mellow underlying hops. The aftertaste is sweet with a vague bitterness that is not prominent. The body is firm.

BIERE DES SANS CULOTTES

TYPE: SPECIAL BREW

ALCOHOL: 7% VOL.

FERMENTATION: TOP

Special remarks:
a blonde top-fermented beer. Sans Culottes was the name given to the French revolutionaries.

KORMA

TYPE: BIERE DE GARDE

ALCOHOL: 5.9% VOL.

FERMENTATION: TOP

Special remarks: this brew with seven different malts is described by its brewer as "a beer for the Gauls." Korma is old Celtic for barley wine. The seven different malts are each chosen for particular properties: one for color, another for aroma etc. The result is an amber ale that has a secondary fermentation with a sweet caramel aroma and sweet rounded taste. The aftertaste is somewhat drying and the body is rounded and firm.

• • •

LA CHOULETTE AMBREE

TYPE: BIERE DE GARDE

ALCOHOL: 7.5% VOL.

FERMENTATION: TOP

Special remarks: a strong amber ale with mainly malty taste and aroma with hints of caramel.

LA CHOULETTE BIERE DE MARS

TYPE: BIERE DE GARDE

ALCOHOL: 5.8% VOL.

FERMENTATION: TOP

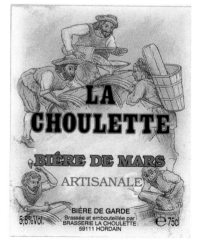

BRASSERIE LA CHOULETTE, HORDAIN

Production in hectoliters: 4,000
Founded: **1885**

The brewer and owner of La Chouette is Alain Dhaussy. From a brewing family, he took over his father's Bourgeois-Lecerf brewery in 1977 and renamed it La Chouette in 1986. He brews by craft methods with coppers dating from 1920. He sells to northern France, and also exports to the UK, Italy, and Canada.

LA CHOULETTE BLONDE

TYPE: BIERE DE GARDE

ALCOHOL: 7.5% VOL.

FERMENTATION: TOP

Special remarks: a malty and robust top-fermented ale with quite a degree of underlying hops.

LA CHOULETTE DE NOËL

TYPE: SPECIAL CHRISTMAS BREW

ALCOHOL: 7% VOL.

FERMENTATION: TOP

LA CHOULETTE FRAMBOISE

TYPE: RASPBERRY BEER

ALCOHOL: 7% VOL.

FERMENTATION: TOP

Special remarks: a craft-brewed beer supplemented with raspberry extract.

• • •

BRASSERIE DE CLERCK, PERONNE

Production in hectoliters: 5,000

Founded: –

A small craft brewery.

COLVERT

TYPE: BIERE DE GARDE

ALCOHOL: 7% VOL.

FERMENTATION: TOP

Special remarks: brewed with malt and hops from the region and allowed eight weeks conditioning at cool temperatures. It is a fairly full ale with sweet aroma of malt. The taste is mellow sweet malt and drying. The aftertaste is also slightly sweet.

• • •

BRASSERIE DUYCK, JENLAIN

Production in hectoliters: 80,000

Founded: 1922

A small family brewery headed by Raymond Duyck. It is a craft brewery close to the border with Belgium. There were once hundreds of such breweries in the north of France on farms but nothing remains of these farm enterprises. The Duyck brewery is one of the survivors and it is still sited on a farm.

JENLAIN

TYPE: BIERE DE GARDE

ALCOHOL: 6.5% VOL.

FERMENTATION: TOP

Special remarks: Jenlain was one of the first beers to create new life for the biãre de garde type of product. It is amber in color with an orange tint. The aroma is mainly of malt but with fruit. The taste is of sweet malt and fruit with underlying hops. There is tartness in the finish. The sensation in the mouth is of warmth from this firm-bodied beer.

• • •

GRANDE BRASSERIE ENFANTS DE GAYANT, DOUAI

Production in hectoliters: 200,000
Founded: 1919

The "children of the giants" brewery results from a merger of four breweries at the end of World War I. Its beers include two lagers brewed using Goldenberg and Saaz hops that are mainly for local sale.

BIERE DU DESERT

TYPE: SPECIAL BREW
ALCOHOL: 7% VOL.
FERMENTATION: BOTTOM

Special remarks: this "desert" beer is a pale blonde with flora hoppy aroma. The taste is neutral with some alcoholic sweetness. The aftertaste is of slightly bitter hops.

ABBAYE DE SAINT LANDELIN BRUNE

TYPE: ABBEY ALE
ALCOHOL: 6.2% VOL.
FERMENTATION: TOP

Special remarks: a dark abbey ale with mild fruity taste and slightly fruity aroma. It is brewed under license from the monks of the Crespin abbey.

LA BIERE DU DEMON

TYPE: LAGER
ALCOHOL: 12% VOL.
FERMENTATION: BOTTOM

Special remarks:
this "devil's beer" doubtfully claims to be the strongest beer in the world.

• • •

ABBAYE DE ST. LANDELIN TRIPLE BRUNE 8°

TYPE: ABBEY ALE
ALCOHOL: 8% VOL.
FERMENTATION: TOP

Special remarks: these dark abbey ales are the only such French beers. They were once brewed by the monks of Crespin. The beer contains water, hops, malt, but also rice and wheat. It has no secondary fermentation. The color is dark brown with a deep red glint. St. Landelin is a full-bodied and warming ale with a sweet taste. The aroma is a mixture of caramel and darker malts. The taste has hints of caramel and roasted malt. The sensation in the mouth is important with this type of beer and the Triple Brune has well-balanced dryness, alcoholic warmth, and roundness or rondeur.

BRASSERIE FISCHER D'ALSACE, SCHILTIGHEIM

Production in hectoliters: 1,200,000
Founded: 1821

Founded by Jean Fischer and known as Fischer P'cheur. It is part of the Heineken group.

DESPERADOS

TYPE: SPECIAL LAGER
ALCOHOL: 5.9% VOL.
FERMENTATION: BOTTOM

Special remarks: a golden lager flavored with tequila. Following the coat tails of the success of Latin American beers in their transparent bottles, Desperados tries to look as Mexican as possible.

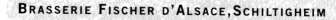

267

FISCHER TRADITION

TYPE: LAGER
ALCOHOL: 6% VOL.
FERMENTATION: BOTTOM

Special remarks: golden lager with a somewhat fruity aroma and a taste that is slightly malty and a touch fruity. The aftertaste is a little malty. The body is medium.

PELFORTH BLONDE

TYPE: SPECIAL LAGER
ALCOHOL: 5.8% VOL.
FERMENTATION: BOTTOM

Special remarks: the golden Pelforth has a slight sweet aroma. The taste is fresh, dry, and slightly of sweet malt. The sensation in the mouth is of dryness and the aftertaste is briefly of sweet malt. The body is thin to medium.

KINGSTON

TYPE: SPECIAL BREW
ALCOHOL: 7.9% VOL.
FERMENTATION: BOTTOM

Special remarks: a rum-flavored beer for a variation on the theme. Perhaps created following the success of whiskey-flavored beers. It is a strong amber beer with a taste of alcohol.

• • •

PELFORTH BRUNE

TYPE: SPECIAL BEER
ALCOHOL: 6.5% VOL.
FERMENTATION: TOP

Special remarks: this reddish-brown ale with a pelican on the label has a fruity aroma with hints of roasted malt. The taste is sweet and is increasingly towards the finish of burnt malt and bitter chocolate. The sensation in the mouth of this well-balanced beer is mainly full and mellow.

BRASSERIES HEINEKEN, RUEIL MALMAISON

Production in hectoliters: 12,000,000
Founded: —

Heineken is the number two brewer in France with large breweries in Marseille, Schiltigheim, and Mons-en-Baroeul.

SPIN

TYPE: LAGER
ALCOHOL: 7.9% VOL.
FERMENTATION: BOTTOM

Special remarks: this golden lager has a fresh neutral taste with sensation of alcohol in its finish without bitterness. The transparent bottle with its name in mirrored script enables it to be known as either Spin or Nips. Part of the web that Heineken weaves surrounding the origins so that these are known only to the brewers themselves.

BRASSERIE HENRY, BAZINCOURT/SAULX

Production in hectoliters: –
Founded: –

BLANCHE DE LA SAULX

TYPE: SPECIAL BREW
ALCOHOL: 5% VOL.
FERMENTATION: TOP

Special remarks: a blonde beer brewed with wheat and barley malt that has a secondary fermentation. The brewer says the sediment includes genuine Bavarian yeast. The cloudy golden beer is extremely lively and has a quite sweet aroma of malt and somewhat sour taste. The aftertaste is a touch bitter. It is medium in body.

LA SAULX

TYPE: SPECIAL BREW
ALCOHOL: 7% VOL.
FERMENTATION: TOP

Special remarks: a dark brown beer with ruby glint that has a secondary fermentation. It is a lively beer with a sparkling creamy-colored head. It is best poured into a large balloon glass with the sediment left in the bottle. The aroma is of malt with fruit and the taste is of sweet malt. The body is firm and the sensation in the mouth reveals alcohol with dryness towards the end. The brief aftertaste brings forth no new tastes.

• • •

BRASSERIE JEANNE D'ARC, RONCHIN

Production in hectoliters: 100,000
Founded: 1898

The brewery was founded in 1898 by Henri Vandamme with his partner Pierre Hovalaque. After the latter departed in 1902 his place was taken by Désiré Desruelle. The brewery passed wholly into Desruelle hands in 1906. The family name of the present owner dates back to a marriage in 1927 when Charles Leclercq took control of the brewery. Today fifty percent of the production is sold locally, thirty-five percent is sold elsewhere in France, and fifteen percent is exported to the UK, Italy, the USA, Canada, and Belgium.

AMBRE DES FLANDRES

TYPE: BIERE DE GARDE
ALCOHOL: 6.4% VOL.
FERMENTATION: BOTTOM

Special remarks: this amber biãre de garde is bottom fermented and has a fully and slightly sweet flavor with a fruity aroma.

BELZEBUTH

TYPE: ALE
ALCOHOL: 15% VOL.
FERMENTATION: TOP

Special remarks: a top-fermented beer with an improbable level of alcohol which dominates the taste and aroma together with considerable sweetness. This pale amber beer is more likely to appeal to the spirits drinker than most lager and Pilsener drinkers. The original gravity is 30.5°. Belzebuth is brewed using pale, Viennese, and amber malts and Hallertau, Brewer's Gold, Styria, and aromatic hops.

GRAIN D'ORGE

TYPE: ALE
ALCOHOL: 8% VOL.
FERMENTATION: TOP

Special remarks: OG 21°. Grain d'Orge (barley) is a strong golden beer in the Flemish mold. The full and rounded taste is predominantly sweet but dominated by the presence of alcohol. The aftertaste, although not strongly so is determined by bitter hops.

ORPAL

TYPE: LAGER
ALCOHOL: 5.2% VOL.
FERMENTATION: BOTTOM

Special remarks: golden lager.

SCOTCH TRIUMPH

TYPE: SPECIAL BREW
ALCOHOL: 6% VOL.
FERMENTATION: TOP

Special remarks: a brown beer with a deep red glint made according to Flemish tradition. Scotch Triumph has a full sweet taste with hints of caramel, a rich aroma, and a warming sensation in the mouth. One real disadvantage is that the bottle is too small.

• • •

BRASSERIES KRONENBOURG SA, STRASBOURG

Production in hectoliters: 25,000,000 (entire group)
Founded: 1664

Kronenbourg is France's largest brewer, owned by the food conglomerate Danone. The group includes Italian Peroni, Belgian Aken-Maes, SCBK in the Congo, and the Spanish breweries of Mahou and San Miguel. The brewery was first established in 1664 by Jérome Hatt.

1664

TYPE: LAGER

ALCOHOL: 6.3% VOL.

FERMENTATION: BOTTOM

Special remarks: named for the founding year of the brewery, abbreviated in French to soixante quatre. It is a blonde lager with light aroma and taste of malt with some hops in the finish. The aftertaste is drying and hoppy.

BLANCHE HERMINE

TYPE: WHEAT BEER

ALCOHOL: 4% VOL.

FERMENTATION: TOP

Special remarks: a pale wheat beer with secondary fermentation. The beer should be served chilled. It has a fresh and fruity aroma. The taste is initially quite malty with suggestions of fruit becoming drying and tart towards the finish. The aftertaste is quite tart.

KRONENBOURG

TYPE: PILSENER

ALCOHOL: 5% VOL.

FERMENTATION: BOTTOM

Special remarks: a neutral blonde Pilsener of an international character with slightly malt taste and modestly hoppy aftertaste.

• • •

DUCHESSE ANNE

TYPE: SPECIAL BREW

ALCOHOL: 6.5% VOL.

FERMENTATION: TOP

Special remarks: Anne de Bretagne was daughter of Duke Francois II in fifteenth century France. This beer is golden in color and has a fresh but sweet scent. The taste is of sweet malt accompanied by a prickling and warm sensation in the mouth. Honey is added to the bottle to cause secondary fermentation.

CERVOISERIE DU MANOIR DE GUERMAHIA, BRASSERIE LANCELOT, ST. SERVANT SUR OUST

Production in hectoliters: 2,000

Founded: 1990

A small craft brewery in Brittany with Belgian-style beers, founded by Bernard Lancelot in an old manor.

BIERE LANCELOT

TYPE: SPECIAL BREW

ALCOHOL: 6% VOL.

FERMENTATION: TOP

Special remarks: Lancelot is an amber malty ale bottled with live yeast. The aroma of malt and fruit is succeeded by a full-blown taste of sweet malt with alcoholic warmth in the finish. Hence Lancelot dries the mouth somewhat. There are underlying Saaz hops to be found. It is very lively when opened but this is not apparent once poured. The brewer describes it as a "Trappist type."

CERVOISE LANCELOT

TYPE: SPECIAL BREW
ALCOHOL: 6% VOL.
FERMENTATION: TOP

Special remarks: this is an "old type beer from the time of the Gauls", brewed with barley malt and given its aroma by seven different herbs and a little honey. It is not filtered and careful pouring is required to leave the sediment behind. It is dark amber topped by a creamy head. It is a fine rounded beer with full-blooded taste of sweet malt and a sweet and fruity aroma. The aftertaste is rather bitter and also slightly tart. The brewer's warning not to attempt more than two or three glasses is a challenge perhaps?

TELENN DU

TYPE: SPECIAL BREW
ALCOHOL: 4.5% VOL.
FERMENTATION: TOP

Special remarks: a dark beer brewed with barley malt and some buckwheat that undergoes secondary fermentation. Once there was a harp on the label of Telenn Du (which is Breton for "black harp") but Guinness did not appreciate this.

• • •

BRASSERIE DE SAINT OMER, ST. OMER

Production in hectoliters: 1,500,000
Founded: 1985

This brewery forms part of the Heineken group. Its brews include Sembrau, Blonderbrau, and Biãre de St. Omer

BRASSERIE DE ST.-SYLVESTRE, ST.-SYLVESTRE-CAPEL

Production in hectoliters: 20,000
Founded: –

A small brewery in the French part of Flanders.

GAVROCHE

TYPE: SPECIAL BREW/ALE
ALCOHOL: 8.5% VOL.
FERMENTATION: TOP

Special remarks: a top-fermented ale with secondary fermentation. In the Belgian way the sediment needs to be left in the bottle when pouring. Once poured it is a coppery ale with an ivory head. Gavroche has an intense and very fruity aroma. This is a lively ale with quite sweet taste with hints or oranges and some floral notes. The finish is drying and the aftertaste is quite bittersweet.

• • •

BRASSERIE METEOR, HOCHFELDEN

Production in hectoliters: 400,000
Founded: 1640

The Meteor brewery has been in the hands of the Haag family since 1844. The brewery was established in an inner courtyard of former cloisters around 1640. Meteor's brews include Meteor, Mortimer, and Ackerland in different versions.

METEOR DE NOËL

TYPE: SPECIAL CHRISTMAS BEER
ALCOHOL: 5.8% VOL.
FERMENTATION: BOTTOM

Special remarks: Christmas beer flavored with oranges.

• • •

BRASSERIE NOUVELLE DE LUTECE BNL, BONNEUIL SUR MARNE

Production in hectoliters: –
Founded: –

LUTECE

TYPE: BIERE DE GARDE
ALCOHOL: 6.4% VOL.
FERMENTATION: TOP

Special remarks: an amber top-fermented beer with a sweet and slightly fruity aroma. The taste is of sweet caramel with hops at the finish. The aftertaste is drying bitterness of hops. Lutãce was the Roman name for Paris.

• • •

BRASSERIE PIETRA SA, FURIANI CORSICA

Production in hectoliters: 50,000
Founded: 1992

A small craft brewery set-up in 1992 by Dominique and Armelle Siaelli. This small eight-man brewery – named after the birth place of the founders – brews Corsican specialties.

PIETRA

TYPE: SPECIAL BREW
ALCOHOL: 6% VOL.
FERMENTATION: TOP

Special remarks: an amber-colored beer with a somewhat malty aroma. The taste is neutral with a hint of malt and slightly bitter aftertaste. Some ground walnut is used in the brewing of Pietra.

• • •

GRANDE BRASSERIE DE LA PATRIE SCHUTZENBERGER, SCHILTIGHEIM

Production in hectoliters: 200,000
Founded: 1740

This still independent brewery is run by Rina Muller--Walters, making it an exceptional case in Europe of a brewery run by a woman. The Grande Brasserie de la Patrie (grand brewery of the fatherland) originated in Strasbourg but moved to Schiltigheim to avoid the flooding that regularly affect the cellars in Strasbourg. The Schutzenberg name became linked with the brewery in 1768 when Jean-Daniel Schützenberger took over the Strasbourg brewery.

COPPER

TYPE: SPECIAL LAGER
ALCOHOL: 7.6% VOL.
FERMENTATION: BOTTOM

Special remarks: this lager is brewed with pale amber malt. The restrained aroma is of malt and the taste is initially of malt followed by a bitter aftertaste. If drunk quickly this bitterness dominates but more slowly consumed – which is advisable with its 7.6% alcohol – then the taste of malt has a chance to come to the fore.

JUBILATOR

TYPE: MALT LAGER/BOCK
ALCOHOL: 6.8% VOL.
FERMENTATION: BOTTOM

Special remarks: the German influence is everywhere in Alsace and also in this double bock. The aroma of this blonde malt lager is markedly of hop flowers. The taste is well developed of malt giving way to bitter hops in the aftertaste. It is well-balanced with a firm body and a sensation in the mouth reveals the 7% alcohol.

PATRIATOR

TYPE: MALT LAGER/BOCK
ALCOHOL: 6.8% VOL.
FERMENTATION: BOTTOM

Special remarks: dark brown malt lager/bock.

TÜTSS

TYPE: ICE BEER
ALCOHOL: 4.8% VOL.
FERMENTATION: BOTTOM

Special remarks: a blonde ice beer with fresh mild taste of malt. It is quite full but mainly neutral. The bottle is wrapped in white foil.

• • •

BIERE SUR SCHUTZENBERGER

TYPE: SPECIAL BREW
ALCOHOL: 6.8% VOL.
FERMENTATION: TOP

Special remarks: this golden ale has a quite hoppy aroma. The taste is mildly hoppy, giving way to a slightly bitter aftertaste. It is firm in body.

GRANDE BRASSERIE MODERNE DE TERKEN, ROUBAIX

Production in hectoliters: 600,000
Founded: 1920

This is a large cooperative brewery with a number of brews including Terken in both blonde and brown versions, Septente 5 or 75 as a biãre de garde, Ubald, Orland, and Breug.

• • •

SCHUTZENBERGER TRADITION

TYPE: LAGER
ALCOHOL: 4.6% VOL.
FERMENTATION: BOTTOM

Special remarks: Tradition is a blonde lager with vaguely malty aroma. The taste is fresh and neutral with underlying dryness. The aftertaste is slightly bitter.

BRASSERIE THEILLIER SARL, BAVAY

Production in hectoliters: 3,500
Founded: –

A small brewery run by the Theillier family. The only product is a biãre de garde.

LA BAVAISIENNE

TYPE: BIERE DE GARDE
ALCOHOL: 7% VOL.
FERMENTATION: TOP

Special remarks: an amber beer with a malty flavor. The aroma is slightly floral and the

aftertaste is of prolonged slight bitterness. It is medium-bodied.

• • •

LA COMPAGNIE DES TROIS EPIS, PARIS

Production in hectoliters: –
Founded: –

The brewery of the three "ears" of corn.

L'EPI BLANC

TYPE: SPECIAL BREW
ALCOHOL: 5.6% VOL.
FERMENTATION: TOP

Special remarks: the "white" version is an oatmeal beer with a mainly neutral taste. The aroma and taste are vaguely malty. The sensation in the mouth is sharp and lively, the aftertaste is drying.

L'EPI NOIR

TYPE: SPECIAL BREW
ALCOHOL: 5.6% VOL.
FERMENTATION: TOP

Special remarks: the "black" version is brewed with some buckwheat. It is an orange-amber beer that is slightly malty with good background of hops that is drying. It is quite thin-bodied.

L'EPI ROUGE

TYPE: SPECIAL BREW
ALCOHOL: 5.6% VOL.
FERMENTATION: TOP

Special remarks: the "red" is a mid brown beer with neutral taste and slight aftertaste of malt.

• • •

UNKNOWN/OTHER BREWERIES

GRANDE RIVIERE

TYPE: SPECIAL BREW
ALCOHOL: 6% VOL.
FERMENTATION: TOP

Special remarks: a filtered top-fermented beer brewed under the name of La Rouget/R.B.M. Perrigny. It is an amber ale with slight aroma of hops. The taste too is slightly hoppy with a drying mildly bitter aftertaste.

LA ROUGET DE LISLE

TYPE: SPECIAL BREW
ALCOHOL: 5.8% VOL.
FERMENTATION: TOP

Special remarks: a blonde top-fermented beer with secondary fermentation brewed by R.B.M. Perrigny. This amber ale has a warm sweet and slightly fruity aroma. The taste is slightly sweet and fairly neutral. The aftertaste is briefly similar.

THOMAS BECKET

TYPE: SPECIAL BREW
ALCOHOL: 6.5% VOL.
FERMENTATION: TOP

Special remarks: this amber secondary fermentation beer is bottled with some honey. Biãre de Sens is brewed by Brasserie des Champs for Valerie Gufflet of Collemiers/ Sens. It is a dark amber ale that undergoes secondary fermentation. The aroma and taste are of sweet caramel. It is a mellow but full-bodied ale with hints of roasted malt. The taste reveals fruit. The aftertaste is drying. It is well-balanced with a rounded body yet refreshing.

BRIMBEL

TYPE: SPECIAL BREW
ALCOHOL: 6% VOL.
FERMENTATION: TOP

Special remarks: brewed with black blueberries by Boissons Sofabo, Lavilledieu. It is amber in color, the taste is fruity and drying with a sour finish. The aftertaste is dry and slightly bitter.

COMBEL

TYPE: SPECIAL BREW
ALCOHOL: 6% VOL.
FERMENTATION: TOP

Special remarks: this top-fermented beer is brewed with chestnuts by Boissons Sofabo Lavailledieu. It is

amber in color with a fruity and nutty aroma. The taste is of sweet fruit but dries in the finish. The aftertaste is bitter. The body is firm.

SAINTE COLOMBE BIERE AMBREE

TYPE: SPECIAL BREW
ALCOHOL: 6% VOL.
FERMENTATION: TOP

Special remarks: brewed by Breton brewers Ste-Colombe G. Keizer of Ste-Colombe. It is a craft-brewed secondary fermentation ale that is neither filtered or pasteurized. The aroma is vaguely of malt but the taste captures the maltiness but hops predominate in the end when alcoholic warmth is also apparent. The aftertaste is slightly bitter.

SAINTE COLOMBE BIERE D'HIVER

TYPE: SPECIAL BREW
ALCOHOL: 8% VOL.
FERMENTATION: TOP

Special remarks: a specialty beer brewed by Breton brewers Ste-Colombe G. Keizer of Ste--Colombe. It is a copper-colored secondary fermentation ale that is neither filtered or pasteurized. Some homey is added at bottling, specially for winter evenings. It has a malty and slightly spice taste. The aftertaste combines bitterness with a drying sensation of alcohol.

SPELTOR

TYPE: SPECIAL BREW
ALCOHOL: **4.8% VOL.**
FERMENTATION: TOP

Special remarks: brewed by Moulin Meckert Diemer, Krautwiller. It is brewed with organic grain. The aroma is of hops, the color is pale blonde, and the taste is slightly hoppy with a very dry finish. There is a slight background of underlying malt with a hint of spice and the body is thin.

KORLENE

TYPE: SPECIAL BREW
ALCOHOL: **6% VOL.**
FERMENTATION: TOP

Special remarks: brewed by Brasserie du Canardou, Nastringues, this copper-colored ale with secondary fermentation is neither filtered or pasteurized. Its taste is of hops with hints of roasted malt. The body is firm and the aftertaste is of prolonged bitterness.

● ● ●

COUNTRY The Czech Republic

The Czech Republic is a small country in Central Europe that has played a major role in the history of beer. Like their western neighbors in Bavaria, the Czechs drink a remarkable quantity of beer. With almost 160 liters per head of population they are number one in the world league of beer drinkers. Local breweries make cheap and light alternatives that are widely consumed in volume. The alcohol content is not indicated in the Czech Republic: instead the original gravity of the wort is given. Hence a beer of 10% is not a really strong one but a light beer of around 4% alcohol by volume. The blonde lagers predominate but there are also darker beers. The Czechs are also aware of the Reinheitsgebot but do not adhere to it strictly for all their brewing. The premium export lagers generally stick to the rules because export to Germany is important.

The influence of foreign breweries is increasing in the Czech Republic and the original and authentic methods are rapidly disappearing in many places. Wooden casks are replaced with stainless steel and open fermentation vessels have largely disappeared. The quality of Czech beers remains good. They also have some renowned types of malt and hops. During the Communist rule the breweries output was solely aimed at the local needs. Beer from other areas was simply not available. The breweries are now operating much more at the entire national and also at export markets. The local character of the beer though has not completely vanished.

RODINNÝ PIVOVAR V HUMPOLCI BERNARD, HUMPOLEC

Production in hectoliters: 110,000
Founded: 1597/1991

Humpolec lies centrally in the Czech Republic on the borders of the provinces of South and East Bohemia. The original founding of the Bernard brewery occurred in 1597. It had a capacity of 2,000 hectoliters per year and by the late nineteenth century it had grown into an industrial concern and was producing 20,000 liters each year. After World War II the brewery became state owned and both quality and quantity suffered as a result of lack of investment. In 1991 the state-owned brewery was taken over by three investors, Stanislav Bernard, Rudolf Smejkal, and Josef Vávra. The brewery was then extensively renovated and its capacity increased five-fold. The brewery is now a modern concern with an eye to producing beer of good quality.

The proprietors of the Bernard brewery.

BERNARD POLOTMAVÉ PIVO 11%

TYPE: LAGER
ALCOHOL: 4.9% VOL.
FERMENTATION: BOTTOM

Special remarks: this light brown lager has a fully-developed taste of malt with underlying dryness. It is also known as Granát.

BERNARD SVĚTLÉ PIVO 10%

TYPE: LAGER
ALCOHOL: 4.5% VOL.
FERMENTATION: BOTTOM

Special remarks: Bernard's 10% is primarily a session beer. The fullness of this beer is good for the level of alcohol with a significant level of sweet malt accompanied by slight bitterness of hops. The aftertaste is briefly of bitter hops.

BERNARD SVĚTLÝ LEŽÁK 12%

TYPE: LAGER
ALCOHOL: 5.1% VOL.
FERMENTATION: BOTTOM

Special remarks: the premium beer from this brewer is the Ležák. It is a bittersweet beer with a substantial sensation in the mouth and fine underlying dryness.

• • •

BUDĚJOVICKÝ BUDVAR, NÁRODNÍ PODNIK, ČESKÉ BUDĚJOVICE

Production in hectoliters: 1,000,000
Founded: 1895

Budweiser beer is the biggest-selling name in the world but by far the majority of it originates from the USA's brewing giant Anheuser-Bush rather than this brewery. Despite this, this brewery has substantial awareness throughout the world with its beer, the name of which means "from Budweis", with people choosing to support the little guy in a David and Goliath contest.

The use of the name Budweiser has been hotly debated and subject of law suits since the start of the twentieth century. Two agreements were concluded in 1911 and 1939 which regulated the use of the name by both parties. Anheuser-Bush is prevented from using the Budweiser name in a few countries in Europe where it must call its beer "Bud." It is doubtful if this has much effect on the European beer drinker, most of whom are unaware of US Budweiser's fame in its native land. After the velvet revolution the US brewer made some efforts to take-over the Czech

company or at least to acquire a significant number of shares in order to settle the matter in its favor. The Czech government though, owner of the Budvar brewery, is entirely aware of the value of its national heritage and at present has been unprepared to do business. The Budvar brewery was established in 1895 by a group of Czech investors for reasons of ethnic pride. At that time the country formed part of the Austro-Hungarian Habsburg empire. One third of the population of Budweis at that time was German-speaking and these people had all the prominent positions. The main brewery, then known as the Budweis Brauberechtigen Burgerliches Brauhaus – now it is the Samson brewery – was in the hands of this minority. A group of Czechs established Český Akciový Pivovar (the Czech brewery Ltd), now known as Budvar. The Samson and Budvar breweries were brought under state control during the Communist regime and traces of this are still

apparent. The two breweries were separated again after 1989, with the Budvar brewery remaining in state hands. Since that time the brewery has been extensively modernized – both in terms of the production processes and the outward appearance. A considerable part of the production is exported and this was even the case during the communist times. The planned economy of the communists was pushed to one side in order to gain valuable finance. Budvar profited from this following 1989 because the Budweiser name and that of Pilsner Urquell is known abroad, unlike that of the other Czech breweries.

BUDĚJOVICKÝ BUDVAR 10%
TYPE: LAGER
ALCOHOL: 4% VOL.
FERMENTATION: BOTTOM

Special remarks: this light Budweiser is aimed at the local market. It is a thin-bodied blonde lager with vague aroma of malt and slightly sweet taste and brief drying finish.

BUDĚJOVICKÝ BUDVAR 12%
TYPE: LAGER
ALCOHOL: 5% VOL.
FERMENTATION: BOTTOM

Special remarks: this version represents the Czech town throughout the world. It is brewed with

Bohemian and Moravian barley, Saazer hops, and well water that is low in sodium. This Budweiser is a blonde lager with a medium body. The taste is slightly sweet with underlying hops. The aftertaste is bittersweet. In contrast with the beer from Pilsen, Budweiser is fuller, sweeter, and less bitter.

EGGENBERG 10%

TYPE: LAGER
ALCOHOL: 3% VOL.
FERMENTATION: BOTTOM

Special remarks: this pale blonde lager has a vague aroma and taste of malt with slight underlying hoppiness. It is thin in body.

• • •

BUDĚJOVICKÝ BUDVAR NEALKOHOLICKÉ PIVO

TYPE: ALCOHOL-FREE LAGER
ALCOHOL: 0.5% VOL.
FERMENTATION: BOTTOM

Special remarks: also known as Budweiser Free. It is a pale blonde non alcoholic lager with an aroma and a thin flavor of wort.

• • •

HOSTAN SRO, ZNOJMO

Production in hectoliters: 200,000
Founded: 1720

Hostan is a medium-sized brewery that mainly produces for its local market. Znojmo is in the southeast of the Czech Republic, close to the border with Austria.

HOSTAN 10%

TYPE: LAGER
ALCOHOL: 4% VOL.
FERMENTATION: BOTTOM

Special remarks: Hostan's 10% is a light lager that is blonde with a slight aroma of hops. The taste is slightly malty with some underlying hops. It is thin in body and is drunk as an everyday thirst-quencher.

SOUKROMÝ PIVOVAR SRO EGGENBERG, ČESKÝ KRUMLOV

Production in hectoliters: 120,000
Founded: 1560

The Eggenberg brewery derives its name from one of the aristocratic families that determined much of the history of the Czechs. The brewery was privatized in 1991 and has Czech shareholders. The brewery has been largely modernized and brews with its own water supply. It produces a diet beer, blonde and dark beers of 10%, and a 12% blonde. The majority of the production is of the 10% blonde.

HOSTAN 10% GRANÁT

TYPE: LAGER
ALCOHOL: 3.8% VOL.
FERMENTATION: BOTTOM

Special remarks: the Granát is a dark brown lager with an aroma containing roasted malt. The flavor is rounded and of malt with hints of coffee. The aftertaste is slightly bitter.

HOSTAN 11%

TYPE: LAGER

ALCOHOL: 4.4% VOL.

FERMENTATION: BOTTOM

Special remarks: Hostan 11% is a fuller blonde lager with a slightly hoppy aroma. The taste is of sweet malt but with a bitter finish. The aftertaste is briefly bittersweet.

OPAT 12%

TYPE: LAGER

ALCOHOL: 5% VOL.

FERMENTATION: BOTTOM

Special remarks: this blonde lager has a somewhat buttery aroma and taste. It is fairly full and has no bitterness but is drying in the finish.

HOSTAN 12%

TYPE: LAGER

ALCOHOL: 5% VOL.

FERMENTATION: BOTTOM

Special remarks: the premium lager is golden in color and has an aroma of malt. The flavor is of malt sweetness through a medium body. The aftertaste is of drying bitter hops.

• • •

OPAT 14%

TYPE: LAGER

ALCOHOL:6.1% VOL.

FERMENTATION: BOTTOM

Special remarks: a medium-bodied blonde lager with a sweet malt taste that gives way to the bitterness of hops.

• • •

PIVOVARY HRADEC KRÁLOVÉ SP, HRADEC KRÁLOVÉ

Production in hectoliters: 200,000

Founded: 1348/1960

Parent brewery of Pivovar Broumov Olivetin of Broumov since 1348.

OPAT 11%

TYPE: LAGER

ALCOHOL: 4.2% VOL.

FERMENTATION: BOTTOM

Special remarks: this blonde malty lager is medium-bodied with slight underground of hops. The aftertaste is briefly and slightly bitter.

PIVOVAR A SODOVKÁRNA JIHLAVA AS, JIHLAVA

Production in hectoliters: 150,000

Founded: 1860

This brewery's history began in 1860 when four German-speaking brewers decided to start-up on their own. At that time the Jihlava brewery was named Iglau (hedgehog) in German. The Czech for this animal is Ježek. This German heritage almost led to the brewery's demise after World War II but it managed to survive. It was able to grow and develop to the extent this was possible under the communist regime as a result of the closure of other local breweries.

That the brewery was not really coping with the change to a market economy became apparent in 1995 when less than half the capacity of the brewery was being utilized and capital was not available for modernization. Jihlava was bought out by the Zwettl brewery in Austria, just over thirty miles to the south. This Austrian brewery is a similar size but had significantly more resources available. Zwettl has made the necessary investment, resulting in the traditional methods being almost entirely replaced by modern techniques. The Austrian brewer saw the acquisition as a springboard into the Czech market. The Austrian influence is readily apparent. The brewery in Jihlava is housed in what for the Czechs is an attractive building with a fine entrance and a restaurant.

The restaurant of the Ježek brewery.

JEŽEK 11%

TYPE: LAGER
ALCOHOL: 4.9% VOL.
FERMENTATION: BOTTOM

Special remarks: this blonde lager is brewed with an original gravity of 11°. It has a slightly malty taste with underlying bitterness of hops. The ever-present bitterness does not overpower.

JEŽEK 12%

TYPE: LAGER
ALCOHOL: 5.2% VOL.
FERMENTATION: BOTTOM

Special remarks: the 12% can be regarded as this brewer's premium Pilsener. It is a firm and full blonde lager with strong bittersweet taste and prolonged bitter aftertaste.

JEŽEK 10%

TYPE: LAGER
ALCOHOL: 4.2% VOL.
FERMENTATION: BOTTOM

Special remarks: this 10% is the local session beer to quench the daily thirst. It is blonde, thin in body and taste of bitter hops.

JEŽEK 10% TMAVÝ

TYPE: DARK LAGER
ALCOHOL: 4.2% VOL.
FERMENTATION: BOTTOM

Special remarks: the dark brown version of the 10% has a fairly malty sweet aroma and malty taste with hints of roasted dryness. The beer has hints of caramel sweetness but is less cloying than some similar beers. The Tmavý has a slightly bitter aftertaste.

JEŽEK 14% SPECIÁL

TYPE: LAGER
ALCOHOL: 5.8% VOL.
FERMENTATION: BOTTOM

Special remarks: the Speciál is a golden to amber lager with a strong aroma of malt and distinct malt flavor too. Only the underlying taste has room for hops but the taste dries and becomes entirely of bitter hops in the aftertaste. The 14% is a real mouthful that imparts the sensation of alcoholic warmth. It is slightly out of balance.

PIVOJ 10%

TYPE: LAGER
ALCOHOL: **4.2%** VOL.
FERMENTATION: BOTTOM

Special remarks: a thin-bodied golden lager with slightly hoppy aroma. The taste is mid-way between malt and hops and dries slightly. The taste is of hops.

• • •

KRAKONOŠ 10%

TYPE: LAGER
ALCOHOL: **4.1%** VOL.
FERMENTATION: BOTTOM

JIHOČESKÉ PIVOVARY AS, ČESKÉ BUDĚJOVICE

Production in hectoliters: **1,200,000** (group)
Founded: **1992**

This brewery group of Southern Bohemia results from merging the Samson, Platan, and Regent breweries. This group was bought out from the Czech government with Czech capital.

The entrance to the Southern Bohemia brewing group.

• • •

KRAKONOŠ SPOL. SRO, TRUTNOV

Production in hectoliters: **160,000**
Founded: **1582**

A small regional brewery.

KRAKONOŠ 11%

TYPE: LAGER
ALCOHOL: **4.3%** VOL.
FERMENTATION: BOTTOM

Special remarks: golden lager with slightly hoppy aroma. The taste is neutral with a touch of hops and body is medium. There is no strong aftertaste.

KRAKONOŠ 12%

TYPE: LAGER
ALCOHOL: **5.1%** VOL.
FERMENTATION: BOTTOM

Special remarks: golden lager with a slight hoppy aroma. The flavor is of dry hops with vague buttery notes. The prolonged aftertaste is modestly of hops.

• • •

KRÁLOVSKÝ PIVOVAR KRUŠOVICE AS, KRUŠOVICE

Production in hectoliters: 750,000
Founded: 1581

The German Binding group has owned a majority of the share in the former Royal brewery of Krušovice since 1994. It is a modern concern where the investment in stainless steel was already made. It is clear from the labels than German marketing ideas have been incorporated.

KRUŠOVICE ČERNÉ 10%

TYPE: LAGER
ALCOHOL: 3.8% VOL.
FERMENTATION: BOTTOM

Special remarks: a dark brown lager with faint aroma of malt. The taste is initially of sweet malt, giving way to roasted notes through a thin body.

KRUŠOVICE LEŽÁK 12%

TYPE: LAGER
ALCOHOL: 5% VOL.
FERMENTATION: BOTTOM

Special remarks: a medium-bodied blonde lager with bittersweet taste and aroma of malt. This is the brewer's premium lager.

KRUŠOVICE SVĚTLÉ 10%

TYPE: LAGER
ALCOHOL: 3.8% VOL.
FERMENTATION: BOTTOM

Special remarks: a pale blonde lager with a reasonable body for an OG of 10°. The taste is slightly malty with

underlying mild bitterness and a slightly drying finish.

• • •

LOBKOWICZKÝ PIVOVAR S R.O., VYSOKÝ CHLUMEC

Production in hectoliters: 75,000
Founded: 1466

This small brewery has its own maltings. It has been in the hands of the Lobkowicz family for four centuries apart from the period of state ownership. After the fall of the communist regime the family regained possession and have subsequently entered into an agreement with the Austrian brewer Brau AG for which it now brews Kaiser Premium.

LOBKOWICZ KLASSIK 10%

TYPE: LAGER
ALCOHOL: 3.7% VOL.
FERMENTATION: BOTTOM

Special remarks: a thin-bodied fresh beer with an aroma of malt and golden color. The taste is immediately of hops, though not intense. This is the brewer's local thirst quencher.

• • •

PIVOVAR LOUNY AS, LOUNY

Production in hectoliters: 300,000
Founded: 1892

This medium-sized brewery exports a small part of its output to Germany and other countries. It brews Prinz von Böhem, Lounský Ležák, and a local 10% blonde lager.

FÜRST VON LOUNY

TYPE: LAGER

ALCOHOL: 4.5% VOL.

FERMENTATION: BOTTOM

Special remarks: this dark lager has a slightly sweet aroma. The taste is of malt with hints of roasted malt over a medium body.

● ● ●

MĚŠŤANSKÝ PIVOVAR HAVLÍČKŮV BROD AS, HAVLÍČKŮV BROD

Production in hectoliters: 150,000

Founded: 1834

This small brewery has its own maltings.

have been combined here with traditional equipment which certainly is not detrimental to the quality.

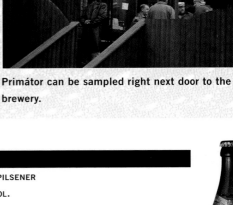

Primátor can be sampled right next door to the brewery.

REBEL 10%

TYPE: LAGER

ALCOHOL: 4.5% VOL.

FERMENTATION: BOTTOM

● ● ●

PIVOVAR NÁCHOD AS, NÁCHOD

Production in hectoliters: 200,000

Founded: 1872

This brewery in the north of the country is sited on the edge of a hill on the edge of Náchod with a view of the castle on the other side of the town. Modern techniques

PRIMÁTOR

TYPE: PREMIUM PILSENER

ALCOHOL: 5% VOL.

FERMENTATION: BOTTOM

Special remarks: this brewery's premium Pilsener is a robust golden lager with full sensation in the mouth and bittersweet taste, hoppy aroma, and bitter aftertaste. Original gravity is 12°.

PRIMÁTOR DIA

TYPE: DIET BEER

ALCOHOL: 4.4% VOL.

FERMENTATION: BOTTOM

Special remarks: this blonde lager is suitable for diabetics (in consultation with their doctor).

PRIMÁTOR NEALKOHOLICKÉ SVĚTLÉ PIVO

TYPE: ALCOHOL-FREE

ALCOHOL: 0.4% VOL.

FERMENTATION: BOTTOM

Special remarks: this non-alcoholic lager is golden in color, has a sweet taste of malt, and an aroma or wort.

• • •

PITO

TYPE: ALCOHOL-FREE

ALCOHOL: 0.7% VOL.

FERMENTATION: BOTTOM

• • •

PIVOVAR PARDUBICE AS, PARDUBICE

Production in hectoliters: 200,000
Founded: 1871

Pardubice brews Pernštejn and Porter brand beers and Linie soft drinks.

9

TYPE: LAGER

ALCOHOL: 3.7% VOL.

FERMENTATION: BOTTOM

Special remarks: this light lager is sold as an everyday thirst quencher. It is golden, has a medium body, is hoppy with a slightly bitter taste with a hint of butter, and has a brief bitter finish which is drying.

PERNŠTEJN DIA PIVO

TYPE: LIGHT BEER

ALCOHOL: 4.2% VOL.

FERMENTATION: BOTTOM

Special remarks: this blonde light lager is a diet beer with an aroma of malt. The taste contains hops over a thin to medium body. The aftertaste is briefly slightly bitter.

JIHOČESKÉ PIVOVARY AS, PLATAN, PROTIVÍN

Production in hectoliters: 370,000
Founded: 1598

The Platan brewery is one of three of the South Bohemia brewery group. The company was formerly owned by an aristocratic family which led to the beers being sold throughout Europe. The Schwarzenberger family rebuilt the brewery in 1876 at its present site beneath plane trees – hence the name from Platanus. This new brewery was suitable for brewing lagers but the brewery has once again been fully modernized.

PLATAN 10%

TYPE: LAGER

ALCOHOL: 3.9% VOL.

FERMENTATION: BOTTOM

Special remarks: this blonde lager with an original gravity of 10° is primarily intended as a cheap alternative for the local market. The pale blonde beer has a thin feeling in the mouth and faint aroma of malt. The taste is also only slightly malty and at first. The aftertaste is bitter.

PLATAN 11%

TYPE: LAGER

ALCOHOL: 4.5% VOL.

FERMENTATION: BOTTOM

Special remarks: a golden lager with a fairly hoppy aroma. The taste is initially of sweet malt but finishes with hops. This thin to medium-bodied beer has a brief aftertaste that is slightly bitter.

• • •

PLZEŇSKÝ PRAZDROJ AS, PIVOVAR PLZEŇ, PILSEN (Pilsner Urquell)

Production in hectoliters: 5,000,000
Founded: 1842

Plzeňský Prazdroj, or Pilsner Urquell – meaning "original source from Pilsen", is the largest brewing group in the Czech Republic. This is hardly surprising since the beer brewed here is the most imitated type of beer in the world: Pilsener or Pilsner. Pilsner Urquell now consists of four breweries: Gambrinus and Pilsner Urquell in Pilsen, and breweries in Karlovy Vary and Domažlice. The group supplies more than a quarter of the Czech market. Gambrinus is responsible for almost two-thirds of the group's production. Almost ten percent of the production is exported to fifty-three different countries, with the biggest importers being Slovakia, Germany, Poland, the USA, and the UK. Gambrinus was established in 1870 by German-speaking businessmen, including Emil Škoda, the

The restaurant of the Pilsner-Urquell brewery.

car manufacturer. The brewery was known as Erste Pilsner Aktienbrauerei and brewed beer sold as Kaiserpils. The brewery was already one of the largest in the region at the start of the twentieth century. Following World War I the company name and Kaiser brand were renamed Gambrinus, a bastardization of Jan Primus, Duke of Brabant. Under communist rule Gambrinus and Urquell were merged together with the breweries in Karlovy Vary and Domažlice. While Urquell is the best-known international brand, Gambrinus is far better known among the Czechs themselves. The inexpensive Gambrinus 10% is the best-selling beer in the Czech Republic. Gambrinus is brewed under license in Lithuania and Slovakia. Pilsner Urquell was set-up in 1842 by a group of Czech brewers to compete with the German dark lagers. They established a new civic brewery or Měšťanský Pivovar, and commissioned the architect Martin Stelzer to design a new brewery for bottom-fermented lagers. Stelzer brought a master brewer, Josef Grolle, from Bavaria, who was skilled in the German lager technique. Grolle intentionally or unintentionally made a clear blonde lager instead of a dark one.

The date of this invention was October 5, 1842 and it coincided with the wider use of glasses which suddenly made color and clarity more important than they had been in a metal or stoneware tankard. This resulted in this clear blonde beer with its flavor of malt and hops quickly becoming very popular and this popularity extended beyond the borders of the Austro-Hungarian empire and the beer became known as Pilsener or Pilsner everywhere. Only Urquell has the right to use the term "original Pilsener." Many "Pilseners" have significantly less character than the original but this happened also with the original when the open wooden fermentation vessels, lager casks, and fermentation vats disappeared.

Urquell has grown rapidly since 1989 and has been extensively modernized with considerable effort going into retention of the flavor and aroma of the beer. Although a great deal of wood has been replaced by stainless steel, they still use Moravian barley, Saazer hops, and the original number one strain of yeast. In order to be able to compare the modern version with the original, the brewery has kept part of the old equipment where Pilsener is still brewed in small amounts under the original conditions.

Karlovy Vary within the group is a small brewery founded in 1879 as the Weber Brauerei. The beers from this brewery were branded as Weber. After the great ridding of German language this brewery changed its name to Pivovar Karlovy

Vary and beer names changed too. Today it brews Karel, Wallenstein, and Primus. Wallenstein originally came from the now closed brewery in Cheb.

The Domažlice brewery is one of the oldest breweries in the Czech Republic with a history dating back to 1341. It is the smallest brewery within the Urquell group. Domažlice's brews include Purkmistr, Radní, and Písař.

GAMBRINUS BLONDE 10%

TYPE: PILSENER
ALCOHOL: 4.1% VOL.
FERMENTATION: BOTTOM

Special remarks: this 10% is a popular beer throughout the country. It is a cheap daily thirst quencher with a fairly malty aroma and hoppy taste with a bitter and drying finish. It is thin in body.

GAMBRINUS BLONDE 12%

TYPE: PILSENER
ALCOHOL: 5% VOL.
FERMENTATION: BOTTOM

Special remarks: the 12% is a premium Pilsener with a malty aroma. The taste is slightly fruity and hoppy with underlying malt. This Pilsener dries to a hoppy finish and has a bitter aftertaste.

GAMBRINUS DARK 10%

TYPE: DARK LAGER
ALCOHOL: 3.8% VOL.
FERMENTATION: BOTTOM

Special remarks: the dark Gambrinus 10% is a rather thin lager with a fresh neutral taste with hints of roasted malt at the finish.

GAMBRINUS MASTER

TYPE: ALCOHOL-FREE
ALCOHOL: 0.5% VOL.
FERMENTATION: BOTTOM

Special remarks: this pale blonde non-alcoholic lager has an aroma and taste of wort.

PRIMUS BLONDE 10%

TYPE: LAGER
ALCOHOL: 3.3% VOL.
FERMENTATION: BOTTOM

Special remarks: this blonde lager from Gambrinus is a light neutral beer with aroma of hops and vague bittersweet aftertaste.

PILSNER URQUELL 10%

TYPE: LAGER
ALCOHOL: 3.3% VOL.
FERMENTATION: BOTTOM

Special remarks: this 10% is aimed at the local market with a cheaper version and is not representative of the Pilsener style. It is a thin lager with slightly malty taste and some bitterness in the finish and aftertaste.

PRIMUS

TYPE: LAGER
ALCOHOL: 4.3% VOL.
FERMENTATION: BOTTOM

• • •

PILSNER URQUELL 12%

TYPE: PILSENER
ALCOHOL: 4.4% VOL.
FERMENTATION: BOTTOM

Special remarks: a close relative of the original Pilsener and the only one permitted to add the word "original" to Pilsener/Pilsner. It is a blonde beer with a floral and hoppy aroma. The taste contains both malt and hops with the balance shifting to hops in the finish. It has medium body and a drying bitter aftertaste of hops.

PRÁVOVAŘEČNÉ MĚŠŤANSTVO V HRADCI KRÁLOVÉ - DRUŽSTVO, HRADEC KRÁLOVÉ

Production in hectoliters: 200,000
Founded: 1844

This brewery produces its own malt.

KRÁLOVSKÁ 8

TYPE: LAGER

ALCOHOL: 3.2% VOL.

FERMENTATION: BOTTOM

Special remarks: a light blonde lager that is quite full for a brew with an OG of 8°. The taste is slightly of malt with vague hops in the finish and there is a slight aroma of malt.

LEV 10% TMAVÉ PIVO

TYPE: DARK LAGER

ALCOHOL: 3.8% VOL.

FERMENTATION: BOTTOM

Special remarks: a sweet caramel taste tending to buttery, slightly drying, and medium in body.

KRÁLOVSKÝ LEV 11%

TYPE: LAGER

ALCOHOL: 4.3% VOL.

FERMENTATION: BOTTOM

Special remarks: this golden lager has an aroma and taste of sweet malt. It has medium body and the aftertaste is sweet.

• • •

PRAŽSKÉ PIVOVARY AS, STAROPRAMEN, PRAGUE 5

Production in hectoliters: 2,700,000
Founded: 1992

The "Prague brewery" is second only in the Czech Republic to the Pilsner Urquell group. It consists of six breweries that were merged, of which Staropramen is the biggest. Bass bought one third of the shares in 1994.

Through Bass the brewers acquires financial resources and expertise. The finances were necessary for the modernization of production and Bass also provided international marketing expertise to break into major markets. The Czech's were at the point of changing their methods when Bass became involved but Bass put the brakes on this and advised them not to change the methods by which they brewed their beer too much to prevent significant changes in the character of their beer. It was essential though to improve efficiency considerably to achieve the desired growth.

The Staropramen brewery was founded in 1869 in the suburb of Smíchov. It is now a modern concern with a new brewery but with traditional brewing methods. Staropramen has its own traditional-style floor malting house which produces half of the malt used.

One of the other partners in the Prague group is Braník. This brewery was founded in 1898 by several Czech brewers who wanted to pool their resources in order to compete with the big industrial-scale breweries. Braník is a go-ahead brewery that has extensively modernized regardless of foreign involvement and mergers. It was the first Czech brewery to install horizontal fermentation vessels.

The Měšťan brewery in the suburb of Holešovice was found in 1895 as První Pražský Měšťanský Pivovar, or "the first Prague people's brewery." In this way the brewery differentiated itself from the other breweries, many of which had aristocratic backgrounds. The brewery has been partially modernized and still uses its own maltings.

The brewery in Liberec, Vratislavice nad Nisou was established in 1872. It brews Vratislav beers in 10, 11, and 12% versions.

The Svijany brewery produces beers under the Svijanská name from the old brewery with a history dating back to 1564. In 1998 Bass proposed this brewery should be sold to its management team.

The Ostrava brewery, founded in 1897, also has its own maltings and brews Ostrava beers.

BRANICKÝ LEŽÁK

TYPE: LAGER

ALCOHOL: 5.3% VOL.

FERMENTATION: BOTTOM

Special remarks: this stronger lager from Braník has a slight aroma of hops and malt and a taste that is initially quite apparent of hops. The slight bitterness endures through to the aftertaste. There is underlying maltiness and slight dryness. This beer has an OG of 12°.

MĚŠŤAN DARK 11%

TYPE: DARK LAGER

ALCOHOL: 4.1% VOL.

FERMENTATION: BOTTOM

Special remarks: a sweet malty dark lager from the Měšťan brewery is known as the "women's beer" and is one of their most popular. It has an aroma of roasted malt found in the taste together with caramel. The aftertaste is slightly bitter.

BRANÍK 10%

TYPE: LAGER

ALCOHOL: 4.2% VOL.

FERMENTATION: BOTTOM

Special remarks: this blonde 10° is a cheap session beer for the local market. It has a slightly hoppy aroma with a hoppy taste and bitter finish. Body is thin to medium.

STAROPRAMEN 10%

TYPE: LAGER

ALCOHOL: 4.2% VOL.

FERMENTATION: BOTTOM

Special remarks:
a golden lager with a slightly sweet taste with underlying bitter hops. It is intended for the local market.

MĚŠŤAN BLONDE 10%

TYPE: LAGER

ALCOHOL: 4% VOL.

FERMENTATION: BOTTOM

Special remarks: a blonde everyday thirst quencher with slightly malty aroma. The taste is of slight bitterness of hops drying towards the end. The aftertaste is of bitter hops and the body is thin.

STAROPRAMEN DARK 11%

TYPE: DARK LAGER

ALCOHOL: 4.6% VOL.

FERMENTATION: BOTTOM

Special remarks: this mellow dark brown lager has a vague aroma of malt. The taste is of sweet malt with hints of burnt malt. The aftertaste is brief with nothing new. It is brewed according to the Reinheitsgebot for the German market.

STAROPRAMEN PREMIUM 12%

TYPE: LAGER

ALCOHOL: 5.2% VOL.

FERMENTATION: BOTTOM

Special remarks: this premium lager, brewed in accordance with the Reinheitsgebot has a rich aroma of malt and hops. The taste is of malt giving way to mild bitterness of hops in the finish. The sensation in the mouth is of fullness and dryness in the finish. There is a prolonged mildly bitter aftertaste.

• • •

PIVOVAR RADEGAST AS, NOŠOVICE

Production in hectoliters: 1,800,000
Founded: 1970

The Radegast brewery was planned and built under communist rule. It has no nationalist upwelling or aristocratic heritage behind its foundation. Purely practical considerations led the communist rulers to build the brewery. After the change in the political scene in the then Czechoslovakia Radegast was a large and relatively modern brewery that with injection of Czech capital was able to compete in the new market economy against other breweries which often had difficulty keeping their antiquated breweries in production. Radegast has more than doubled its production since 1989. In 1995 Radegast took over the Sedlec brewery in Most.

RADEGAST TRIUMF

TYPE: LAGER

ALCOHOL: 3.9% VOL.

FERMENTATION: BOTTOM

Special remarks: a cheaper version aimed at the local market with an OG of 10° and slightly sweet malty taste.

• • •

PIVOVAR RADEGAST SEDLEC AS, MOST

Production in hectoliters: –
Founded: –

Subsidiary of the Radegast brewery.

PIVRNEC

TYPE: LAGER

ALCOHOL: 4.5% VOL.

FERMENTATION: BOTTOM

Special remarks: this blonde lager with an OG of 11° is named after the Czech comic. It is a golden beer with sharp and somewhat spicy taste and aroma of hops. The aftertaste is quite bitter.

RADEGAST PREMIUM

TYPE: LAGER

ALCOHOL: 5.1% VOL.

FERMENTATION: BOTTOM

Special remarks: Radegast's premium lager has an OG of 12°. It is a blonde beer with slight fruity and malt aroma with a slight taste of malt which becomes drying and slightly hoppy towards the finish.

RADEGAST DARK

TYPE: DARK LAGER

ALCOHOL: 3.6% VOL.

FERMENTATION: BOTTOM

Special remarks: this dark brown lager has a vague aroma of malt and sweet taste of malt with hints of roasted malt. The aftertaste is brief.

• • •

JIHOČESKÉ PIVOVARY AS, REGENT, TŘEBOŇ

Production in hectoliters: 430,000
Founded: 1379

The Regent brewery is part of the Southern Bohemia brewing group. It is one of the oldest breweries of the Czech Republic that was founded by the aristocratic Rosenberger family. The coat of arms of the Rosenbergers can still be found in the label. Later owners, the Schwarzenbergers, moved the brewery to the armory of their castle, which they had extensively rebuilt. The Regent brewery is still sited in this location and is a very traditional firm that still produces its own malt on a malting floor. The inexpensive 10% blonde lager accounts for the majority of the production. Some of the more limited production of premium beers is exported.

REGENT 10%
TYPE: LAGER
ALCOHOL: 3.3% VOL.
FERMENTATION: BOTTOM

Special remarks: a blonde daily thirst quencher with faintly hoppy aroma. The taste is neutral with vague flavor of malt. The aftertaste is briefly and slightly bitter.

REGENT 12%
TYPE: LAGER
ALCOHOL: 4.9% VOL.
FERMENTATION: BOTTOM

Special remarks: the premium 12% lager is a pale blonde with somewhat hoppy aroma and full bittersweet taste. It has a medium body and slightly bitter aftertaste.

• • •

JIHOČESKÉ PIVOVARY AS, SAMSON, ČESKÉ BUDĚJOVICE

Production in hectoliters: 400,000
Founded: 1795

The Samson brewer – part of the Southern Bohemia brewing group – is a century older than its rival Budvar in the same city. The brewery was founded in 1795 as civic brewery by German-language brewers. In 1865 the Samson name was adopted. At first this brewery also brewed beer with the Budweiser name but the Budvar brewery was more successful than the Samson brewery. During communist times the two

breweries were merged. After the end of communism Samson was privatized while Budvar remains in state hands. Samson still has its own maltings. The Samson brewery contrasts sharply with the modernized structure of the Budvar brewery.

SAMSON BLONDE 10%
TYPE: LAGER
ALCOHOL: 3.3% VOL.
FERMENTATION: BOTTOM

Special remarks: a cheap regional blonde lager with slightly hoppy aroma. The taste is neutral with a touch of hops and dry finish. The aftertaste is of dry hops.

SAMSON BLONDE 12%

TYPE: LAGER

ALCOHOL: 5% VOL.

FERMENTATION: BOTTOM

Special remarks:
the Samson brewery's premium lager is golden with quite and aroma of malt with a hint of hops. The taste is of sweet malt with slight bitterness of hops in the finish. It has medium body and a brief bitter aftertaste.

• • •

STAROBRNO DRAK 14%

TYPE: LAGER

ALCOHOL: 5.7% VOL.

FERMENTATION: BOTTOM

Special remarks: this golden premium lager has a firm rounded body but is not too sweet. Hops are firmly present but in a gentle mild form. The aftertaste is slightly bitter. Drak means "dragon."

STAROBRNO AS, BRNO

Production in hectoliters: 550,000

Founded: 1872

Starobrno is owned by Austrian Brau AG. The brewery was founded in 1872 with capital from the Mandel and Hayek families. Prior to this there is a history of brewing in Brno by monks. During the 1920s and 1930s the Starobrno brewery bought up many small local breweries to strengthen its local position. During communist rule of course the brewery had a monopoly in the city of Brno and surrounding area. Competition only slowly became apparent following the revolution. The involvement of Brau AG has led to modernization.

Brno is second only in size in the Czech Republic to Prague.

STAROBRNO PREMIUM 12%

TYPE: LAGER

ALCOHOL: 5.2% VOL.

FERMENTATION: BOTTOM

Special remarks: this blonde premium lager has an aroma and taste of malt. It has medium body and a somewhat bittersweet aftertaste.

STAROBRNO TRADIČNÍ SVĚTLÉ PIVO 10%

TYPE: LAGER

ALCOHOL: 4.3% VOL.

FERMENTATION: BOTTOM

Special remarks: this pale blonde lager is destined for the local market. It has a vague aroma and slight taste of malt with a drying and slightly bitter finish through to the aftertaste.

ČERVENÝ DRAK

TYPE: LAGER

ALCOHOL: 6% VOL.

FERMENTATION: BOTTOM

Special remarks: this amber lager has a firm rounded body and slightly sweet taste with an aroma of hops. The OG is 15°.

STAROBRNO ŘEZÁK 10%

TYPE: LAGER

ALCOHOL: 4.1% VOL.

FERMENTATION: BOTTOM

Special remarks: this dark amber lager has a somewhat malty aroma and a flavor of malt with hints of burnt malt. The aftertaste contains more hops.

NEKTAR GOLD 10%

TYPE: LAGER

ALCOHOL: 4% VOL.

FERMENTATION: BOTTOM

Special remarks: this lager has a vague aroma of hops. The taste too is slightly hoppy with a drying finish. It has a medium body and a fairly prolonged slightly bitter aftertaste.

• • •

ZLATÝ TRUMF 10%

TYPE: LAGER

ALCOHOL: 4.3% VOL.

FERMENTATION: BOTTOM

Special remarks: produced for the local market, this blonde lager has a slight aroma of malt and sweet taste of malt with a thin body.

• • •

PIVOVAR A SODOVKÁRNA SVITAVY AS, SVITAVY

Production in hectoliters: 200,000

Founded: 1888

This medium-sized brewery brews both Svitavák and Bruno brands.

SVITAVÁK 10%

TYPE: LAGER

ALCOHOL: 3.6% VOL.

FERMENTATION: BOTTOM

Special remarks: a blonde light lager aimed at the local populace. The golden color tends towards orange. There is a slight taste of malt with sugar sweetness breaking through. The aftertaste is more pronounced but briefly bitter with the slightly tart beer.

• • •

PIVOVAR STRAKONICE, STRAKONICE

Production in hectoliters: 200,000

Founded: 1649

This brewery and the brewery in Pelhřimov form a small group still owned by the Czech state that is managed from the Budweiser brewery.

PIVOVAR VELKÉ POPOVICE AS, VELKÉ POPOVICE

Production in hectoliters: 850,000
Founded: 1874

This brewery is also known as Kozel or "goat." It was founded by German-speaking Czech Franz Ringhoffer. This is a large brewery that owns some "pubs" in the British manner.

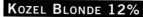

KOZEL BLONDE 12%

TYPE: LAGER
ALCOHOL: 5% VOL.
FERMENTATION: BOTTOM

Special remarks: this golden blonde premium lager has a more pronounced aroma of hops and the taste to is of hops, especially in the drying finish. There is underlying malt. The aftertaste is of bitter hops and it has a medium body.

KOZEL BLONDE 10%

TYPE: LAGER
ALCOHOL: 4% VOL.
FERMENTATION: BOTTOM

Special remarks: this beer is the brewer's most popular thirst quencher. It is an inexpensive lager for the regional market. It is golden with slightly malty aroma and taste and has a thin body.

KOZEL DARK 10%

TYPE: DARK LAGER
ALCOHOL: 3.8% VOL.
FERMENTATION: BOTTOM

Special remarks: the dark brown Kozel is somewhat malty with a touch of fruit in aroma with a taste of malt containing hints of roasting. It has a thin to medium body and somewhat drying aftertaste.

• • •

COUNTRY | The Slovak Republic/Slovakia

The Slovaks are not such great beer drinkers as their Czech neighbors and wine is of at least equal importance to them. Slovak beer labels are well organized with both the consume by and production dates indicated. You will also find the level of alcohol, the original gravity, the amount of kilojoules (calories) per liter, the volume, and the main ingredients all indicated.

PIVOVAR ILAVA, ILAVA

Production in hectoliters: 80,000
Founded: –

Part of the KK Group of Vlkanová.

MARTINER RICHTÁR

TYPE: LAGER
ALCOHOL: 4.6% VOL.
FERMENTATION: BOTTOM

Special remarks: brewed with an original gravity of 12°. It is blonde with a fine deep tinge of gold. Both the aroma and taste are of malt with hints of butter and hops, with a slightly bitter aftertaste.

MARTINER VARTÁŠ

TYPE: LAGER
ALCOHOL: 3.8% VOL.
FERMENTATION: BOTTOM

Special remarks: a light lager with an OG of 10° and a blonde color. It reveals an aroma of sweet malt and caramel from a watery, thin body. The taste is of malt with hints of sweet caramel but this is less intense than the aroma suggests. There is virtually no aftertaste.

• • •

PIVOVAR MARTIN, MARTIN

Production in hectoliters: 300,000
Founded: 1893

The Martin brewery is part of the KK Group with its headquarters in Vlkanová.

MARTINSKÝ ZDROJ 10%

TYPE: LAGER
ALCOHOL: 3.3% VOL.
FERMENTATION: BOTTOM

Special remarks: this blonde lager has an aroma of malt. Its body is thin and it dries in its finish. The aftertaste is a little bitter.

• • •

PIVOVAR ŠARIŠ AS, VEĽKÝ ŠARIŠ

Production in hectoliters: 750,000
Founded: –

This medium-sized brewery exports to Moscow, the Ukraine, the UK, France, and Sweden. Malt is also produced, mainly for own use. The shares are largely owned by South African Breweries.

ŠARIŠ SVĚTLÉ PIVO 10%

TYPE: LAGER
ALCOHOL: 3.6% VOL.
FERMENTATION: BOTTOM

Special remarks: this golden blonde 10% has an aroma mid-way between malty and hoppy and this is true too of the taste. Neither is

intense. The body is thin to medium and the aftertaste is brief.

SMÄDNÝ MNÍCH EXPORT BEER PREMIUM

TYPE: LAGER
ALCOHOL: 5.1% VOL.
FERMENTATION: BOTTOM

Special remarks: a blonde lager with an OG of 12°. It is a fairly robust golden blonde beer with slightly buttery aroma and taste of sweet malt with dry and slightly hoppy undertones.

SMÄDNÝ MNÍCH NEALKOHOLICKÉ PIVO

TYPE: ALCOHOL-FREE
ALCOHOL: 5.1% VOL.
FERMENTATION: BOTTOM

• • •

PIVOVAR STEIGER, EDUARD RADA SRO BANSKÁ ŠTIAVNICA

Production in hectoliters: 150,000
Founded: 1473

The Steiger brewery of Rada has two sites of almost equal size: this one and another in Vyhne. This brewer is represented in the UK by the Hell UK company and Hell lager is sold in Tesco supermarkets.

HELL

TYPE: LAGER

ALCOHOL: 4.9% VOL.

FERMENTATION: BOTTOM

Special remarks: the aroma of this golden lager is quite hoppy and the taste is slightly bitter hops. The body is thin to medium and the aftertaste is bitter.

STEIN SVĚTLÉ PIVO 10%

TYPE: LAGER

ALCOHOL: 3.5% VOL.

FERMENTATION: BOTTOM

Special remarks: both the date of production and drink by date are indicated on the label of this blonde lager brewed for daily consumption in the Slovak capital. It is a light beer ,brewed with water, malt, sugar, and hops. It has a slight aroma of malt and somewhat bittersweet taste. Body is thin to medium and the aftertaste is mildly bitter.

STEIGER 10%

TYPE: LAGER

ALCOHOL: 3.6% VOL.

FERMENTATION: BOTTOM

Special remarks: this blonde lager is brewed with an OG of 10°. The aroma is quite sharply hoppy and prominent, The taste too is of hops with slight flavor of underlying malt. The body is thin to medium and the aftertaste is slightly bitter.

STEIN SVĚTLÉ PIVO 12%

TYPE: LAGER

ALCOHOL: 4.5% VOL.

FERMENTATION: BOTTOM

Special remarks: a lager with an OG of 12°. This blonde beer is reasonably full with an aroma that reveals both malt and hops. The taste is also a balance of these two and the aftertaste is briefly slightly bitter. It has medium body.

STEIGER 11%

TYPE: DARK LAGER

ALCOHOL: 4.3% VOL.

FERMENTATION: BOTTOM

Special remarks: an almost black lager with an aroma of sweet malt. The taste is sweet with hint of caramel and burnt malt. It has a rounded body.

• • •

STEIN TMAVÉ PIVO 11%

TYPE: DARK LAGER

ALCOHOL: 3.5% VOL.

FERMENTATION: BOTTOM

Special remarks: a dark brown lager with a cream-colored head. The taste is of sweet caramel and the aftertaste is slightly sweet.

• • •

PIVOVAR STEIN AS, BRATISLAVA

Production in hectoliters: 300,000

Founded: 1873

A medium-sized brewery that mainly concentrates on exports to Russia, the Ukraine, and Hungary.

PIVOVAR TOPVAR AS, TOPOĽČANY

Production in hectoliters: 570,000
Founded: –

A medium-sized brewery with its own maltings. Topvar exports ten percent of its production to more than ten countries, including the Ukraine, the UK, the USA, and Germany.

TOPVAR 10%

TYPE: LAGER
ALCOHOL: 4 % VOL.
FERMENTATION: BOTTOM

Special remarks: the inexpensive 10% light blonde lager of Topvar has an OG of 10° and slight aroma of malt with hint of butter. Both determine the taste which is succeeded by a brief and slight bitter aftertaste. This all lurks beneath a cream-colored head.

TOPVAR 12% PIVO

TYPE: LAGER
ALCOHOL: 5.2 % VOL.
FERMENTATION: BOTTOM

Special remarks: a blonde lager with an OG of 12°. It has a strong taste of bitter hops with underlying dryness. The aroma is floral with a hint of butter and well-developed hints of hops. It is well-balanced but the full flavor of mild bitterness leaves the main impression.

• • •

PIVOVAR ZLATÝ BAŽANT AS, HURBANOVO

Production in hectoliters: 500,000
Founded: –

Heineken has a majority stake in this brewery. It is both a brewery and maltings. Zlatý Bažant means "golden pheasant."

ZLATÝ BAŽANT 12% SVĚTLÉ PIVO

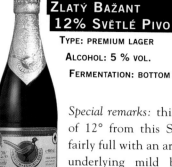

TYPE: PREMIUM LAGER
ALCOHOL: 5 % VOL.
FERMENTATION: BOTTOM

Special remarks: this premium lager of 12° from this Slovak brewer is fairly full with an aroma of malt and underlying mild bitterness. This blonde beer is malty in character and well-balanced. The brief aftertaste is bitter.

ZLATÝ BAŽANT 13% TMAVÉ PIVO

TYPE: DARK LAGER
ALCOHOL: 5 % VOL.
FERMENTATION: BOTTOM

Special remarks: this dark full lager has a compact head and it has underlying slight dryness. The taste is a little sweet with hints of roasted malt. It is well balanced.

ZLATÝ BAŽANT NEALKOHOLICKÉ

TYPE: ALCOHOL-FREE
ALCOHOL: 0.75 % VOL.
FERMENTATION: BOTTOM

Special remarks: a blonde non-alcoholic lager with strong aroma of wort and the taste is determined by this oppressive taste of moist malt.

• • •

COUNTRY Hungary

Hungary was part of the Austro-Hungarian empire for a long time and the influences of the neighboring Austrians are still apparent. A number of Austrian brewers have investments in Hungary but other international brewers have also become involved.

Hungarian beer is generally lager, often brewed with sugar and corn (maize) but there are also darker beers similar to porter and malt beer (bock). The ten million Hungarians have a broad choice of both wine and beer so that like their northern neighbors in the Slovak Republic they drink on average eighty-five liters of beer per head.

Hungarian beer terms

sör	beer
világos sör	blonde beer
barna sör	porter
csapolt sör	draught beer
sorgyar	brewery
hagyomány	traditional
készült	made from
víz	water
cukor	sugar
árpa	barley
kétsoros árpa	two-row barley
hatsoros árpa	winter barley
maláta	malt
kucorica	corn (maize)
kukoricadara	corn meal
komló	hops
élestö	yeast

AMSTEL SÖRGYÁR, KOMÁROM

Production in hectoliters: 500,000
Founded: 1988

This brewery is a fully-owned subsidiary of Heineken and it brews Talléros, Amstel Pils, Amstel Bock, Amstel Gold, and Buckler.

TALLÉROS

TYPE: LAGER
ALCOHOL: 5 % VOL.
FERMENTATION: BOTTOM

Special remarks: a thin gold lager with none too pleasing sharp aroma of hops. The taste is slightly hoppy, drying in the finish when bitterness re-emerges.

• • •

BORSODI SÖRGYÁR, BÖCS

Production in hectoliters: 2,000,000
Founded: 1972

This brewery produces beer and malt. Interbrew of Belgium has a three-quarter stake and in addition to its own brands, Stella Artois is also brewed.

BORSODI BARNA

TYPE: LAGER
ALCOHOL: 7.2 % VOL.
FERMENTATION: BOTTOM

Special remarks: barna is "brown" and barna sör is translated as "porter." This dark brown beer has a light brown head. The aroma is of roasted malt and this determines the taste too. The taste becomes bitter. The body is firm and rounded, not dry, and slightly unbalanced. Sweet alcohol comes to the fore in the mouth.

BORSODI PÓLÓ

TYPE: ALCOHOL-FREE
ALCOHOL: 0.5 % VOL.
FERMENTATION: BOTTOM

Special remarks:
a non-alcoholic lager brewed with water, malted barley, corn (maize), aromatic malt, hops, and yeast.

BORSODI SÖR

TYPE: LAGER
ALCOHOL: 4.6 % VOL.
FERMENTATION: BOTTOM

Special remarks: a blonde lager brewed with water, corn (maize), malted barley, hops, and yeast. It has a thin and dry body. The taste is slightly hoppy with a dry finish.

• • •

DREHER SÖGYÁRAK, BUDAPEST

Production in hectoliters: 2,500,000
Founded: 1854

Fully owned by South African Breweries.

ARANY ÁSZOK

TYPE: LAGER
ALCOHOL: 4.7 % VOL.
FERMENTATION: BOTTOM

Special remarks: a pale blonde lager that is clear and slightly malty with a drying finish. The body is thin to medium. There is no bitterness. This beer with nothing to upset anyone could be an international lager.

KANIZSAI VILÁGOS

TYPE: LAGER
ALCOHOL: 4.4 % VOL.
FERMENTATION: BOTTOM

Special remarks: a light blonde lager
with a somewhat malty taste with
slightly hoppy undertones. It dries
and has a sweet aftertaste.

SZALON SÖR

TYPE: LAGER
ALCOHOL: 4.6 % VOL.
FERMENTATION: BOTTOM

Special remarks: this blonde lager has
a slightly hoppy aroma. It has a thin
body, a sweet taste, with underlying
slight dryness and an sweet
aftertaste.

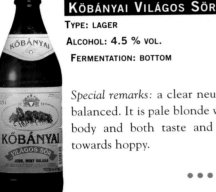

KÖBÁNYAI VILÁGOS SÖR

TYPE: LAGER
ALCOHOL: 4.5 % VOL.
FERMENTATION: BOTTOM

Special remarks: a clear neutral lager that is well
balanced. It is pale blonde with thing to medium
body and both taste and aftertaste that tend
towards hoppy.

• • •

SZALON BARNA

TYPE: DARK LAGER
ALCOHOL: 5.8 % VOL.
FERMENTATION: BOTTOM

Special remarks: a dark brown lager with a cream-
colored head. The slightly sweet aroma is not
distinct. The taste is initially slightly sweet
caramel but this is replaced by roasted notes.

• • •

PÉCSI SÖRFÖZDE RT, PÉCS

Production in hectoliters: 500,000
Founded: 1848

In addition to their own brands this brewery produces
Goldfassl under license from Ottakringer of Austria.

SOPRONI SÖRGYAR / BRAU UNION HUNGARIÁ, SOPRON

Production in hectoliters: 1,500,000
Founded: 1895

Brau AG of Austria has a three-quarter stake in this
brewery. it brews Zipfer, Schwechater, Gösser, and Kaiser in
addition to Hungarian brews.

HÁROM KIRÁLYOK

TYPE: LAGER
ALCOHOL: 6.4 % VOL.
FERMENTATION: BOTTOM

Special remarks: this pale blonde lager
has a very compact white head. It is a
full and fairly neutral beer that is
slightly sweet.

SOPRONI ÁSZOK

TYPE: LAGER
ALCOHOL: 4.6 % VOL.
FERMENTATION: BOTTOM

Special remarks: brewed with an
original gravity of 10.5°, this blonde
lager has little aroma. The trace there
is reveals some hops. The taste is of
sweet malt with underlying hops. It
dries towards the end.

• • •

COUNTRY Austria

That Austria is a neighbor of Germany is plain to see in its beer. The Austrian market consists of a sizable number of regional breweries and a couple of bigger national ones. The beers are predominantly ordinary blonde lagers, similar to German and Czech beers.

FREISTÄDTER BIER MÄRZEN

TYPE: MÄRZEN
ALCOHOL: 4.9 % VOL.
FERMENTATION: BOTTOM

Special remarks: this Märzen from the Freistadt brewery is not pasteurized. It is a pale blonde beer with a fairly hoppy aroma. The taste is of malt with underlying hops and the slightly drying aftertaste is briefly somewhat bitter.

FREISTÄDTER BIER RATSHERNN TRUNK

TYPE: LAGER
ALCOHOL: 5.3% VOL.
FERMENTATION: BOTTOM

BRAUCOMMUNE IN FREISTADT, FREISTADT

Production in hectoliters: 50,000
Founded: 1777

A small brewery in the north of Austria.

Special remarks: brewed with an OG of 12.5°, Austrian-grown malting barley, and Muhlviertaler hops. It is conditioned for six weeks and not pasteurized or preserved in any way. The pale blonde lager has a fine clean white head. The aroma is slightly hoppy. It is a fairly firm-bodied lager with a slightly hoppy taste and brief aftertaste of slight bitterness.

FOHRENBURGER JUBILÄUM

TYPE: PREMIUM LAGER
ALCOHOL: 5.5% VOL.
FERMENTATION: BOTTOM

Special remarks: the original gravity of the "jubilee beer" is 12.9° and it has an aroma of malt. The taste is also initially of malt but quickly becomes hoppy, extending to a slightly bitter finish. The aftertaste adds nothing new. It has medium body.

FREISTÄDTER BIER SPEZIALBRÄU DUNKEL

TYPE: DUNKEL
ALCOHOL: 5.1 % VOL.
FERMENTATION: TOP

Special remarks: this dark dunkel is not pasteurized and conditioned for six weeks. Almost black it has a syrupy character with taste of sweet malt and caramel with hints of roasted malt. It has medium body that is softened by the sweetness.

• • •

FOHRENBURGER SPEZIALBIER

TYPE: PREMIUM LAGER
ALCOHOL: 5.5% VOL.
FERMENTATION: BOTTOM

Special remarks: the original gravity is 12.9°

BIERBRAUEREI FOHRENBURG GMBH & CO, BLUDENZ

Production in hectoliters: 270,000
Founded: 1881

The Fohrenburg brewery sits amid the Austrian Alps, surrounded by snow-capped peaks and mountain streams. The presence of such natural water was the reason why Ferdinand Gassner chose this location to build a brewery in 1881.
Fohrenberg concentrates on premium lagers that are stronger than the run of the mill. The water used for brewing comes from one of two own sources which is pumped to the coppers without treatment. The brewer uses Bohemian Saazer, Bavarian Hallertau, and Austrian hops. The malt is mainly from Austria. Brewing is in accordance with the Austrian version of the Reinheitsgebot, or Codex, without pasteurization.

FOHRENBURGER STIFTLE

TYPE: PREMIUM LAGER
ALCOHOL: 5.1% VOL.
FERMENTATION: BOTTOM

Special remarks: a "full" Austrian beer of 11.9° with a fairly malty aroma and somewhat sweet taste of malt. Otherwise this beer is relatively neutral.

• • •

BRAUEREI EGGENBERG STÖHR & CO, VORCHDORF

Production in hectoliters: 150,000
Founded: 1681

This brewery has been in the hands of the Stohr family for almost two centuries. Prior to this it was owned by the nobles of the castle of Eggenberg.

EGGENBERG URBOCK 23%

TYPE: MALT LAGER/BOCK
ALCOHOL: 9.6% VOL.
FERMENTATION: BOTTOM

Special remarks: its OG of 23° gives this Urbock a full and robust body. The golden beer is hoppy with bittersweetness and has a somewhat fruity aroma with prominence of alcohol. Its firm body is rounded. The brewer claims it to be the world's strongest beer and while there are certainly stronger beers they may not be brewed according to the Reinheitsgebot as this one is.

HOPFENKÖNIG

TYPE: PILSENER
ALCOHOL: 5.1% VOL.
FERMENTATION: BOTTOM

Special remarks: a full malt beer with fine mellow bitter taste and full sensation in the mouth.

MÄRZEN BIER

TYPE: MÄRZEN
ALCOHOL: 4.9% VOL.
FERMENTATION: BOTTOM

Special remarks: a pale blonde Märzen with neutral taste going on sweet. There is no aftertaste or any bitterness.

SPEZIAL BIER

TYPE: PREMIUM LAGER
ALCOHOL: 5.2% VOL.
FERMENTATION: BOTTOM

Special remarks:
a slightly malty beer with a bitter, somewhat dry undertones and medium body.

BRAUEREI FRANZ WURMHÖRINGER, ALTHEIM

Production in hectoliters: 50,000
Founded: 1652

This small private brewery employs seven and brews only bottom-fermented beers.

• • •

MÄRZEN BIER

TYPE: MÄRZEN
ALCOHOL: 4.7% VOL.
FERMENTATION: BOTTOM

Special remarks:
a blonde lager with a malty aroma and taste. It has medium body and has mild hoppiness.

• • •

BRAUEREI GRIESKIRCHEN-AG, GRIESKIRCHEN

Production in hectoliters: 110,000
Founded: 1708

Steirerbrauer AG of Graz has a majority stake in this brewery.

MÄRZEN

TYPE: MÄRZEN
ALCOHOL: 5% VOL.
FERMENTATION: BOTTOM

Special remarks: this pale blonde Märzen has a medium body with a sweet taste of malt. There is no bitterness and no strong taste is left in the mouth.

• • •

BRAUEREI HIRT GMBH, HIRT

Production in hectoliters: 150,000
Founded: 1270/1846

Independent family brewery.

HIRTER MORCHL

TYPE: DARK LAGER
ALCOHOL: 5% VOL.
FERMENTATION: BOTTOM

Special remarks: a very dark, almost black lager, brewed with caramel malt and dark malts. It is not pasteurized. The taste is of roasted malt and slightly sweet. Underlying is slight dryness. It is medium in body and very smooth.

HIRTER PRIVAT PILS

TYPE: PILSENER
ALCOHOL: 5.2% VOL.
FERMENTATION: BOTTOM

Special remarks: a pale blonde Pilsener with a firm head. The beer beneath is equally firm with full taste of malt and fine mellow bitter finish.

• • •

BRAUEREI JOSEF BAUMGARTNER, SCHÄRDING

Production in hectoliters: 100,000
Founded: 1609

This medium-sized brewery brews Baumgartner Pils, Lager, Dunkel, and Export.

BAUMGARTNER MÄRZEN

TYPE: MÄRZEN
ALCOHOL: 5.1% VOL.
FERMENTATION: BOTTOM

Special remarks: brewed with an original gravity of 12.3°. This Märzen is pale blonde and has a distinct aroma of malt. The taste is a touch bitter and there is bitterness too briefly in the aftertaste.

• • •

PRIVATBRAUEREI JOSEF SIGL KG, OBERTRUM

Production in hectoliters: –
Founded: 1775

A small family brewery with fifty-five employees. They brew a Pils, Märzen, and Weizengold.

TRUMER PILS

TYPE: PILSENER
ALCOHOL: 4.9% VOL.
FERMENTATION: BOTTOM

Special remarks: brewed with an original gravity of 11.5°. The brewer describes this Pilsener as "extra dry". It is light but has underlying hop bitterness and is drying towards the finish.

• • •

BRAUEREI KAPSREITER AG, SCHÄRDING

Production in hectoliters: 80,000
Founded: 1590

KAPSREITER HOPFENKRONE

TYPE: LAGER
ALCOHOL: 5% VOL.
FERMENTATION: BOTTOM

Special remarks: a blonde lager brewed to 12.6° in accordance with the Reinheitsgebot. Hofenkrone has a vaguely aroma and sweet malty taste with underlying hops. The aftertaste is slightly hoppy. It has medium body.

KAPSREITER LANDBIER BOCK

TYPE: MALT LAGER/BOCK
ALCOHOL: 6.9% VOL.
FERMENTATION: BOTTOM

Special remarks: this bock has an OG of 16.3°, is fermented for ten days, and conditioned for 105 days. It is brewed according to the Reinheitsgebot. This blonde bock initially has a grassy aroma, is slightly sweet malt in taste, rounded, and has no strong aftertaste.

KAPSREITER LANDBIER GOLDBRAUN

TYPE: LAGER
ALCOHOL: 4.4% VOL.
FERMENTATION: BOTTOM

Special remarks: an amber lager with an OG of 12.8° that is fermented for eight days and conditioned for sixty-six days. Roasted malt is used for the Goldbraun to create a darker color.

The lager has an aroma and full flavor of malt and is medium bodied. It dries towards the finish.

KAPSREITER MÄRZEN

TYPE: MÄRZEN
ALCOHOL: 5.1% VOL.
FERMENTATION: BOTTOM

Special remarks: this blonde Märzen has a vague aroma with some hops and malt. It has an original gravity of 12.2°. The taste is of sweet malt and the slightly hoppy aftertaste is somewhat drying. It has medium body.

KAPSREITER PILS TYP

TYPE: PILSENER
ALCOHOL: 6% VOL.
FERMENTATION: BOTTOM

Special remarks: this Pilsener is brewed with an OG of 12.5°. It is a golden blonde lager with a sharp aroma of hops and the taste is also hoppy with a short bitter aftertaste. It has medium body.

• • •

RITTERBRÄU PRIVATBRAUEREI NEUMARKT GMBH & CO. KG, NEUMARKT

Production in hectoliters: 140,000 (including soft drinks)
Founded: 1609

Ritterbräu is a small brewery employing forty-five people. Under the management of Johan Zeiger, six different beers are brewed according to Reinheitsgebot rules.

MÄRZENBIER

TYPE: MÄRZEN
ALCOHOL: 5.1% VOL.
FERMENTATION: BOTTOM

Special remarks:
a traditional bottom-fermented dark blonde with a malty and slightly hoppy taste. The original gravity is 12.3°.

EDEL-PILS

TYPE: PILSENER
ALCOHOL: 5% VOL.
FERMENTATION: BOTTOM

Special remarks:
Rittenbräu's blonde Pilsener has an aroma of hops and an OG of 11.8°.

JUBILÄUMSBIER

TYPE: LAGER
ALCOHOL: 5.2% VOL.
FERMENTATION: BOTTOM

Special remarks: this blonde "jubilee beer" has an original gravity of 12.5°.

EXPORT DUNKEL

TYPE: SPECIAL BREW (DUNKEL/DARK LAGER)
ALCOHOL: 5.5% VOL.
FERMENTATION: BOTTOM

Special remarks: the export dark lager has a malty taste and an OG of 13.5°.

URTRUNK

TYPE: PREMIUM LAGER
ALCOHOL: 5.3% VOL.
FERMENTATION: BOTTOM

Special remarks: a slightly stronger version with an original gravity of 12.8°. It is blonde with a vague aroma of malt and malty taste that gives way to mild hops. The aftertaste is slightly bitter but not at all intense. It has medium body.

WEIHNACHTS BOCK

TYPE: CHRISTMAS MALT LAGER/BOCK
ALCOHOL: 7.4% VOL.
FERMENTATION: BOTTOM

Special remarks: this bock is popular around Christmas time. It's OG is 16.5°. It is a full-bodied beer with a sturdy hoppy character.

BRAUEREI SCHWECHAT, SCHWECHAT

Production in hectoliters: —
Founded: 1632

This brewery is part of Österreichische Brau AG of Linz.

DREHER'S SCHWARZBIER

TYPE: BLACK BEER
ALCOHOL: 5.3% VOL.
FERMENTATION: BOTTOM

Special remarks: named after Anton Dreher, one of the pioneers of bottom-fermented beers who was based here in Schwechat. Although Dreher was renowned for his amber-red beers, brewed with Viennese malt, the proprietor of the brewery today has coupled his name to this specialty. Dreher would not be ashamed. It is a very dark lager with a fine aroma of burnt malt. The taste is complex with equally fine hints of roasted malt and slight sweetness. This black beer has a short dry aftertaste.

• • •

BRAUEREI WIESELBURG, WIESELBURG

Production in hectoliters: —
Founded: 1650

A subsidiary of Österreichische Brau AG

KAISER MÄRZEN FAßTYP

TYPE: MÄRZEN
ALCOHOL: 5.2% VOL.
FERMENTATION: BOTTOM

Special remarks: a golden lager with aroma and taste of malt. The background is slightly dry and the body is medium.

WIESELBURGER BIER DAS STAMBRÄU

TYPE: LAGER
ALCOHOL: 5.4% VOL.
FERMENTATION: BOTTOM

Special remarks: this is a fairly robust pale blonde lager with a slightly hoppy aroma. The taste is of malt which recurs in the aftertaste with underlying hops.

• • •

BRAUEREI ZIPF, ZIPF

Production in hectoliters: 1,000,000
Founded: 1858

The Zipf brewery was originally a family concern, founded in 1858 by Frans Schaup but has been part of Brau AG of Linz since 1970.

ZIPFER MÄRZEN

TYPE: MÄRZEN
ALCOHOL: 5.2% VOL.
FERMENTATION: BOTTOM

Special remarks: a pale blonde Märzen with an aroma of malt. The taste is of sweet malt with a touch of spice. It has a medium body and dries slightly towards the finish. The aftertaste is briefly somewhat bitter. The beer is brewed under license in the Wieselburg brewery.

ZIPFER ORIGINAL

TYPE: LAGER
ALCOHOL: 5.4% VOL.
FERMENTATION: BOTTOM

Special remarks: this hoppy lager is brewed according to the Reinheitsgebot. The shape of the bottle of this Zipfer and neck label and twist knob is similar to the American Michelob.

ZIPFER URTYP

TYPE: LAGER
ALCOHOL: 5.4% VOL.
FERMENTATION: BOTTOM

Special remarks: a pale yellow lager with aroma of malt and hops. The taste is sharp, slightly bitter, with underlying dryness and a short bitter finish.

ZIPFER URTYP MEDIUM

TYPE: LAGER
ALCOHOL: 3% VOL.
FERMENTATION: BOTTOM

Special remarks: for those who are thirsty and wish to avoid the negative side of a lot of alcohol, Zipfer has this lower alcohol version of the Urtyp. This pale blonde lager has a taste that is initially of sweet malt that becomes bitter hops. There is a drying and mild bitter aftertaste. The medium body is not readily apparent.

• • •

BRAUEREI ZWETTLER, ZWETTL

Production in hectoliters: 210,000
Founded: 1708

Books trace the brewing activities of Zwettl in Austria to 1306. The family brewery though was founded as the Stiegenbrauerei in the suburb of Syrnau in 1708. In 1890 it passed into the hands of Georg Schwarz, a brewer from Bavaria. The fifth generation of Schwarz, Mag. Karl Schwarz is now at the helm.

For true enthusiasts, Zwettl organizes three different seminars about beer each year and trips to study the beers of foreign countries. In addition to the beers described here, Zwettl also brew a number of unfiltered beers that are only available on draught.

ICE BIER

TYPE: LAGER/ICE BEER
ALCOHOL: 4.7% VOL.
FERMENTATION: BOTTOM

Special remarks:
Zwettler is following the trend of
Canadian and America brewers for
ice beers.

ZWETTLER EISBIER

TYPE: LAGER/ICE BEER
ALCOHOL: 4.7% VOL.
FERMENTATION: BOTTOM

STIFTSBRÄU

TYPE: LAGER
ALCOHOL: 4% VOL.
FERMENTATION: BOTTOM

Special remarks: this light blonde
thirst quencher has an original
gravity of 9.8°, which is apparent in
its thin body, The aroma is slightly
malty. The taste is neutral to slightly
sweet.

ZWETTLER EXPORT

TYPE: EXPORT LAGER
ALCOHOL: 4.8% VOL.
FERMENTATION: BOTTOM

Special remarks: this export is aimed
at the beer drinker who prefers a
malty beer with little in the way of
hops.

ZWETTLER DUNKLES

TYPE: DARK LAGER/DUNKLE
ALCOHOL: 3.2% VOL.
FERMENTATION: BOTTOM

Special remarks: with is OG of 11° the
alcohol of this dark beer is quite low.
The sweet malty taste and aroma
are a direct consequence.

ZWETTLER KEUNRINGER FESTBOCK

TYPE: MALT LAGER/BOCK
ALCOHOL: 6.8% VOL.
FERMENTATION: BOTTOM

Special remarks:
this is Zwettler's
strongest beer,
intended for feast
days. It is a blonde
bock of 16° OG
which keeps the
malt and hops in
balance.

ZWETTLER ORIGINAL 1890

TYPE: PILSENER
ALCOHOL: 4.9% VOL.
FERMENTATION: BOTTOM

Special remarks: a premium Pilsener brewed solely with local ingredients. It is blonde with a vaguely malty aroma and somewhat sweet taste of malt. It has medium body and the aftertaste contains more hops.

ALPIN RADLER

TYPE: BEER AND SOFT DRINK MIX
ALCOHOL: 2.8% VOL.
FERMENTATION: BOTTOM

Special remarks: this is a mixture of 55% beer and 45% herbal lemonade.

ZWETTLER PILS

TYPE: PILSENER
ALCOHOL: 4.7% VOL.
FERMENTATION: BOTTOM

Special remarks: this Pilsener is lighter in brew at 11.5° than the Original but it clearly has several different types of hops present.

KAISER GOLD QUELL SPEZIAL

TYPE: EXPORT LAGER
ALCOHOL: 5.7% VOL.
FERMENTATION: BOTTOM

Special remarks: a medium-bodied blonde lager with a hoppy aroma. The taste is a fine balance of malt and hops that is drying towards the finish.

• • •

ÖSTERREICHISCHEN BRAU-AG BRAU UNION, LINZ

Production in hectoliters: 10,000,000
Founded: **1992**

Brau AG, Austria's largest drinks company, resulted from mergers between many different breweries, including Schwechater in Linz, Steirerbrau in Graz, and the breweries in Zipf and Wieselburg.
Three foreign breweries were added later, including Starobrno of Brno in the Czech Republic and the Soproni brewery in Hungary.

SCHLOßGOLD ALKOHOLFREIES BIER

TYPE: ALCOHOL-FREE
ALCOHOL: –
FERMENTATION: –

Special remarks: a non-alcoholic lager brewed by Brau AG under license from the Swiss brewer Feldschlössen.

SCHÜTZEN BRÄU

TYPE: LAGER
ALCOHOL: 4.4% VOL.
FERMENTATION: BOTTOM

Special remarks: a pale yellow lager with a somewhat sweet malt taste and slight underlying dryness. The aftertaste is briefly quite bitter and body is thin to medium.

SCHWECHATER BIER

TYPE: LAGER
ALCOHOL: 5.2% VOL.
FERMENTATION: BOTTOM

Special remarks: a very pale blonde lager with a neutral taste that has a slightly sharp edge to it.kant.

SPORT RADLER

TYPE: BEER AND SOFT DRINK MIX
ALCOHOL: 3.2% VOL.
FERMENTATION: BOTTOM

Special remarks: the Sport Radler is a mix of 60% beer and 40% lemonade.

•••

BRAUSTÄTTE DER STEIRERBRAU AG, GRAZ

Production in hectoliters: 2,500,000
Founded: 1977

Steierbrau results from a merger in 1977 between the Gösser brewery, set-up in 1893 by Max Kober and the brewery of the Reininghaus brothers which had merged in 1922 with Österreichische Brau to from Brau-Union of Linz.

PUNTIGAMER

TYPE: LAGER
ALCOHOL: 5.1% VOL.
FERMENTATION: BOTTOM

Special remarks: this fairly full-bodied blonde lager has an aroma and taste of hops, with slight bitterness. The brief aftertaste is also bitter.

GÖSSER

TYPE: LAGER
ALCOHOL: 5% VOL.
FERMENTATION: BOTTOM

Special remarks: a blonde lager with an aroma that is slightly malty and hoppy. The taste is of malt with underlying hops and the brief aftertaste is bittersweet. The label indicates the original gravity but not the level of alcohol.

GÖSSER MÄRZEN

TYPE: MÄRZEN
ALCOHOL: 5.2% VOL.
FERMENTATION: BOTTOM

Special remarks: a full-flavored blonde beer with an aroma of malt. It has medium body with a taste of malt and somewhat sharp hops. The aftertaste is drying and slightly bitter.

•••

HOFBRÄU KALTENHAUSEN, KALTENHAUSEN

Production in hectoliters: –
Founded: 1475

Part of Österreichische Brau AG.

EDELWEISS HEFETRÜB

TYPE: WHEAT BEER
ALCOHOL: 5.5% VOL.
FERMENTATION: TOP

Special remarks: a cloudy and lively wheat beer and is somewhat sharp and fresh with a slight aroma of citrus fruit. Underlying this is slight dryness.

EDELWEISS WEISSBIER DUNKEL

TYPE: DARK WHEAT BEER

ALCOHOL: 5.5% VOL.

FERMENTATION: TOP

Special remarks: this beer has a fruity aroma of banana, a cloudy amber color, and full but mellow and sweet flavor with a hint of spice. It is lively.

• • •

MOHRENBRAUEREI AUGUST HUBER, DORNBIRN

Production in hectoliters: 200,000

Founded: 1834

Mohrenbrauerei August Huber is a family-run brewery.

MOHREN PFIFF

TYPE: LAGER

ALCOHOL: 4.9% VOL.

FERMENTATION: BOTTOM

Special remarks: this medium-bodied blonde lager has a slightly hoppy aroma and taste. It is briefly bitter at the finish.

MOHREN SPEZIAL

TYPE: LAGER

ALCOHOL: 5.6% VOL.

FERMENTATION: BOTTOM

Special remarks: this full-flavored beer has medium body. It is a blonde neutral lager with slight hoppiness. It is briefly bitter at the end and out of balance.

• • •

OTTAKRINGER BRAUEREI HARMER-AG, WIENNA

Production in hectoliters: 585,000

Founded: 1837

Ottakringer is a brewery which mainly serves its local market of which it has about a twenty percent share.

GAMBRINUS

TYPE: LAGER

ALCOHOL: 5% VOL.

FERMENTATION: BOTTOM

Special remarks: a full-flavored beer which is name in honor of the beer's original patron.

GOLDFASSL PILS

TYPE: PILSENER

ALCOHOL: 4.6% VOL.

FERMENTATION: BOTTOM

Special remarks: a blonde Pilsener with an original gravity of 11.2°. This fresh clear Pilsener has a pronounced hoppy character with bitter taste and aftertaste, though not excessively so or prolonged. The body is thin to medium.

GOLDFASSL SPEZIAL

TYPE: SPECIAL BREW

ALCOHOL: 5.6% VOL.

FERMENTATION: BOTTOM

Special remarks: a robust lager with an OG of 13.2°. It is blonde in color and the aroma is of hops. It has good body with a flavor of hops giving way to mellow bitterness against underlying dryness.

EGGER LEICHT

TYPE: LIGHT BEER

ALCOHOL: 3.5% VOL.

FERMENTATION: BOTTOM

Special remarks: a blonde lager with an aroma of malt and somewhat hoppy taste and a thin body.

NULL KOMMA JOSEF

TYPE: ALCOHOL-FREE

ALCOHOL: –

FERMENTATION: BOTTOM

Special remarks: an aroma of sweet malt with hints of the wort and this is true of the taste too in which hops come to the fore. This blonde non-alcoholic beer has forty percent fewer calories than the Helles.

EGGER NATURBRÄU

TYPE: LAGER

ALCOHOL: 5.2% VOL.

FERMENTATION: BOTTOM

Special remarks: this dark blonde lager is sweet with a medium body. It has no aftertaste but does dry towards the finish. There is some vague bitterness in the background.

OTTAKRINGER HELLES BIER

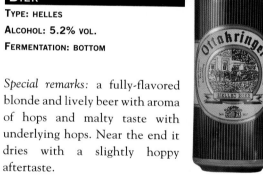

TYPE: HELLES

ALCOHOL: 5.2% VOL.

FERMENTATION: BOTTOM

Special remarks: a fully-flavored blonde and lively beer with aroma of hops and malty taste with underlying hops. Near the end it dries with a slightly hoppy aftertaste.

• • •

PRIVATBRAUEREI FRITZ EGGER GMBH, UNTERRADLBERG

Production in hectoliters: 320,000

Founded: 1675

Medium-sized family brewery.

EGGER NATURGOLD

TYPE: LAGER

ALCOHOL: 5.1% VOL.

FERMENTATION: BOTTOM

Special remarks: a golden premium lager brewed according to the Reinheitsgebot. The aroma is slightly hoppy, the taste is of malt with gentle underlying hops, the brief aftertaste is slightly bitter, and it has medium body.

• • •

STIEGLBRAUEREI ZU RIEDENBURG BEI SALZBURG, SALZBURG

Production in hectoliters: 650,000
Founded: 1492

Stieglbrauerei of Riedenberg near Salzburg is the largest privately-owned brewery of Austria.

GAUDI RADLER HIMBEER

TYPE: BEER AND SOFT DRINK MIX
ALCOHOL: 2.5% VOL.
FERMENTATION: BOTTOM

Special remarks: Gaudi Radler must mean something like "the cheerful cyclist." Whatever, it is a blend of Goldbräu and raspberry lemonade.

GAUDI RADLER ZITRONEN

TYPE: BEER AND SOFT DRINK MIX
ALCOHOL: 2.5% VOL.
FERMENTATION: BOTTOM

Special remarks: a mix of Stiegl Goldbräu and lemonade.

STIEGL GOLDBRÄU

TYPE: LAGER
ALCOHOL: 4.9% VOL.
FERMENTATION: BOTTOM

Special remarks: the brewer is proud of the fact that Goldbräu is brewed with an original gravity of 12°. This golden lager has a malty aroma and taste which endures.

STIEGL LEICHT

TYPE: LIGHT BEER
ALCOHOL: 3.3% VOL.
FERMENTATION: BOTTOM

Special remarks:
brewed in accordance with the Reinheitsgebot with an OG of 7.9°. It is pale blonde and has a slight malty aroma. The taste is of dry hops. The brief aftertaste is somewhat bitter. The thin body is masked by significant presence of hops.

• • •

COUNTRY Switzerland

BRASSERIE DU BOXER SA, ROMANEL SUR LAUSANNE

Production in hectoliters: 14,000
Founded: 1960

BOXER OLD LAGER

TYPE: LAGER
ALCOHOL: 5.2% VOL.
FERMENTATION: BOTTOM

Special remarks: a blonde premium lager that should not be drunk too cold, allowing it to become more mellow and fuller in the glass. It is a fresh beer with underlying dryness and a slight aroma of hops and a brief bitter finish.

• • •

BRASSERIE DU CARDINAL FRIBOURG, FRIBOURG

Production in hectoliters: 1,470,000
Founded: 1788

This big brewery was opened in 1788 and now has a capacity of 1,470,000. It is part of Feldschlössen-Hürlimann of Rheinfelden.

CARDINAL ORIGINAL DRAFT

TYPE: LAGER
ALCOHOL: 4.9% VOL.
FERMENTATION: BOTTOM

Special remarks: a clear pale blonde lager with malty aroma and fresh sweet taste of malt with no bitterness that is mellow and quite smooth and of medium body. It is a mystery where this beer originates for the label gives no information and what is said is in English.

• • •

BRAUEREI FALKEN AG, SCHAFFHAUSEN

Production in hectoliters: 47.000
Founded: 1899

FALKEN HELL

TYPE: LAGER
ALCOHOL: 4.8% VOL.
FERMENTATION: BOTTOM

Special remarks: a fine blonde lager of medium body and full flavor. It is hoppy and malty with not too much bitterness.

• • •

BRAUEREI FRAUENFELD AG, MARTIN WARTMANN, FRAUENFELD

Production in hectoliters: 2,500
Founded: –

A small brewery that uses equipment of Haldengut in nearby Winterthur.

ITTINGER KLOSTERBRÄU

TYPE: LAGER
ALCOHOL: 6% VOL.
FERMENTATION: BOTTOM

Special remarks: connoisseurs regard this amber Klosterbräu as one of Switzerland's best beers. In view of the rich flavor and fine balance this view is not entirely misplaced. The aroma of hops is succeeded by a slightly sweet hoppy taste accompanied by a mild underlying bitterness. Towards the finish Klosterbräu dries and remains slightly bitter in its aftertaste. The hops used are grown in the gardens of the Carthusian monastery of Ittinger.

• • •

BRAUEREI KARL LOCHER, APPENZELL

Production in hectoliters: –
Founded: –

APPENZELLER NATURPERLE

TYPE: LAGER
ALCOHOL: 4.8% VOL.
FERMENTATION: BOTTOM

Special remarks: this lager has a malty aroma and taste with underlying dryness and a hint of sharpness and bitterness. It is a cloudy blonde unfiltered beer with a vague aroma of citrus fruit. It is brewed with malted barley and hops of organic origin.

ORIGINAL QUÖLLFRISCH

TYPE: LAGER
ALCOHOL: 4.8% VOL.
FERMENTATION: BOTTOM

Special remarks: this unfiltered lager has a cloudy peach coloring. It is malty, slightly hop bitter, with a brief bitter aftertaste and underlying dryness.

• • •

BRAUEREI SCHÜTZENGARTEN AG, ST. GALLEN

Production in hectoliters: 130,000
Founded: 1779

The medium-sized brewery was originally located in a shooting association from which the brewery gets its name.

BILLWILLER

TYPE: PILSENER
ALCOHOL: 4.6% VOL.
FERMENTATION: BOTTOM

Special remarks:
this blonde Pilsener is brewed according to the Reinheitsgebot. It has an aroma of malt and the taste is initially of malt but is succeeded by bitterness of hops. The aftertaste is prolonged hop bitterness with some malt recurring in the finish.

EDELSPEZ

TYPE: PREMIUM LAGER
ALCOHOL: 5.2% VOL.
FERMENTATION: BOTTOM

Special remarks:
a blonde lager in accordance with the Reinheitsgebot. It has a slight aroma of hops with medium body and a mellow flavor of hops that is flows into a faintly bitter aftertaste.

EDELSPEZ DUNKEL

TYPE: DARK LAGER/DUNKEL
ALCOHOL: 5% VOL.
FERMENTATION: BOTTOM

Special remarks: brewed according to the Reinheitsgebot. A dark lager with strong aroma of malt. The taste is also dominated by malt with suggestions of roasted malt mid-way and then drying. The aftertaste is of roasted malt going on bitter.

EDELSPEZ LIGHT

TYPE: LIGHT BEER
ALCOHOL: 2.8% VOL.
FERMENTATION: BOTTOM

Special remarks: brewed according to the Reinheitsgebot with the same ingredients as the Edelspez Hell but with less alcohol and fewer calories. It has a aroma and taste of unfermented malt.

FESTBIER

TYPE: OKTOBERFEST BEER
ALCOHOL: 5.2% VOL.
FERMENTATION: BOTTOM

Special remarks: this Swiss festival beer has a somewhat malty aroma and taste of sweet malt. The color is blonde and it has a drying sensation in the mouth. The aftertaste is quite sweet.

SCHÜTZENGARTEN LAGER HELL

TYPE: LAGER
ALCOHOL: 4.8% VOL.
FERMENTATION: BOTTOM

Special remarks: a golden lager of medium body and slight flavor of malt. It is fairly neutral with no bitterness and no strong aftertaste.

ST. GALLER KLOSTERBRÄU

TYPE: LAGER
ALCOHOL: 5.2% VOL.
FERMENTATION: BOTTOM

Special remarks: an unfiltered amber lager that is slightly cloudy. The taste is obviously fruity with a medium and rounded body. It dries towards the finish but with a sweet taste briefly apparent.

• • •

CALANDA HALDENGUT AG, CHUR-GRAUBUNDEN

Production in hectoliters: 500,000
Founded: 1780

The Calanda-Haldengut brewery results from a merger of two breweries of these names in 1990. Heineken acquired a majority stake in 1994.

CALANDA MEISTER BRÄU

TYPE: LAGER
ALCOHOL: 5.7% VOL.
FERMENTATION: BOTTOM

Special remarks: a slightly malty blonde lager of medium body and modest hops.

HALDEN KRONE

TYPE: LAGER
ALCOHOL: 5.2% VOL.
FERMENTATION: BOTTOM

Special remarks: the brewer regards this as the pinnacle of his career. This blonde lager lurks beneath a compact white head, has medium body, and a flavor balanced between slightly malty and brief mild bitterness. The aroma is slightly hoppy.

321

HALDENGUT DUNKEL

TYPE: DARK LAGER/DUNKEL
ALCOHOL: 5.2% VOL.
FERMENTATION: BOTTOM

Special remarks: this dark lager is of a remarkably mellow nature. The drying taste tends towards slight roasted malt flavor.

BIRELL

TYPE: ALCOHOL-FREE
ALCOHOL: 0.38% VOL.
FERMENTATION: BOTTOM

Special remarks: Birell is an non alcoholic beer brewed in accordance with the Reinheitsgebot by the Eggenberg brewery. It is a blonde beer with an aroma of malt and slightly sweet malty taste with vague underlying hints of hops.

HALDENGUT HELL

TYPE: HELLES
ALCOHOL: 4.8% VOL.
FERMENTATION: BOTTOM

Special remarks: a mild blonde lager with an aroma and taste of malt. Hops come to the top in the aftertaste. The body is thin to medium.

• • •

CARDINAL LAGER

TYPE: LAGER
ALCOHOL: 4.8% VOL.
FERMENTATION: BOTTOM

Special remarks: the brewery says "pure malt" on the label. The pale blonde lager has an aroma of malt with hints of hops. The flavor is a good balance of malt and hops and there is underlying dryness. The aftertaste is prolonged dryness.

FELDSCHLÖSSEN-HÜRLIMANN-HOLDING, RHEINFELDEN-ARGAU

Production in hectoliters: 2,300,000
Founded: 1874/1865

The Feldschlössen and Hürlimann breweries merged in January 1966. The Felschlössen brewery was founded in 1874 by Théophil Roniger. The brewery's name is derived from the castellated form of the building with its many towers. It is a folly rather than a genuine castle. The Cardinal brewery in Rheinfelden and Fribourg and a number of other breweries and companies make up SIBRA Holdings within this group. The Hürlimann brewery in Zurich was founded in 1865 by Albert Hürlimann and became famous for the development of specific strains of yeast. The Zurich brewery is now closed and brewing transferred to Rheinfelden. The Löwenbrau brewery in Zurich, that formed part of the group, is also shut with its brewing shifted to Rheinfelden. The group has a joint cooperation agreement with the French KSN/Kronenbourg group.

DUNKLE PERLE

TYPE: DARK LAGER/DUNKEL
ALCOHOL: 5.5% VOL.
FERMENTATION: BOTTOM

Special remarks: the "dark pearl" of this Swiss brewer is an almost black beer. It is fresh and malty with hints of roasted malt and a touch of sweetness. There is underlying dryness.

FELDSCHLÖSSEN HOPFENPERLE

TYPE: LAGER

ALCOHOL: 5.2% VOL.

FERMENTATION: BOTTOM

Special remarks: a pale malty lager with a fine balanced flavor and aroma of hops. The finish is dry with somewhat sharp hoppiness.

ICE BEER

TYPE: ICE BEER

ALCOHOL: 5% VOL.

FERMENTATION: BOTTOM

Special remarks: a blonde lager filtered over ice with no discernible aroma, although when warmer a hint of malt. The taste is of sweet malt without an aftertaste. The medium body is fuller than most ice beers but this one too is unlikely to offend or excite.

LÖWENBRÄU ZÜRICH

TYPE: LAGER

ALCOHOL: 4.8% VOL.

FERMENTATION: BOTTOM

Special remarks: this golden lager has a vague aroma with a hint of malt. The taste is slight of hops with a hint of bitterness and slightly dry undertones. It has a thing to medium body and the aftertaste is slightly bitter.

ORIGINAL

TYPE: LAGER

ALCOHOL: 4.8% VOL.

FERMENTATION: BOTTOM

Special remarks:
a slightly malty blonde lager with underlying bitterness and a dry, briefly bitter finish.

SAMICHLAUS BIER

TYPE: SPECIAL BREW

ALCOHOL: 14% VOL.

FERMENTATION: BOTTOM

Special remarks: the Hürlimann brewery was a leader in the field of developing special strains of yeast. This renown led in 1980 to the brewing of the first Samichlaus beer which is one of the world's strongest brews, with an entry in The Guinness Book of Records. Yeast converts the malt sugars present into alcohol and carbon dioxide. The alcohol produced initially retards fermentation and so it is a matter of skill to select strains of yeast that are the least retarded by alcohol. This eventually resulted in brewing a Samichlaus of 16% alcohol by volume. This was brewed as a special occasion beer in 1980 and it is now brewed each December 6 for the festival of St. Nicholas. Since the beer is conditioned for a year it is necessary to wait a year for the effect of this beer. Originally both a blonde and dark version were brewed but now only the dark one is produced. It is reddish-brown with a sweet malty taste that is entirely dominated by alcohol. The brews differ from year to year and the length of time this strong beer is left to further condition has a great bearing on the taste. There is a rumor though that the now commercially-aggressive group has no place for such an oddball.

• • •

BRAUEREI LÖWENGARTEN, RORSCHACH

Production in hectoliters: 60,000
Founded: 1871

LÖWENGARTEN EXPORT HELL

TYPE: HELLES
ALCOHOL: 4.8% VOL.
FERMENTATION: BOTTOM

Special remarks: a light malty lager with both and aroma and aftertaste of hops, though the general impression is neutral.

• • •

SONNENBRÄU AG, REBSTEIN

Production in hectoliters: 25,000
Founded: 1891

This family brewery was founded in 1891 by Eduard Graf and is now run by a third generation of the Graf family.

ICE BEER

TYPE: ICE BEER
ALCOHOL: 5% VOL.
FERMENTATION: BOTTOM

Special remarks: brewed and then stored so cold that ice crystals form. The colorless bottles are sealed with a pull-off top. It is blonde with slightly sweet taste and vague hints of vanilla. Sonnenbräu Ice Beer is in any event very easily swallowed.

LAGER-HELL

TYPE: HELLES
ALCOHOL: 4.8% VOL.
FERMENTATION: BOTTOM

Special remarks: a sharply hopped and thin-bodied lager.

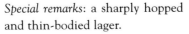

RHEINTALER MAISBIER

TYPE: LAGER
ALCOHOL: 5% VOL.
FERMENTATION: BOTTOM

Special remarks: while some brewers anxiously conceal the use of corn (maize) others such as Sonnenbräu use it as a sales pitch. The corn used is guaranteed to originated from the Rhine valley and like the malt used is from organic agriculture. The result of these efforts is a pale blonde lager with a slightly malty aroma and taste verging on sweetness of medium body.

• • •

WÄDI-BRÄU-HUUS AG, WÄDENSWIL

Production in hectoliters: 7,500
Founded: 1991

A pub brewery that has brewed organic beers since 1991. It brewed the first hemp beer in 1996 after being granted permission from the Swiss minister of health. Part of the production is undertaken by the H. Müller brewery of Baden.

HANF

TYPE: LAGER
ALCOHOL: 5.8% VOL.
FERMENTATION: BOTTOM

Special remarks: an organic beer brewed with organically grown ingredients, including water, yeast, malted barley, hops, and also hemp (hanf) blossoms. It is not filtered and thus a cloudy golden-blonde color. The taste is of malt with hints of citrus fruit. It is a sweet, drying, and mellow beer.

• • •

COUNTRY Poland

Poland is one of major growth markets for beer in Europe. With average consumption of around forty liters per head the Poles are way behind their western neighbors. With the growth of the Polish economy and adoption of westernized life styles it is anticipated that beer consumption in Poland will double in the next decade. Western breweries have therefore rushed to buy stakes in Polish breweries. Heineken, Bittburger, and SAB are all clearly involved in Poland with major investments to capture a slice of the Polish market. Polish beer is generally lager but stronger bock (malt lager) is also popular.

ELBREWERY COMPANY LTD, ELBLAG
Production in hectoliters: 1,300,000
Founded: 1991

This large brewery employing 1,500 people also sells Dutch Grolsch in the Polish market in addition to its own brews. Heineken acquired a 51% stake in 1998.

Special remarks: a pale blonde Pilsener with an original gravity of 11°. It has a slight aroma of hops with a fresh hoppy taste giving way to some bitterness. It has thin to medium body and a fine balance with an aftertaste that yields dry hops.

EB SPECJAL PILS
TYPE: PILSENER
ALCOHOL: 5.5% VOL.
FERMENTATION: BOTTOM

SPECJAL MOCNY
TYPE: LAGER
ALCOHOL: 7% VOL.
FERMENTATION: BOTTOM

Special remarks: this lager has a neutral to slightly bitter taste without a dominant aftertaste. It is rather thin for a beer of 14.5° original gravity.

• • •

ZAKLADY PIWOWARSKIE W LEZAJSKU SA, LEZAJSK

Production in hectoliters: 300,000
Founded: 1525

The medium-sized brewery produces Kristall and Gold in addition to Trunk.

LEZAJSK TRUNK

TYPE: DARK LIGHT BEER
ALCOHOL: 1.2% VOL.
FERMENTATION: BOTTOM

Special remarks: a dark brown beer with a light brown head and aroma of wort. The taste is entirely dominated by an oppressive sugary sweetness.

• • •

BROWARY KARKONOSKIE SA, LWÓWEK SLASKI

Production in hectoliters: —
Founded: 1872

GÓRNICZE

TYPE: LAGER
ALCOHOL: 6.2% VOL.
FERMENTATION: BOTTOM

Special remarks: a pasteurized blonde lager of 12.5° OG. The aroma is slightly hoppy with vague maltiness. The taste is of hops with a bitter finish and there is a slight undertone of malt. Sweetness dominates the aftertaste.

KSIAZECE

TYPE: LAGER
ALCOHOL: 6.2% VOL.
FERMENTATION: BOTTOM

Special remarks: a pasteurized blonde lager of 12.5° OG. The aroma and taste are similar to Górnicze: hops with a faint undertone of malt.

MOCNE DOBRE

TYPE: LAGER
ALCOHOL: 7% VOL.
FERMENTATION: BOTTOM

Special remarks: Mocne Dobre is a pasteurized blonde lager of 15° OG. The aroma is slightly hoppy and the taste is sweet with underlying hops that is not entirely balanced. The aftertaste is slightly bitter and body is rounded and firm.

MURZYNEK

TYPE: DARK LIGHT BEER
ALCOHOL: 1.2% VOL.
FERMENTATION: BOTTOM

Special remarks: this almost black beer has a pale brown head. The aroma is of roasted malt while the taste is syrupy sweet with a sweet aftertaste.

PREMIER

TYPE: LAGER
ALCOHOL: 5.7% VOL.
FERMENTATION: BOTTOM

Special remarks: a pale blonde lager of 12° OG. The taste is of malt with underlying hops and the aroma is slightly hoppy. It has medium body.

• • •

OKOCIM KARMI

TYPE: LIGHT BEER
ALCOHOL: 1.2% VOL.
FERMENTATION: BOTTOM

Special remarks: a dark lager of 10.4° OG with very low level of alcohol.

BROWAR OKOCIM, BRZESKO

Production in hectoliters: 900,000
Founded: 1845

The goat on the labels of this brewer's beers are a reference to the symbol of the town in which the beer is brewed. This is a large brewery employing about 1,200 people with its own maltings, three brewing sites, and exports to various countries, including the USA.

OKOCIM LIGHT BEER

TYPE: LIGHT BEER
ALCOHOL: 1.2% VOL.
FERMENTATION: BOTTOM

Special remarks: this pale blonde lager has a malty aroma with some sharp undertones of hops. The aftertaste is slightly hoppy with a dry finish.

OKOCIM MOCNE

TYPE: LAGER
ALCOHOL: 7.8% VOL.
FERMENTATION: BOTTOM

Special remarks: a gold-blonde rounded lager of 15.1° OG with a full malty flavor. It is slightly sweet but also fresh. The aroma is of malt and there is no bitterness.

OKOCIM PIWO JASNE

TYPE: LAGER
ALCOHOL: 5.5% VOL.
FERMENTATION: BOTTOM

Special remarks: a pasteurized pale blonde lager of 11° OG. It is medium in body with an aroma of malt and hops without either dominating and the taste is similar. The aftertaste is initially and briefly bitter before sweetness comes to the fore.

• • •

BROWAR PIASTOWSKI, WROCLAW

Production in hectoliters: 750,000
Founded: 1893

A large brewery with its own maltings.

KSIAZ

TYPE: LAGER

ALCOHOL: 5.7% VOL.

FERMENTATION: BOTTOM

Special remarks: this Polish lager of 12° OG is golden-blonde and has an aroma of malt. The taste is sweet with underlying hops before a bitter aftertaste. Its body is rounded and it is drying.

• • •

TERMINATOR 10.5

TYPE: LAGER

ALCOHOL: 5.3% VOL.

FERMENTATION: BOTTOM

Special remarks: a special occasion beer to celebrate the New Year.

• • •

LECH BROWARY WIELKOPOLSKI SA, POZNAN

Production in hectoliters: 1,500,000
Founded: –

This large brewery employs almost 1,200 people. The shares are owned by South African Breweries.

LECH MOCNY

TYPE: LAGER

ALCOHOL: 5.7% VOL.

FERMENTATION: BOTTOM

Special remarks: a slightly sweet blonde lager with a hint of bitterness and fairly full sensation in the mouth. It is brewed with and OG of 14.8°.

LECH PREMIUM

TYPE: LAGER

ALCOHOL: 5.3% VOL.

FERMENTATION: BOTTOM

Special remarks: this blonde lager has an original gravity of 10.5°. The taste is slightly hoppy with underlying malt giving way to some bitterness. The body is thin to medium but thins in the mouth.

BROWAR SZCZECIN, SZCZECIN

Production in hectoliters: 350,000
Founded: 1848

This brewery is a subsidiary of Bittburger. It is situated in the Polish port town of Szcezcin and has a history dating back to 1848. At the end of World War II the brewery was named Bohrische Brauerei AG Stettin after is proprietor. From then on it became a state-owned business until 1992 when it once more returned to private hands. The brand name of "Bosman" (or bosun) is prompted by the brewery's waterside location. The German owners, Bittburger, have great plans for this brewery in Stettin (the German name for the town). The brewery was not entirely decrepit when it was taken over in 1997 but it required an investment of fifty million

Deutschmarks. The production is to be doubled to 600,000 hectoliters per annum and the Bosman brand has to be changed from regional to national brand.

BOSMAN FULL

TYPE: LAGER

ALCOHOL: 5.6% VOL.

FERMENTATION: BOTTOM

Special remarks: Full is blonde lager with an original gravity of 12.5° with a slightly hoppy aroma. The taste is of hops too without real bitterness. Body is thin to medium with a full mouth sensation. It is well-balanced and fairly neutral.

BOSMAN PILS

TYPE: LAGER

ALCOHOL: 5.3% VOL.

FERMENTATION: BOTTOM

Special remarks: a pale blonde Pilsener with an original gravity of 11° with a slightly hoppy taste and dry undertones. The aroma is vaguely hoppy and the body is thin to medium.

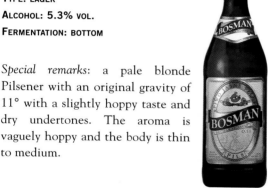

BOSMAN SPECJAL

TYPE: LAGER

ALCOHOL: 6.8% VOL.

FERMENTATION: BOTTOM

Special remarks: a blonde lager with an original gravity of 14° that is filtered and pasteurized. It is robust with medium body and a neutral taste verging on sweet with a bitter finish. Alcohol rises to the fore.

● ● ●

BROWAR ZACHODNIE LUBUSZ SA, ZIELONA GÓRA

Production in hectoliters: 60,000

Founded: 1872

A medium-sized brewery with its own maltings and soft drinks production. They brew a Pils, Kosher, Gambrinus, and Ulan in addition to Jubilat.

JUBILAT

TYPE: PREMIUM LAGER

ALCOHOL: 6.2% VOL.

FERMENTATION: BOTTOM

Special remarks: a golden-blonde lager with an original gravity of 13°. It has the firmness and rondeur of a bock. The taste is of prolonged hop bitterness. It is brewed according to the Reinheitsgebot.

● ● ●

BROWAR ZYWIEC, ZYWIEC

Production in hectoliters: 1,300,000

Founded: 1856

Zywiec is one of the largest Polish breweries. Its beers are exported to the USA, Canada, the UK, and Russia. Heineken has owned fifty percent of the shares since 1998 and are likely to extend this to a 75% stake although the Polish Stock Exchange has set some restrictions.

ZYWIEC

TYPE: LAGER

ALCOHOL: 5.8% VOL.

FERMENTATION: BOTTOM

Special remarks: a pale blonde lager with a somewhat malty taste but no bitterness of aftertaste. It is brewed to an original gravity of 12.5° and is pasteurized.

ŻYWIEC PORTER

TYPE: PORTER

ALCOHOL: 9.2% VOL.

FERMENTATION: BOTTOM

Special remarks: brewed to a recipe dating from 1881. This dark black porter has a full flavor of roasted malt that is rounded and sweet with a drying finish, giving way to bitterness and accompanied from the outset by alcohol.

MALOPOLSKI BROWAR STRZELEC, JEDRZEJÓW

Production in hectoliters: –

Founded: 1995

STRZELEC JASNE PELNE

TYPE: LAGER

ALCOHOL: 5.5% VOL.

FERMENTATION: BOTTOM

Special remarks: a pale blonde lager with an original gravity of 11°. The aroma is of malt and hops and the taste is defined by hops, concluding with a bitter finish. It has medium body.

COUNTRY Denmark

'Where a small country can be big' certainly applies to Denmark as far as beer is concerned. The United Brewers, easily the most dominant of all Danish brewers, comprises of two brewers that are responsible for two world famous beers, namely Carlsberg and Tuborg. The small population of five million does not exactly mean a large consumer market for this Danish brewer. The export market is therefore especially important for the Carlsberg/Tuborg Group to withstand the pressures exerted by the other large international brewers groups. However, the Danes are so taken by their own beer that they drink an average of 380 bottles per person per year, 80% of which is produced by their largest brewer. The Danes prefer to drink straight out of the bottle. Well, once you've been raised on a bottle.....

ALBANI BRYGGERIERNE, ODENSE

Production in hectoliters: approx. 1,000,000
Founded: 1859

Albani breweries include the Slotmfillen brewery in Kolding and the Maribo brewery in Lolland.
Albani brews a Pilsener, an export beer, a strong sweetish beer known as Giraffe, a dark beer, and a seasonal beer at Easter and Christmas.

• • •

BRYGGERIERNE FAXE JYSKE, FAXE

Production in hectoliters: approx. 2,700,000 (concern)
Founded: –

This is also the main branch of the Bryggerigruppen A/S (Danish brewers groups) which include the breweries Ceres and Thor. The Faxe beers are brewed here, including Faxe Light, Faxe Premium, Faxe Fad and Lys Faxe.

• • •

BRYGGERIET APOLLO, COPENHAGEN

Production in hectoliters: 1,500
Founded: 1990

This brewery produces Apollo beer and an organic beer known as Clemens.

• • •

BRYGGERIET S.C. FUGLSANG, HADERSLEV

Production in hectoliters: –
Founded: 1865

This small brewery and maltings produces beers known as Fugslang, Hertug Hans Pilsner and Golden Bird.

• • •

BRYGGERIET SLOTSMØLLEN KOLDING AS, KOLDING

Production in hectoliters: 250,000
Founded: 1570

Queen Dorethea, wife of King Christian 111 of Denmark, founded Slotsmfillen in 1570. Throughout the centuries this has remained a small local brewery. It is currently a subsidiary of the Albani group. Their beers are brewed from a mixture of 80% malt, and 20% corn (maize).

24.12

TYPE: LAGER

ALCOHOL: 5.4% VOL.

FERMENTATION: BOTTOM

Special remarks: 24.12 is a seasonal beer brewed for Christmas.

SLOTS GULD

TYPE: LAGER

ALCOHOL: 5.7% VOL.

FERMENTATION: BOTTOM

SLOTS HERKULES

TYPE: LAGER

ALCOHOL: 7.5% VOL.

FERMENTATION: BOTTOM

SLOTS PILSNER

TYPE: LAGER

ALCOHOL: 4.6% VOL.

FERMENTATION: BOTTOM

VÅRBRYG

TYPE: LAGER

ALCOHOL: 5.5% VOL.

FERMENTATION: BOTTOM

Special remarks: This strong lager is brewed for the spring.

•••

BRYGGERIET THOR BREWERY GROUP DENMARK A/S, RANDERS

Production in hectoliters: –

Founded: –

Thor, together with the Ceres and Faxe breweries, form the second largest brewers group in Denmark. One of the Thor brand names is "Buur", which actually means "beer". Buur is a strong blonde lager, full-bodied and malty with the resulting hoppy aftertaste. Other beers from this brewery include Thor Beer, a blonde balanced lager with nuances of malt and hops with a dry hoppy aftertaste, and Danish Gold, another blonde, strong hoppy lager, with a medium-body.

•••

BRYGGERIET VESTFYEN, ASSENS

Production in hectoliters: 250,000

Founded: 1885

This independent brewery exports to Germany, Sweden, and Iceland. This brewery's products include Prins Kristian, Danish Pride and Vestfyen Pilsener.

•••

CARLSBERG BRYGGERIERNE A/S KGL. DÄNISCHER HOFLIEFERANT, COPENHAGEN

Production in hectoliters: 32,000,000

Founded: 1847

This brewery is one of two breweries that make up the Carlsberg Group, also known as United Breweries. This international group with dozens of subsidiaries throughout the world now exports to more than one hundred countries. Carlsberg's history started early in the nineteenth century, when Jacob Christian Jacobson, together with his brother, started his own brewery in Copenhagen, where he embraced modern techniques and science. Jacob's son went to work for the Spaten brewery in Bavaria, just at the time when Gabriel Sedlmayr was in the process of brewing the first dark lager. Jacobson, armed with what he had learned, returned to Denmark, and started brewing his own lagers in 1846. When Jacobsen had a new brewery built on a hill near Copenhagen, he named it after his son Carl: Carl's hill - Carlsberg. In 1875, Jacobson set up his own laboratory where Emil Hansen developed a yeast strain, which was to guarantee the consistent quality of the beer.

CARLSBERG BEER

TYPE: PILSENER
ALCOHOL: 5.5% VOL.
FERMENTATION: BOTTOM

Special remarks: Carlsberg is one of a group of international lagers that owes its world-wide fame to an absence of marked elements in its taste, combined with a strong marketing strategy. This is not to say that it is poor quality beer, on the contrary, Carlsberg is without doubt a quality lager, with a beautiful full head and a yellow golden color. The taste of this somewhat full lager with a light to medium body is slightly sweet. It has a light hoppy aroma and a neutral aftertaste. An important part of the marketing strategy is the slim bottle, instantly recognized throughout the world, with the green label around the bottle neck.

CARLSBERG ICE

TYPE: ICE BEER
ALCOHOL: 5% VOL.
FERMENTATION: BOTTOM

Special remarks: This beer is brewed in accordance with the Reinheitsgebot by the Hannen brewery in Germany, a subsidiary of Carlsberg. It has nothing to offer a beer lover who wishes to be excited by aroma and taste. Ice is an excellent thirst quencher, and provided it is drunk well chilled will disappoint few drinkers. Carlsberg Ice is a clean tasting, smooth beer with just a hint of maltiness.

ELEPHANT BEER

TYPE: MALT LAGER/BOCK
ALCOHOL: 7.2% VOL.
FERMENTATION: BOTTOM

Special remarks: The word treacherous usually has negative connotations. However, for a beer

connoisseur this word can be hiding a challenge and a pleasant surprise. Elephant beer with its sweet malty taste and its rich aroma of hops does not give the immediate impression that it is a strong beer with a high level of alcohol. The name actually refers to an enormous brewery gate, supported on both sides by a life size elephant.

• • •

TUBORG BREWERIES LTD CARLSBERG INTERNATIONAL A/S, HELLERUP-COPENHAGEN

Production in hectoliters: -
Founded: 1873

Tuborg, the other large part of the Carlsberg concern. Tuborg-fabrieken NV was founded on 13 May, 1873, by a group of financiers and bankers. The ultimate goal was to become an export brewery. Export sales failed to meet expectations, however home sales exceeded them. The now familiar light gold Pilsener was introduced on 1 May 1880. The bond between the two brewers was forged in 1903, when they decided to share all profits and losses until the year 2000. In 1970, both companies merged, while still retaining their separate identities.

TUBORG GOLD LABEL

TYPE: PILSENER
ALCOHOL: 5.8% VOL.
FERMENTATION: BOTTOM

Special remarks: Gold Label is one Tuborg's top brands. This beer has a hoppy aroma, is golden in color, and has a smooth full balanced taste with a dry finish. Gold Label Pilsener was one of the first international premium beers, and is now exported to more than one hundred countries.

TUBORG STRONG BEER

TYPE: MALT LAGER/BOCK
ALCOHOL: 7.2% VOL.
FERMENTATION: BOTTOM

Special remarks: This robust golden lager is the Portuguese version. Strong Beer has a robust body, a hoppy and malty aroma and a malty taste, which imparts a somewhat alcoholic glow.

• • •

TUBORG JULEBRYG

TYPE: SPECIAL CHRISTMAS BREW
ALCOHOL: 5.5% VOL.
FERMENTATION: BOTTOM

Special remarks: Julebryg is the Danish word for Christmas. Several Danish breweries release a special beer to celebrate the Christmas season. This particular Tuborg beer is amber in color.

CERES BRYGGERIERNE BREWERY GROUP DENMARK A/S, AARHUS

Production in hectoliters: —
Founded: —

Ceres, is part of the second largest brewers group in Denmark. This concern also includes the Thor brewery in Randers and the Faxe brewery in Faxe. Ceres brews a dry malty stout, the strong dortmunder Ceres Dansk Dortmunder, a full-bodied malty Ceres Strong Ale and Ceres Royal Export.

TUBORG PÅSKEBRYG

TYPE: SPECIAL EASTER BREW
ALCOHOL: 7.8% VOL.
FERMENTATION: BOTTOM

Special remarks: This is another amber-colored seasonal beer, and is brewed to celebrate Easter.

RED ERIK

TYPE: LAGER
ALCOHOL: 6.5% VOL.
FERMENTATION: BOTTOM

Special remarks: this amber-colored lager is named after Erik the Red who discovered Greenland. This is also intended to denote something of the strength of this beer. It is a strong lager with a rich palette of aromas and flavors from sweet through to bitter, accompanied by a well-developed warmth in the mouth. The aftertaste is of prolonged bitterness.

FREDERICIA BRYGGERI, FREDERICIA

Production in hectoliters: 2,700,000
Founded: 1979

The Frederica brewery is a full subsidiary of Carlsberg and its products include Tuborg and Carlsberg beers.

•••

HANCOCK BRYGGERIERNE, SKIVE

Production in hectoliters: 2,300,000
Founded: 1876

This brewer's products include Hancock Pils and Old Gambrinus.

•••

HARBOE'S BRYGGERI, SKAELSOR, SJAELLAND

Production in hectoliters: –
Founded: 1883

This medium-sized brewery's products include Harboe Pilsener, Let Pilsener, Easter and Christmas beers and a Bjfirne Bryg beer.

•••

MARIBO BRYGHUS, MARIBO

Production in hectoliters: –
Founded: 1896

This brewery is a subsidiary of the Albani group and has approximately eighty employees.

•••

SCT. CLEMENS, AARHUS

Production in hectoliters: 2000
Founded: 1992

This small independent brewery has a high Holy content. Their brews include Sct. Clemens Special, Sct. Own Porter, Sct. Clemens Red Christmas, Augustijn and an organic beer known as Green Beer.

•••

THISTED BRYGHUS, THISTED

Production in hectoliters: 30,000
Founded: 1902

This brewery brews an organic beer, a whole host of beers with the word "Thy" included in their names, a dark beer known as Limfjords, and a number of Pilsener type beers.

•••

WIIBROE'S BRYGGERI, HELSINGOER

Production in hectoliters: 100,000
Founded: 1840

Carl Wiibroe founded this brewery in 1840. This brewery currently brews a Pilsener and a premium lager, both of which bear the founder's name, an Imperial Stout, and an alcohol-free beer.

•••

COUNTRY Sweden

The fact that the beer enthusiast is not exactly spoilt for choice in Sweden certainly cannot be blamed on the brewers in the extreme north of the country. The Swedish Government has always suppressed the beer culture as much as possible under pressure from anti-alcohol lobbying. The general sale of beer in Sweden is no longer allowed. Only beer with an alcohol level of less than 3.6% volume may be freely sold. Beer in higher categories may only be sold in state shops (systembolaget), pubs and certain restaurants and then at highly inflated prices. The minimum age for purchasing alcohol from a state shop is twenty years old, with the minimum age in pubs and restaurants being eighteen years old. The range on offer in the state shops varies, but is generally very limited. All this means Swedish brewers have never been able to offer a wide selection, resulting in only three brewers of any significance surviving. In spite of this, Sweden, with an average annual consumption of 65 liters per person, has not totally turned its back on alcohol. Sweden has been subject to European legislation since joining the European Union, which enables the Swedes to cross the border to Denmark and purchase 15 liters of beer per person tax free. Swedish beer lovers make grateful use of this not least because beer in Denmark is considerably cheaper than in Sweden. In order to combat this urge to import, the Swedish government has lowered the enormous tax levied on its own beers, making the import of Danish beer less attractive. A side effect of this is the influx of Fins on the other side of Sweden, who cross the border to buy their own Lapin Kulta. This is likely to continue for some time until the individual European member countries have adjusted to each other's individual legislative measures.

ÄBRO BRYGGERI AB, VIMMERBY

Production in hectoliters: 800,000
Founded: 1856

A medium-sized brewery owned by the Dunge family since 1898, and still family run after four generations. Apart from their own beer, they brew Gösser in various strengths and are wholesale distributors of a number of imported beers. They also brew a whole range of lagers using their own spring water, including Weigickl Pils, named after their current Master Brewer. Their strongest variety is Gorilla, a strong lager with 7.6% volume.

• • •

FALCON BRYGGERIER AB, FALKENBERG

Production in hectoliters: 1000,000
Founded: 1896

Danish Carlsberg has a majority stake in Falcon brewery, acquired from Unilever. This brewery was founded by John Laurentius Skantze, the son of a captain who learned brewing in Copenhagen and Berlin. The brewery was built on the west coast of Sweden next to a natural spring and is still there to this day. The beers from the Falcon brewery are Falcon in a standard variety or Falkenberger beer in the Viennese style, a Christmas beer called Julöl and Carlsberg.

GAMMELBRYGD 1993

TYPE: MALT LAGER/BOCK
ALCOHOL: 5.6% VOL.
FERMENTATION: BOTTOM

Special remarks: Gammelbrygd is a beer that is brewed annually on November 1. The brew year is added to the label after the beer has been allowed to mature for more than a year. Gammels means old. It has an intense aroma and with its roasted malt and sweetening, is somewhat Port like. Its black color is hidden beneath a small cream-colored head. The taste is dry and particularly of a sweet roasted nature, with an aftertaste that is brief and vaguely bitter. This is a rich and finely balanced lager with robust body.

•••

GOTLANDS BRYGGERI, VISBY

Production in hectoliters: 5000
Founded: 1995

The Gotlands brewery (a Swedish island in the Baltic Sea) fulfills Spendrup's wishes for a small scale brewery for public relations purposes that can be used for experimental brewing. Spendrup distributes the beers brewed in the picturesque Visby throughout the country. One of these is Wisby Klosteröl, an ale in the Belgium style with 6% abv and with a measure of wheat, neither filtered or pasteurized. Another bottled beer from this brewery is the Wisby Munköl, an unpasteurized dortmunder with 5.5% volume. Gotlands also brew the Scottish MacLay & Thistle MacLay's Stout under license.

•••

GREBBESTADS BRYGGERI, GREBBESTAD

Production in hectoliters: –
Founded: 18 December 1995

Grebbestads brewery is a small microbrewery on the west coast of Sweden, founded by Lars Wenneræs. In 1996, this newcomer took over another newcomer, the brewery tenant Bohus, enabling Grebbestad to produce their two robust hoppy Pilseners.
Apart from the two Bohus Pilseners, Grebbestad also brews two lagers, Granit and Koster.

•••

KÄLLEFALLS BRYGGERI AB, TIDAHOLM

Production in hectoliters: 5000
Founded: 1992

This microbrewery exclusively brews top fermented beer in the English style. In all probability the beer monitoring body, Campaign for Real Ale (CAMRA), awakened their enthusiasm. Their beers are Pale Ale, Brown Ale, Strong Ale, Jul Öl and Skarabôrjarn.

•••

KUNGSHOLMENS KVARTERSBRYGGERI AB, STOCKHOLM

Production in hectoliters: 7500
Founded: 1997

The Kungsholmens brewery is a new microbrewery, and was started by seven home-brewers who were dissatisfied by the beers being brewed by the big players. The jewels in the crown of this brewery are Håkan Lundgren and O.P. Vikström. This brewery's aim is to brew lagers and ales, following the old traditions. Their beers are Lundrens Lager and King's Dog Ale, both of which have limited availability in Stockholm.

•••

MUNKBO ÄNGBRYGGERI, SMEDJEBACKEN

Production in hectoliters: –
Founded: 1996

Ängbryggeri means "steam brewery", and refers to the steam heated mash kettle. This microbrewery is housed in a brewery formerly started in 1856, following its closure in 1988, and where Spendrup was at the helm for about eight years. They now brew a number of non-pasteurized lagers, which include Munkbo lager 5.6%, Old Swedish Lager and Örebro Slottsöl.

• • •

NYA BANCO BRYGGERIER I SKRUV AB, SKRUV

Production in hectoliters: 70,000
Founded: –

This is a small brewery with about 45 employees. All beers produced by this brewery include the word "Banco" in their name

• • •

PIVOVAR PAJALA, PAJALA

Production in hectoliters: –
Founded: 1998

This is a small pub microbrewery that has found a superb form of development by collaborating the Czech brewery Humpolec Bernard, and brewing their beers under license.

• • •

PRIPPS RINGES AB, STOCKHOLM

Production in hectoliters: 15,000,000
Founded: 1880

Pripps-Ringes is a large international concern with breweries in seven countries: Norway, Sweden, Russia, Estonia, Latvia, Lithuania and the Ukraine. There are 8600 employees within the group. Pripps-Ringes and the Finnish brewer Oy Hartwell form Baltic Beverage Holdings.
This brewery produces a whole range of lagers with names like Pripps, Arboga, Bulldozer 8% volume, Eagle, K2 Ice, Sarek Export, TOP and Three Towns. Pripps also brews Carnegie Pale Ale, Carnegie Porter, Ross Creek Red Beer, an American amber ale and Carlsberg and Fosters under license.

• • •

SOFIERO BRYGGERI, LAHOLM

Production in hectoliters: 10,000
Founded: 1888

This small brewery produces a variety of lagers including Sofiero 1888 Pils, Mörk Guld and Sofiero Whiskey Malt. Sofiero is also a wholesaler of various imported beers such as Pilsener Urquell and King & Barnes. This brewery was taken over by Pripps in 1989, after brewing for over one hundred years. Pripps intended closing the brewery down but this was avoided through a management buy-out. Sofiero brews in open copper kettles heated over open fires. This traditional method results in the slightly burnt taste. Laholm is in Southern Sweden, close to the Danish border, which is convenient location.

• • •

COUNTRY Latvia

ALDARIS BREWERY, RIGA

Production in hectoliters: –
Founded: 1865

The Aldaris brewery is part of the Swedish/Finnish Pripps-Hartwall corporation, and has approximately four hundred employees.

ALDARIS PORTERIS

TYPE: PORTER
ALCOHOL: 7% VOL.
FERMENTATION: TOP

Special remarks: this rounded sweetish porter is jet black in color, and has a light dry finish. The aroma is rich and complex with light herb nuances. Alderis Porteris is a mild, non-bitter porter.

ALDARIS ZELTA

TYPE: LAGER/PILSENER
ALCOHOL: 5% VOL.
FERMENTATION: BOTTOM

Special remarks: Zelta is a blonde lager with a malty, slightly sweetish taste. The aroma is slightly hoppy and this beer has a light bitter finish. Zelta leaves a slight sensation of alcohol in the mouth.

• • •

COUNTRY Italy

The boot of Italy is not overflowing with blonde frothy malted brew. Beer has never been traditional in Italy and is only drunk by younger Italians. Italians prefer to drink wine even more than the French.

In the nineteenth century, Northern Italy fell under the rule of the Austrian-Hungarian Empire, which has left a small legacy in the form of a few Viennese style lagers, however the beer culture in Italy has never followed that of Austria.

With an average annual consumption of twenty-five liters per person, Italy is firmly seated at the bottom of the ladder of beer drinking folk. Nevertheless, Italy has a population of sixty million people, and the interest in beer is increasing. The younger generation, along with large numbers of tourists from Northern Europe likes to be served with a cold glass of beer in this country, which is invariably hot. This potential growth market has attracted the main world brewers. Heineken has already a finger in the pie with Dreher and Moretti making it the largest Italian group. Carlsberg has their foot in the door at Poretti, and BSN/Kronenbourg has become involved with Peroni. This means that by far the largest market share in Italy is in the hands of foreign companies. It follows therefore that the beers that dominate the Italian market are the universal international lagers. There has been a noticeable growth in the availability of stronger beers with more character but demand is still very low. However, a trend has started in the large Italian cities, which has seen the opening of several "real" old English pubs. So maybe all is not yet lost with the Italians.

Italy is vast, which has led to the large brewers setting up a number of different brewing locations throughout the country. The Italians clearly indicate on the packaging of each product exactly where it was brewed.

HEINEKEN ITALIA SpA, MILAN

Production in hectoliters: 5000,000
Founded: 1974

Heineken Italy is a holding that includes eight different breweries with the best known being Dreher and Moretti. It is the largest group in Italy with a third of the market. Dreher was founded by Anton Dreher in Trieste in Northern Italy in 1865. Moretti, formerly owned first by Labatt and then by Interbrew was founded in 1859, in the then Austrian province of Friuli near Udine. The Moretti La Rossa, still brewed in the Viennese style, serves as a reminder to the old ties with Austria. Messina Nuova Birra, is just one of the other breweries that make up the group.

BAFFO D'ORO

TYPE: LAGER
ALCOHOL: 4.6% VOL.
FERMENTATION: BOTTOM

Special remarks: "brewed with pure malt" gives the Moretti an abundance of maltiness. At first, the sweet malty taste reminds the drinker of an alcohol-free beer. Baffo D'Oro means "golden mustache" and is a reference to the brewery's trademark: The man with a mustache is shown on the label.

DREHER

TYPE: LAGER
ALCOHOL: 4.7% VOL.
FERMENTATION: BOTTOM

Special remarks: the blonde Dreher has a slightly hoppy aroma. The taste is slightly malty, but is dominated by the hops. The aftertaste is short and somewhat bitter.

BIRRA MORETTI

TYPE: PILSENER
ALCOHOL: 4.6% VOL.
FERMENTATION: BOTTOM

Special remarks: this Moretti Pilsener is a light blonde lager with a faint hoppy aroma. The taste is hoppy and dry, and flows into a short somewhat bitter aftertaste.

MESSINA

TYPE: LAGER
ALCOHOL: 4.7% VOL.
FERMENTATION: BOTTOM

SANS SOUCI

TYPE: EXPORT
ALCOHOL: 5.6% VOL.
FERMENTATION: BOTTOM

Special remarks: "without worries" is the name of this export variety of the Morreti range. Sans Souci is a light blonde lager. The aroma is faint, floral, hoppy and slightly malty. The taste is malty, fresh and has a hoppy finish. The aftertaste is slightly bitter.

• • •

BIRRA FORST SpA, LAGUNDO

Production in hectoliters: 700,000
Founded: 1857

Birra Forst is a medium-sized and bilingual brewery, using both the Italian and German languages. This brewery collaborates with Weihestephan for the brewing their wheat beers. Forst brews include Forst Pils, Forst Luxus Light, Forst Kronen in export style, and Forst St. Sixtus a somewhat heavier abbey beer. Manabrea in Biella is a subsidiary of the Forst brewery.

• • •

BIRRA MENABREA, BIELLA

Production in hectoliters: 60,000
Founded: 1846

This small brewery has a number of English beers and German Palmbräu in its assortment in addition to its own beer. Menebrau is owned by Forst.

MENABREA

TYPE: LAGER
ALCOHOL: 4.8% VOL.
FERMENTATION: BOTTOM

Special remarks: a blonde export lager with a hoppy aroma. The taste is slightly hoppy as is the dry aftertaste.

• • •

BIRRA PERONI INDUSTRIALE SPA, ROME

Production in hectoliters: 4000,000
Founded: 1846

Peroni is owned by the French Kronenbourg/BSN concern, and after Heineken is the biggest player in the Italian market.

NASTRO AZZURO

TYPE: EXPORT LAGER
ALCOHOL: 5.2% VOL.
FERMENTATION: BOTTOM

Special remarks: Nastro Azzuro from the Peroni brewery is a blonde export lager with a slightly sharp hoppy aroma. The taste is hoppy with undertones of malt. It has a light bitter finish, resulting in a dryness. It has a light to medium body. Nastro Azzuro means "blue ribbon" and is one of the best selling beers in Italy.

PERONI

TYPE: LAGER

ALCOHOL: 4.7% VOL.

FERMENTATION: BOTTOM

Special remarks: this blonde lager has a slight aroma of malt with vague hoppiness. The taste is of hops, leading to a slightly bitter finish. It has medium body and the aftertaste is dry, hoppy, and slightly bitter.

INDUSTRIE PORETTI SPA, MILAN/INDUNO OLONA

Production in hectoliters: 2,000,000

Founded: 1877

In addition to their own brands this brewery produces Carlsberg under license.

SPLÜGEN

TYPE: LAGER

ALCOHOL: 4.5% VOL.

FERMENTATION: BOTTOM

Special remarks: a blonde lager with slightly sharp aroma of hops. The taste is lightly hoppy with a brief bitter and drying finish. It has thin to medium body.

● ● ●

Portugal

The ten million Portuguese drink an average of sixty-five liters of beer per person each year. The majority of this beer comes from the country's two largest breweries, Unicer and Central de Cervejas. The Portuguese beers appear to be influenced by German lagers, which entirely suits tourists from northern Europe.

SA CENTRAL DE CERVEJAS, LISBON

Production in hectoliters: 3,200,000
Founded: 1934

Apart from owning a variety of breweries and a maltings, Central de Cervejas also has interests in other companies. Their most important beers are: Sagres; Europa; Golden; Topázio; Onix; Jansen Light; Bohemia; St. Jorge. Central's main export markets are Angola and Spain.

IMPERIAL

TYPE: LAGER
ALCOHOL: 5.1% VOL.
FERMENTATION: BOTTOM

Special remarks: this is a blonde neutral lager with a faint slightly hoppy aroma. The taste of hops and malt comes through, but very reluctantly. Imperial has a medium body and is slightly dry towards the finish.

JANSEN SEM ÁLCOOL

TYPE: ALCOHOL-FREE BEER
ALCOHOL: -
FERMENTATION: BOTTOM

Special remarks: a blonde alcohol-free beer with a worty aroma and an acute smell of hops. The taste is light, slightly malty, with a tinge of sweetness in the aftertaste. This is neither hoppy or bitter.

SAGRES

TYPE: LAGER
ALCOHOL: 5.1% VOL.
FERMENTATION: BOTTOM

Special remarks: Sagres is one of the best-known beers of Portugal. It is a blonde lager with a malty taste, accompanied by quite a strong taste of hops. Sagres has a light to medium body.

SAGRES DARK

TYPE: LAGER
ALCOHOL: 4.3% VOL.
FERMENTATION: BOTTOM

Special remarks: this is a jet black beer with a light brown head. The aroma is malty and slightly burnt. The taste is also malty, with coffee like traits, but is especially reminiscent of burnt toast, all be it not overpowering. Sagres has quite a sturdy body. The dark variety of Sagres is dry as the finish is approached, and has no pronounced aftertaste.

● ● ●

FABRICIA DE CERVEJA JOÃO DE MELO ABREU, PONTA DELGADA

Production in hectoliters: 61,000
Founded: **1893**

The most important beers are Especial, Concha and Petra Doce (alcohol-free). This brewery has 150 employees and exports to the USA and Canada.

• • •

SA UNICER UNIÃO CERVEJEIRA, MAMEDE DE INFESTA

Production in hectoliters: 3,500,000
Founded: **1890**

Unicer is one of the two largest breweries in Portugal, with Carlsberg owning a third of the shares. Their most important beers are Superbock; Cristal; Cristal Tipo Munique; Carlsberg and Tuborg.

CHEERS

TYPE: ALCOHOL-FREE
ALCOHOL: 0,5% VOL.
FERMENTATION: BOTTOM

Special remarks: gold blonde in color, with a malty aroma. The taste is also malty with worty undertones.

CRISTAL PILSENER

TYPE: PILSENER
ALCOHOL: 5.1% VOL.
FERMENTATION: BOTTOM

Special remarks: Cristal is one of the most widely known Pilseners in Portugal. It has a light blonde color with a slightly hoppy aroma. The taste has a tinge of hops and the aftertaste is dry and somewhat briefly bitter. This Pilsener has a medium body.

SUPERBOCK

TYPE: MALT LAGER/BOCK
ALCOHOL: 5.8% VOL.
FERMENTATION: BOTTOM

Special remarks: although the term Superbock sounds very German, this light blonde lager is one of the best-known Portuguese beers. The taste is sweetish and lightly malted with an underlying hoppy flavor. Superbock has a medium to robust body.

• • •

COUNTRY Spain

The Spanish like the French are really wine drinkers and do not really have their own beer culture with its own traditions. Even in the former Spanish colonies there is no real evidence of Spanish beer. Despite this, the Spanish market is still of great interest to European brewers. Not only are there forty million Spaniards but hordes of tourists from Germany, Belgium, The Netherlands and the UK who represent a significant market that much greater than the combined Benelux countries. The principal beers are once again lagers, and the market is dominated by northern European brewers such as Heineken, BSN, Guinness and Carlsberg.

GRUPO CRUZCAMPO, SEVILLA

Production in hectoliters: 6,600,000
Founded: 1904

Almost ninety percent of Cruzcampo is owned by Guinness, with Carlsberg owning the remaining ten percent. Cruzcampo is a large group with five production centers in Seville, Madrid, Navarra, Valencia and Jean. Cruzcampo distributes Guinness and Kilkenny and produces Carlsberg, Kaliber, Keler, Victoria, Skol, Alcázar, Estrella del Sur, Calatrava, Oro Lujo, Henninger and Cruzcampo.

• • •

MAHOU SA, MADRID

Production in hectoliters: 4,500,000
Founded: –

Mahou is part of the BSN/Kronenbourg group.

• • •

FABRICAS DE CERVEZA Y MALTA SA SAN MIGUEL, MADRID

Production in hectoliters: 3,500,000
Founded: –

The "beer and malt factories" of San Miguel are part of the BSN/Kronenbourg group.

SA EL AGUILA, MADRID

Production in hectoliters: 9,000,000
Founded: 1900

El Aquila brews at three centers in Spain: Valencia, Madrid and San Sebastian. Heineken has a majority stake in these breweries, that brew Buckler and Heineken, and distribute Murphy's stout, in addition to brewing Aquila.

SAN MIGUEL EXPORT

TYPE: EXPORT LAGER
ALCOHOL: 5.4% VOL.
FERMENTATION: BOTTOM

Special remarks: a blonde lager with a faint malty aroma. It has a lightly malted taste, with a slightly dry and hoppy finish. The aftertaste is lightly malted. This export is brewed with water, malt, hops, yeast, antioxidant and a preservative.

COUNTRY Croatia

ZAGREBACKA PIVOVARA, ZAGREB

Production in hectoliters: 1,200,000
Founded: 1892

This is the largest brewery in Croatia with approximately six hundred employees, and it is half owned by Belgium's Interbrew. It mainly brews for the home market with export sales accounting for just 3% of production. As well as their own beers, this brewery produces Stella Artois as a premium luxury beer under license.

OZUJSKO PIVO

TYPE: LAGER
ALCOHOL: 5% VOL.
FERMENTATION: BOTTOM

Special remarks: Ozujsko means "March beer". March was formerly the best month for brewing lager before the advent of industrial cooling. Ozujsko is now the number one brewery in Croatia with a market share of around 35%.

TOMISLAV PIVO

TYPE: DARK LAGER
ALCOHOL: 6% VOL.
FERMENTATION: BOTTOM

Special remarks: Tomislav is named after the first Queen of Croatia. This dark lager was launched in 1926 to celebrate the thousandth anniversary of the coronation of Tomislav, and is now the biggest selling dark lager in Croatia.

•••

COUNTRY Bosnia Hercogovina

PIVOVARA BIHACKA, BIHAC

Production in hectoliters: –
Founded: –

PREMINGER

TYPE: LAGER
ALCOHOL: 5% VOL.
FERMENTATION: BOTTOM

Special remarks: this dark blonde pasteurized lager has an original gravity content of 12°.

UNSKI BISER

TYPE: LAGER
ALCOHOL: 4.3% VOL.
FERMENTATION: BOTTOM

Special remarks: this blonde light variety has an original gravity content of 11.3°.

•••

COUNTRY Greece

NORTHERN GREECE BREWERIES SA, THESSALONIKI

Production in hectoliters: –
Founded: –

AEGEAN LAGER BEER

TYPE: LAGER

ALCOHOL: 5% VOL.

FERMENTATION: BOTTOM

Special remarks: this is blonde lager, lightly malted with a somewhat sharp hop presence. It has a light to medium body.

• • •

COUNTRY Malta

Malta is a small, heavily-populated island just to the south of Italy. It came under British rule for a time and this influence is still apparent. Where most people of the Mediterranean prefer to quench their thirst with a cool lager because of the warm climate, the Maltese still have a brewer of real ales. Löwenbräu arrived in Malta in 1992 and in addition to their lagers, also import a range of English ales.

SIMONDS FARSONS CISK LTD, THE BREWERY, MRIEHEL

Production in hectoliters: 200,000
Founded: 1927

This Maltese brewery was originally founded by Faruggia & Sons, shortened to Farsons, supported by the English brewer Simonds. Cisk is the shortened version of the family name Scicluna, who also own shares in the brewery. Apart from their own ales and lagers this brewery produces soft drinks, fruit juices and mineral water and brews Carlsberg under license. This brewery has developed a system that collects and stores rainwater that can be used in the event of a drought.

FARSONS STRONG ALE

TYPE: ALE

ALCOHOL: 6.7% VOL.

FERMENTATION: TOP

Special remarks: this robust amber colored ale has a sweetish fruity aroma. The taste is slightly sweet with a dry bitter finish.

• • •

The Americas

The Americas

COUNTRY Canada

The Canadian market is not tremendously different to that of the USA. It is almost totally controlled by two foreign groups, Labatt and Molson, with some room for American imports and a few European beers. In the last few years a small group of microbreweries and pub breweries have sprung up to pick up a slice of the cake but as with their southern neighbors, this slice is not really significant.

Thirty million Canadians are not really big drinkers, with an average annual consumption of sixty-five liters per head of population.

British immigrants originally established the beer traditions but ultimately the market was almost entirely taken over by lagers, under influence of US breweries. Canada too like the USA had a period of prohibition. The restrictions varied between provinces, with some having a total ban on brewing while others only permitted brewing for export. Even the "temporary beer" with a maximum alcohol of two percent was available in one province but not in another. Government restrictions on brewers selling to other provinces have only helped the survival of giants at the expense of smaller brewers.

BRASAL BREWERY INC, LASALLE QUEBEC

Production in hectoliters: –
Founded: 1989

Brasal claims to be the only brewery in Quebec still brewing lager in the German style in accordance with the Reinheitsgebot. Brasal brews include Brasal Bock, Brasal Légãre, Hopps Bräu, Hopps aux Pommes, Sans Fontiãre Ambré and Sans Fontiãre Blonde.

BRASAL BIERE AMBRÉE SPÉCIALE

Type: LAGER
Alcohol: 6.1% VOL.
Fermentation: BOTTOM

Special remarks: this amber-colored lager has a slightly roasted malt aroma, together with a slightly roasted taste. This lager is medium bodied with an aftertaste leaving a sensation of alcohol warmth.

•••

LE CHEVAL BLANC, MONTREAL

Production in hectoliters: 5,000
Founded: 1987

Le Cheval Blanc, or white horse, is a pub brewery with a Master Brewer by the name of Jerôme Denys. Thebrews include Blanche Originale, Loch Ness, Titanic and Cap Tourmente.

BIÉRE AMBREE TRADITIONNELLE

Type: ALE
Alcohol: 8% VOL.
Fermentation: TOP

Special remarks: this sturdy ale has secondary fermentation in the bottle.

BIERE ROUSSE LEGENDAIRE

Type: ALE
Alcohol: 5% VOL.
Fermentation: TOP

Special remarks: this amber-colored ale has a somewhat fruity aroma and a soft sweetish caramel taste with a fruity nuance.

•••

LES BRASSEURS GMT INC, MONTREAL, QUEBEC

Production in hectoliters: 50,000
Founded: 1988

This microbrewery's range consists solely of lagers, including Biãre de Noel 6%, Belle Guele 5.2%, Belle Gueule Rousse 5.2% and Canon 7.6%.

TREMBLAY

Type: LAGER
Alcohol: 5% VOL.
Fermentation: BOTTOM

Special remarks: a blonde, reasonably full bodied lager has a somewhat hoppy aroma. The taste is softly hoppy with a touch of floral freshness, supported by sufficient maltiness. The mouth sensation is dry and the aftertaste hoppy, without bitter accents.

•••

THE HART BREWING CO LTD, CARLETON PLACE ONTARIO

Production in hectoliters: –
Founded: –

As well as the Festive Brown, this small brewery's range includes an Amber Ale and a Cream Ale.

HART

TYPE: AMERICAN ALE
ALCOHOL: 6% VOL.
FERMENTATION: TOP

Special remarks: medium brown in color, this ale is light bodied with a taste of burnt malt, not intense, but somewhat bitter.

• • •

LABATT BREWERIES LTD, LONDON

Production in hectoliters: 11,500,000
Founded: 1847

This company is one of Canada's brewing giants, and has a market share of around 45%. Labatt has been part of Belgium's Interbrew since 1995.
The history of Labatt, began with John Kinder Labatt, an Irish immigrant, who took over the Simcoe Street brewery in London, Ontario, in 1847, together with his partner Samuel Eccles. In 1853, John Labatt became the sole owner of the brewery, and renamed it John Labatt's Brewery. Labatt had already started to expand in the nineteenth century, thanks in part to the laying of the railroad which enabled distribution to other Canadian provinces. At the start of the twentieth century, Labatt had to cope with the Canadian prohibition that took different forms in the various provinces. Labatt survived due to production of export beer and 'temporary beer', with alcohol of just 2%. This period lasted from 1915 until 1926. Labatt was nationalized in 1945. In 1951, Labatt launched a Pilsener that was given the nickname "Blue" because of the color of its label and sponsorship of the American football team, The Blue Bombers. Labatt Blue has been the best-selling Canadian lager since 1979. Labatt also brews John Labatt Classic, Labatt Genuine Draft, Labatt Wildcat, Labatt Ice, Labatt 50, Labatt Select, Labatt Lite and Blue Lite, Labatt 5 and Labatt Extra Dry. Labatt also brews a number of beers under license, including, Budweiser and Bud Lite, Carlsberg and Guinness, along with a number of other brands for the local market. In 1993, Labatt was the first to introduce ice beer, using a patented method. In total, Labatt brews around fifty types of beer. Labatt has currently eight breweries in five different provinces.

LABATT ICE

TYPE: ICE BEER
ALCOHOL: 5.6% VOL.
FERMENTATION: BOTTOM

Special remarks: ice beer is brewed in the same way as lager. It is then chilled to such a degree that ice crystals form. These crystals are filtered out of the beer, resulting in – according to the brewer – a mellow, evenly-balanced beer, with slightly higher level of alcohol. Labatt Ice is a golden beer with a sweet malty taste with sufficient support from the hops.

• • •

MOLSON BREWERIES, TORONTO

Production in hectoliters: 14,000,000
Founded: 1786

Three Canadian breweries were behind the birth of the Molson brewery. John Molson founded Molson in 1786. The two breweries with which Molson merged in 1989, were Carling, founded by Thomas Carling in 1840, and O'Keefe founded by Eugene O'Keefe in 1862. These two breweries had already merged in the nineteenth century and at the time of the merger with Molson the company was bought up by the Australian brewery, Fosters (CUB). In 1993, Miller obtained a small stake in Molson, giving the company an improved international status. Molson is the largest brewery in Canada with eight breweries, and brews the following brands, and a whole range of different varieties: Molson, Carling, O'Keefe, Alpine, Red Dog, Old Vienna and for the Canadian market, Miller and Coots, Fosters, Amstel and Asahi.

MOLSON DRY

TYPE: LAGER

ALCOHOL: 5% VOL.

FERMENTATION: BOTTOM

Special remarks: Molson Dry is a light lager with a slightly malty taste that has a tinge of dryness which remains through to the finish.

• • •

MOOSEHEAD BEER

TYPE: LAGER

ALCOHOL: 5% VOL.

FERMENTATION: BOTTOM

Special remarks: Moosehead is a blonde lager with a sweetish aroma that has a suggestion of malt. It is light bodied with a light malt taste and a dry aftertaste.

• • •

MOOSEHEAD BREWERIES LIMITED, SAINT JOHN

Production in hectoliters: –
Founded: 1867

This brewery was started in 1867 with investment of $9,600 by Captain De Winton and two local businessmen. These financiers were impressed with the brew of Susannah Oland, wife of John James Dunn Oland, the brewery manager.
This brewery has had its ups and downs, but is still an independent family brewery run by an Oland. Moosehead currently brews a top fermenting Ale, an Ice Beer, Dry Beer and a Light Beer, in addition to its lagers.
Moosehead owns the Premium Beer Company, a Canadian wholesaler which distributes imported beers of Scottish & Newcastle, Tetley, Bass, Beck, Beamish and Bulmer's cider.

UNIBROUE INC, CHAMBLY QUEBEC

Production in hectoliters: 100,000
Founded: 1990

The history of the Unibroue brewery dates back to 1990 when André Dion and Serge Racine took over a loss-making Massawippi brewery. At the time it was less complicated to take over an existing brewery than start a new one, because this avoided the need for a Canadian government license. In collaboration with a Belgium brewer, Unibroue launched the first of its current ten bottle-conditioned special beers of Belgian style in 1992. The Brewer Gino Vantieghem is also of Belgian descent. Unibroue beers are brewed exclusively with natural ingredients and bottle conditioning gives them a long shelf life, which is far easier for export. Unibroue does not concentrate solely on the Canadian market, with sales to the USA and Europe, particularly to France and Switzerland. Unibroue's production process takes about eight weeks. In addition to the beers reviewed, Unibroue brews Blanche de Chambly, Raft-man, Quelque Chose, 1837 and Marie Clarisse. The bottles and labels are of interest, even though the printing in typical Belgian style leaves much to be desired.

EAU BENITE

TYPE: SPECIAL BREW

ALCOHOL: 7.7% VOL.

FERMENTATION: TOP

Special remarks: this golden bottle-conditioned beer has a fruity aroma. The taste is somewhat fruity, and it has a malty, slightly sour finish. The aftertaste could be described as vaguely hoppy.

LA GAILLARDE

TYPE: SPECIAL BREW

ALCOHOL: 5.0% VOL.

FERMENTATION: TOP

Special remarks: La Gaillarde, or the gay affair, is a blonde bottle conditioned beer with a whitish haze. This beer has a small pure white head. The aroma is sweet and fruity. The taste is sour and dry with shades of citrus. This is a reasonably balanced beer with a slightly sour aftertaste.

LA FIN DU MONDE

TYPE: SPECIAL BREW

ALCOHOL: 9% VOL.

FERMENTATION: TOP

Special remarks: the brewer has named this beer "the end of the world". This is a golden, somewhat cloudy bottle-conditioned beer with a sweet fruity aroma of caramel and oranges. The taste is sweetish and rich with herbs and fruit, and at the finish dry and warming. The 9% is cleverly concealed in the background, so watch out!

MAUDITE

TYPE: SPECIAL BREW

ALCOHOL: 8% VOL.

FERMENTATION: TOP

Special remarks: this amber-colored bottle conditioned beer has a taste that develops. The aromas of the hops and malt are also accompanied by one of alcohol. The taste is malty and complex with a herbal sourness approaching the finish with a certain hoppiness in the background. This beer has a robust body, and leaves a lively and warming sensation in the mouth.

TROIS PISTOLES

TYPE: SPECIAL BREW

ALCOHOL: 9% VOL.

FERMENTATION: TOP

Special remarks: a dark brown beer with an intense sweet and fruity aroma. The taste is full and sturdy. The start is very dry and sweetish, with something of a sour finish. Trois Pistoles has full roasted malt taste. The alcohol of this well-balanced beer is kept beautifully in the background. Qua style, this could almost be a robust Belgium abbey beer. The aftertaste is briefly somewhat bitter, but this is dominated by its dryness.

COUNTRY USA

In terms of their individual consumption, Americans are not the biggest beer drinkers in the world, but with an annual consumption of eighty-five liters per head each year, they are not doing badly. In terms of beer production though America is in a league of its own with an annual production of around three hundred million hectoliters, making them the worlds biggest producers of beer. The majority of growth among US brewers has largely been evident in the export sector.

There has actually been a shift in the types of beer being drunk by the Americans. Imported beer accounts for a little less than 10% of American beer market, while around 30% of the total production is exported. There has been a move away from light lagers marketed by the major breweries, to more specialist beers produced by pub breweries and microbreweries. A large number of these small breweries have been founded since the mid 1980's, a few of which can hardly be considered as microbreweries any more, given the volume of special beer they now produce. Generally speaking, these "craft" breweries follow German and English traditions. The Americans now have ales, stouts, Hefeweizen and Oktoberfests on their shelves, not surprising considering the large numbers of early immigrants from these countries, many of whom have a good understanding of brewing. Many large breweries were set-up by either German or English founders, although this did not prevent them eventually turning their backs on European traditions in favor of the light lagers.

Prohibition between 1920 and 1933 had an enormous influence on the development of the American breweries, which were forbidden from brewing beer with any alcoholic content, except those for export. A few US states even had bans on alcohol that pre-date Prohibition. After this period, the brewing industry became industrialized, and some of the brewing traditions did not return. In the first decade, the growth of the specialty beer was enormous, often in factors of tens of percentage points. However the total amount of special beer is not really worth mentioning, because it accounts for less than three percent of all sales. This seems unlikely to increase as growth appears to have run its course.

Meanwhile, the giant breweries were well aware of the trend towards specialty beers, and used the enormous strength of their advertising and distribution might to overpower small brewers. To a certain extent they blocked trading of the microbreweries by forcing wholesalers exclusively to stock their own product range. Microbreweries are now also experiencing competition between themselves and some large breweries have introduced their own competitive specialist beers, by brewing it themselves, or taking a stake in a microbrewery. It is all part of the mature state of the US beer market in which a handful of giant brewers dominate the industry. There are more than 1,500 breweries in the United States, of which more than half are pub breweries. Almost five hundred breweries call themselves microbreweries, which means that they do not brew more than 25,000 hectoliters per year.

ALASKAN BREWING COMPANY, JUNEAU

Production in hectoliters: 80,000
Founded: **1986**

Brewing beer in the northern most states of America is a task that can present a few snags. Nevertheless, after realizing that moving the glaciers, bears and mountains to warmer regions was just not on, the founders of the Alaskan brewery, Geoff and Marcy Larson, decided to start brewing their beer here. In 1995, this brewery opened a new 100-barrel brewing house, together with extended storage and bottling facilities, enabling them to achieve a growth up to 120,000 barrels. The Alaskan brewery distributes to six American states and also exports their beer to Japan.

ALASKAN AMBER

TYPE: ALT
ALCOHOL: 5% VOL.
FERMENTATION: TOP

Special remarks: this alt was the brewery's debut beer, brewed to a recipe of an old Juneau brewery, dating from the gold rush. The Amber is a medium malty alt with a mild hoppy character. This beer is brewed with Crystal and Klages malt and with Cascade and Saaz hops.

ALASKAN FRONTIER

TYPE: AMERICAN ALT
ALCOHOL: 5% VOL.
FERMENTATION: TOP

Special remarks: this was originally an autumn beer, but has actually been brewed throughout the year since 1996. This copper colored ale has a roasted malt taste and a somewhat bitter finish.

ALASKAN PALE

TYPE: ALE
ALCOHOL: 4.6% VOL.
FERMENTATION: TOP

Special remarks: this brewery has been making this beer since 1988 as a light alternative to the Amber. This is a light malty beer with just a tinge of citrus aroma and a hoppy finish. The Pale is especially recommended as a thirst quencher in warm weather. The malts used are Klages pale and Münchener, together with Tettnang, Willamette and Chinook hops.

ALASKAN SMOKED PORTER

TYPE: PORTER
ALCOHOL: 5.9% VOL.
FERMENTATION: TOP

1995 SMOKED PORTER

Special remarks: the Smoked Porter is brewed with malt that is roasted above alder wood, which gives it the distinct roasted taste. This is a very dark beer with underlying dryness. The bottling year is printed on the label.

• • •

ANCHOR BREWING CO, SAN FRANCISCO

Production in hectoliters: 150,000
Founded: 1896

Although the Anchor brewery's history goes back as far as 1896, this brewery was given a second wind a few decades ago thanks to the current owner, Fritz Maytag. On hearing in 1968 that Anchor, the brewer of his favorite beer was about to close he decided to buy them out. This led to Maytag becoming acknowledged as one of the pioneers of the American microbreweries. Apart from Porter, other beers in the Anchor range include Steam Beer, Liberty Ale, Old Foghorn Barley wine, Wheat Beer and Our Special Ale.

ANCHOR PORTER

TYPE: PORTER
ALCOHOL: 5.7% VOL.
FERMENTATION: TOP

Special remarks: this very dark porter is a full malt beer with a strong malty aroma with a lightly burnt subtlety. It has a sweetish malty taste that is drying until the bitter hoppy aftertaste with its cherry like tints. This porter leaves a full and rounded mouth sensation, and is easy to drink.

ANCHOR STEAM BEER

TYPE: STEAM BEER
ALCOHOL: 4.8% VOL.
FERMENTATION: BOTTOM AT HIGH TEMPERATURES

Special remarks: this is not only an exceptional beer at the Anchor brewery, this steam beer is exceptional in the whole brewing world. Its name has very little to do with steam machines as is the case with some European steam beers. When bottom fermenting became popular in America some Californian brewers were using bottom fermenting yeast strains for brewing their beer without being able to cool it. This meant that their beers could not mature fully, resulting in the continuation of the fermenting process. This resulted in a lot of "hissing" barrels, which probably led to the beer being called steam beer. The Steam Beer brewed by Anchor nowadays no longer "hisses" due to it being pasteurized. This process gives the beer its cloudy nature. This amber-colored beer has a fruity smell approaching raspberries. The taste is clean and neutral with soft fruity nuances and a softly bitter background. Steam Beer is medium bodied.

• • •

ANHEUSER-BUSCH INC, ST. LOUIS

Production in hectoliters: 130,000,000
Founded: 1852

Georg Schneider laid the foundations of the largest brewery concern in the world, when he started the Bavarian Brewery in St. Louis in 1852. In 1860, Eberhard Anheuser, who at the time was a wealthy soap manufacturer, bought this brewery out. Through the brewery, the Anheuser family came in contact with Adolphus Busch, a merchant of brewery requirements. Busch married Lily Anheuser, Eberhard's daughter on 7 March 1861. He then went to work for the E. Anheuser Co.'s Brewing Association, and became chairman when Eberhard Anheuser died on 2 May 1880. The brewery, under the new name of Anheuser-Busch, grew into a large concern producing more than one million hectoliters of beer per year before the turn of the century. To this day, a Busch family member has always headed this concern since the death of Adolphus Busch in 1913. Budweiser was introduced in 1876. This concern has twelve breweries, serving almost half of the total US market. Anheuser, having exhausted the potential growth within the American market and are now feverishly trying to develop new markets in Europe and Asia. Continental Europe was somewhat disappointing for Anheuser because of the limitations on their use of the Budweiser brand because of its Czech namesake.

This brewing giant has a fairly traditional outlook on the world: It is the only brewery in the USA that still maintains a stable of Clydesdale horses and its St. Louis brewery radiates past heritage.

BUD ICE

TYPE: ICE BEER
ALCOHOL: 5.2% VOL.
FERMENTATION: BOTTOM

Special remarks: the blonde Bud Ice has an extremely neutral taste thanks to the ice filtering process. The brewer says this beer is "remarkably easy to drink" and this is true. Especially when drunk cold, Bud Ice has an almost spring water taste. The malt can just about be detected. A real thirst quencher for people who are not keen on the taste of beer.

BUDWEISER / BUD

TYPE: LAGER
ALCOHOL: 4.8% VOL.
FERMENTATION: BOTTOM

Special remarks: Budweiser is marketed under the slogan "King of Beers" probably derived from the preference shown by Bohemian monarchs for the Budweis beers. Budweiser is brewed with two-row and six-row barley malt with rice. The barley is home grown and is processed in three maltings. Although the use of rice is often treated with disdain, AB sees it as an addition that contributes to the drinking ability of Budweiser. They make no attempt to conceal the fact, indeed AB maintains the addition of rice and the extra processing it requires makes brewing more rather than less expensive. The hop content consists of no less than ten different types of whole hops. AB have their own hop fields in both the United States and Europe (Hallertau). New cultures of the yeast used by AB are derived from pure cultures that are flown every week to the thirteen local breweries. The beer is conditioned in large sealed tanks to which beech wood chips are added. Additional yeast is added and the beer is then allowed three weeks to condition. Budweiser is everybody's friend, with a light taste and a low bitter content.

MICHELOB

TYPE: LAGER
ALCOHOL: 5% VOL.
FERMENTATION: BOTTOM

Special remarks: AB has actually brewed Michelob since 1896 but it was not bottled until 1960. Michelob is named after Michalovce, a place in Slovakia. This is a light lager with a light malty taste. Somewhat drying towards the finish and with a degree of hops.

MICHELOB GOLDEN DRAFT

TYPE: LAGER
ALCOHOL: 5% VOL.
FERMENTATION: BOTTOM

Special remarks: the Golden variety is a beer which is easy to drink. It has a light malty taste and is somewhat sweet. The aftertaste is drying and malty.

• • •

THE BOSTON BEER COMPANY, BOSTON

Production in hectoliters: 2,000,000
Founded: 1985

This brewery is fifty times smaller than the largest in the same country, not a very appealing title, but when that country happens to be the USA, and this brewer is in the tenth place by size it is very impressive. The Boston Brewery Company (BBC) is accomplished, and is therefore a fine example to those breweries that would still like to expand while brewing beer in a traditional manner. BBC's flagship beer is the Samuel Adams Boston Lager, brewed to an old recipe from the ancestors of James Koch, the founder. The brewery insists its beer must be brewed with water, hops, yeast and barley malt, and this helped Samuel Adams Boston Lager become the first American beer to be imported by Germany.

During the early years, Koch determined not to allow the Boston brewery to grow into a mega-brewery but rather to leave the brewing to mostly de-centralized breweries, including a number in Stroh.

BOSTON LIGHTSHIP

TYPE: LIGHT LAGER
ALCOHOL: 2.8% VOL.
FERMENTATION: BOTTOM

Special remarks: this light beer has an original gravity of 7.6° and is brewed with Saaz, Hallertau and Tettnanger hops. As the brewers would say the Lightship is "healthily dry hopped".

SAMUEL ADAMS BOSTON ALE

TYPE: ALE
ALCOHOL: 4.9% VOL.
FERMENTATION: TOP

Special remarks: Boston ale is brewed with Harrington and caramel malt with Saaz, Fuggles and Goldings hops. This red to amber colored ale is warmly fermented but the conditioning takes place at a lower temperature. Boston Ale is cool-stored.

SAMUEL ADAMS BOSTON LAGER

TYPE: LAGER
ALCOHOL: 4.75% VOL.
FERMENTATION: BOTTOM

Special remarks: this blonde Boston Lager is brewed using two-row and Harrington malt, a small amount of caramel malt, with Hallertau and Tettnager hops. This beer has an original gravity of 13°. The taste is malty, slightly sweet with a hoppy aroma. The Boston Lager is dry-hopped.

SAMUEL ADAMS CHERRY WHEAT

TYPE: WHEAT/FRUIT BEER
ALCOHOL: 5.3% VOL.
FERMENTATION: BOTTOM

Special remarks: BBC brews this "warm weather beer" with a combination of Harrington and caramel barley malt, wheat malt, cherries and cherry extract with Tettanger and Saaz hops.

SAMUEL ADAMS CREAM STOUT

TYPE: STOUT
ALCOHOL: 4.7% VOL.
FERMENTATION: TOP

Special remarks: this Cream Stout is brewed with Harrington malt, wheat malt, roasted barley, caramel malt and chocolate malt. The hops used are Fuggles and Goldings. The result is a robust stout with a sweetish taste and clear roasted nuances.

SAMUEL ADAMS DARK WHEAT

TYPE: WHEAT BEER
ALCOHOL: 5% VOL.
FERMENTATION: TOP

Special remarks: this dark wheat from BBC is brewed with an original yeast strain that originates from the Weihenstephan brewery. This deep brown wheat beer is brewed towards the end of spring.

SAMUEL ADAMS SCOTCH ALE

TYPE: ALE
ALCOHOL: 5.9% VOL.
FERMENTATION: TOP

Special remarks: the ingredients of this sturdy ruby red ale include peat-smoked malt. The original gravity is 16.3°. The hops used are Fuggles and Goldings. The taste clearly betrays the chocolate malt and the smoked malt.

SAMUEL ADAMS OCTOBERFEST

TYPE: OCTOBERFEST
ALCOHOL: 5.7% VOL.
FERMENTATION: BOTTOM

Special remarks: BBC brews this dark reddish lager early in the spring. This seasonal beer brewed with Münchener malt with Saazer and Tettnanger hops has an especially malty character.

SAMUEL ADAMS DOUBLE BOCK

TYPE: MALT LAGER/BOCK
ALCOHOL: 7.2% VOL.
FERMENTATION: BOTTOM

Special remarks: the original gravity of 22° is achieved with generous doses of Harrington and caramel malt, which also gives this double bock a considerable fullness and malt character. This ruby-red ale, brewed with Hallertau and Tettnanger hops, is cool-stored for a long period.

SAMUEL ADAMS WINTER LAGER

TYPE: WHEAT BOCK
ALCOHOL: 6.9% VOL.
FERMENTATION: BOTTOM

Special remarks: an amber-colored wheat bock, brewed around November. This is a full, malty beer with a complex aroma.

SAM ADAMS TRIPLE BOCK

TYPE: MALT BEER/BOCK

ALCOHOL: 17.5% VOL.

FERMENTATION: TOP

Special remarks: starting with an original gravity of 40° this ruby-red beer achieves the incredible alcohol level of 17.5%. Harrington and caramel malt is brewed with Hallertau hops and is bombarded with two different top fermenting yeast strains. Maple syrup is added and the beer is allowed to mature in barrels formerly used for whisky storage.

• • •

BROOKLYN LAGER

TYPE: LAGER

ALCOHOL: 5.1% VOL.

FERMENTATION: BOTTOM

Special remarks: this lager is the flagship of the Brooklyn Brewery. It has a deep golden color with a floral hoppy aroma with evidence of malt. The taste is lightly malt with a hoppy background and a light bitter finish that develops into a dry bitter aftertaste.

• • •

BROOKLYN BREWERY, BROOKLYN NEW YORK

Production in hectoliters: 30,000
Founded: 1987

New York's Brooklyn brewery was set up in 1987 by journalist, Steve Hindy and banker, Tom Potter, with the intention of breathing new life into traditionally crafted beers that existed before Prohibition. Due to the limited money they decided to have their beer brewed by the FX Matt brewery in Utica. William M. Moeller, a fourth generation brewer with a German background was taken on to supply the recipe. The large distributors showed little enthusiasm for the small quantities produced by the Brooklyn Brewery forcing them to make their own deliveries. This activity was later expanded with the distribution on behalf of other microbreweries and eventually with the import and distribution for products from Belgium, The Netherlands, the UK, and Germany. On 28 May 1996, Brooklyn opened their own brewery and their first beer was the Brooklyn Weisse. Beers currently brewed include, Brooklyn Brown Ale, Brooklyn East India Pale Ale, Brooklyn Black Chocolate Stout, Brooklyn Pilsener, Brooklyn Pennant Pale Ale '55, Brooklyner Weisse, Brooklyner Dunkel Weisse, Breukelen Abbey Ale, Blanche de Brooklyn and a beer with limited availability, the Brooklyn Monster Ale with alcohol of 11%.

CELIS BREWERY, AUSTIN

Production in hectoliters: 50,000
Founded: 1991

The founder of this brewery also founded Belgium's De Kluis brewery, after a passage of thirty years and a shift in continent. After a fire in his brewery in 1985,

Pierre Celis was forced to link up with Stella Artois, that become part of Interbrew group. In 1990, after disputes with Interbrew, Celis decided to leave the group and moved to Austin, Texas. At 65 years old, Celis started up again with a tradition in beer that was entirely unknown to Americans. The Celis brewery is primarily a family company, run by his daughter, Christine together with her brother-in-law and brewer Peter Camps. In order to achieve better distribution and marketing, Celis decided to make an agreement with Miller, but because of his past experiences with larger brewing concerns, he ensured the recipes and brewing techniques remained within his family. In addition to the beers reviewed below, Celis also brews Celis Dubbel Ale in the tradition of abbey beers.

CELIS GOLDEN

TYPE: PILSENER
ALCOHOL: 4.8% VOL.
FERMENTATION: BOTTOM

Special remarks: the Golden is a Pilsener brewed with American barley malt and Czech Saaz hops. It needs six weeks to mature. Celis Golden is medium-bodied with a hoppy aroma. The taste has a good balance of hops and malt. The aftertaste is drying and hoppy bitter.

CELIS GRAND CRU

TYPE: SPECIAL BREW
ALCOHOL: 8.75% VOL.
FERMENTATION: TOP

Special remarks: the Grand Cru is a robust ale brewed with pale lager malt, Saaz and Cscade hops, Curacao peel and a variety of herbs. The taste and aroma is determined by the malt and herbs, brought about by amongst other things, cloves.

CELIS PALE BOCK

TYPE: BELGIAN ALE
ALCOHOL: 4.8% VOL.
FERMENTATION: TOP

Special remarks: a copper-colored ale with a fruity malty aroma. The taste is sweet malt, with caramel and an evidence of fruit. The aftertaste is drying and a shade hoppy. This top fermenter is brewed with a variety of malts, Saaz, Willamette and Cascade hops.

CELIS RASPBERRY

TYPE: FRUIT BEER
ALCOHOL: 4.8% VOL.
FERMENTATION: TOP

Special remarks: the Celis raspberry beer is brewed with 30% wheat and Cascade, Willamette and Goldings hops. The raspberry taste is created by adding the raspberries during the secondary fermentation. The aroma is without doubt that of raspberries as is the taste, which is dry and slightly sour. The aftertaste is sour, but this leads to a sweet raspberry finish.

CELIS WHITE

TYPE: WHEAT BEER
ALCOHOL: 4.8% VOL.
FERMENTATION: TOP

Special remarks: the Celis White is brewed with 50% wheat and 50% Texas winter malt. The hops used are Willamette and Cascade. Other ingredients include coriander and Curacao orange peel. It has an orange and herb aroma. The taste of this orange hazy beer is softly sweet and sour with overtones of herbs and fruit.

• • •

ADOLF COORS BREWERY, GOLDEN, COLORADO

Production in hectoliters: 25,000,000
Founded: 1873

The Coors brewery is a family company founded Adolf Coors, and Jacob Scheuler, who left after a few years when the brewery became known as the Adolf Coors Golden Brewery. The brewery at Golden is one of the largest in the world. Apart from this brewery, Coors also has a brewery in Memphis, Tennessee. Coors uses water from the Rocky Mountains. They do not pasteurize their beer and use hops and barley from their own farms. Coors beers include, Coors Beer, Coors Light, Coors Extra Gold, Coors Winterfest, Coors Eisbock, Coors Oktoberfest Märzen and Coors Weizenbeer.

COORS EXTRA GOLD

TYPE: PILSENER
ALCOHOL: 5% VOL.
FERMENTATION: BOTTOM

Special remarks: the Coors Extra Gold has a neutral taste and a light body. The malt and hops are vaguely recognizable. This is a very clean tasting beer but lacks character.

• • •

THE DOCK STREET BREWING COMPANY, BALA CYNWYD, PHILADELPHIA

Production in hectoliters: 40,000
Founded: 1986

The Dock Street brewery was founded in 1986 by Jeffrey D. Ware. After a thorough schooling as manager in a variety of restaurants, and after being infected by the passion of CAMRA, he decided to set up his own brewery, where he could brew beers of character following traditional techniques. Dock Street has won a number of impressive awards for their four bottled beers that are brewed in accordance with the Reinheitsgebot. Apart from the brewery, Dock Street also owns restaurants with pub breweries in both Philadelphia and Washington.

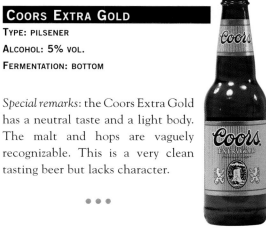

DOCK STREET AMBER BEER

TYPE: AMBER ALE
ALCOHOL: 5.3% VOL.
FERMENTATION: TOP

Special remarks: the Dock Street Amber Beer is an amber-colored ale brewed with pale malt, caramel malt and Cascade hops. This debut beer from Dock Street is dry-hopped.

DOCK STREET BOHEMIAN PILSENER

TYPE: PILSENER
ALCOHOL: 5.3% VOL.
FERMENTATION: BOTTOM

Special remarks: Bohemian Pilsener is a serious attempt to brew a true Pilsener. This blonde lager was launched in 1992 and is brewed with Saaz and Hallertau hops. It has a hoppy aroma and a well balanced taste of malt and hops. The aftertaste is drying and hoppy.

DOCK STREET EXTRA BEST PALE ALE

TYPE: PALE ALE
ALCOHOL: 5.3% VOL.
FERMENTATION: TOP

Special remarks: this ale is brewed following the traditions of the English Ales from Burton on Trent. It is brewed using Cascade hops and is dry-hopped with East Kent Goldings hops while maturing. It has a hoppy aroma and its taste has a malty background. The after taste is hoppy and drying.

DOCK STREET ILLUMINATOR

TYPE: MALT LAGER/BOCK

ALCOHOL: 7.5% VOL.

FERMENTATION: BOTTOM

Special remarks: Illuminator is a double bock brewed according to German tradition with Tettnang and Hallertau hops. This is an amber-colored double bock with a rounded malt taste with roasted nuances. The aftertaste is roasted malt, slightly warming with a vague hoppy bitterness.

• • •

FRANKENMUTH BREWERY, FRANKENMUTH

Production in hectoliters: 80.000
Founded: 1987

Frankenmuth, is a small place known as Michigan's Little Bavaria, and is visited annually by a large numbers of tourists. The Frankenmuth brewery has strong ties with the "homeland". The beers are brewed following German traditions and in accordance with the Reinheitsgebot.
A German company fitted out the brewery, and they even have an Oktoberfest and a Biergarten. The brewery is owned by the Heine family.
Apart from their own beers, Frankenmuth also brews under a number of private labels. Frankenmuth also brews Old Detroit, a beer intended for those less German orientated.

FRANKENMUTH BOCK

TYPE: MALT LAGER/BOCK

ALCOHOL: 6.4% VOL.

FERMENTATION: BOTTOM

Special remarks: a dark bock, brewed in accordance with the Reinheitsgebot and conditioned for three months. This is a sturdy bock with a malty aroma and a sweet malt fruity taste with roasted elements. The aftertaste is malty and drying.

FRANKENMUTH DARK

TYPE: DUNKEL

ALCOHOL: 5.2% VOL.

FERMENTATION: BOTTOM

Special remarks: another beer following the Reinheitsgebot, this dunkel is dark amber colored as a result of the use of black malt. The taste is malty, drying and roasted. The aftertaste is malty and drying.

FRANKENMUTH EXTRA LIGHT

TYPE: LIGHT BEER

ALCOHOL: 4% VOL.

FERMENTATION: BOTTOM

Special remarks: the Light is primarily a low-calorie beer. It is a light blonde lager with a light body and a light malt taste followed by one of hops.

FRANKENMUTH PILSENER

TYPE: PILSENER

ALCOHOL: 5.2% VOL.

FERMENTATION: BOTTOM

Special remarks:
the Frankenmuth Pilsener
is a blonde lager with a light
hoppy and malt aroma. The
taste is of hops with malt in
the background. This is
a medium bodied lager with
a drying hoppy aftertaste.
This beer is brewed in
accordance with the Reinheitsgebot.

with fruity malt aroma and a malty taste with
a drying hoppy finish and a hoppy bitter aftertaste.

• • •

D.L. GEARY BREWING, PORTLAND

Production in hectoliters: 40,000
Founded: 1983

David Geary, who started this
brewery together with his wife
Karen, learned the brewing
trade at several of small
British breweries. At first,
Geary was invited to work
for Peter Maxwell Stuart at
the Traquair House brewery.
In 1986, on returning to his
own country, he set about brewing

his first pale ale, making him one of the pioneers of the
microbrewery. The four Geary beers are available in
seventeen states. Hampshire Special Ale is a seasonal
beer and is only available in the winter months.

FRANKENMUTH WEISSE

TYPE: WHEAT BEER
ALCOHOL: 4.5% VOL.
FERMENTATION: TOP

Special remarks: the Weisse is
brewed as a summer beer. It is an
unfiltered wheat beer brewed in the German
tradition in accordance with the Reinheitsgebot.
It has a somewhat fruity aroma with a fruity wheat
taste with an underlying taste of herbs. Herbs
dominate the aftertaste.

OLD DETROIT RED LAGER

TYPE: LAGER
ALCOHOL: 4.8% VOL.
FERMENTATION: BOTTOM

Special remarks: Red Lager is
an amber colored lager with
a sweet malt aroma. The
taste is light sweet and
malty, drying towards the
finish. This is a medium
bodied lager.

OLD DETROIT AMBER ALE

TYPE: ALE
ALCOHOL: 5.9% VOL.
FERMENTATION: TOP

Special remarks: this is
a light amber colored ale

GEARY'S AMERICAN ALE

TYPE: ALE
ALCOHOL: 4.8% VOL.
FERMENTATION: TOP

Special remarks: this American Ale is
brewed with English malt and Mt.
Hood and Tettnang hops. It is a golden
ale, lightly malt with a mild hoppy
finish.

GEARY'S LONDON STYLE PORTER

TYPE: PORTER
ALCOHOL: 4.2% VOL.
FERMENTATION: TOP

Special remarks: this London Porter is
brewed with English malts, pale,

crystal, chocolate and black. The hops used are the Cascade, Willamette and Goldings. This very dark porter as a robust roasted aroma and a roasted malty taste, moving towards coffee and chocolate. The body is light to medium. The aftertaste is drying, bitter and roasted.

fermented at higher temperatures. It is a yellow gold beer with a light taste, with evidence of malt and hops. It has a dry background and is light to medium bodied.

GEARY'S PALE ALE

TYPE: ALE
ALCOHOL: 4.5% VOL.
FERMENTATION: TOP

Special remarks: this English pale ale is brewed with two-row malts, pale crystal and chocolate and Cascade, Mt. Hood, Tettnang and Fuggle hops. This is a copper colored ale with a fruity aroma and a fruity malt taste with a hoppy finish and a hoppy bitter aftertaste. The mouth sensation is drying when approaching the finish.

• • •

HUDEPOHL-SCHOENLING BREWING CO, CINCINNATI OHIO

Production in hectoliters: 500,000
Founded: 1986

This Cincinnati brewery is the result of a merger between the Hudepohl brewery, founded in 1855, and the Schoenling brewery that was set up in 1934. Their beers include Hudepohl, Moerlein, Little King and Schoenling. In 1997, this brewery was taken over by the Boston Beer Company, and was renamed The Samuel Adams Brewery.

LITTLE KINGS CREAM ALE

TYPE: CREAM ALE
ALCOHOL: 5% VOL.
FERMENTATION: BOTTOM

Special remarks: this Cream Ale is not actually an ale as the name implies, but a lager that is

INDEPENDENCE BREWING COMPANY, PHILADELPHIA

Production in hectoliters: 15,000
Founded: 1994

Independence is one of the "state of the art" microbreweries that prefer to give the Americans variation rather than mass-produced products. Apart from the reviewed  beers, this brewery, influenced by both England and Germany, also produce the following: Gold and mild ale at 4.8%, Porter, a full dark seasonal beer at 4.8%; Betsy Ross Kristall Wheat, a blond seasonal beer brewed in the German tradition, filtered and with a volume of 4.5%. Independence beers, none of which are pasteurized do not have any added chemicals.

INDEPENDENCE ALE

TYPE: ALE
ALCOHOL: 4.7% VOL.
FERMENTATION: TOP

Special remarks: this amber colored ale is brewed using six different malts and American and English hops. This is a full-bodied ale with a hoppy character.

INDEPENDENCE WINTER WARMER

TYPE: ALE

ALCOHOL: 8% VOL.

FERMENTATION: TOP

Special remarks: the hop varieties used for the Winter Warmer are Fuggle and Goldings together with a whole range of malts. The result is a strong full bodied bronze colored ale, intended as a boost on those cold winter evenings.

INDEPENDENCE FRANKLINFEST

TYPE: LAGER/MÄRZEN

ALCOHOL: 5% VOL.

FERMENTATION: BOTTOM

Special remarks: Benjamin Franklin is rather frivolously portrayed on the label of this Oktoberfest beer wearing Lederhöse, and so it follows that this independent brewer only uses German ingredients in this lager. This sweet malted beer is available throughout the year.

• • •

LATROBE BREWING CO, LATROBE PENNSYLVANIA

Production in hectoliters: 2,000,000
Founded: 1893

The Latrobe brewery is an old brewery taken over by Labatt in 1987. Due to the contribution made by Labatt, of the Interbrew Group, Latrobe has seen substantial growth in the past ten years, with their most important beer being Rolling Rock. Latrobe also produce light, bock, and ice versions of their premium beer.

ROLLING ROCK PREMIUM BEER

TYPE: LAGER

ALCOHOL: 5% VOL.

FERMENTATION: BOTTOM

Special remarks: Rolling Rock comes in a printed bottle, a practice that used to be quite common. This gives it something extra, as discovered by the South American Sol and Corona, who have also successfully applied a similar technique. This is a blonde lager with a light aroma, malty with a hint of hops. The taste is malty with a hoppy finish. The aftertaste is lightly drying with a hoppy bitterness.

• • •

MENDOCINO BREWING COMPANY, HOPLAND

Production in hectoliters: 25,000
Founded: 1983

This brewery's success story started with three home brewers that decided to take advantage of the growing demand and the changing legislation to try their luck in the brewing world. On 14 August 1983 they opened the first pub brewery in California since the Prohibition. About the same time, the New Albion brewery closed down, and two of the brewers were given jobs at Medocino, where they were later to become the fourth and fifth partners. This brewery has been growing ever since the opening, and the continuous demand has led to collaboration with the Indian UB group from Bangalore. This led to a capacity being realized in 1997 of 320,000 hectoliters. Apart from the beers reviewed, MDC also produces the blonde ale Peregrine Ale, and the seasonal beers, Yuletide Porter, Springtide Ale and Frolic Shipwreck Ale.

RED TAIL ALE

TYPE: AMBER ALE

ALCOHOL: 6.6% VOL.

FERMENTATION: TOP

Special remarks:
this non-pasteurized beer is bottled with yeast. This is the brewery's flagship beer, and accounts for 80% of the total production capacity. It was also the first beer ever to be brewed at this pub brewery in 1983, when it was only available in pints or in the world's largest six pack – six 1.5 liter bottles. Red Tail Ale is brewed with two-row malt, whole Cascade and Cluster hops, water and home cultivated yeast. The recommended serving temperature is between 10 and 15° C.

BLUE HERON PALE ALE

TYPE: INDIA PALE ALE

ALCOHOL: 6.6% VOL.

FERMENTATION: TOP

Special remarks:
this golden ale is brewed in the English tradition with strong hoppy character. It was never this brewer's intention for Blue Heron to resemble the original, but to create a variety with a little more balance. This beer is bottled with yeast and is a fine compliment to an Asiatic meal. The serving temperature range is between 10–12°C (50–53.6°F). This Blue Heron was introduced on 17 March, 1985, is non-pasteurized and has a shelf life of four months.

BLACK HAWK STOUT

TYPE: STOUT

ALCOHOL: 5.2% VOL.

FERMENTATION: TOP

Special remarks: as stouts go, Black Hawk is not that strong, and was one of the initial brews when the brewery was opened in 1983. This stout is brewed following the Irish traditions and has a dry aftertaste and an obvious roasted malt taste.

EYE OF THE HAWK

TYPE: ALE

ALCOHOL: 7.2% VOL.

FERMENTATION: TOP

Special remarks: a robust ale that is brewed between the months of July and October. This is a copper colored ale with a complex taste experience.

• • •

MILLER BREWING CO, MILWAUKEE, WISCONSIN

Production in hectoliters: 75,000,000
Founded: 1855

The Miller brewery is one of the largest breweries in America and is battling with Heineken for the second place in the world ratings. The Miller brewery was originally called the Charles Best Plank Road Brewery. Frederic Miller bought the brewery in 1855, and it was to remain in family hands for more than a century. In 1969, Miller was taken over by the cigarette manufacturer Philip Morris. Since then, the brewery has experienced enormous growth, due in no small part to the success of Miller Lite, which was one of America's first low-calorie beers, which suited the Americans with their constant desire to be slimmer. Miller has a majority holding in a number of other breweries, such as Celis Brewery, Jacob Leinenkugel Brewing and Shipyard Brewery, with a minority holding in the Canadian Molson. Miller has five large breweries in America.

Miller's beers include Miller Lite, Miller Reserve Amber Ale (a real top fermenting ale brewed with one hundred percent barley malt), Miller Reserve Velvet Stout, Miller Ice and Miller High Life.

MILLER GENUINE DRAFT

TYPE: LAGER

ALCOHOL: 4.7% VOL.

FERMENTATION: BOTTOM

Special remarks: this golden lager has a malty aroma. The taste is also malty, drying when approaching the finish.

• • •

MINNESOTA BREWING, ST. PAUL

Production in hectoliters: 3,000,000
Founded: 1991

This Minnesota brewery brews a whole range of beers under contract.

APOLLO

TYPE: LAGER

ALCOHOL: 4.5% VOL.

FERMENTATION: BOTTOM

Special remarks: Apollo was introduced by the Big Bang Brewery. With its blue colored bottle, it has without doubt a striking packaging, not to mention the contents. It actually looks more like an ale, with its amber color and cream colored head. The moderate carbon dioxide content and the hoppy aroma is also reminiscent of an ale. The taste is hoppy and dry developing into a short light bitter finish, with sufficient maltiness. Apollo is a medium bodied lager.

• • •

NEW BELGIUM BREWING, FORT COLLINS

Production in hectoliters: 50,000
Founded: 1991

This successful brewery was founded by Jeffrey Lebesch. He became inspired by the Belgian beers while touring Belgium on a mountain bike. On returning to the USA, Lebesch and his wife Kim, set up a small brewery in the cellar of their house. One of their first brewing successes was Fat Tire, which led them to moving to a former railroad building in 1992. About the same time, Brian Calahan became a partner the New Belgium brewery. The

second move came in November 1995, when they relocated to a newly built brewery, where around sixty employees brew Belgium beers. The mountain bike still has a role within the company, where it has become a tradition for every employee to be given a mountain bike after one year's loyal service. Apart from the reviewed beers, New Belgium also produces a Trippel; Sunshine, a wheat beer flavored with coriander and orange peel; Saison; Frambozen and Porch Swing.

ABBEY

TYPE: SPECIAL BREW/ABBEY BEER

ALCOHOL: 6.9% VOL.

FERMENTATION: TOP

Special remarks: a brown unfiltered secondary fermentation beer with a sweet malty aroma and malty taste that has a slightly sour finish. It has a robust body and the aftertaste strongly hopped and drying.

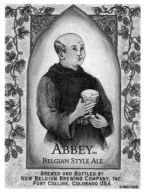

FAT TIRE

TYPE: AMBER ALE

ALCOHOL: 5.2% VOL.

FERMENTATION: TOP

Special remarks: this amber-colored ale has a hoppy aroma. The taste is one of light sweet malt with caramel nuances. Fat Tire, also the nickname of the notorious mountain bike, is neither pasteurized or filtered, resulting in a small amount of sediment.

OLD CHERRY ALE

TYPE: SPECIAL BREW/CHERRY BEER

ALCOHOL: 6.5% VOL.

FERMENTATION: TOP

Special remarks: sweet and sour ale with a cherry like fruitiness. Old Cherry Ale has an amber ale base, and is fermented with real cherries.

• • •

NORTH COAST BREWING CO
ACME ALE COMPANY, FORT BRAGG

Production in hectoliters: 20,000
Founded: 1988

The management of the North Coast Brewing Co. is made up of three people who combined their skills to found this brewery in 1988. With the availability of an historic building in the center of Fort Bragg, a new pub brewery was created. Mark Reudrich, who had gained brewing experience in the UK and the United States, introduced his wife Merle to the business, and she now runs the brewery restaurant. Joe Rosenthal, a builder, paid for and carried out the construction work. The third partner, Tom Allen provided the skills he gained during managing restaurants. Meanwhile, the brewery has grown beyond the pub format, and has had to build a new brewery in order to satisfy continuing demand. Apart from their own vast line of beers, North Coast Brewing also brews a number of specialty beers, such as a bock, an alt and an Oktoberfest. The Acme line is an old Californian brand that the brewery resurrected in 1996.

ACME CALIFORNIA BROWN ALE

TYPE: BROWN ALE

ALCOHOL: 5.4% VOL.

FERMENTATION: TOP

Special remarks: this reddish brown ale is brewed with dark malt that is lightly apparent in the aroma and is mildly hopped with Tettanger and Hallertau hops.

ACME CALIFORNIA PALE ALE

TYPE: PALE ALE

ALCOHOL: 5.3% VOL.

FERMENTATION: TOP

Special remarks:
this light variety of Acme is a light amber colored beer with a sweetish taste and a light dry finish. This easy drinking Pale Ale is brewed with Yakima Valley hops and American two-row malt with a small amount of English malt.

BLUE STAR

TYPE: WHEAT BEER

ALCOHOL: 4.9% VOL.

FERMENTATION: TOP

Special remarks: this cloudy unfiltered wheat beer is light in color and body, with a fruity clean taste. The brewer recommends the addition of a lemon slice to Blue Star.

PRANQSTER

TYPE: SPECIAL BREW/BELGIAN ALE

ALCOHOL: 6.9% VOL.

FERMENTATION: TOP

Special remarks: a robust gold colored ale brewed in the Belgian tradition. This is a rounded beer with a fruity sweetish taste and a hoppy aroma.

OLD NO. 38 STOUT

TYPE: STOUT/DRY

ALCOHOL: 5.4% VOL.

FERMENTATION: TOP

Special remarks: a deep dark stout with a robust mouth sensation and an obvious roasted malt taste with coffee and caramel subtleties and a light bitter background. No. 38 was the steam locomotive that once pulled the wagons from Fort Bragg to Willis.

RED SEAL ALE

TYPE: PALE ALE

ALCOHOL: 5.6% VOL.

FERMENTATION: TOP

Special remarks:
Red Seal Ale is an amber colored American ale with a reasonable fullness and a hoppy bitter end.
The label announces,
"Ingredients: water, hops, yeast, malt and that's all".

OLD RASPUTIN RUSSIAN IMPERIAL STOUT

TYPE: IMPERIAL STOUT

ALCOHOL: 8.9% VOL.

FERMENTATION: TOP

Special remarks: with an OG of 1090, this old Russian is a sturdy stout, jet black with a red blaze. This full bodied stout as a complex aroma which includes fruit, roasted malt and chocolate nuances. The rounded sweet taste has a bitter drying finish. Since its debut in 1995, Old Rasputin has won a respectable amount of awards.

SCRIMSHAW PILSNER STYLE BEER

TYPE: PILSENER

ALCOHOL: 4.2% VOL.

FERMENTATION: BOTTOM

Special remarks: Scrimshaw was the name given to a figure that used to be whittled by seamen from ivory or shells. This is a light blonde beer, lively with a light malty sweet taste and a mild hoppy aroma. It is brewed with Munich and Klages malt with Hallertau and Tettnang hops.

• • •

ODELL BREWING COMPANY, FORT COLLINS

Production in hectoliters: 30,000
Founded: 1989

The Odell brewery is a family brewery where Doug Odell is the brewer. The brewery aimed to brew following English traditions, and originally only produced draft beer. The first bottled varieties were launched in 1996 and are now distributed to its enthusiasts in nine American states. Apart from the reviewed beers, Odell also produces barley wine known as Odell's Curmudgeon's Nip.

ODELL'S 90 SHILLING

TYPE: ALE
ALCOHOL: 5.5% VOL.
FERMENTATION: TOP

Special remarks:
90 Shilling is an amber-colored ale, brewed with two-row, Vienna, Crystal and Chocolate malt, Northern Brewer and Cascade hops, with a top fermenting ale yeast.

ODELL'S LEVITY

TYPE: ALE
ALCOHOL: 5% VOL.
FERMENTATION: TOP

Special remarks: this "light-hearted" blonde ale will appeal to the lovers of a milder ale. It is brewed with Munich, Caramel and honey malt with Northern Brewer, Mount Hood and Saaz hops.

ODELL'S EASY STREET WHEAT

TYPE: WHEAT BEER
ALCOHOL: 4.7% VOL.
FERMENTATION: TOP

Special remarks:
Easy Street Wheat is an unfiltered wheat beer brewed with wheat malt, two-row barley malt, Crystal and Munich malt, and Cascade, Tetnanger and Saaz hops.

CUTTHROAT PORTER

TYPE: PORTER
ALCOHOL: 5.3% VOL.
FERMENTATION: TOP

Special remarks:
Cutthroat Porter is a Porter brewed in the London tradition: dark and robust, brewed with two-row barley malt, Chocolate, Crystal and Aber malt, with Galena, English Kent and Northern Brewer hops.

ODELL'S HOLIDAY SHILLING

TYPE: ALE
ALCOHOL: 5.7% VOL.
FERMENTATION: TOP

Special remarks:
Holiday Shilling is an ale that is brewed especially for Christmas, and is based on the 90 Shilling. The brewing involves replacing some of the hops with herbs including cinnamon, nutmeg, ginger, rose hips, cardamom and fennel.

PETE'S BREWING COMPANY, PALO ALTO CALIFORNIA

Production in hectoliters: 500,000
Founded: 1986

Pete's brewery, known for the Pete's wicked brand, was founded in 1986 by Pete Slossgerg a passionate home brewer, who was able to set up a new brewery thanks to the success of his American ale and financial support from his friends. Pete's brewery became a fast rising star between 1986 and 1996 when it was placed several times in the top one hundred of the fastest growing American companies. This brewery is now the second largest "craft brewery", and just as with the other microbreweries is confronted with an ever maturing market, where growth figures of a thousand percent are no longer so common. Pete's Wicked beers are brewed by the Stroh brewery in St. Paul, Minnesota. The Pete's Wicked range includes a variety of twelve beers.

PETE'S WICKED ALE

TYPE: AMERICAN ALE
ALCOHOL: 5% VOL.
FERMENTATION: TOP

Special remarks:
This ale was the first to be brought on the market by Pete Slossberg. It is a light brown ale with a roasted malt aroma. The taste is one of roasted malt, lightly fruity with caramel and a good balance of hops towards the finish. The aftertaste is drying and lightly hopped. This is a medium bodied ale and is brewed with pale, caramel and chocolate malts with Cascade and Brewers Gold hops.

PETE'S WICKED HONEY WHEAT

TYPE: WHEAT BEER
ALCOHOL: 4.8% VOL.
FERMENTATION: TOP

Special remarks: brewed with wheat, malt, pale and caramel malt, honey, with Tettnang and Cascade hops. This is an unfiltered cloudy blonde variety with a fruity aroma and a sweetish taste. The aftertaste is somewhat drying, and has some hoppy bitterness, together with a honey like sweetness.

PETE'S WICKED OKTOBERFEST

TYPE: MÄRZEN
ALCOHOL: 5.6% VOL.
FERMENTATION: BOTTOM

Special remarks: the Oktoberfest is a copper-colored lager brewed with pale and caramel malt. The hops are Yakima Cluster, Cascade, and Tettnang. The aroma is sweetish and this medium bodied lager has a sweetish caramel taste.

PETE'S WICKED PALE ALE

TYPE: PALE ALE
ALCOHOL: 5% VOL.
FERMENTATION: TOP

Special remarks: The Wicked pale ale is a light amber colored ale with a fruity aroma and a taste that is especially influenced by the intense presence of hops.

PETE'S WICKED STRAWBERRY BLONDE

TYPE: FRUIT BEER
ALCOHOL: 5.1% VOL.
FERMENTATION: TOP

Special remarks: a blonde fruit beer that is sweetened with raspberries. It is brewed with wheat, pale malt, Yakima Cluster and Tettnang hops with fresh raspberries.

PETE'S WICKED SUMMER BREW

TYPE: FRUIT BEER/LEMON

ALCOHOL: 4.6% VOL.

FERMENTATION: TOP

Special remarks: Summer brew is a pale ale with a dash of lemon juice. It is brewed with pale and wheat malt with Tettnang hops.

PETE'S WICKED WINTER BREW

TYPE: FRUIT BEER

ALCOHOL: 5.1% VOL.

FERMENTATION: TOP

Special remarks: Winter Brew is a seasonal beer brewed sweetened with raspberries. It is amber-colored with a pinkish glint.
The raspberries, with a background of herbs dominate the aroma and taste. The aftertaste is more drying and hoppy, but the raspberries are still in evidence. Winter Brew is brewed with pale and caramel malt, Cascade, Tettnang and Saaz hops with raspberries and nutmeg.

• • •

PLANK ROAD BREWERY, MILWAUKEE, WISCONSIN

Production in hectoliters: –
Founded: 1855

The Plank Road brewery is the original name of the brewery taken over by Frederic Miller. The Plank Road Brewery is an up-market subsidiary of Miller, that brews special beers following the old traditions.

RED DOG

TYPE: LAGER

ALCOHOL: 5% VOL.

FERMENTATION: BOTTOM

Special remarks: this is a blonde lager with a vanilla like maltiness in the aroma. The taste is lightly malt and somewhat sweet with a light body. Miller, the Canadian concern Molson and the Australian Mathilda brewery, owned by CUB, all brew Red Dog.

• • •

SAXER BREWING COMPANY, LAKE OSWEGO

Production in hectoliters: 40,000
Founded: 1993

The Saxer brewery has taken its name from a German immigrant, Henry Saxer, who founded the first brewery in the north west in Portland, Oregon. This German pioneer inspired this new brewery to brew a miscellany of German lagers along with their variations, and distribute them to thirty-two American states. Chuck Taylor and Kerry Gilbert were also there at the birth of the Saxer brewery, Taylor's place later being taken by Steve Goebels. Saxer's brewer is Tony Gomes, who was educated in Germany, and who completed his studies at Munich University. The growth of the brewery was rapid, which included a turnover growth of 68% in 1996, however Steve Goebels has indicated that they have no intention of exceeding the 50,000 hectoliter annual production. Saxer claims to be the only lager brewery in the north west with their own double decoction system. Apart from the reviewed beers, Saxer also produces: Dark Bock, 7.2%; Three Finger Jack Summer 5.6%, flavored with Curacao peel and coriander. After taking over the Nor'Wester brewery, Saxer adopted six other beers into their range. This demanded quite a shake up within the brewery, as Nor'Wester had four ales in their range, two of which were wheat beers. The other beers that carry the Nor'West flag are : Smith Rock Bock 7.3%; Black Rail, a black bottom fermenting seasonal beer 5.1%; and White Forest, a Scottish ale at 5.5%.

JACK FROST WINTER DOPPELBOCK

TYPE: MALT LAGER/DOUBLE BOCK

ALCOHOL: 8% VOL.

FERMENTATION: BOTTOM

Special remarks: this double bock achieved Saxer's third gold medal at the "Great American Beer Festival" in 1996. This dark robust beer is brewed with Cascade hops and a variety of American and imported malts. The original gravity is 18.5°. This winter beer is allowed a cold conditioning period of eight weeks.

NOR'WESTER BLACKSMITH PORTER

TYPE: PORTER

ALCOHOL: 5.1% VOL.

FERMENTATION: TOP

Special remarks: a deep dark brown porter with a medium body, a roasted taste and a coffee like aroma.

NOR'WESTER HEFE WEIZEN

TYPE: WHEAT BEER

ALCOHOL: 5.1% VOL.

FERMENTATION: TOP

Special remarks: this is a light hazy blonde wheat beer brewed with 55% wheat malt.

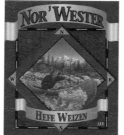

NOR'WESTER RASPBERRY

TYPE: FRUIT BEER

ALCOHOL: 5.5% VOL.

FERMENTATION: TOP

Special remarks: an amber-colored wheat beer with raspberry extract. Gomes changed the time for the addition of the raspberries from just

before the bottling to a few days before the end of the maturing time, to limit further fermentation.

SAXER BOCK

TYPE: MALT LAGER/BOCK

ALCOHOL: 7.2% VOL.

FERMENTATION: BOTTOM

Special remarks: this "Helles" from the Saxer Bock range is available throughout the year. This beer is allowed to mature for six weeks, is golden and has a reasonable bitterness that is accompanied by a malty background.

SAXER'S LEMON LAGER

TYPE: FRUIT LAGER

ALCOHOL: 3.8% VOL.

FERMENTATION: BOTTOM

Special remarks: a light lager with an original gravity of 10°, brewed with two-row pale malt and Yakima Valley Perle and Saaz hops. Inspired by the German beer and lemonade mixtures, Gomes adds lemon extract to this beer during the maturing process. This beer has become the pride of the Saxer brewery.

THREE FINGER JACK AMBER

TYPE: MÄRZEN

ALCOHOL: 4.8% VOL.

FERMENTATION: BOTTOM

Special remarks: brewed with caramel, Münchener and pale malt, and a mixture of Saaz and Hersbrucker hops. This Oktoberfest beer is amber in color and has an original gravity of 12.8°. This beer won a gold medal in the Oktoberfest category at the 1995 "Great American Beer Festival".

THREE FINGER JACK ROASTED RED HEFEDUNKEL

TYPE: DUNKEL

ALCOHOL: 4.8% VOL.

FERMENTATION: BOTTOM

Special remarks: this American variety of the first German lagers is unfiltered. This red-brown dunkel is brewed with Hersbrucker, Münchener, caramel and roasted malt. This dunkel once won a gold medal in the dark lager category at the "Great American Beer Festival".

THREE FINGER JACK STOUT

TYPE: STOUT

ALCOHOL: 4.9% VOL.

FERMENTATION: BOTTOM

Special remarks: "the only lagered stout we know about" announces the brewer on the label of this jet-black specialty. Whether or not this beer can actually be called a stout is still a subject for discussion. It is however brewed with Cascade hops with Münchener, pale and roasted malt.

• • •

SIERRA NEVADA BREWING CO INC, CHICO, CALIFORNIA

Production in hectoliters: 300,000
Founded: 1978

The Sierra Nevada brewery started in a time when microbreweries and pub breweries were not as common as they became a decade later. The two founders, Ken Grossman and Paul Camusi had mutual hobbies of cycling and brewing. They decided to set up a small brewery where they could expand their home brewing activities.

Ken Grossman, one of the founders of the Sierra Nevada Brewing Co.

With financial help from their parents, and equipment that was largely home-made from old equipment scavenged from old breweries, ice cream manufacturers and lemonade producers, they eventually launched their first beer in 1981. Sierra Nevada's growth was explosive, for many years doubling their sales. In 1989, they opened their new brewery where they brew beer in the traditional way using copper kettles and open fermenting tanks. Sierra Nevada brew using exclusively whole hop flowers. Their beers are secondary fermenters, so pasteurized beers are out of the question. Apart from beer, this brewery also markets mustard. Sierra Nevada beers other than those reviewed include, Pale Bock, Big Foot, Barley Wine, Celebration Ale and the bottom fermenting Summerfest.

The Sierra Nevada Brewery.

SIERRA NEVADA PALE ALE

TYPE: PALE ALE

ALCOHOL: 5.5% VOL.

FERMENTATION: TOP

Special remarks: this amber colored Pale Ale has a rich hoppy aroma with a fruity maltiness. The taste is of hops, malty and robustly hoppy at the finish, developing into a long light bitter aftertaste.

SIERRA NEVADA PORTER

TYPE: PORTER

ALCOHOL: 5.9% VOL.

FERMENTATION: TOP

Special remarks: sturdy dark porter with a sweet malty aroma and hoppy nuances. The taste is more roasted with a hoppy finish. The body is robust. The aftertaste is one of roasted malt with a hoppy bitterness.

SIERRA NEVADA STOUT

TYPE: STOUT
ALCOHOL: 6% VOL.
FERMENTATION: TOP

Special remarks: this is a deep dark colored stout with an aroma of roasted malt. The taste is one of roasted malt and somewhat sweet. This stout has a sturdy body and a roasted aftertaste.

• • •

SMUTTYNOSE BREWING CO, PORTSMOUTH

Production in hectoliters: 20,000
Founded: 1994

Smuttynose is an American microbrewery that has manage to take a small slice of the market by doggedly following tradition. The brewery results from the merger of two breweries, and is named after an island off the coast of New Hampshire. Smuttynose beers are available in New Hampshire and neighboring states. They also brew an export pale ale for the UK.

SHOALS PALE ALE

TYPE: PALE ALE
ALCOHOL: 5.3% VOL.
FERMENTATION: TOP

Special remarks:
a light amber-colored ale, unfiltered, with a slightly sweet taste and hoppy aroma. The house on the label is that of Samuel Haley, the only one on Smuttynose Island.

**The two versions of
Shoal's Pale Ale.**

OLD BROWN DOG ALE

TYPE: AMERICAN BROWN ALE
ALCOHOL: –
FERMENTATION: TOP

Special remarks: this is a dark amber ale with a malty taste, medium body, and a light fruity and sweet aroma. Old Brown Dog has existed longer than the Smuttynose brewery as it was first brewed by the Northampton brewery.

CHUCK WHEAT ALE

TYPE: WHEAT BEER
ALCOHOL: 5% VOL.
FERMENTATION: TOP

Special remarks: this is light wheat beer recommended for drinking with fish and pasta dishes.

• • •

THE STROH BREWERY COMPANY, DETROIT, MICHIGAN

Production in hectoliters: 30,000,000
Founded: 1850

Stroh is the third largest brewery in America, and is in the top twenty of the largest breweries in the world. This brewery is a family concern with Bernard Stroh having founded the brewery in Detroit. The Stroh family are descendants of a German brewing family, with a brewing tradition going back to the year 1700. The brewery has been in the hands of the Stroh family ever since. Peter Stroh is the current chairman of a brewery that largely consists of a collection of breweries taken over by Stroh. The first was the Goebels brewery, also of Detroit, taken over after being

**Bernard Stroh, founder
of the Stroh Brewery.**

381

forced to close. The Goebels brewery was founded in 1842 by a German immigrant, August Goebels. This was followed in 1981 by acquisition of the Schaefer brewery of New York, with its Piels brand. Then in 1982, the takeover of the Josef Schlitz Brewing Co. of Milwaukee was finalized. The most recent acquisition was in 1996 with the takeover of the G. Heileman Brewing Co. of La Crosse in Wisconsin.

*Peter W. Smith,
head of the Stroh brewery.*

This company brought with it quite a slice of history as over the years Heileman themselves had swallowed up around ten breweries. Stroh currently owns eight breweries employing more than 4000 people. Their flagship brand of Stroh's together with a number of other beers are still brewed in fire–stoked brewing coppers, which gives a different character to the beer than steam heated coppers. This collection of breweries has resulted in a tremendous range of beers. These beers are: Stroh's, Stroh's Light, Stroh's Non-Alcoholic, Signature, Old Milwaukee, Old Milwaukee Light, Old Milwaukee Red, Old Milwaukee Ice, Old Milwaukee Non-Alcoholic, Old Style, Old Style Light, Schaefer, Schaefer Light, Schlitz, Schlitz Light, Schlitz Ice, Schlitz Non–Alcoholic, Schmidt's, Schmidt's Light, Schmidt's City Club, Lone Star, Lone Star Light, Rainier, Rainier Light, Rainier Ice, Rainier Ale, Yakima Red, Yakima Honey Wheat, Yakima Pale Ale, Colt 45, Schlitz Malt Liquor, Bull Ice, Red Bull Malt Liquor, Silver Thunder Malt Liquor, Mickey's, St. Ides Malt Liquor, St. Ides Gold, St. Ides Special Brew, Crooked I Ice Tea, Champale, Goebels, Piels, Piels Light, Altes, Red White & Blue, Blatz, Black Label, Primo, Heileman's Special Export, Heileman's Special Export Light, Henry Weinhard's Private Reserve, Henry Weinhard's Porter, Henry Weinhard's Amber Ale, Henry Weinhard's Blackberry Wheat, Weinhard's Pale Ale, Weinhard's Red, Weinhard's Ice Ale, Weinhard's Hefeweizen, Weinhard's Dark, Augsburger Bock, Augsburger Oktoberfest, Augsburger Winter Festbier, Augsburger Weiss, Augsburger Alt, Augsburger Red, First Reserve Lager, Red River Valley Red Lager. Stroh also produces a number of beers under license.

MICKEY'S

TYPE: LAGER
ALCOHOL: 5.6% VOL.
FERMENTATION: BOTTOM

Special remarks: Mickey's is packaged in accordance with European standards in a strange looking bottle with a screw cap. It is a light bodied lager, with a clean light taste. The aroma is slightly hoppy and somewhat floral, with a slightly sharp taste, lightly hopped.

STROH'S

TYPE: LAGER
ALCOHOL: 5% VOL.
FERMENTATION: BOTTOM

Special remarks:
Stroh's is this brewery's flagship beer. It has a somewhat hoppy aroma and a hoppy taste with a malty background. It is medium bodied, with a drying and hoppy aftertaste. Stroh's is a well-balanced lager.

• • •

SUMMIT BREWING COMPANY, ST. PAUL

Production in hectoliters: 50,000
Founded: 1986

Summit is one of the most rapidly expanding microbreweries and has bombarded the local market with special beers. In spite of this market sector being one of less than spectacular growth, the director and founder, Mark Stutrud has taken the risk of having a new brewery built with an eventual annual production capacity of 250,000 hectoliters. Summit's loyalties are divided between traditional English ale and a number of German varieties.

SUMMIT ALT BIER

TYPE: ALT
ALCOHOL: 4.9% VOL.
FERMENTATION: TOP

Special remarks: this alt is brewed in the Dusseldorf tradition and is available from September to November. This beer is brewed with four different malts and Northern Brewer, Saaz and Tettnang hops. This alt has a deep copper color.

SUMMIT EXTRA PALE ALE

TYPE: ALE
ALCOHOL: 4.9% VOL.
FERMENTATION: TOP

Special remarks: this extra pale ale is the flagship beer of the Summit brewery. This is an amber colored ale with an average fullness and a light fruity character.

SUMMIT GREAT NORTHERN PORTER

TYPE: PORTER
ALCOHOL: 5.4% VOL.
FERMENTATION: TOP

Special remarks:
Summit brews this London style porter with a malty, sweetish character and a deep dark color.

SUMMIT HEFE WEIZEN

TYPE: WHEAT BEER
ALCOHOL: 4.1% VOL.
FERMENTATION: TOP

Special remarks: to quench those thirsts in the summer months, Summit has brewed this German variety of wheat beer. This is a clean tasting beer with a light haze and is available from May until September.

SUMMIT INDIA PALE ALE

TYPE: ALE/IPA
ALCOHOL: 5.9% VOL.
FERMENTATION: TOP

Special remarks: this dark India Pale Ale has been dry hopped by Summit which gives it that hoppy aroma.

SUMMIT WINTER ALE

TYPE: ALE
ALCOHOL: 6.2% VOL.
FERMENTATION: TOP

Special remarks: Summit markets this Winter Ale from November until February. This is a slightly more robust ale for those cold winter evenings.

• • •

TABERNASH BREWING, DENVER

Production in hectoliters: 15,000
Founded: 1993

Tabernash was founded by George Barela, Jeff Mendel, Mark Lupa, and Eric Werner, the brewer who was awarded a diploma at Weihenstephan in honor of his knowledge of beer. The four founders felt that their enterprise was well worth the risk, due in part to the absence of a traditional German microbrewery in Colorado. The Bavarian "temple of brewing" of Weihenstephan also supplies the yeast strains used to brew Tabernash beers.

TABERNASH AMBER

TYPE: AMERICAN STEAM BEER

ALCOHOL: 5.4% VOL.

FERMENTATION: BOTTOM

Special remarks:
this amber-colored American steam beer is brewed with bottom fermenting yeast at high temperatures, after which it is allowed a cold maturing period. This gives the beer the clarity of a lager with the richer aroma of an ale.

TABERNASH GOLDEN

TYPE: PILSENER

ALCOHOL: 5.3% VOL.

FERMENTATION: BOTTOM

Special remarks: this blonde Pilsener from Tabernash is brewed with Gambinus, Münchener and Caramel malt with Perle-Hersbrucker and Saaz hops. This Pilsener is given an adequate six weeks to mature.

TABERNASH MUNICH

TYPE: MÜNCHENER/DUNKEL

ALCOHOL: 4.9% VOL.

FERMENTATION: BOTTOM

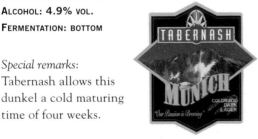

Special remarks:
Tabernash allows this dunkel a cold maturing time of four weeks.

TABERNASH WEISS

TYPE: WHEAT BEER

ALCOHOL: 5.7% VOL.

FERMENTATION: TOP

Special remarks:
totally in the German tradition, this is an unfiltered wheat beer with a clean and fruity character.

• • •

WIDMER BROTHERS BREWING CO, PORTLAND, OREGON

Production in hectoliters: 250,000
Founded: 1984

This brewery primarily produces German-oriented beers and is run by Kurt and Rob Widmer with their father, Ray. The brothers learned the craft of brewing in Germany, and even use the German Weihenstephan yeast for

The Widmer brothers.

their flagship Widmer Hefeweizen beer. The brothers have an agreement with Anheuser-Busch, which allows them to use this brewing giant's distribution network in exchange for shares in Widmer. In addition to the beers reviewed, Widmer also brews the following: Big Ben Porter; Ray's Amber Lager, a Viennese style lager in honor of their father Ray; Hop Jack for lovers of a well hopped lager; Pilsener; Altbier and Wildwood. Widmer also brews a number of seasonal beers including an Oktoberfest and a double bock. Considering the creative urge of the Widmer's couple with other new possibilities, a shift in the product range can be expected.

WIDMER AMBERBIER

TYPE: AMBER BEER

ALCOHOL: 5.2% VOL.

FERMENTATION: TOP

Special remarks: an amber-colored ale with a malty somewhat fruity aroma. The taste is reminiscent of roasted malt, slightly sweet with a bitter finish. The aftertaste is drying and bitter.

WIDMER HEFEWEIZEN

TYPE: WHEAT BEER
ALCOHOL: 4.3% VOL.
FERMENTATION: TOP

Special remarks:
an unfiltered hazy blonde wheat beer with a lively character.

WIDMER WIDBERRY

TYPE: FRUIT BEER
ALCOHOL: 4.5% VOL.
FERMENTATION: TOP

Special remarks:
this traditional Belgian beer is sweetened with raspberries and hopped with Tettnang. This beer has a sweet and sour fruit taste with a somewhat hoppy background.

• • •

YBOR CITY BREWING COMPANY, TAMPA

Production in hectoliters: 20,000
Founded: 1994

YCBC is a local microbrewery that sells its beers exclusively in Florida. The brewery is in a former cigar factory, of which there were once around two hundred in Ybor City. The restored factory gives this brand new brewery a nostalgic flavor. The founder, Humberto Perez, is also responsible for small piece of history, being a third generation brewer. YCBC presents itself as a craft brewer, using no preservatives or chemical additives, and aims to become thenumber one microbrewery in Florida.

YBOR GOLD

TYPE: LAGER
ALCOHOL: 4.9% VOL.
FERMENTATION: BOTTOM

Special remarks:
YCBC Gold is the flagship beer of YCBC. This is a light, amber colored lager with a medium body.

YBOR CALUSA WHEAT

TYPE: AMERICAN WHEAT BEER
ALCOHOL: 3.9% VOL.
FERMENTATION: TOP

Special remarks: a blonde light wheat beer brewed with two-row barley malt and wheat malt. Recommended to be served with light meals and fish dishes.

YBOR BROWN ALE

TYPE: ALE
ALCOHOL: 4.4% VOL.
FERMENTATION: TOP

Special remarks: this copper to brown colored ale has a reasonable fullness and its brewing ingredients include chocolate malt and caramel malt. Recommended with, chicken, other poultry and wild game.

GASPAR'S ALE

TYPE: PORTER
ALCOHOL: 5.2% VOL.
FERMENTATION: TOP

Special remarks: this dark brown porter is a seasonal beer introduced for the winter months. YCBC are planning other seasonal beers for future production.

• • •

COUNTRY Mexico

Bordering on the United States of America, Mexico, with its population of more than ninety million, has a vast and wealthy export market on its doorstep. With its Spanish background and indigenous populations, Mexico has an entirely different culture to that of its northern neighbor.

The Mexicans are Latin Americans; but their beers resemble the German lagers. Perhaps even more surprising is the presence of a number of traditional Viennese-style lagers.

Two large breweries, Cuauhtémoc and Modelo dominate the Mexican market.

CERVECERÍA CUAUHTÉMOC MOCTEZUMA, MONTERREY

Production in hectoliters: 20,000,000
Founded: 1890/1894

Cuauhtémoc and Modelo are both part of a holding known as Femsa, making it the largest brewery group in Mexico. Interbrew owns a 22% stake thanks to their ownership of the Canadian brewery Labatt.

Cuauhtémoc was founded by Isaac Garza and José Calderón, with help from the American Joseph Schnaider, whose beer was distributed by Garza and Calderón. In 1894, the new brewery was opened in Monterrey under the name of Cerveceria Cuauhtémoc. In 1896, Guillermo Hasse, together with Cuno Von Halte and Emilia S. Mantey opened a brewery known as the Guillermo Hasse y Compañía in Orizaba. This brewery was renamed the Cerveceria Moctezuma in 1896. These breweries merged in 1985 and became part of the Femsa holding. Their beers are brewed at Tecate, established in 1943 with a capacity of 3,8 million hectoliters; Navojoa, established in 1991, has a capacity of 4.2 million hectoliters; Monterrey, the oldest brewery in Mexico has a capacity of 6.6 million hectoliters; Guadalajara, established in 1970 has a capacity of 3.1 million hectoliters; Toluca, established in 1969 has a capacity of 5.4 million hectoliters; and Orizaba established in 1894 has a capacity of 6.6 million hectoliters. The Holding, Fomento Económico Mexicano encompasses not just six breweries but also factories producing glass, malt, labels and packaging. They also run OXXO one of the largest supermarket chains in Mexico. Fomento's beers include Bohemia, Carta Blanca, Dos Equis, Tecate, Tecate Light, Sol, Noche Buena, Superior, XX Lager and India.

BOHEMIA

TYPE: PILSENER
ALCOHOL: 4.8% VOL.
FERMENTATION: BOTTOM

Special remarks: this is a blonde Pilsener with a malty aroma. The taste is sweet malt with a hoppy and slightly floral background. The Bohemia is reasonably intense with a drying and hoppy aftertaste. A well-balanced lager.

DOS EQUIS

TYPE: VIENISSE STYLE
ALCOHOL: 4.8% VOL.
FERMENTATION: BOTTOM

Special remarks: the many Austrian immigrants introduced this traditional Austrian beer to Mexico. It is an amber-colored lager reminiscent of the German dunkel. It is lightly malted with a slightly fruity aroma and a vaguely roasted clean malty taste.

DOS EQUIS SPECIAL LAGER

TYPE: LAGER
ALCOHOL: 4.5% VOL.
FERMENTATION: BOTTOM

Special remarks: a blonde lager, slightly malty with a hoppy finish. The aroma is floral and hoppy. This special has a drying and lightly hopped aftertaste.

SOL

TYPE: LAGER
ALCOHOL: 4.5% VOL.
FERMENTATION: BOTTOM

Special remarks: Sol is the Mexican counterpart of Corona. It does not have an exceptional taste or intensity, but is a great thirst quencher when served well chilled.

TECATE

TYPE: PILSENER
ALCOHOL: 4.6% VOL.
FERMENTATION: BOTTOM

Special remarks: Tecate is a Pilsener with a somewhat light body. The taste and aroma is one of subtle hops and malt. The aftertaste is slightly more drying and hoppy.

• • •

CERVECERÍA MODELO, MEXICO-STAD

Production in hectoliters: 27,000,000
Founded: 1925

Modelo is the second largest brewery in Mexico with 38,000 employees. Apart from its eight breweries, it has its own maltings, barley fields, and factories producing their own bottles and packaging. Modelo even owns the mines that produce the raw materials used in their glass production. Modelo has recently opened a new brewery in Zacatecas with a production capacity of 15 million hectoliters. In a single move this has increased their total capacity by one third to forty million hectoliters, more than adequate to cope with demand for the foreseeable future. Modelo's other breweries are in Mexico City, Guadalajara, Tuxtepec, Torreon, Ciudad Obregon, Mazatlan and Merida. An important part of the Modelo beer production, with especially that of Corona is intended for the export market. Anheuser Busch has a minority stake in Modelo. All of the Modelo export beers are brewed in their own breweries in Mexico.

CORONA EXTRA

TYPE: LAGER

ALCOHOL: 4.6% VOL.

FERMENTATION: BOTTOM

Special remarks: Corona is nothing special but it has managed to topple Heineken from the number one spot of the American imported beer charts. It is a light lager, particularly neutral, being slightly drying and hoppy. Corona is often served with a slice of Lemon, a habit that did not originate in Mexico, as Corona was only originally intended as a cheap lager, a daily thirst quencher for Mexican workers. The American yuppies started pushing a slice of lemon through the neck of the bottle, setting a trend to be followed by other Americans, Europeans and even the Mexicans. Corona is brewed with corn (maize), rice, malt, hops, yeast and ascorbic acid. This beer contains no artificial additives or preservatives.

NEGRA MODELO

TYPE: LAGER

ALCOHOL: 5.3% VOL.

FERMENTATION: BOTTOM

Special remarks: this red-brown lager has a roasted malt aroma, slightly sweet. The taste is rounded with evidence of sweet roasted malt. The aftertaste is drying, lightly bitter with a hint of chocolate. Negra (black) is not exactly a crafted beer, but does have an intensive taste and aroma.

PACÍFICO CLARA

TYPE: LAGER

ALCOHOL: 4.5% VOL.

FERMENTATION: BOTTOM

Special remarks: this lager is brewed at the Mazatlán brewery that was founded in 1900 by Jacob Scheule. This is a blonde lager with a floral hoppy aroma and a light hoppy and malty taste. The aftertaste is drying and slightly hoppy.

• • •

COUNTRY Brazil

Brazil's surface area makes it one of the largest countries in the world, with a population of more than 190 million. Until 1925 it was a Portuguese colony, with Portuguese being the official language. Despite this the traditional Brazilian beers are once more based on German/Czech traditions such as Pilsener and bock beers. With an average consumption of approximately fifty liters per head per year, the Brazilians are not exceptional beer drinkers, and yet Brazil is the world's fourth largest beer-producing nation.

COMPANHIA CERVEJARIA BRAHMA, RIO DE JANEIRO

Production in hectoliters: 40,000,000
Founded: 1888

Brahma is one of the world's top five breweries. Its product range includes Brahma Chopp, Brahma Light, Brahma Extra, Brahma Bock and Malzbier. Skol. The second most popular brand in Brazil, is now also owned by Brahma giving them approximately half of the Brazilian market. Brahma's premium export beers are Carlsberg and Miller.

BRAHMA CHOPP

TYPE: PILSENER
ALCOHOL: 5% VOL.
FERMENTATION: BOTTOM

Special remarks: this is the export variety of Brahma. Around 25 million hectoliters of Brahma Chopp are sold annually worldwide. The sharp hoppy aroma of Brahma is evident initially, but soon fades. This light blonde lager as a very soft malty sweet taste and a light body.

• • •

CERVEJARIA INDEPENTE, TOLEDO

Production in hectoliters: –
Founded: –

XINGU BLACK BEER

TYPE: BLACK LAGER
ALCOHOL: 5.7% VOL.
FERMENTATION: BOTTOM

Special remarks: Xingu is a modern version of a native drink that used to be made by the native people of the Amazon region. Xingu has been taken from the Brazilian river of the same name. This black lager is brewed from burnt malt and maze, and is fermented using wild yeast strains. The current version just comes from a brewery and can best be described as being similar to sweet stout, although Xingu is bottom fermenting. Xingu is opaque black with a brown head which is light in color at the top, fading towards the bottom. The aroma is one of roasted malt and is slightly coffee-like. The intense rich taste is reminiscent of caramel, coffee and toffee, in a bitter chocolate coating. This beer is sweet, but certainly not sticky. Curiously, although Xingu is a very complex beer, it is not that full bodied, which is probably due to being well diluted. Xingu is not dry and is not that bitter setting it apart from stout.

• • •

UNKNOWN BREWER, CANTINO DO BRAZIL

Production in hectoliters: –
Founded: –

CARIOCA

TYPE: LAGER
ALCOHOL: 5% VOL.
FERMENTATION: BOTTOM

Special remarks: Carioca is a light blonde lager with a neutral taste and a slightly hoppy finish.

• • •

COUNTRY Peru

UNIÓN DE CERVECERÍAS PERUANAS BACKUS & JOHNSTON SA, RÍMAC

Production in hectoliters: –
Founded: 1955

Unión de Cervecerías Peruanas Backus & Johnston SA. resulted from a merger between Cervecería Backus y Johnston S.A, Compañia Nacional de Cervezas SA. Sociedad Cervecera de Trujillo SA. and Cerveza del Norte SA. Their beers include: Cristal, Pilsen Callao, Pilsen Trujillo, Garza Real, Maltina, Pantera, Sansón, Morena, Guarana, Viva Backus and Champale. This is the largest brewing group in Peru.

CRISTAL

TYPE: LAGER
ALCOHOL: 5% VOL.
FERMENTATION: BOTTOM

Special remarks: Cristal is a blonde neutral lager with a clean, vaguely malty taste.

PILSEN CALLOA

TYPE: PILSENER
ALCOHOL: 5% VOL.
FERMENTATION: BOTTOM

Special remarks: this is a blonde Pilsener with a vague hoppy aroma. This is a light-bodied beer with the taste of hops and malt, all be it slight. Calloa is a well-balanced beer with a lovely soft character.

• • •

COUNTRY Columbia

CERVEJARIA ANCLA, BOGOTÁ

Production in hectoliters: –
Founded: –

ANCLA
TYPE: LAGER
ALCOHOL: 4.8% VOL.
FERMENTATION: BOTTOM

Special remarks: a well–balanced blonde lager with a hoppy aroma and a full malty. Ancla has a hoppy background, and is drying towards the finish. This is a medium-bodied lager with a hoppy bitter aftertaste.

• • •

CERVEJARIA AGUILA, BARRANQUILLLA

Production in hectoliters: –
Founded: –

AGUILA
TYPE: LAGER
ALCOHOL: 4% VOL.
FERMENTATION: BOTTOM

Special remarks: this is a light blonde lager with a sharp hoppy aroma. The taste is lightly malted with an initial sharp tang of hops, which is later lost in the glass. Aguila is light-bodied with a drying and slightly bitter aftertaste.

• • •

COUNTRY Bolivia

CERVECERIA BOLIVIA NACIONAL SA, LA PAZ

Production in hectoliters: –
Founded: –

Cerveceria is a large national brewery.

PACEÑA CENTENARIO BEER

TYPE: LAGER
ALCOHOL: 5.2% VOL.
FERMENTATION: BOTTOM

Special remarks: this is a blonde lager brewed with water, yeast, hops, malt and rice. The aroma is malty The taste is malty and slightly sharp with a hoppy dry finish.

● ● ●

COUNTRY Suriname

PARBO BREWERY, PARAMARIBO

Production in hectoliters: –
Founded: –

DJOGO PILSENER BIER

TYPE: PILSENER
ALCOHOL: 5% VOL.
FERMENTATION: BOTTOM

PARBO BIER

TYPE: PILSENER
ALCOHOL: 5% VOL.
FERMENTATION: BOTTOM

Special remarks: this is a light blonde Pilsener, with a light sweet malty taste with in the background a sharp hoppy bitterness.

• • •

COUNTRY Cuba

MAYABE BREWERY, HATUEY, HOLGUIN

Production in hectoliters: –
Founded: 1926

Hatuey, (pronounced 'ahtway') was first brewed by the Cuban Bacardi Rum Company. The Bacardi family recruited the German Georg Friederic from the USA to brew them a good quality Pilsener. Joaquin Bacardi later became Cuba's first master brewer after learning the brewing trade in Copenhagen. This led to Hatuey accounting for around half of the Cuban market before the Cuban revolution. Hatuey was a legendary Cuban native who fought the Spanish. The Pilsener that bears his name is now brewed in the USA by the Bacardi Company Inc.

HATUEY

TYPE: LAGER
ALCOHOL: 4.8% VOL.
FERMENTATION: BOTTOM

Special remarks: this blonde, slightly cloudy lager has a neutral and somewhat malty taste with an aftertaste that is vaguely hoppy and malty.

COUNTRY Jamaica

Jamaica is a Caribbean island, south of Cuba, with a population of approximately two and a half million that was under colonial English rule for a long time. Almost half of the national income is derived from tourism, assuring the continuing demand for a cold lager, not to mention Jamaican stout.

DESNOES & GEDDES LTD, KINGSTON

Production in hectoliters: –
Founded: 1918

The Desnoes & Geddes brewery, named after its founders, is actually owned by Guinness. It is a medium-sized brewery with Red Stripe lager being the jewel in its crown.

RED STRIPE

TYPE: LAGER
ALCOHOL: 4.7% VOL.
FERMENTATION: BOTTOM

Special remarks: this is light blonde lager with a hoppy aroma. The taste is malty with a slightly drying finish and a light malt aftertaste.

DRAGON STOUT

TYPE: STOUT
ALCOHOL: 7.5% VOL.
FERMENTATION: BOTTOM

Special remarks:
this bottom fermented stout from DG is opaque and very dark in color. It initially gives a full, almost creamy mouth sensation that warms towards the finish. It has a fruity aroma, slightly cherry-like with a rounded sweet burnt taste. The aftertaste is warming, slightly drying with a tinge of chocolate bitterness.

Asia

Asia

Japan

With a population of 125 million with among the highest average incomes in the world, Japan is a major market for beer market, even though average annual consumption per person is only sixty liters. Japan has four large independent brewery groups which more than hold their own without any help from American or European brewers. Any collaboration entered into by Japanese brewers with other brewers has been to penetrate markets outside of Japan, due to stagnation in the domestic market. Sapporo and Asahi merged in 1949 to form a single giant, but were de-merged following government intervention. Pub breweries are increasingly popular in Japan, following changes in legislation.

ASAHI BREWERIES LTD, TOKYO

Production in hectoliters: 19,000,000
Founded: 1889

Asahi is the second largest brewery in Japan and has approximately one third of the Japanese market. Asahi Super Dry is the brewery's flagship beer, and this is sold in more than thirty countries. Due to stagnation of the domestic market, Asahi has started to concentrate on foreign markets. Towards the end of 2000, Asahi started a joint venture to build a new brewery with the Tsingtao Brewery Company based in China, to serve what is probably the world's largest market for beer. Asahi is now also working with Miller in North America, where Asahi Super Dry is brewed in Canada by Molson and distributed in the USA by Molson USA (owned by Miller). Furthermore, Asahi has ties with Foster's, Bass and Löwenbräu. Asahi has nine breweries in Japan. This concern's products include Asahi Super Dry, Asahi Kuronama (Black Draft Beer) and Asahi First Lady. Asahi breweries also distributes Löwenbräu Pilsener which they brew under license together with the imported Miller Special and Bass Pale Ale. Apart from beer, Asahi also produces wine, spirits and pharmaceutical products.

KIRIN BREWERY CO, TOKYO

Production in hectoliters: 40.000.000
Founded: 1885

This Japanese brewing giant takes its name from a mythological half dragon known as the Kirin. An American, William Copeland and German brewer Herman Heckland founded the Spring Valley Brewery in 1870 but this brewery went bankrupt in 1884 and was reopened in 1885 by a group of American and English businessmen, renamed as The Japan Brewery Company.

They first brewed the lager known as Kirin in 1888. In 1907 the brewery came into the hands of the Mitsubishi family and was acquired its current name of Kirin Brewery. Kirin expanded to become the largest brewery in Japan with almost forty percent of the market, which also places it in the top ten of the world's biggest breweries. In addition to brewing beer, Kirin has a number of other activities. With Anheuser Busch, they built a new brewery in Los Angeles in 1997 to satisfy American demand for fresh Kirin. Besides Kirin Lager this brewery also produces Ichiban, a premium beer 5% alcohol, Kirin Light with 3.5% alcohol and Draft, requiring no explanation.

SAPPORO BREWERIES, TOKYO

Production in hectoliters: –
Founded: 1880 / 1949

The Sapporo brewery is one of the major players in the Japanese market with ten breweries and six thousand employees. Sapporo produces wine and also owns a number of hotels and restaurants. The pressures of the home market have resulted in Sapporo searching for markets overseas. A joint venture with Guinness has led to Guinness producing Sapporo for the European market and Sapporo importing and distributing Guinness in Japan. Sapporo helps with the hop cultivation in the Czech Republic and works with universities in Australia and Canada in the development of new yeast strains.

Sapporo has started working with Chinese brewers and since 1984 has had a sales office in the USA where they deal with the sales orders for the best-selling Japanese beer in America, Sapporo Draft. The brewery's flagship beer is Sapporo Black Label. Their other beers include Yebisu, Drafty Special and Drafty Black Special, Super Star, Hokkaido, Calorie Half, Classic, The Winter Tale and Haru Ga Kita.

KIRIN LAGER

TYPE: LAGER
ALCOHOL: 4.8% VOL.
FERMENTATION: BOTTOM

Special remarks: Kerin is brewed under license in a variety of countries with barley malt, rice, maize and hops. This is a light neutral malty lager with nuances of Saaz and Hallertau hops.

• • •

SAPPORO PREMIUM LAGER

TYPE: LAGER
ALCOHOL: 4.5% VOL.
FERMENTATION: BOTTOM

Special remarks: this premium lager is brewed by Guinness Ireland and contains water, malt, hops and maize. The result is a gold blonde lager, lightly malty with a subtle dry background, the mouth sensation is light, and even somewhat watery.

• • •

SUNTORY BREWERY, TOKYO

Production in hectoliters: –
Founded: 1899 / 1963

The Suntory brewery did not start brewing until 1963 and is part of a much larger concern with a variety of divisions.

Suntory's flagship beer is Malt's. Their other beers include Super Hop's, Daichi to Mizu no Megumi and Dynamic. Suntory also brews Carlsberg under license. Suntory has interests in China as well as Japan.

• • •

COUNTRY India

Much of the beer brewing in India has been placed on hold because of regional and national legislation dictating that the breweries are only permitted to produce a beer of a certain quantity, although this legislation is widely ignored. British colonial rule has obviously influenced the traditional Indian beer, although international-style lager is the most widely available.

MYSORE BREWERY, BANGALORE

Production in hectoliters: –
Founded: –

COBRA

TYPE: LAGER
ALCOHOL: 5% VOL.
FERMENTATION: BOTTOM

Special remarks: a blonde, light, malty lager. The taste is slightly sweet, drying towards the finish and with a scarcity of hops.

SHAW WALLAGE & CO, CALCUTTA

Production in hectoliters: 12,000,000 (including spirits)
Founded: 1886 / 1815

This brewery was founded in 1886 by David Shaw and C.W. Wallace, and merged in 1945 with the Cutler Palmer & Co. brewery that was founded in 1815.

LAL TAFOON

TYPE: LAGER
ALCOHOL: 4.6% VOL.
FERMENTATION: BOTTOM

Special remarks: Lal Tafoon means "Red Storm" and is named after the desert storms of Rajastan. This blonde light bodied lager is brewed with rice. It has a dry taste and a light bitter aftertaste.

UNITED BREWERIES, BANGALORE

Production in hectoliters: –
Founded: 1857

United Breweries is a large international brewery that is led by Vijay Mallya. Apart from breweries, this group also includes produces spirits and soft drinks.

KINGFISHER

TYPE: LAGER
ALCOHOL: 4.8% VOL.
FERMENTATION: BOTTOM

Special remarks: Kingfisher is one of the most widely available of the Indian beers. This is a blonde light lager with an especially malty character. The aroma is one of hops and malt. The body is light to medium.

COUNTRY China

In spite of its low individual beer consumption, with a population of more than one billion, China remains an interesting market for beer. The world's giant beer brewers are now working with the existing Chinese brewers to build new breweries that will soon satisfy the demand of the world's biggest market for beer.

TSINGTAO BREWERY CO LTD, TSINGTAO

Production in hectoliters: –
Founded: –

Some Germans who ran a trading post in Tsingtao founded the Tsingtao brewery at the end of the nineteenth century.

TSINGTAO BEER

TYPE: PILSENER
ALCOHOL: 4.5% VOL.
FERMENTATION: BOTTOM

CHINESE GINSENG BEER

TYPE: LAGER
ALCOHOL: 4.1% VOL.
FERMENTATION: BOTTOM

Special remarks: this is a blonde lager brewed with water, roasted wheat, caramel, malt, hops, ginger, ginseng, and beer head stabilizer.

ZHU JIANG BEER

TYPE: LAGER
ALCOHOL: 5.2% VOL.
FERMENTATION: BOTTOM

Special remarks: a blonde neutral lager brewed by Interbrew for the Zhu Jiang Group.

COUNTRY Singapore

ASIA PACIFIC BREWERIES, SINGAPORE

Production in hectoliters: –
Founded: 1931

Asia pacific was founded in 1931 as the Malayan Breweries Ltd, after collaboration between Fraser & Neave and Heineken. This modern brewery now has fifteen subsidiaries in Singapore, Vietnam, Malaysia, Cambodia, Thailand, New Zealand and Papua New Guinea.

TIGER LAGER BEER

TYPE: LAGER
ALCOHOL: 5% VOL.
FERMENTATION: BOTTOM

Special remarks: Tiger is one of the biggest Asian brands with an impressive trophy cabinet. The taste is light malt and sweetish with a somewhat floral aroma.

COUNTRY Thailand / Muang Thai

BOON RAWD BREWERY CO LTD, BANGKRABUE

Production in hectoliters: –
Founded: 1933

The Bhirombhakdi family owns seventy percent of the Boon Rawd brewery. This company has around 1,300 employees.

SINGHA

TYPE: LAGER
ALCOHOL: 6% VOL.
FERMENTATION: BOTTOM

Special remarks: Singha is a blonde lager with a hoppy aroma with a hint of lemon. The taste is malty with a sturdy hop accompaniment. The aftertaste is soft, but is dominated by a hoppy bitterness. Singha is medium-bodied.

COUNTRY Philippines / Pilipina

SAN MIGUEL BREWERY, MANILLA

Production in hectoliters: 15,000,000
Founded: 1890

San Miguel no longer has any ties with the Spanish brewery of the same name. This is one of the larger groups in Asia, with a number of breweries, including one in Hong Kong.

SAN MIGUEL PALE PILSEN

TYPE: PILSENER
ALCOHOL: 5% VOL.
FERMENTATION: BOTTOM

Special remarks: this Pilsener is brewed with malt, hops, sugar, citric acid, caramel and stabilizer.

COUNTRY South Korea / Taehan–Min'guk

ORIENTAL BREWERY CO LTD, SEOUL

Production in hectoliters: –
Founded: –

OB BEER

TYPE: LAGER
ALCOHOL: 4.5% VOL.
FERMENTATION: BOTTOM

Special remarks: this is a gold blonde lager with a malty aroma and a sweet malt taste. The aftertaste is somewhat drying.

COUNTRY Israel

TEMPO BEER INDUSTRIES LTD, NETANYA

Production in hectoliters: / Founded: –

Tempo Beer Industries with five breweries is the largest brewing group in Israel, with Maccabee as the best selling beer. All of the brewery's beers are kosher.

MACCABEE

TYPE: LAGER
ALCOHOL: 4.9% VOL.
FERMENTATION: BOTTOM

Special remarks: this is a blond lager with a malty aroma. The taste malty accompanied by a degree of sharp maltiness and drying towards the finish.

GOLDSTAR

TYPE: LAGER
ALCOHOL: 4.9% VOL.
FERMENTATION: BOTTOM

Special remarks: this is a light amber colored lager with a malty aroma and a medium body. It has a malty taste with a malty drying finish. Goldstar also contains grain as well as malt.

MALT STAR

TYPE: ALCOHOL–FREE
ALCOHOL: 0.5% VOL.
FERMENTATION: –

Special remarks: this is a ruby red non–alcoholic beer with a sweet malty taste. Malt Star contains water, malt, sugar, caramel and hops.

COUNTRY The Lebanon

BREWERY AND MALTINGS, ALMAZA SAL, ALMAZA

Production in hectoliters: –
Founded: **1933**

According to the label, this company brews in association with and under the technical supervision of the Amstel brewery in The Netherlands.

ALMAZA

TYPE: PILSENER
ALCOHOL: 4.5% VOL.
FERMENTATION: BOTTOM

Special remarks: this Lebanese Pilsener is light blonde in color with a somewhat malty aroma. The taste is malty. There is practically no evidence of hops in Almaza, except in the aftertaste, and then only very slight.

COUNTRY Turkey

When thinking of Turkey, beer is not a thing that immediately springs to mind. After all, alcohol and Islam do not exactly go hand in hand. However, Turkey has a number of breweries, of which the Efes breweries are the largest group. Tuborg has also had a small brewery and maltings in Turkey since 1967. Large numbers of Turks have emigrated to Africa and Europe, resulting in a considerable export market for Efes.

EFES-BREWERY, ISTANBUL

Production in hectoliters: 3,000,000
Founded: **1967**

This large brewery has subsidiaries in Izmir and Ankara. Apart from their brewery, Efes also owns a number of maltings. As well as their Pilsener, they also produce a light and an alcohol-free beer.

EFES PILSENER

TYPE: PILSENER
ALCOHOL: 5% VOL.
FERMENTATION: BOTTOM

Special remarks: a blonde Pilsener with a somewhat sharp, hoppy and somewhat floral aroma. The taste is light and sweetish, with just a touch of hops at the finish.

• • •

Africa

Africa

5

COUNTRY Egypt

With a population of sixty million, and a blistering climate, Egypt is an interesting market for the beer industry. Especially when you consider that beer brewing came out of the cradle of the Egyptian civilization around six thousand years ago. Strict limitations on imports, together with government interference and the anti-alcohol teaching of the religion followed by sixty million of the population has put pay to all of that. There are only a million Christians in Egypt and they are not renowned as the biggest drinkers in the world. Tourists and the less devout therefore account for most of the sales of beer from a brewery that until recently was the monopoly state-run brewery. The German brewer Löwenbrau has now taken over the brewery with permission from the Egyptian government to continue brewing.

PYRAMIDS BEVERAGES CO, CAîRO

Production in hectoliters: –
Founded: 1898

The name Stella that appears on the label of every bottle that leaves this brewery is probably a strong reminder of the Belgian brewer, Stella Artois. Belgians were indeed responsible for the birth of the Pyramid Brewery around one hundred years ago. The brewery experienced enormous growth during World War II when half the armies of the world's were roaming across Egypt. All Egyptian companies were nationalized in the 1960s and the two remaining breweries were forced to merge.

STELLA LAGER BEER

TYPE: LAGER
ALCOHOL: 5% VOL.
FERMENTATION: BOTTOM

Special remarks: this blonde lighter version of Stella has a sharp hoppy aroma and taste. It is just a shade insipid and thin-bodied with a slightly bitter and drying aftertaste.

STELLA LAGER EXPORT BEER

TYPE: LAGER
ALCOHOL: 5% VOL.
FERMENTATION: BOTTOM

Special remarks: this is a gold blonde reasonably full beer, malty with a soft hoppy bitterness. The background is slightly dry.

• • •

COUNTRY Namibia

Namibia is one of the African countries where growing prosperity and an increase in foreign tourism has led to a rise in demand for good thirst quenchers. The sweltering temperatures and the lack of safe drinking water makes Namibia fertile territory for the brewing industry. Namibia is adjacent to South Africa, on the southwest coast of the African mainland. The economy of this country, with its population of 1,6 million is in fact largely dependent on its larger neighbors to the south. The capital of Namibia is Windhoek, where they speak English, German and/or one of the many African languages.

NAMIBIA BREWERIES LTD, WINDHOEK
Production in hectoliters:
Founded: 1920

Namibia Breweries have a large brewery with a strong export market in South Africa. Its German past is instantly recognizable due to its beers being brewed in accordance with the Reinheitsgebot. There has even been a conflict with the South African Brewer SAB concerning the use of the term "Hofbrau".

WINDHOEK EXPORT
TYPE: LAGER / PREMIUM
ALCOHOL: 4.5% VOL.
FERMENTATION: BOTTOM

Special remarks: this lager is brewed in accordance with the Reinheitsgebot. This blonde export lager starts with a somewhat sharp hoppy aroma that becomes considerably softer after a time. The taste is malty and a shade sweet. This lager has a hoppy background, a medium body and is dry and smooth. Certainly a beer to be recommended.

WINDHOEK SPECIAL
TYPE: LAGER
ALCOHOL: 5.3% VOL.
FERMENTATION: BOTTOM

Special remarks: this lager is also brewed in accordance with the Reinheitsgebot. The gold blonde Windhoek Special has a malty aroma with a malty taste and a hoppy background. It is a robust beer with the roundness of a bock. The Special has little bitterness, but it remains a beer full of character.

• • •

COUNTRY Kenya

Kenya is a country in Africa with a population of approximately twenty-five million spread over around forty different tribes. It has an English colonial past, and the English language is widely spoken.

The beers are mainly lagers, many produced by Kenya Breweries, whose main competitors are SAB.

Furthermore, a number of native beer varieties are brewed with alcohol volumes up to 15%. These brews often lead to uncontrolled intoxication and in extreme cases even death.

The larger breweries fall under a high taxation group, making their beer relatively expensive. This has made the market very receptive for the native brews.

KENYA BREWERIES LTD, NAIROBI

Production in hectoliters: –
Founded: 1920

Kenya Breweries is the second largest African Brewery after SAB, and has around 3000 employees. This brewery was originally founded by English colonialists using English equipment.

Apart from Tusker, Kenya Breweries produces White Cap also available throughout Kenya.

TUSKER PREMIUM LAGER

TYPE: LAGER
ALCOHOL: 5% VOL.
FERMENTATION: BOTTOM

Special remarks: this premium lager has a somewhat malty aroma. The taste is light malt with a somewhat hoppy background. Tusker is medium–bodied with a drying hoppy aftertaste.

• • •

COUNTRY Zimbabwe

NATIONAL BREWERIES ZIMBABWE, HARARE

Production in hectoliters: –
Founded: –

ZAMBEZI

TYPE: LAGER
ALCOHOL: 4.5% VOL.
FERMENTATION: BOTTOM

Special remarks: this is a clear blonde beer with a light malty taste and a slightly hoppy background. The aftertaste is one of a light hoppy bitterness.

• • •

COUNTRY South Africa

SOUTH AFRICAN BREWERIES (SAB), JOHANNESBURG

Production in hectoliters: 43,000,000
Founded: 1862

SAB is the result of a merger between a variety of breweries in South Africa that came about as a result of the demand for beer by different groups of immigrants. The Germans, British, and Dutch all had their own breweries which mainly brewed lagers, in keeping with the hot climate.

In 1956, Castle and Lion Beer merged, forming the largest brewery on the African continent. SAB is now one of the world's five largest breweries, and has currently over 80,000 employees and brews in seventy countries, primarily concentrated in Africa, (ten breweries), Central Europe (seven breweries) and China (five breweries). In addition, SAB has seven breweries in South Africa, with a total capacity of twenty-five million hectoliters. As well as breweries, SAB also own hotels, maltings, hop gardens, and factories where they produce soft drinks, fruit juices and sorghum beer. The beers, together with those brewed under license by SAB, are all lagers, and include Castle Lager, Castle Lite, Castle Milk Stout, Lion Lager, Ohlsson's Lager, Hofbräu, Redds, Dooleys, Hansa Pilsener, Amstel and Carling Black Label. SAB imports Heineken, Guinness and Kilkenny.

SAB also owns a further twenty breweries that brew sorghum beer known as Chibuku Sorghum, a modern version of an old type of beer based on the tropical grain sorghum or millet.

CASTLE LAGER

TYPE: LAGER
ALCOHOL: 5% VOL.
FERMENTATION: BOTTOM

Special remarks: this is the flagship beer of SAB. A blonde lager with a somewhat hoppy aroma. The taste is hoppy and somewhat sharp. Castle is medium-bodied with a hoppy and drying aftertaste.

• • •

BAVARIA BRÄU, CENTURION PARK

Production in hectoliters: –
Founded: –

This is a small brewery that leans towards the old brewing craft traditions. They brew in accordance with the Reinheitsgebot and their export markets include England.

RORKE'S REAL LAGER

TYPE: LAGER
ALCOHOL: 5% VOL.
FERMENTATION: BOTTOM

Special remarks: this is blonde lager with a strong aroma of grain. The taste is malty, with a malty and slightly sharp hoppy background. The aftertaste is short with a hoppy bitterness.

• • •

Oceania

Oceania

6

COUNTRY Australia

Australia is well known for being "the land down under". This large island has an abundance of English influences thanks to its alliance with the UK, which started at the end of the eighteenth century.

Australia is a fairly hot country, with about seventy percent of the land being desert. English ales are not really suited to this hot climate, so lagers have replaced them, even though these are masquerade under the description of bitter or ale. The American Foster brothers started this transition and in 1887 they founded Foster's brewery in Melbourne. Their brewery employed the latest lager brewing techniques available with the cooling playing an essential role. The brothers later returned to America but left their legacy in Australia in the form of a new type of beer. The Australians are average beer drinkers, consuming around one hundred liters per person annually, primarily cold lagers. The Australian breweries, especially the two largest, CUB and Lion Nathan, have always worked feverishly at exporting in view of the small Australian population of fewer than eighteen million. Thanks to foreign takeovers and their export markets, these breweries have achieved considerable growth.

FOSTER'S
AUSTRALIA'S FAMOUS BEER

TASMANIAN BREWERIES PTY LTD, TASMANIA

Production in hectoliters: –
Founded: 1927

The Tasmanian brewing group is made up of the Boag's brewery in Launceston and the Cascade brewery in Hobart. Both have a long history, but merged in 1927. All beers bear either the name of Boag's or Cascade on the label. Large quantities of hops and brewer's barley are cultivated on the island of Tasmania.

JAMES BOAG'S PREMIUM
TYPE: EXPORT SLAGER
ALCOHOL: 5% VOL.
FERMENTATION: BOTTOM

Special remarks: this premium export lager is gold in color and has a hoppy aroma. The taste is one of light malt and is lightly hopped. The aftertaste is hoppy and slightly drying.

• • •

CARLTON & UNITED BREWERIES LTD, MELBOURNE

Production in hectoliters: 27,000,000
Founded: 1887

Carlton & United breweries Ltd are part of Elders Holding. It is Australia's largest brewing concern, owning several other breweries. They brew under a variety of names including Tooth, Carlton, Abbots and Reschs.

FOSTER'S ICE BEER
TYPE: ICE BEER
ALCOHOL: 5% VOL.
FERMENTATION: BOTTOM

Special remarks: this gold blonde ice filtered lager has a light slightly malty taste.

FOSTER'S LAGER
TYPE: LAGER
ALCOHOL: 5% VOL.
FERMENTATION: BOTTOM

Special remarks: this amber-colored lager has a light hoppy and malty aroma. The taste is lightly hopped, with malty sweetness in the background. The body is light to medium. The aftertaste is drying. Foster's is a widely available international lager.

VICTORIA BEER
TYPE: LAGER
ALCOHOL: 4.9% VOL.
FERMENTATION: BOTTOM

Special remarks: this blonde lager is light and has a sweet malty taste with evidence of more hops at the finish.

• • •

COOPER'S BREWERY LTD, ADELAIDE

Production in hectoliters: –
Founded: 1862

While almost all Australian breweries have switched from the brewing of ale to lager, Coopers have always stuck to the top fermenting techniques. Cooper's have their own maltings. This brewery was founded by Thomas Cooper, an English immigrant. His descendants are still brewing ales following English traditions, some of which are bottled secondary fermenters.

COOPER'S BEST EXTRA STOUT

TYPE: STOUT
ALCOHOL: 6.8% VOL.
FERMENTATION: TOP

Special remarks: this black stout is bottled with a small amount of unfermented wort, and a little sugar to start the secondary fermentation process. This beer has an aroma of burnt malt and a robust burnt taste with coffee like nuances. The aftertaste is drying with a light bitterness.

COOPER'S EXPORT

TYPE: ALE
ALCOHOL: 4.9% VOL.
FERMENTATION: TOP

Special remarks: this Cooper's Export is a gold blonde ale with a somewhat sweetish and slightly fruity aroma. The taste is sweet malt with a hoppy background. The body is medium and slightly rounded. The aftertaste is drying and hoppy, but has a slightly sweetish finish.

COOPER'S SPARKLING ALE

TYPE: ALE
ALCOHOL: 5.8% VOL.
FERMENTATION: TOP

Special remarks: this blonde Sparkling Ale has a light haze due to the presence of yeast sediment in the bottle. This beer has a lively mouth sensation and a fruity aroma. The taste is fruity, with evidence of herbs and malt. The aftertaste conveys a little more hoppy bitterness.

• • •

MATILDA BAY BREWING CO LTD, NORTH FREEMANTLE

Production in hectoliters: 400,000
Founded: 1984

The Matilda Bay brewery was founded under the name of Brewtech in 1984. A number of local entrepreneurs bought a hotel in Freemantle and renamed it the Sail and Anchor. A small annexed pub brewery was opened where the guests could enjoy fresh and special beers. A small microbrewery was later set up in Nedland. In 1990, Carlton and United secured a majority holding in this brewery which has led to the unprecedented growth of Matilda Bay whose beers also include Bitter Beer and Red Dog.

DOGBOLTER

TYPE: LAGER
ALCOHOL: 5.2% VOL.
FERMENTATION: BOTTOM

Special remarks: Dogbolter is a brown lager with an aroma of roasted malt. The taste is malty and roasted. This lager has a robust body with drying aftertaste of roasted malt.

FREEMANTLE BITTER ALE

TYPE: ALE

ALCOHOL: 4.9% VOL.

FERMENTATION: TOP

HAHN BREWING CO PTY LTD / LION NATHAN, CAMPERDOWN

Production in hectoliters: –

Founded: 1988

Originally the Hahn brewery was set up to be a microbrewery. Lion Nathan took over the brewery in 1996 and has given the old Hahn labels a new lease of life. The brewer at Lion Nathan's Toohey brewery is Chuck Hahn.

REDBACK BEER LIGHT

TYPE: WHEAT BEER

ALCOHOL: 3.4% VOL.

FERMENTATION: TOP

Special remarks: this is the light version of Redback and is a somewhat lighter wheat beer with a malty taste and a drying finish. The brewer recommends the addition of a slice of lemon.

HAHN ICE BEER

TYPE: ICE BEER

ALCOHOL: 4.9% VOL.

FERMENTATION: BOTTOM

HAHN LONGBREW LAGER

TYPE: LAGER

ALCOHOL: 4.5% VOL.

FERMENTATION: BOTTOM

Special remarks: Longbrew is a diet beer, brewed with a lower carbohydrate content.

REDBACK ORIGINAL

TYPE: WHEAT BEER

ALCOHOL: 4.7% VOL.

FERMENTATION: TOP

Special remarks: the Original is a filtered wheat beer that resembles neither the Belgian or German varieties. It has a fruity aroma that is more reminiscent of an English ale. The taste is malty initially, becoming dryer and somewhat hoppy towards the finish. The wheat content gives the Original a slightly dry sourness and typical liveliness. The aftertaste is brief and is once again vaguely hoppy. The color is golden blonde approaching amber.

HAHN PREMIUM

TYPE: LAGER

ALCOHOL: 5% VOL.

FERMENTATION: BOTTOM

Special remarks: this golden blonde lager has a somewhat sweet malt aroma. This is a medium-bodied lager with slightly hoppy background. The aftertaste is malty and softly bitter. Hahn premium is a full malt beer, brewed in copper brewing kettles and allowed four weeks to mature. Hahn Premium is this brewery's flagship beer in direct competition with premium import lagers.

• • •

• • •

TOOHEYS LTD, SYDNEY

Production in hectoliters: 7,000,000
Founded: **1869**

Tooheys is the largest brand within Lion Nathan. This brewery has been owned by a New Zealand concern since 1990.

TOOHEYS BLUE LABEL BITTER

TYPE: LIGHT LAGER
ALCOHOL: 2.7% VOL.
FERMENTATION: BOTTOM

Special remarks: Tooheys has been brewing this light lager as a thirst quencher for the more sporting types since 1991. It is a light brown beer with a somewhat hoppy aroma. The taste is light, clean and slightly malty with a somewhat hoppy finish.

TOOHEYS EXTRA DRY

TYPE: LAGER
ALCOHOL: 5% VOL.
FERMENTATION: BOTTOM

Special remarks: this light blonde lager is light-bodied and easy to drink. Both the aroma and taste are slightly malty. Extra Dry has a lightly drying finish.

TOOHEYS GOLD

TYPE: LAGER
ALCOHOL: 3.5% VOL.
FERMENTATION: BOTTOM

Special remarks: this golden light lager was launched in 1993.

TOOHEYS OLD BLACK ALE

TYPE: ALE
ALCOHOL: 4.4% VOL.
FERMENTATION: TOP

Special remarks: this copper-colored ale has a somewhat malty and fruity aroma. The taste is of roasted malt. Old Black has a medium body and an aftertaste reminiscent of roasted malt. It is one of the oldest beers brewed by Tooheys. The brewer maintains that this ale is brewed with an ale yeast strain that has been used at the brewery since 1900.

TOOHEYS RED BITTER

TYPE: LAGER
ALCOHOL: 4.9% VOL.
FERMENTATION: BOTTOM

Special remarks: this golden lager has a hoppy aroma. The taste is hoppy with some bitterness towards the finish. Tooheys Red is medium-bodied with a drying hoppy aftertaste.

TOOHEYS SYDNEY'S FAVOURITE

TYPE: LAGER
ALCOHOL: 5% VOL.
FERMENTATION: BOTTOM

Special remarks: Whitbread brews this golden blonde lager for the UK market under license from the Australian brewery.

• • •

COUNTRY New Zealand

British influences in New Zealand may be less readily apparent to the casual visitor compared with their neighbors in the enormous country of Australia, yet there is little difference between the beer cultures of the two countries. New Zealand, with a population of just less than four million prefer to drink their lagers chilled. The market is dominated by two large brewery groups, and although a couple of pub breweries have sprung up in the meantime, the special beers have had very little influence on the market.

Emma Hunt, brewer at the Waitemata Brewery

DB BREWERIES LIMITED, AUCKLAND

Production in hectoliters: 1,600,000
Founded: 1930

DB Breweries has a majority stake in Asia Pacific Breweries, with Heineken holding a third stake. The board is thus comprised of representatives from these brewing giants, with Heineken Technical Services playing a role. Heineken is brewed under license by DB, which accounts for forty-four percent of the New Zealand beer market. The drink merchant Henry Kelliher and the brewer William Coutts founded this brewery in 1930, originally from cologne. The brewery in Waitemata has been expanded with breweries in Mangatainoka, Greymouth (Montieth's) and Timaru.

DB NATURAL BEER

TYPE: ALE
ALCOHOL: 4% VOL.
FERMENTATION: TOP

Special remarks: New Zealand ale is not pasteurized. This is considered unnecessary by the brewers, as the ale is micro-filtered, a process that retains the taste properties. This amber ale has a sweet malty taste with a dry background and a medium body. The finish is prolonged and lightly hoppy.

DB BITTER BEER

TYPE: LAGER
ALCOHOL: 4% VOL.
FERMENTATION: BOTTOM

Special remarks: a light brown lager with a somewhat malty aroma. The taste is light hoppy with a slightly drying hoppy aftertaste.

DB DRAUGHT BEER

TYPE: LAGER
ALCOHOL: 4% VOL.
FERMENTATION: BOTTOM

Special remarks: an amber colored lager with a light hoppy aroma. The taste is hoppy with a malty background. The body is medium and the aftertaste is hoppy and drying. This is one of the best selling beers in New Zealand.

DB EXPORT DRY

TYPE: EXPORT LAGER
ALCOHOL: 5% VOL.
FERMENTATION: BOTTOM

Special remarks: this blonde lager has a light malty aroma and a light malty taste. This light-bodied Export Dry is drying towards the end.

DB EXPORT GOLD

TYPE: EXPORT LAGER
ALCOHOL: 4% VOL.
FERMENTATION: BOTTOM

Special remarks: a light malty gold blonde lager with a light malty taste.

DB DOUBLE VITA STOUT

TYPE: STOUT
ALCOHOL: 4% VOL.
FERMENTATION: TOP

Special remarks: this dark stout is one of the smaller products produced by DB. Both the aroma and taste are of roasted malt. Double Vita has a drying finish.

DOUBLE BROWN BEER

TYPE: LAGER

ALCOHOL: 4% VOL.

FERMENTATION: BOTTOM

Special remarks: this is an amber-colored lager with a malty aroma. The taste is malty and the aftertaste is drying with a slightly hoppy bitterness.

MAKO SPECIAL BITTER BEER

TYPE: LIGHT LAGER

ALCOHOL: 2.5% VOL.

FERMENTATION: BOTTOM

Special remarks: this is the best selling light beer in New Zealand, and is a brown beer with a light malty taste.

NUGGET GOLDEN LAGER

TYPE: LAGER

ALCOHOL: 5% VOL.

FERMENTATION: BOTTOM

Special remarks: the Golden Lager is brewed by the Monteiths's brewery in Greymouth. DB assigned this brewery to cater for the specialty beer market. (New Zealanders call specialty beers "boutique beers"). Nugget is a full premium beer brewed in small batches.

TUI EAST INDIA PALE ALE

TYPE: ALE

ALCOHOL: 4% VOL.

FERMENTATION: TOP

Special remarks: this ale has been brewed in the Tui brewery in Mangatainoka since 1889. It is an amber-colored ale with a malty aroma, a malty taste and a hoppy background.

• • •

LION NATHAN BREWERIES LIMITED, AUCKLAND

Production in hectoliters: –

Founded: –

Lion Nathan is one of the largest brewers in New Zealand, with large business interests in Australia. Lion Nathan beers include Rheineck, Lion Brown and Red, Speights and Leopard.

STEINLAGER

TYPE: LAGER

ALCOHOL: 5% VOL.

FERMENTATION: BOTTOM

Special remarks: Steinlager is an international lager and is exported to more than fifty countries. It has a light hoppy aroma and a hoppy taste with a malty background. The aftertaste is hoppy and drying.

• • •

Index *(List of Beers)*

A

F

G

Kozel Blonde 10% – 297
Kozel Blonde 12% – 297
Kozel 10% – 297
Krakonoš 10% – 284
Krakonoš 11% – 284
Krakonoš 12% – 284
Královská 8 – 291
Královský Lev 11% – 291
Kriek – 150
Kriek Boon – 131
Kriek Girardin – 139
Kristall Weizen – 215
Kritzenthaler Alkoholfreies Pils – 201
Kronenbourg – 271
Kroon Pilsener – 240
Krušovice Černé 10% – 285
Krušovice Ležák 12% – 285
Krušovice Světlé 10% – 285
Ksiaz – 329
Ksiazece – 326
Kylian – 253

L

L'Angelus – 264
L'Epi Blanc – 275
L'Epi Noir – 275
L'Epi Rouge – 275
La Bavaisienne – 274
La Bière du Demon – 267
La Binchoise Blonde – 128
La Chouffe – 122
La Choulette Ambrée – 265
La Choulette Biére de Mars – 265
La Choulette Blonde – 266
La Choulette de Noël – 266
La Choulette Framboise – 266
La Divine – 161
La Fin du Monde –358
La Gaillarde – 358
La Gauloise Ambree – 130
La Gauloise Blonde – 131
La Gauloise Brune – 131
La Guillotine – 143
La Rouget de Lisle – 275
La Saulx – 269
La Trappe Dubbel – 245

La Trappe Enkel – 245
La Trappe Quadrupel – 245
La Vieille Salme – 122
Labatt Ice – 356
Lagerbier Hell – 182
Lager-Hell – 324
Lal Tafoon – 400
Lambton's – 96
Lamme Goedzak – 256
Lamoral Tripel – 132
Lancashire Strong Brown Ale – 93
Lapin Kulta Export – 342
Lech Mocny – 328
Lech Premium – 328
Leichte Weisse – 215
Lezajsk Trunk – 326
LEV 10% Tmavé Pivo – 291
Licher Ice Beer – 199
Licher Pilsner Premium – 199
Licht van Troost – 256
Liempd's Gildebier Antonius Abt – 229
Lieve Royale – 232
Lightfoot – 93
Lindeboom Lente Bock – 243
Lingen's Blond – 253
Little Kings Cream Ale – 370
Livinus Blonde – 139
Lobkowicz Klassik 10% – 285
Loburg – 126
London Pride – 75
Loteling Blond – 170
Loteling Bruin – 171
Löwenbräu Alkoholfrei – 200
Löwenbräu Export – 200
Löwenbräu Hefe Weissbier – 200
Löwenbräu Ice Beer – 200
Löwenbräu Kristallweizen – 200
Löwenbräu Original Münchner Hell – 200
Löwenbräu Premium Pils – 200
Löwenbräu Schwarze Weisse – 200
Löwenbräu Zürich – 323
Löwengarten Export Hell – 324
Lucifer – 158
Lutéce – 273
Luxembourg Black Lager – 260
Luxembourg Export – 260
Luxembourg Lager – 261

O

O'schterbéier – 261
Oatmeal Stout – 90
OB Beer – 402
Oberdorfer Weissbier Dunkel – 213
Oberdorfer Weissbier Helles – 213
Odell's 90 Shilling – 376
Odell's Easy Street Wheat – 376
Odell's Holiday Shilling – 376
Odell's Levity – 376
Oeral – 135
Oerbier – 136
Okocim Karmi – 327
Okocim Light Beer – 327
Okocim Mocne – 327
Okocim Piwo Jasne – 327
Old Brewery Pale Ale – 90
Old Brown Dog Ale – 381
Old Cherry Ale – 374
Old Detroit Amber Ale – 369
Old Detroit Red Lager – 369
Old Devil – 101
Old Dick – 92
Old Hooky – 78
Old Jock – 105
Old Nick – 102
Old No. 38 Stout – 375
Old Peculier – 93
Old Rasputin Russian Imperial Stout – 375
Old Slug Porter – 84
Old Speckled Hen – 83
Old Stockport Bitter – 86
Old Thumper – 85
Old Timer – 98
Old Tom – 87
Old Winter Ale – 75
Op-Ale Speciale – 164
Opat 11% – 282
Opat 12% – 282
Opat 14% – 282
Opus' 97 – 153
Oranjeboom Oud Bruin – 257
Oranjeboom Premium Malt – 257
Oranjeboom Premium Pilsener – 257
Original – 323
Original HB München – 222

Original Münchner – 205
Original Münchner Dunkel – 206
Original Oetringer Kristall Weizen – 204
Original Oettinger Alt – 204
Original Oettinger Dunkles Hefeweizen – 204
Original Oettinger Export – 204
Original Oettinger Hefeweissbier – 204
Original Oettinger Hell – 204
Original Oettinger Leicht – 205
Original Oettinger Leichte Weisse – 205
Original Oettinger Pils – 205
Original Oettinger Schwarzbier – 205
Original Quöllfrisch – 320
Orkney Dark Island – 111
Orpal – 270
Orval – 155
Ottakringer Helles Bier – 317
Oud Kriekenbier – 134
Oud Zottegems Bier – 134
Outlaw Brewing Co First Gold – 87
Ozujsko Pivo – 350

P

Paceña Centenario Beer – 393
Pacífico Clara – 388
Paderborner Pilsener – 205
Palm Speciale – 156
Paranoia Groen – 171
Paranoia Roze – 171
Parbo Bier – 394
Parel – 239
Pastor Ale – 264
Pater Lieven – 132
Pater Lieven Blond – 132
Patriator – 274
Paulaner Hefe–Weissbier – 206
Paulaner Hefe–Weissbier Dunkel – 206
Paulaner Premium Leicht – 206
Paulaner Premium Pils – 206
Paulaner Weissbier Kristallklar – 206
Pauwel Kwak – 132
Pecheresse – 151
Pedigree Bitter – 82
Pelforth Blonde – 268
Pelforth Brune – 268
Père Noël – 157

R

S

Sam Adams Triple Bock – 365
Samichlaus Bier – 323
Samson Blond 10% – 294
Samson Blond 12% –295
Samuel Adams Boston Ale – 363
Samuel Adams Boston Lager – 363
Samuel Adams Cherry Wheat – 363
Samuel Adams Cream Stout – 364
Samuel Adams Dark Wheat – 364
Samuel Adams Double Bock – 364
Samuel Adams Octoberfest – 364
Samuel Adams Scotch Ale – 364
Samuel Adams Triple Bock – 365
Samuel Adams Winter Lager – 364
San Miguel Export – 349
San Miguel Pale Pilsen – 402
Sans Souci – 345
Sanwald Hefeweizen – 192
Sanwald Kristallweizen – 192
Sanwald Weizen Dunkel – 192
Sapporo Premium Lager – 399
Šariš Světlé Pivo 10% – 299
Satan Gold – 130
Satan Red – 130
Saxer Bock – 379
Saxer's Lemon Lager – 379
Scanlon's Middlesex Gold – 89
Schäff's Helle Weisse – 213
Schiehallion – 106
Schlösser Alt – 213
Schloßgold Alkoholfreies Bier – 314
Schmucker Hefe Weizen Dunkel – 216
Schneider Weisse Kristall – 217
Schneider Weisse Light – 217
Schneider Weisse Original – 217
Schneider Weisse Weizenhell – 217
Schöfferhofer Dunkles Hefeweizen – 187
Schöfferhofer Kristallweizen – 187
Schuitheiss Diät – 219
Schultheiss Lager – 219
Schultheiss Lager Schwarz – 219
Schultheiss Mix – 220
Schultheiss Original Berliner Weisse – 220
Schultheiss Pilsener – 220
Schutzenberger Bière sur Lie – 274
Schutzenberger Tradition – 274
Schnützen Bräu – 314
Schützengarten Lager Hell – 321
Schwaben Bräu Märzen – 192

Schwaben Bräu Meister Pils – 192
Schwaben Bräu Meister Weizen – 192
Schwaben Bräu Urtyp Export – 193
Schwarze Weisse – 222
Schwechater Bier – 315
Schweiger Schmankerl Weisse – 220
Scorpion – 96
Scotch Ale – 108
Scotch Triumph – 270
Scottish Oatmeal Stout – 105
Scrimshaw Pilsner Style Beer – 375
Sezoens Blond – 153
Sezoens Quattro – 153
Shoals Pale Ale – 381
Siegel Pils – 195
Sierra Nevada Pale Ale – 380
Sierra Nevada Porter – 380
Sierra Nevada Stout – 381
Simon Pils – 261
Simon Regal – 261
Sinebrychoff Porter –342
Singha – 402
Sion Kölsch – 185
Sjoes – 250
Skullsplitter – 111
Sleutel Bokbier – 253
Sloeber – 161
Slots Guld – 332
Slots Herkules – 333
Slots Pilsner – 333
Smädný Mních Export Beer Premium – 299
Smädný Mních Nealkoholické Pivo – 299
Snapdragon – 88
Sol – 387
Soproni Ászok – 304
Spaten Alkoholfrei – 221
Spaten Diät–Pils – 221
Special London Ale – 102
Specjal Mocny – 325
Special Roman – 161
Speculation Ale – 73
Speltor – 277
Spendrup's Old Gold – 339
Spendrup's Original – 339
Spezial Bier – 307
Spezial–Export – 226
Spitfire – 89
Splügen – 346
Sport Radler – 315

T

U

V

W

X

Y

Z

Index *(List of Breweries)*

C

D

E

F

I

Independence Brewing Company, Philadelphia – 370
Industrie Poretti, Milan/Induno Olona – 346
Interbrew SA, Louvain – 143

J

Jacob Stauder, Essen – 222
Jantjes, Uden – 254
Jeanne D'Arc, Ronchin – 269
Jersey Brewery, Ann Street Brewery, St. Helier, Jersey – 79
Jihočeské Pivovary a.s., České Budějovice – 284
Jihočeské Pivovary a.s., Samson, České Budějovice – 294
Jihočeské Pivovary, Platan, Protivín – 287
Jihočeské Pivovary, Regent, Třebon –294
John Martin, Genval, Waals Brabant – 144
John Smiths Brewery, Tadcaster, North Yorkshire – 89
Johnston, Rímac – 391
Josef Baumgarrner, Schärding – 308
Josef Sigl, Obertrum – 308
Joshua Tetley & Son, The Brewery, Leeds, West Yorkshire – 92

K

Källefalls, Tidaholm – 337
Kapsreiter AG, Schärding – 309
Karkonoskie, Lwówek Slaski – 326
Karl Locher, Appenzell – 320
Kasteelbrouwerij de Dool, Houthalen-Helchteren – 136
Kenya Breweries Ltd, Nairobi – 408
Kerkom, Kerkom-St.Truiden – 144
Kimberley Brewery, Hardys & Hansons PLC, King & Barnes Ltd, The Horsham Brewery, Horsham, West Sussex – 79
Kirin Brewery Co, Tokyo – 399
Weltenburg Abbey Brewery, Kelheim – 226

Krakonoš spol. s.r.o., Trutnov – 284
Královský pivovar Krušovice, Krušovice – 284
Kronenbourg, Strasbourg – 270
Kungsholmens Kvartersbryggeri, Stockholm – 337

L

La Binchoise, Binche Henegouwen – 128
La Choulette, Hordain – 265
La Compagnie des Trois Épis, Paris – 275
Labatt Breweries Ltd, London – 356
Latrobe Brewing Co, Latrobe, Pennsylvania – 371
Le Cheval Blanc, Montreal – 355
Lech Browary Wielkopolski, Poznan – 328
Lefèbvre, Quenast – 147
Leffe Abbey, Dinant – 148
Leroy, Boezinge – 149
Les Brasseurs GMT Inc, Montreal, Quebec – 355
Licher Brewery, Jhring-Melchior GmbH & Co KG, Lich – 199
Liefmans, Oudenaarde – 150
Lindemans, Vlezenbeek – 150
Lion Brewery, Morrells Brewery Ltd, Oxford, Oxfordshire – 82
Lion Nathan, Camperdown – 419
Lobkowiczký Pivovar, Vysoký Chlumec – 285
Louwaege, Kortemark – 152
Löwenbräu A.G., Munich – 199
Löwengarten, Rorschach – 324

M

Maasland, Oss – 254
L. Macks, Ølbryggeri & Mineralvandfabrik, Tromsø – 340
MacLay & Co, The Thistle Brewery, Alloa, Clackmannanshire – 108
Mahou, Madrid – 349
Malopolski Browar Strzelec, Jedrzejów – 330
Mansfield Brewery PLC, formerly of Mansfield, Nottinghamshire – 81
Maribo Bryghus, Maribo – 335
Markt Schwaben – 220

N

O

P

W

Y

Z

Glossary

A

Additives: there are two types of additives – adjuncts i.e. all other grains other than barley which render fermentable sugar and sugar itself, and true additives such as chemical compounds or biological matter used in the brewing process. Both big and small-scale brewers make use of both.

Alcohol: an organic chemical compound containing ethanol C_2H_6O (ethyl alcohol) as a by-product of fermentation.

Ale: any top-fermented beer that is fermented at higher temperatures; generally refers to British types of beer.

Aroma: perception of smell through the nose. Beer often has an aroma of hops and malt but fruit and spices can also be detected without these actually being present in the beer.

B

Balling: Czech scientist who first produced a scale for expressing the density of beer. This was later refined by the German scientist Plato. Plato is the most widely used but degrees are expressed in some countries as degrees "B".

Bitterness units: a scale against which the bitterness of beer can be expressed. Known as IBU (International Bitterness Units).

Body: the extent of the fullness of beer, largely determined by the unfermented sugars and proteins still present.

Bouquet: a refined term for the aroma.

C

CAMRA: Campaign for Real Ale, a British organization that campaigns to maintain real ales on the market and to counter the moves of major breweries that are more interested in efficiency, cost, and volume than craftsmanship and quality.

Carbon Dioxide CO_2 gas: the gas that causes bubbles in beer. Beer without carbon dioxide is still. It can be artificially added to beer but is formed naturally by keeping beer under pressure during fermentation or secondary fermentation.

Chaff: the hard outer casing of a grain (as in the case of barley) that protects it. Plays an important role as a filter in brewing.

Chalk: rock formed by the skeletons of marine organisms. Used for filtration.

Clarification vessel: vat in which the wort is clarified or made clear by filtration. The bottom has slots in which the chaff from the malted grain becomes lodged and these act as natural filters for the wort. In traditional breweries this is often a fine looking object with rows of brass taps.

Conditioning: the storage at a specific temperature in order to mature beer by allowing natural biological process to do their work. This is usually one in a cool place.

Cooper: craftsman who makes and repairs wooden barrels and casks. Only a small number of breweries employ their own coopers.

Crown cap: the most commonly-used form of closure used for bottles. It is a metal plate with a plastic seal (formerly cork) that was invented by William Painter in 1892 to replace corks. In the USA in addition to crown caps bottles are also fitted with screw-top closures that are opened by twisting.

Cuvée: Belgian term, derived from wine terminology, used for beer intended for a special occasion. It is often used more as a marketing tool than having any special significance or respect for the original meaning.

Cylindrical fermentation vats: large breweries increasingly use horizontal stainless steel tanks in which beer is both fermented and conditioned. This huge vats or tanks have tapered undersides in which the yeast collects when it has more or less finished fermentation. Once the yeast is removed the immature beer remains in the vat for a few weeks in order to condition. The outside of these vats are cooled so that the beer is kept at the required temperature.

D

Decoction: concentration through boiling; in brewing refers to a method of forming the mash where part of the wort is heated in a separate copper before being added to the rest in order to raise the overall temperature.

Dextrin: a carbohydrate gum formed from unfermented sugar that largely determines the body and sweetness of beer.

Diacetyl: by-product of fermentation that disappears if the beer is given time to condition. It can produce a buttery aroma and flavor.

Diatase: a group of enzymes that convert starch into sugar, consisting of alfa and beta amylase that are stored in malt.

Dubbel/Double: a Belgian term for abbey or Trappist beers that refers to the original gravity of the wort. Double is not twice as high as Enkel (or single) but mid-way between enkel and tripel or triple. Alcohol level is usually between 6 and 7.5%.

E

EBC: European Brewing Convention, based in Zoeterwoude. An association of European brewers. EBC is also the color scale used by brewers for both malt and beer.

Enkel/Single: a rarely-used term. It is the base level that determines the dubbel and tripel levels of Belgian abbey or Trappist beers. Once enkel was the daily thirst quencher for the monks.

Esters: volatile organic compounds in beer that provide fruity and spicy aromas and flavors. They are formed at the beginning of fermentation, normally at high temperatures and hence ales generally have higher levels of esters than lagers. Esters can form into an acid and an alcohol.

F

Filter plates: plates filled with an inert filter substance such as chalk or fine grit that remove residue from the wort.

G

Gambrinus: the patron of beer or Jan Primus. Jan I, Duke of Brabant, born in Brussels in 1252, died 1294. It is said he gave his soldiers free beer. Gambrinus is often depicted with a beer tankard in his hand.

Grand cru: some Belgian brewers use this wine term for their best product but it says nothing whatever about the type of beer.

Gravity: the extent of non-dissolved sugars in a liquid. Original gravity is measured prior to fermentation and final gravity or density after fermentation.

H

Heavy brewing: American brewers with a lack of space use this method in which less water is used to produce a wort of much higher density. The required amount of water is added at the end of the brewing process to achieve the desired density. This enables a brewer to expand capacity by a quarter without investment in new tanks, tuns, fermentation vessels, or storage tanks.

Hop sieve:

Hot water tanks: some brewers heat water separately and add it, already heated, to the mash tun or copper. Other treatment can also be carried out in these separated water tanks.

Hydrometer: instrument used for measuring the density of the wort. Brewers use hydrometers at various stages of the brew.

I

IBU: International Bitter Units: unit of expressing the level of bitterness of a beer.

Infusion: method of mashing in which the temperature is gradually raised in the same copper.

Isinglass: substance used to clarify liquids, naturally occurring in the swim-bladders of some freshwater fish.

L

Lactose: a disaccharide sugar present in milk and also known as milk sugar ($C_{12} H_{22} O_{11}$). A sugar that does not ferment and hence gives body and fullness to beer. It is especially used for sweet stouts.

Lager: term used for bottom-fermented beers that are conditioned under cool temperatures.

Late hopping: addition of hops in storage tanks or casks in order to add extra aroma. Late hopping does not increase bitterness.

Lintner: measurement for expressing the quantity of enzymes that must convert starch into sugars. This power of enzymes in malt is given in degrees of Lintner.

Lovibond: an international unit to express the color of malt. Comparable with EBC and SRM.

whirlpool in which solids are separated by remaining in the center.

Wort: once a liquid has been formed from the mash it is known as the wort.

M

Maltose: a disaccharide ($C_{12} H_{12} O_{11}$) consisting of glucose residues formed by the hydrolysis of starch: the most important sugar to be derived from malt.

Mash tun: the vessel in which liquid is added to the malt in order to form the mash. Some mash tuns have rotors in to agitate the mash.

P

Plato: see Balling.

R

Rolling: the process of crushing malt (or other grain) in a roller mill, without removing its chaff.

S

Secondary fermentation: further fermentation that occurs in a bottle. It is primed by adding sugar or fresh yeast or some fermented wort.

Sediment: remnants of fermentation found at the bottom of casks or bottles.

SRM: Standard Reference Method: a scale for expressing the color of beer. Comparable with EBC.

W

Whirlpool: brewers that do not use whole hops cannot therefore use the hops themselves as filters. They use a form of centrifuge known as a

Y

Yeast starter: a quantity of yeast to start the process of fermentation in an acceptable period of time. In theory just a single cell of yeast is sufficient but this would need so much time to reproduce that the wort would decay.